Re

THE STASI

THE STASI: MYTH AND REALITY

MIKE DENNIS

With the assistance as translator of
Peter Brown

PEARSON
Longman

PEARSON EDUCATION LIMITED

Head Office:
Edinburgh Gate
Harlow CM20 2JE
Tel: +44 (0)1279 623623
Fax: +44 (0)1279 431059

London Office:
128 Long Acre
London WC2E 9AN
Tel: +44 (0)20 7447 2000
Fax: +44 (0)20 7447 2170
Website: www.history-minds.com

First edition published in Great Britain in 2003

© Pearson Education Limited 2003

The right of Mike Dennis to be identified as Author
of this Work has been asserted by him in accordance
with the Copyright, Designs and Patents Act 1988.

ISBN 0 582 41422 9

British Library Cataloguing in Publication Data
A CIP catalogue record for this book can be obtained from the British Library

Library of Congress Cataloging in Publication Data
A CIP catalog record for this book can be obtained from the Library of Congress

10 9 8 7 6 5 4 3 2 1

Set in 10.5/12pt Bembo by Graphicraft Limited, Hong Kong
Printed and bound in China

The Publishers' policy is to use paper manufactured from sustainable forests.

CONTENTS

LIST OF TABLES

PREFACE

At the end of August 1989, ten weeks before the fall of the Berlin Wall, the veteran Minister of State Security, Erich Mielke, anxiously asked a group of his leading officers if an uprising on the scale of 17 June 1953 was imminent. The spectre of another major revolt against communist rule was hovering over the leaders of the GDR[1] confronted with the escalation of protests on the streets and the flight of East Germans to the West. Mielke may have drawn some comfort from his colleagues' assurance that this would not occur as the Stasi was well prepared to protect state and party. In more stable times the officers' optimism would have been justified, for the ministry, a central prop of communist rule for almost 40 years, had created a system of panopticism par excellence. Its foreign agents were entrenched in the economic, political, scientific and industrial nerve centres of West Germany, the nemesis and main adversary of the East German state. In any given year throughout the 1980s, about one in 50 of the country's 13.5 million adults were working for the Stasi on the home front, either as an officer or as an informer, thus enabling Mielke's security forces not only to penetrate the niches of East German society but also to maintain the reputation of the GDR as one of the most stable states in the Soviet Union's East European empire. Drawing on the rich vein of original sources in the archive of the former Ministry of State Security, this book will examine how the Stasi was able to invade people's lives and all spheres of society – whether the alternative sub-cultures of punks, skins and ecologists or the state-run factories and sports institutions. It will also investigate the Stasi's organisational structure, the ideological faith of officers, the motivation and activities of the army of 176,000 informers and the monitoring of the opinions and attitudes of ordinary East Germans.

But the book will also explore a paradox, that is, the ministry's 'weakness in omnipotence', in particular during the years from 1971 to 1989 when the autocratic Erich Honecker ruled over the GDR. The central paradox lay in the contrast between, on the one hand, the ubiquitous Stasi's all-pervasive system of surveillance and its extensive powers of interrogation and coercion and, on the other hand, a security force bedevilled not only by the problems endemic in any overbloated bureaucracy but also by its symbiotic links to the ruling Communist party. Take the first point. Whereas the Stasi had collected

---

[1] GDR is the abbreviation for the German Democratic Republic which existed as a separate state between 1949 and 1990.

a mountain of data on its own citizens as part of the minister's aim 'to know everything and to report on everything worth knowing',[2] Mielke and his colleagues should have taken note of the inherent constraints on the pursuit of omniscience encapsulated in the admonition of Dean Rusk, President Kennedy's Secretary of State, that: 'Providence has not provided human beings with the capacity to pierce the fog of the future'.[3] And even though East Germany's leaders were so well informed and their population in general quiescent, they themselves did not sleep easily at night for they could not ignore the greater appeal of the West for their own citizens. It was this fundamental legitimacy deficit of the GDR – the less prosperous and the more repressive of the two German republics – which would cause the party and the Stasi to come tumbling down after the fall of the Berlin Wall, the ugly symbol of the Cold War and the GDR's ultimate protective barrier.

---

[2] Naimark N. M. 1995: 366.
[3] Cited in Johnson L. K. 1996: 204.

ACKNOWLEDGEMENTS

The author is grateful to numerous people who willingly gave of their time to illuminate aspects of the East German state security system. Particular mention should be made of Josef Budek, Jörg Driselmann, Klaus Farin, Wolfgang Hartmann, Hagen Koch, Petra Morave and Wolfgang Rüddenklau. The interviews were conducted by Dr Norry Laporte, who was a stimulating and energetic research assistant; he also wrote a substantive draft of Chapters 12 and 13. A great debt is owed to two advisers at the BStU, Frau Jaensch and Frau Scharfenberg, who responded with great patience and understanding to the many requests for documents on a wide range of subjects. My appreciation is extended to the British Academy for the award of a Small Grant to enable research to be conducted at the BStU archive in Berlin. Likewise, I am most appreciative of the advice and guidance given by two of my colleagues in the Modern German History group at the University of Wolverhampton, Professor Eva Kolinsky and Dr Dieter Steinert, and by Professor Karin Weiss, who was a Visiting Leverhulme Foundation Fellow during the academic year 2002–2003. Finally, a special word of thanks to a former colleague at the University, Dr Peter Brown, who provided translations into English of the Stasi's version of the German language and helped to remove the many weaknesses in the manuscript's style and presentation.

The publishers are grateful to Ch. Links Verlag GmbH for permission to reproduce a table from *Die hauptamtlichen Mitarbeiter der Staatssicherheit* by Jens Gieseke, pp. 552–7.

In some instances we have been unable to trace the owners of copyright material and would appreciate any information that would enable us to do so.

LIST OF ABBREVIATIONS

AKG	Auswertungs- und Kontrollgruppe (Assessment and Control Group)
AG	Arbeitsgruppe (Working Group)
BfV	Bundesamt für Verfassungsschutz (Federal Office for the Protection of the Constitution – West Germany)
BND	Bundesnachrichtendienst (Federal Intelligence Service – West Germany)
BStU	Bundesbeauftragte für die Unterlagen des Staatssicherheitsdienstes der ehemaligen Deutschen Demokratischen Republik (Federal Commissioner for the Records of the State Security Service of the Former German Democratic Republic)
BV	Bezirksverwaltung (Regional Administration)
CC	Central Committee
CDU	Christlich-Demokratische Union (Christian Democratic Union)
CIA	Central Intelligence Agency (America)
COCOM	Coordinating Committee for Multilateral Export Controls
COMECON	Council for Mutual Economic Aid
CPSU	Communist Party of the Soviet Union
DVU	Deutsche Volksunion (German People's Party)
DHfK	Deutsche Hochschule für Körperkultur (German College of Higher Education for Physical Culture)
DM	Deutsche Mark (West German currency)
DTSB	Deutscher Turn- und Sportbund der Deutschen Demokratischen Republik (German Gymnastics and Sports Association of the GDR)
DVdI	Deutsche Verwaltung des Innern (German Administration of the Interior in the Soviet Zone of Occupation)
ECCI	Executive Committee of the Comintern
EU	European Union
EV	Ermittlungsverfahren (Preliminary Criminal Proceeding)
FBI	Federal Bureau of Investigation (America)
FDGB	Freier Deutscher Gewerkschaftsbund (Confederation of Free German Trade Unions)
FDJ	Freie Deutsche Jugend (Free German Youth Organisation)
FDP	Freie Demokratische Partei (Free Democratic Party)

FIM	Inoffizieller Mitarbeiter für Führung anderer Inoffizieller Mitarbeiter (Unofficial Collaborator in Charge of other Unofficial Collaborators)
FKS	Forschungsinstitut für Körperkultur und Sport (Research Institute for Physical Culture and Sport)
FRG	Federal Republic of Germany
GDR	German Democratic Republic
GI	Geheimer Informator (Secret Informer)
GMS	Gesellschaftlicher Mitarbeiter für Sicherheit (Societal Collaborator for Security)
GPU	Soviet Secret Police
GST	Gesellschaft für Sport und Technik (Society for Sport and Technology)
HA	Hauptabteilung (Main Department)
HIM	Hauptamtlicher Mitarbeiter (Full-time Collaborator)
HV A	Hauptverwaltung Aufklärung (Main Administration for Reconnaissance)
HVzSV	Hauptverwaltung zum Schutz der Volkswirtschaft (Main Administration for the Protection of the National Economy)
IFM	Initiative Frieden und Menschenrechte (Initiative for Peace and Human Rights)
IM	Inoffizieller Mitarbeiter (Unofficial Collaborator)
IMB	Inoffizieller Mitarbeiter zur unmittelbaren Bearbeitung im Verdacht der Feindtätigkeit stehender Personen (Unofficial Collaborator for Dealing with Persons under Suspicion of Hostile Activity)
IME	Inoffizieller Mitarbeiter für einen besonderen Einsatz (Unofficial Collaborator for a Special Task)
IMK	Inoffizieller Mitarbeiter zur Sicherung der Konspiration und des Verbindungswesens (Unofficial Collaborator for Aiding Conspiracy and Securing Communications)
IMS	Inoffizieller Mitarbeiter zur politisch-operativen Durchdringung und Sicherung des Verantwortungsbereiches (Unofficial Collaborator for the Political-Operative Investigation and Securing of an Area of Responsibility)
IMV	Inoffizieller Mitarbeiter mit vertraulichen Beziehungen zu im Vorgang bearbeiteten Personen (Unofficial Collaborator with Close Contact to Persons under Investigation; from 1979 IMB)
K-5	Kommissariat 5
KD	Kreisdienststelle (District Service Unit)
KGB	Soviet Committee of State Security
KoKo	Kommerzielle Koordinierung (Commercial Coordination)

KPD	Kommunistische Partei Deutschlands (Communist Party of Germany)
MfS	Ministerium für Staatssicherheit (Ministry of State Security – also Stasi)
MGB	Soviet Ministry of State Security
MVD	Soviet Ministry of Internal Affairs
NATO	North Atlantic Treaty Organisation
NES	New Economic System of Planning and Management
NKGB	People's Commissariat of State Security (Soviet)
NKVD	People's Commissariat of Internal Affairs (Soviet)
NSDAP	Nationalsozialistische Deutsche Arbeiterpartei (National Socialist German Workers' Party)
NVA	Nationale Volksarmee (National People's Army)
OD	Objektdienststelle (Object Service Unit)
OG	Operationsgebiet (Operation Area)
OibE	Offizier im besonderen Einsatz (Officer on Special Assignment)
OPK	Operative Personenkontrolle (Operational Personal Check)
OV	Operativer Vorgang (Integrated Operational Clandestine Campaign or Operational Case)
PDS	Partei des Demokratischen Sozialismus (Party of Democratic Socialism)
PID	Political-Ideological Diversion
RAF	Red Army Faction (West German terrorist group)
Rechtsstaat	A state under the rule of law
RIAS	Radio in the American Sector (West Berlin)
SAPMO	Stiftung Archiv der Parteien und Massenorganisationen der DDR (Berlin Branch of the Federal Archive of the Foundation for the Parties and Mass Organisations of the GDR)
SD	Sicherheitsdienst (Nazi Security Service)
SED	Sozialistische Einheitspartei Deutschlands (Socialist Unity Party of Germany)
SMAD	Soviet Military Administration in Germany
SMD	Sportmedizinischer Dienst (Sports Medical Service)
SPD	Sozialdemokratische Partei Deutschlands (Social Democratic Party of Germany)
SOUD	KGB-administered computerised storage of intelligence data
Stasi	see MfS
SVP	Sachverhaltsprüfung (Check on the Facts of a Case)
SWT	Sektor Wissenschaft und Technik (Scientific and Technical Section)
Unrechtsstaat	A state not under the rule of law
VKU	Vorkommnisuntersuchung (Enquiry into an Incident)

ZA	Zentralarchiv (Central Archive)
ZAIG	Zentrale Auswertungs- und Informationsgruppe (Central Assessment and Information Group)
ZKG	Zentrale Koordinierungsgruppe (Central Coordinating Group)
ZOV	Zentraler Operativer Vorgang (Central Operational Case)

Note: Where reference is made in the footnotes to MfS ZA, this denotes the central archival materials of the Ministry of State Security held by a special federal agency, the BStU.

INTRODUCTION

AN ORWELLIAN NIGHTMARE

The Ministry of State Security,[1] popularly known as the Stasi, was an integral element of communist rule in the German Democratic Republic between the ministry's establishment in 1950 to its dissolution in 1989. The GDR itself was founded in 1949, as Stalin's 'unwanted child' of the Cold War. Despite the popular uprising in 1953 against the Stalinist system which had been imposed on the GDR and despite the mass exodus of East Germans to the West, the new state managed to survive until its next major test in 1961. The Berlin Wall, erected by the East German communists with Soviet endorsement, arrested in a brutal manner the haemorrhaging of the population, thereby stabilising the system behind the ugly barrier which soon came to symbolise the totalitarian nature of communism. A combination of social incentives, economic growth and more subtle forms of coercion subsequently enabled the GDR's rulers to consolidate their position and, in the era of superpower détente, to gain international recognition for their country. However, the Soviet Union's retreat from empire under Gorbachev and the GDR's chronic economic malaise exposed the frail legitimacy of the communist social and political order. When the Berlin Wall eventually fell, on the evening of 9–10 November 1989, it was an act of desperation by East Germany's bewildered rulers to save an obsolescent system which neither they nor their security and military forces could prevent from disintegrating under the twin pressures of popular demonstrations and mass flight.

Following in the footsteps of its Soviet counterpart, the KGB, the Ministry of State Security functioned for almost four decades as the sharp sword and trusty shield of the GDR's key institution, the ruling Socialist Unity Party (SED).[2] Such was the ministry's power and ubiquity that one author, Alexandra

---

[1] The German term is *Ministerium für Staatssicherheit*, abbreviated to MfS.
[2] The SED was founded in the Soviet zone of occupation in 1946 as the result of a merger between the German Communist Party (KPD) and the Social Democratic Party

Richie, refers to it as exercising, in the 1980s, 'almost complete control over the captive population of East Germany'.[3] And, indeed, the comprehensive surveillance of the population by a vast army of informers and a plethora of scientific and technical devices lends substance to the claim by the historian Christoph Klessmann that George Orwell's *1984* was realised to a greater extent in the GDR than was ever the case in the Third Reich.[4] When, in addition, the Stasi's success in planting agents in all areas of West German political and cultural life is borne in mind, then it is tempting to concur with Anne Appelbaum's verdict that it was 'the most pervasive and efficient secret service in history'.[5]

Former high-ranking officers of the Stasi seize eagerly on this notion of efficiency as part of a well-packaged defence of what they regard as the ministry's honourable and legitimate role in protecting the East German state against a legion of external and internal enemies. This kind of argument is also used to combat the denigration of the MfS as part of what the officers perceive to be a continuation into the new Germany of the traditional anti-communist doctrine of the old Federal Republic (FRG).[6] The elements of the defamation campaign which they allege is being conducted by the mass media and the 'political class' encompass forced adoptions, the murder of babies, the use of torture in MfS pre-trial detention centres and assisting terrorists in West Germany's notorious Red Army Faction. Not only does this litany of infamy – most of which can be substantiated – serve to discredit the Stasi by association with the murderers of the Gestapo but by depicting the ministry as the centre of evil it adds grist to the mill of those who seek to condemn the GDR as a totalitarian state, thereby justifying the whole-sale dismantling of the former GDR's institutions and the socio-economic upheaval since the country's incorporation into the Federal Republic in October 1990.[7]

Although the self-portrayal of a dedicated, professional service class helps to sustain the officers' feelings of worth and identity in a world transformed,

---

(SPD). The new party soon attired itself in Stalinist clothing and, despite the existence of four other political parties, became the dominant political force in East Germany. The term 'East Germany' will be used to refer to the period from the foundation of the GDR in 1949 to the unification of the two German republics in 1990. The term 'east Germany' is used as an alternative to the 'Soviet zone of occupation' of 1945 to 1949 and to the former GDR after unification in October 1990. Similarly, 'East Berlin' refers to the capital city of the GDR.

[3] Richie A. 1998: 758.

[4] Klessmann C. 1998: 43.

[5] *The Sunday Telegraph*, 21 February 1999, book section, p. 13.

[6] See in particular the declaration of 19 March 2001 published in the daily newspaper *Junge Welt*: http://www.jungewelt.de/2001/03-19/011.shmtl, pp. 1–2.

[7] See the interviews with former Stasi officers in *Junge Welt* in http://www.jungewelt.de/2001/04-20/011.shtml, pp. 2–3, and in http://www/jungewelt.de/1999/08-27/016.shtml, pp. 2–3.

it too often masks the darker, repressive side of the GDR which is so closely associated with the totalitarian paradigm. One of the central sub-themes in the highly controversial debate on the applicability, and the value, of the totalitarian label to the GDR concerns the centrality of the role of the Stasi within the system. Rather than being – as its long-serving minister, the autocratic Erich Mielke, insisted – the loyal and trustworthy agent of the SED's will, the ministry is sometimes depicted as a 'state within a state' whose clandestine operations were not rigorously controlled and monitored by party organs. Egon Krenz, the former head of the SED's Central Committee Department for Security Questions and the SED's last leader, subscribes to the latter argument, partly because it helps to relieve him of some of the burden of responsibility for the Stasi's excesses and abuse of human rights. The myth of an ultra-efficient and omnipotent intelligence and security service has also come under challenge on the grounds that the Stasi was submerged in a flood of data, much of it mindless trivia. Tina Rosenberg has depicted the minutiae, or what she calls the thousands of tons of 'shit' under the nuggets of gold, in graphic detail:

> The Stasi knew where Comrade Gisela kept the ironing board in her apartment . . . and how many times a week Comrade Armin took out his garbage and what color socks he wore with his sandals while doing it . . . The Stasi kept watch on trash dumps and lending libraries – the names of those who checked out books on hot air balloons or rock-climbing equipment were of particular interest – and tapped the booths of Catholic confessionals and the seats at the Dresden Opera. Stasi cameras monitored public toilets . . . Some of its dossiers on East Germans had a hundred categories of information – even the number, location, and design of tattoos. The Stasi kept a library of smells: a few hundred glass jars containing bits of dissidents' dirty underwear, so trained dogs could sniff and match the smell to an antigovernment pamphlet found on the sidewalk.[8]

Complementary to the 'drowning-men of the Stasi' thesis is the view that the ministry was incapable of controlling the disparate social, economic and political currents in a state bedevilled by a pronounced legitimacy deficit and highly vulnerable to Western influences. One leading German historian, Lutz Niethammer, takes up this theme, arguing that the Stasi, 'an uncontrolled and paranoid military bureaucracy', far from being the core of the regime should be placed at the edge on the grounds that the mass of society had either been integrated or immobilised and, furthermore, that the ministry fostered rather than reduced opposition. By the late 1980s, it had come to personify an outmoded anti-fascism and Chekist steel fist.[9] While the interpretation of a floundering Stasi is certainly not without substance, the Stasi cannot, of

---

[8] Rosenberg T. 1995: 290–91.

[9] Niethammer L. 1997: 308, 332–4, 339. The Cheka – the Extraordinary Commission for Combating Counterrevolution and Sabotage – was the original Soviet secret service on which the MfS was modelled.

course, be relegated to a peripheral role in the light of its multiplicity of functions as guardian of the verities of Marxist–Leninist ideology, its ruthless implementation of the socialist revolution of the 1950s, its upholding of the communist power monopoly against perceived enemies at home and abroad, its crucial part in the acquisition of hard currency and scientific and technical know-how from the West, and its snooping into the intimate details of people's lives. Far from being a blunt sword and rusty shield, the Stasi was an indispensable instrument of the communist power elites in the global struggle against their capitalist rivals in the West, even though it should be stressed that in some spheres, especially the vital one of the economy, the Stasi's autocratic minister, Erich Mielke, often resembles a Don Quixote tilting at socialist windmills.

THE STASI IN COMPARATIVE PERSPECTIVE

To what extent was the Stasi *sui generis*, at least in German history? A comparison with its nearest pre-war equivalent, the Gestapo, reveals that the Stasi soon evolved into a much larger organisation than the former and was far more reliant on a structured network of agents than on the kind of voluntary 'spite informers' who supplied denunciatory information to the Gestapo.[10] For example, in 1937, the Gestapo employed probably no more than 7,000 officials out of a population of 66 million. In contrast, the MfS, a mere 2,700 in 1950, had reached 48,786 in 1971 and over 91,000 full-time staff out of a population of about 16.4 million in 1989. Furthermore, the MfS, like its KGB counterpart, housed both foreign intelligence and counter-intelligence under one roof, whereas the Gestapo was but one element in the Third Reich's system of policing, state security and counterintelligence. One of the other key agencies was the Security Service (SD) of Himmler's *Schutzstaffel* or SS, and whereas SD informers reported on popular opinion, the Gestapo agents concentrated on 'political crimes'. The number of SD agents is difficult to assess; some historians speculate that the total may have been between 100,000 and 120,000 in 1939.[11] And, as will be stressed in this book, during the course of the 1960s, MfS staff became increasingly professional and more proficient at subtle forms of repression; on the other hand, the professionalism of the Gestapo's early officers – a legacy of the Weimar Republic – was eroded by less qualified new recruits and the organisation was caught up in the growing barbarism of the Third Reich. The contrast is captured in Heiner Geißler's differentiation between the mountain of corpses and files left behind by the Third Reich and the GDR respectively.

Other countries, too, have been unable to dispense with intelligence and security services. In the adversarial atmosphere of the Cold War, the

---

[10] See Gellately R. 1996.
[11] Diewald-Kerkmann G. 1995: 25.

intelligence services of both West and East experienced an exponential growth and were extremely costly to run. They generated a paper mountain of data, suffered information overload, were adept at justifying their existence and evading public accountability, and were pervaded by a conspiratorial view of the world and what Philip Knightley has called 'an obligatory paranoia'. They vied with each other in the use of advanced technology to spy on friend as well as foe and to turn each other's agents.[12] Moreover, the hidden hand of the CIA extended beyond low-level covert operations such as the funding of anti-communist trade unions, political parties and newspapers to the covert 'hot zone' of seeking to overthrow governments in Iran, Guatemala, Nicaragua and Cuba. The overthrow of the Iranian prime minister and the restoration of the Shah in 1953 and the 'Bay of Pigs' fiasco in 1961 illustrate the extremes to which the CIA was prepared to go. But covert activities were also practised at home, notably by J. Edgar Hoover, the long-time head of the FBI, who in the 1960s, according to the National Commission on the Causes and Prevention of Violence, 'helped spread the view among the police that any kind of mass protest is due to a conspiracy promulgated by agitators, often Communists, "who misdirect otherwise contented people"'.[13] As a purveyor of the Red Scare in American politics, Hoover was not too dissimilar from Mielke as the propagator of the Imperialist Scare in the GDR.

It is little wonder that East Germany's legendary spymaster Markus Wolf stresses the basic similarity in methods and goals between the secret services of the Cold War rivals. They were, he claims, vital to the preservation of peace as they gave statesmen security from being taken by surprise. Not only was he therefore performing a task analogous to that of his West German counterparts in the BND[14] but also, in his words, 'Our sins and mistakes were those of every other intelligence agency'.[15] What Wolf conveniently downplays is that a deep-rooted insecurity pervaded the entire East German leadership class and, secondly, that a symbiotic relationship existed between beauty and the beast, that is, between his elitist foreign intelligence service and the Stasi's enormous apparatus of domestic repression. In the West, there was a clearer, though by no means sharp, differentiation between these two services – in America the CIA and FBI and in Britain MI5 and MI6. In this respect, the Stasi is closer to the KGB whose ruthless and uncompromising campaigns against real or imagined enemies at home and its centrality to the preservation of the Soviet system distinguished it from the intelligence communities of the West.[16] The outcome of the Stasi's dual task of external intelligence and the ubiquitous system of surveillance and intimidation at home was an agency

---

[12] Knightley P. 1987: 4–7, 342.
[13] Cited in Blum W. 1986: 9.
[14] Wolf M. 1997: 342.
[15] Ibid., p. xi.
[16] Andrew C. and Mitrokhin V. 1999: 708–14.

many times larger than any Western intelligence or security service, including the Stasi's West German counterparts, the BND and BfV.

One of the most striking features of the Stasi was its sheer size – 91,105 full-time staff and about 176,000 informers shortly before the fall of the Berlin Wall – which, together with an elaborate system of postal and telephone monitoring, enabled the ministry to conduct an almost blanket surveillance of society. The ratio of Stasi employees to the East German population as well as the intensity of surveillance may well have been unprecedented in modern history. While the degree of monitoring and intrusion may have been exceptional, the practices were not peculiar to East Germany as the Cold War spurred the antagonists, in both the East and the West, to penetrate each other's countries as well as their own society. Yet, even the MfS has been outstripped by the electronic monitoring capability now available to modern states. At the time of writing this book, in the summer of 2002, EU governments are considering acquiring access to and storing for one year the records of personal communications, including all emails and telephone calls, a concept of universal surveillance which would have delighted the Stasi's monitors.

THE STASI RECORDS AND THE GAUCK AUTHORITY

A comparative study of the Stasi and the KGB is not easily undertaken as the Russian archives are far less accessible to scholars than the mountain of files of the former GDR agency, a comment which is also true of the classified materials relating to the BND and other Western services. After all, no security agency, or its successor, willingly divulges its innermost secrets. Access to the highly sensitive KGB materials is limited at best and sometimes reliant on money oiling the wheels of approval by the Russian authorities, and it was not until the early 1970s that the British security agencies were forced into admitting, after an elaborate cover-up, to the existence of the breaking of the German codes by Ultra and its vital contribution to the victory over the Third Reich.

The materials of the MfS are held by the *Bundesbeauftragte für die Unterlagen des Staatssicherheitsdienstes der ehemaligen Deutschen Demokratischen Republik* (BStU) in English, the Federal Commissioner for the Records of the State Security Service of the Former German Democratic Republic. Care must be taken in the use of the term BStU for, as the author discovered when trying to locate the site on the Internet, it is also an acronym for 'Brawny Surfed Tanned Upper Bodies' and 'Best Served with Tepid Utensils'. Luckily, the agency is known for short as the Gauck Authority after the name of its first head, Joachim Gauck, a former Lutheran pastor in Rostock-Evershagen. Although it is also referred to as the Birthler Authority after Gauck's successor, Marianne Birthler, who took office in 2000, the title of Gauck Authority or the abbreviation BStU will be used in this book for purposes of brevity. The agency, which was set up by the Law on the Records of the Security Service of the Former German Democratic Republic promulgated by the Bundestag in December 1991, has about 3,000 employees in its Berlin and regional offices.[17] As is explained in Chapter 15, the agency's functions include the provision of information relating to the prosecution of crimes, the rehabilitation of, and compensation for, victims of repression, and the historical reappraisal of the Stasi and its employees. The act thereby entitles not only public bodies and employees to check personnel but also gives individuals the right to consult their personal files.

When individuals have inspected the files compiled from information supplied by Stasi agents, many have been shocked at the details they contain about their political and social activities and their private lives, much of it trivial but some of it extremely sensitive and hurtful. Whereas one can usually live with entries on when the lights were switched off at home or when household rubbish was emptied into a bin, it is difficult to come to terms with the discovery that one's husband or brother had acted as an informer or that trusted work colleagues or members of a peace group had reported your views to their Stasi controlling officer. This was the experience of Vera Wollenberger, who discovered that her husband, Knud (codename IMB 'Donald'), had been reporting for many years not only on her activities in the peace and ecological movement but also on the details of their private life.[18] Many others have found similar traces of betrayal in their files.

As far as historians are concerned, the Stasi records held by the Gauck Authority are an invaluable source for the study not only of the ministry itself but also for the broader history of the GDR.[19] Given the extent of the archival holdings – the shelves would stretch for 185 kilometres – scholars are in a particularly favourable position compared to students of other secret services, even though many of the ministry's foreign intelligence files were destroyed or damaged immediately after the fall of the SED. The records held by the Gauck Authority divide into two broad groups, the administrative records and the files on individuals, albeit with considerable overlap between the two categories. The former, comprising about 20 per cent of the total holdings, cover matters such as ministry guidelines, regulations, service instructions, planning documents and statistical data. The preponderance of individual files in the overall holdings is the result of the Stasi's concern with individual persons as the primary security targets. Much of this material relates to security checks on individuals, campaigns against targets, interrogations of suspects, and the recruitment and running of informers. And not only do the records contain data on individuals and groups which are difficult to

---

[17] *Vierter Tätigkeitsbericht* 1999: 90.
[18] Wollenberger V. 1992.
[19] On this topic, see Engelmann R. 1995 and Schröter U. 1995.

retrieve from other sources, such as the numbers and activities of opposition groups, but they also shed light on developments in Western countries and among the GDR's socialist allies. While the records of a secret police apparatus have to be treated with circumspection, the MfS was most anxious that surveillance reports were both accurate and relevant and, therefore, carried out a variety of checks. Spies informed on each other, blissfully unaware that they were working for the MfS. Wollenberger's husband was described by other Stasi agents as a 'negative, hostile element'. One highly contentious issue concerns individuals who were registered as informers by controlling officers without their agreement and sometimes without their knowledge. The MfS was aware of this and sought to stamp it out; investigations by the Gauck Authority have shown that cases of 'fictional informers' are rare.[20]

The Stasi archival materials cannot be accepted unreservedly; they need to be used in conjunction with other forms of documentary information and oral testimonies. Some of the potential pitfalls in using the Stasi materials can be mentioned here. Take the example of controllers' reports on clandestine meetings, or *Treffs*, with informers. A report was based on information received, either in written or verbal form, from the agent and was thus the controller's version of what he regarded as significant from the agent's original record. Secondly, in the case of interrogation protocols, especially from the 1950s, confessions or statements may have been extracted by force or fear. Despite regular monitoring by the ministry, the accuracy of intelligence data could not be guaranteed. Its estimates of the numbers of skinheads, punks, heavy metals and so forth had inbuilt flaws as individuals were attached to highly fluid and volatile sub-cultures with which Stasi officers and informers were often unfamiliar. Furthermore, given the ideological lens through which the ministry viewed the world darkly the motives and behaviour of alleged 'hostile forces' were easily misinterpreted. One final point: in the Honecker era, the decision-making process is not easy to track as the protocols of the meetings of the leading bodies of the SED and the Stasi – the Politbüro and the Collegium respectively – tended to record decisions rather than debates, and security issues were often dealt with in private conversations between the top leaders of the SED and the MfS.

SOURCES

This book is based on a range of secondary texts, memoirs, interviews, published compilations of primary sources as well as on extensive archival materials from the Gauck Authority and, to a much lesser extent, the Matthias Domaschk Archive and the Foundation for the Parties and the Mass Organisations of the GDR (SAPMO). Most of the primary materials consulted by

---

[20] Geiger H. 1993: 66–7.

the author come under the following categories: the work of informers; the interaction between the Stasi and specific groups and areas in society such as skinheads and punks, the churches, and sport; voluntary forms of denunciation; and the ministry's assessment of popular opinion. Other areas include the internal workings of the ministry, especially the training of officers, disciplinary measures and staff grievances.

Turning to the secondary texts and other published sources which were also consulted, the origins of the Stasi are delineated by Norman Naimark (1995) as part of his stimulating study of the Russians in Germany. Three general surveys of the MfS exist in English: Childs and Popplewell (1999) provide a clear overview of Stasi activities; Wolfe (1991) produced the earliest survey in English of the Stasi and the People's Police; and Koehler (1999) offers a racy account of foreign intelligence. A fourth book in English, by Tim Garton Ash (1997), draws on materials extracted from his personal Stasi file and a series of searching interviews with former officers and spies. Those who read German can refer to the pioneering study by Karl Wilhelm Fricke (1984), which has stood the test of time remarkably well. His updated version of 1991 and Gill and Schröter's anatomy of the ministry (1991) provide a balance between interpretation and archival sources and are crucial for an understanding of the ministry's mode of operation and its mindset. Both Gill and Schröter were intimately involved in the dissolution of the Stasi in 1990 and Fricke was a victim of the Stasi, having been abducted from West Berlin in 1955. More recently, in 2001, Jens Gieseke, a researcher at the Gauck Authority, synthesised primary and secondary materials in a lucid analysis of the development and structure of the Stasi. Gieseke (2000) has also written an outstanding monograph on the social structure, the ideology, the training and the numerical expansion of the ministry's full-time staff. The ministry's own internal survey of staff numbers and of their distribution across the many departments on the eve of communism's collapse can be found in Wiedmann (1996).

The work of Gieseke, Fricke and Wiedmann is complemented by the memoirs of, and interviews with, former officers. The views and judgements of the head of foreign intelligence, Markus Wolf, are elaborated in *Man without a Face* (Wolf 1997), and the intransigence of the long-serving minister, Erich Mielke, leaps from his interview in the German weekly magazine *Der Spiegel* (31 August 1992). Interviews of varying quality with high-ranking officers can be found in Karau (1995), Wilkening (1990), Villain (1990) and Rieckert, Schwarz and Schneider (1990). One of Jean Villain's interlocutors was Wolfgang Schwanitz, the last Minister of State Security. Werner Stiller, who defected in 1979, produced an informative account of the foreign intelligence arm (HV A) and its Scientific and Technical Section several years before the demise of the GDR (Stiller 1992); Klaus Roßberg (1996) looks back at his involvement in the infiltration of the churches; and Josef Schwarz (1994) reflects on work in a regional administration. Two further memoirs, the first by Werner Großmann (2001), Wolf's successor as leader of HV A, and the second by Alexander Schalck-Golodkowski (2000), a Stasi Officer on Special Assignment and head of the shadowy trading organisation KoKo, give little away. Mielke and Wolf have been the subject of several biographies. Wilfried Otto (2000) tracks Mielke along every stage of his career and, as befits a journalist with personal experience of the GDR, Colitt (1995) offers a lively examination of Wolf's career and personality.

As for the agents of the Stasi, Barbara Miller (1999) presents a challenging assessment of the work and motives of IMs[21] and Müller-Enbergs (1993 and 1995b) has written a series of important essays on the motivation of informers and the explosion in their numbers. Hubertus Knabe (1999) has conducted detailed research into HV A's penetration of West German society and politics; he stresses that the issue of informers and collaboration is one shared by both West and East Germany. Not only has Müller-Enbergs (1998) undertaken a critical assessment of the Stasi's informers in the West but he also produced, in 1996, a similar documentary collection and commentary on East German informers. Both books contain the full text of all the ministerial guidelines for work with agents. Several other edited collections of documents reveal the complex and shifting nature of collaboration between the Stasi and eminent writers such as Christa Wolf and Hermann Kant and officials from various parts of the system, among them Manfred Stolpe of the Protestant churches. A highly critical assessment of Stolpe's Stasi contacts appears in Neubert (1993). A sample of documents from Christa Wolf's Stasi files was edited by Vinke (1993), Stolpe's by Reuth (1992), and Kant's by Corino (1995). Files on one of the Stasi's main victims, Reiner Kunze, are printed in *Deckname 'Lyrik'*. Reference has already been made to the case of Vera Wollenberger, whose 1992 publication *Virus der Heuchler*, containing details from her Stasi files, reveals the thoroughness and perniciousness of Stasi operations against her and her colleagues in Pankow. A comparative study of the Gestapo and the Stasi, which draws a contrast between the ways in which the two agencies gathered intelligence, has been undertaken by the American historian Robert Gellately (1996), and Herbert Reinke (1997) has located the MfS within the broader context of political policing in Germany since the early nineteenth century.

The ministry's comprehensive surveillance of society has been well researched: Vollnhals (1996a) and Besier/Wolf (1992) have scrutinised MfS relations with the churches; MfS controls over the legal system and the judiciary are examined by Vollnhals (1999) and Raschka (2000); Joachim Walther (1996) has produced an exhaustive account of the collaboration with the Stasi of so many GDR writers; and Maria Haendke-Hoppe-Arndt (1997) leaves no stone unturned in her examination of the structure and activities of Main Department XVIII in the economic sphere. The latter is part of a multi-volume handbook on the structure of the MfS compiled under the

---

[21] IM is the abbreviation for *Inoffizieller Mitarbeiter* – unofficial collaborator or informer.

auspices of the Gauck Authority. Other volumes in the series include Main Department II (counterespionage) and the Central Coordinating Group, which was responsible for combating flight and emigration from the GDR. The oppositional political culture, which consisted of a kaleidoscope of peace, human rights, women's and ecological groups, is the focus of many studies. Two significant works, which are also based on the perspectives of insiders, are the volume edited by Ulrike Poppe, Rainer Eckert and Ilko-Sascha Kowalczuk (1995) and the account by Wolfgang Rüddenklau (1992). The various strains of non-conformist youth culture such as skinheads and punks are investigated by Ross (2000), Süß (1996) and Michael (1999). Top-level sport, especially football and the doping of athletes, is the subject of the documentary study, *MfS und Leistungssport* (1994). Doping malpractices have been exposed by Spitzer (1998a) and Berendonk (1992).

The lines of communication between the SED and the Stasi and the difficult question of Stasi autonomy have been assessed by Fricke (1991), Suckut (1997) and Süß (1997). Despite the general pacification of society, the Stasi's intrusion into society and the deployment of multiple control mechanisms, both the SED and the Stasi imploded in the autumn of 1989. The agony of the MfS in its final year has been uncovered in a series of documents edited by Mitter and Wolle (1990), which became a bestseller immediately after publication, and in Walter Süß's impressive combination of theoretical issues with an exhaustive combing of the archives in a monograph published in 1999.

THE KEY ISSUES

What are the key issues surrounding the Stasi which will be addressed in this book? Some have already been touched upon: the ministry's relationship with the SED; the value to the historian of the Stasi records; the image of the Stasi as a ubiquitous and highly efficient intelligence-gathering agency both at home and abroad; the complexity of the interaction between society and the instruments of coercion; and the legacy of the Stasi for the political culture of contemporary Germany. In addition to exploring these issues further, the ensuing chapters will address aspects such as the motives behind collaboration with the Stasi; and the extent to which the Stasi officers constituted a cohesive and privileged elite. It is the working premise of this book that the GDR was a dictatorship of the SED party leadership and that during the later Ulbricht era and throughout the Honecker years, the system may be characterised as a post-totalitarian dictatorship. While the basic administrative command structures remained intact and the law was often flouted, the latter concept denotes the less brutal and terroristic form of rule which emerged gradually from the chrysalis of Khrushchev's deStalinisation campaigns. In contrast to the Stalinist era, compliance rather than revolutionary dynamic pervaded the system, a limited but highly contested degree of space existed for a parallel society, and the top leaders tended to be more bureaucratic and state-technocratic than charismatic. In view of the Stasi's role as a junior ally of the SED, the label post-totalitarian party police state might also be regarded as appropriate. This underlines the dictatorial nature of SED rule and the fact that, unlike in Poland in the 1980s, the East German secret services remained subject to the overall political and normative control of the Communist party even though their operational latitude may have been greater than is often believed.[22]

After a brief survey in Chapter 1 of the origins and development of the Stasi, the discussion will focus on the years 1971–89, that is, the period when Erich Honecker presided over country and party and the Stasi was in 'full bloom'. In the early 1970s, the GDR emerged from its diplomatic isolation and appeared to be a stable member of the international community. Despite this improvement in its status and despite the protection afforded by the construction of the Berlin Wall in 1961, the GDR's rulers remained allergic to the 'imperialist' threat and suspicious of the loyalty of their subjects. The closer relations with West Germany following the Basic Treaty between the GDR and the FRG in 1972, the country's entry into the United Nations in the following year and the signing of the Helsinki Final Act in 1975 stimulated popular hopes of an improvement in human rights and of a relaxation of restrictions on contacts with the West. But from the point of view of the regime, and particularly with memories of the Prague Spring of 1968 still very much alive, the new situation was seen as potentially destabilising. Hence, the Stasi was called upon to play a major role in countering the negative aspects of détente. Furthermore, as the terroristic methods of the 1950s and early 1960s were becoming increasingly inappropriate, the Stasi was also expected to carry out a multiplicity of tasks aimed at maintaining the SED system in all walks of life. Such was its apparent success in performing this function that as late as the spring of 1989 German unification appeared inconceivable. Why, despite its enormous potential for coercion, the Stasi was unable to halt the implosion of the GDR, as well as its own disintegration, will conclude the investigation into the 'firm' and the paradox of omnipotence.

---

[22] See Chapman B. 1970: 119–21 and Los M. and Zybertowicz A. 2000: 17–18, 29–31.

Part I

THE ORIGINS AND DEVELOPMENT OF THE EAST GERMAN SECURITY SERVICE, 1945–71

Chapter 1

FROM WEIMAR REPUBLIC
TO GDR

THE KPD CRUCIBLE

The role model of the Stasi was the Cheka, the Soviet secret police founded by Felix Dzerzhinsky in 1917. However, the Stasi also saw itself as the heir to the secret apparatus of the German Communist Party (KPD), whose development before 1945 sheds light on some of the traditions which helped to shape the security doctrine and the working methods of the Stasi. The construction of a secret party apparatus was a compulsory condition of membership of the Communist International (Comintern), as set out in the '21 Conditions' of entry adopted by its Second World Congress in 1920. The secret underground structures were originally justified by the expectation that the period of legality enjoyed by foreign communist parties would end as the revolution in the developed western world approached. They also derived from the communists' belief that they belonged to a conspiratorial confraternity, an attitude which would be reinforced by their experiences in the Nazi period. The secret apparatus was initially subdivided into two sections, the *Nachrichtendienst* (Intelligence Service or N–Group) and the *Militärdienst* (Military Service or M–Group). The former was responsible for 'special political tasks' and the latter for the organisation of the movement's armed uprising.[1] Although formally subordinate to the KPD's German leadership, in practice they were financed and run by the Moscow-based Executive Committee of the Comintern (ECCI). The domination of Moscow's instructors is illustrated by their role in the preparations for the abortive revolution in October 1923. Soviet military advisers, who were present in force since the occupation of the Ruhr by French and Belgian troops in January 1923, took control of the crucial stages of preparations for the uprising.

The failure to ignite a revolution in Germany to overthrow the hated Weimar Republic had a direct impact on the policies of the Comintern, to

---

[1] Fricke K. W. 1984: 17–18.

which the KPD, as a national section, was subordinated. The Comintern, which had always paid close attention to the interests of the Soviet Union, increasingly placed the decisive emphasis on the foreign policy objective of breaking Russian 'encirclement' by the 'imperialist' powers. Germany, which since the Rapallo Treaty (1922) had opened diplomatic and trade relations with Moscow, was central to the Bolsheviks' geopolitical strategy. These developments also had an impact on the function of the KPD's secret apparatus. As the expectation of revolution receded, the M-Group was downscaled; perhaps symbolically, it was renamed the AM (Anti-Military) Group in 1928. The head of the M-Group during these years, Erich Wollenberg, described how the secret apparatus had changed from the military spearhead of a German revolution into a foreign adjunct of department four of the Red Army.[2] However, with the reorientation in communist policy, the functions of the N-Group were constantly expanded from the mid-1920s to suit the new demands made of the secret apparatus. Above all, these involved spying for the Soviets and eliminating Stalin's opponents in the KPD's factional struggles. For these ends, the N-Group was organisationally divided into two main departments, internal party counterintelligence (*Abwehr*) and subversion or decomposition (*Zersetzung*).

Walter Krivitsky, a senior KGB officer, wrote in his memoir-cum-exposé of Soviet secret service practices that: 'Out of the ruins of the Communist revolution we built in Germany a brilliant Intelligence Service, the envy of every other nation'.[3] Whatever the substance of this claim, the success of the Nazis would demonstrate the limitations of a secret service in achieving a party's broader political goals. Under Hans Kippenberger, the head of the KPD's intelligence service, an extensive spy network extended through the army, police, the government and the political parties. Kippenberger himself was appointed to the Reichstag's defence committee in 1927, furnishing Moscow with insider information.[4] So-called 'worker correspondents', who officially wrote for the KPD press, also unofficially provided reports on the situation in their factories and industrial branches and on technical developments, from which edited extracts were forwarded to Moscow. By the later 1920s, the communist movement had a large and diverse group of Soviet secret agents, facilitating the penetration of all areas of German society. The suitability and loyalty of prospective agents in the service of Soviet intelligence was put to the test in a series of minor assignments.[5]

During the second half of the 1920s, the N-Group played an important part in the party's all-consuming factional struggles, in which Stalin's opponents were purged from the party parallel to developments in the CPSU.

---

[2] Wollenberg E. 1951: 14; Weber H. 1969: 347–8.
[3] Krivitsky W. G. 1992: 59–60.
[4] Fischer R. 1948: 510–11.
[5] Ibid., 512–14; Dallin D. J. 1956: 95–9.

During this process, the installation of a tightly centralised structure on the model of the Bolsheviks' 'democratic centralism' played a crucial role. For this purpose, the creation of a new highly disciplined group of functionaries trained in the methods of party organisation was an essential prerequisite. Stalin's German expert, Manuilsky, identified a group of loyal functionaries who were then trained in the Comintern's Lenin School. Among this group who served the Comintern as well as the Soviet secret police, GPU, was Walter Ulbricht, the KPD's new head of organisation. Ulbricht attended the Lenin School in 1924–25 before returning to Germany to resume his work with the all-important Organisational Department of the KPD's Central Committee. An early biographer of Ulbricht writes: 'During the Weimar Republic, Ulbricht unfailingly represented Moscow's interests in the KPD. And just as unfailingly, he helped to eliminate those who had other ideas'.[6] Other functionaries trained in Moscow who later attained prominent positions in the SED and Stasi were Erich Mielke, Markus Wolf, Wilhelm Zaisser and Ernst Wollweber.

The Stalinisation of the KPD, that is the imposition of a centralistic, bureaucratic organisation and ideological conformity, received a decisive impulse with the acceptance of the principle of Leninist democratic centralism at the 1925 Party Congress. This fundamentally eroded the confederal structures and the original ideological diversity of the party by strengthening the central organs, such as the Small Secretariat. The disciplining of the party culminated, in the later 1920s, in the fusion of the Stalin faction, headed by Ernst Thälmann, and the party apparatus functionaries who constituted the party's nerve centre. Thälmann, from a working-class background, became chairman in 1925, bound the KPD ever closer to Moscow and fostered the personality cult of Stalin.

Throughout the history of the KPD, the party leadership had to tolerate the presence of senior Comintern officials, who reported directly to Moscow. However, what changed after 1926 was the GPU's penetration of the wider German party structures through the conduit installed by the secret apparatus. According to Ruth Fischer, the KPD leader in 1924–35, N-Group functionaries pursued opposition activists by raiding their meetings, searching their flats and conducting interrogations.[7] Her claim has broadly been substantiated by new documentary evidence. In Saxony, the mood in the party turned sour as dissident functionaries were placed under surveillance and their flats searched for literature.[8]

After promoting the Stalinisation of the KPD during the Weimar Republic, the N-Group fell victim to a factional struggle in the leadership-in-exile during the mid-1930s. Many of the apparatus functionaries died during the

---

[6] Stern C. 1963: 47.
[7] Fischer R. 1948: 507.
[8] SAPMO 1 3/8/25, 'Protokoll', 1928, pp. 357–8, 390.

Great Purges and in 1937, Kippenberger was executed as an alleged spy and saboteur. Against this background, Ulbricht and the ECCI's cadre department replaced the existing N-Group with a new cadre organisation, which was entrusted with the security of the small leadership group around Pieck and Ulbricht. These changes were accompanied by a purge of Political Bureau members and candidates who had taken the 'wrong side' in the policy debate, thus transferring the locus of power to a Small Secretariat (see below).

THE KPD BETWEEN HITLER AND STALIN

Soon after the establishment of the Nazi regime in 1933, the Gestapo destroyed the KPD's legal party organisation as well as the illegal, secret apparatus which had, ironically, been created for such an eventuality. The Communists were the first major target of Nazi repression. The KPD fell like a pack of cards. As many as 60,000 to 100,000 Communists were interned by the end of 1933. At a KPD conference in Moscow in October 1935, Pieck reported that of 422 leading functionaries in Germany, 24 had been murdered, 219 had been arrested and 125 had found exile in the Soviet Union.[9] The party's highly centralised organisational structure, which had been used to eliminate dissent during the Weimar Republic, proved to be counterproductive as it undermined the efforts of grassroots activists to coordinate any political initiative from below. Under these conditions, the KPD was reduced to little more than a party in exile, even though many thousands of Communists, both at home and abroad, engaged in a variety of resistance activities.

Nor did it help Communist resistance activities in Germany that the party was subordinated to Moscow's interests and its policy prescriptions. Stalin was not interested in rebuilding the KPD and the exile leaders were obliged to fall into line behind the 1935 shift in Comintern policy towards cooperation with social democracy, hitherto regarded as communism's main enemy. At its World Congress in 1935, the Communist movement was instructed to form an anti-fascist, united front not only with Social Democrats but also with bourgeois opponents of fascism. The Popular Front had to be abandoned, however, following the conclusion of the non-aggression pact between Germany and the Soviet Union in the summer of 1939. The KPD leadership in exile was obliged to sanction the dramatic change in policy on the basis that it was a 'success' for the Soviet Union's peace policy. Having been abandoned by the West, Moscow was presented as merely acting to break the 'encirclement' by hostile powers. Until the launching of Operation Barbarossa in 1941, the Comintern returned to the ultra-left policy that social democracy was the main enemy of communism.

Shifts in Stalin's policy also had significant – and sometimes fatal – consequences for the KPD leadership. Dissenters from the 1935 line on the

---

[9] Weber H. 1990: 18.

Popular Front were purged. At the KPD's 'Brussels' conference in October 1935 the main dissidents, Hermann Schubert and Fritz Schulte, were removed from the party hierarchy and the Pieck–Ulbricht axis strengthened; Ackermann and Wehner became candidates of the Political Bureau.[10] The purge of dissenters in the KPD leadership – as was also the case with the other parties in the Comintern – flowed into the Great Terror of the mid-1930s. Some 70 per cent of the KPD émigré functionaries and members were arrested between 1936 and 1938.[11] And more leading functionaries died in the Soviet Union than in Nazi Germany. Of the 43 members and candidates who belonged to the Political Bureau between 1920 and 1933, five members were murdered by the Nazis and five members and two candidates in the Stalinist purges, including Hugo Eberlein and Fritz Schulte. Eberlein's son, Werner, would become a member of the SED Politbüro in 1983. If one looks at the entire leadership corps of about 500 in the 1920s, then 102 lost their lives under Hitler and 41 under Stalin.[12] As indicated above, among Stalin's victims was Hans Kippenberger, the head of the M-P Group, who was executed in Moscow in October 1937. Although the charge was spying for the Western intelligence service and organising terrorist attacks, his real crime was his opposition to Ulbricht and Pieck during the struggles within the KPD leadership in 1935. He also clashed with them over their attempt to tighten party control over the apparatus and to carry out a constant screening and permanent surveillance of the party and its cadres.[13] The apparatus was closed down in 1937.

STALIN'S FAITHFUL SERVANTS

Until the Comintern's dissolution in 1943, as a concession to Moscow's Western allies, no consistent attempt had been made to rebuild the KPD cadre organisation in Germany. However, with the war running in favour of the anti-Hitler coalition, the KPD leaders in Moscow turned their attention, under the close supervision of Dimitrov and Moscow officials, to the construction of a new order in post-war Germany. While they strongly favoured a Soviet-type system, practicalities dictated a gradual transition to this goal. The immediate goal was to be the realisation of the bourgeois–democratic programme of 1848 by means of a 'bloc of fighting democracy' in which the KPD would play the key role. It was from the group of proven Soviet loyalists – Ulbricht, Pieck, Ackermann and Herrnstadt – that the core of the GDR's leaders would be drawn. Pieck, who became President of the GDR in 1949, had been associated with the Spartacus League and had served the Comintern in various positions in the 1920s and early 1930s. Herrnstadt, a

---

[10] Weber H. 1969: 155–7; Podewin N. 1995: 108–10.
[11] Ibid., 133–4.
[12] Weber H. 1998: 23–4.
[13] Kaufmann B., Reisener E., Schwips D. and Walter H. 1993: 9, 43–6.

gifted journalist, was involved in espionage for Red Army intelligence between 1933 and 1939 before fleeing to Moscow. Ackermann, who did illegal work for the KPD after Hitler came to power, served in the Spanish Civil War and in 1940 was smuggled to Moscow by Soviet agents; he would become the first head of GDR foreign intelligence in 1951. What characterised this inner group of leaders? They had survived by demonstrating their loyalty and obedience to Stalin and the Soviet system and they had acquired practical skills on the organisation of a rigidly centralised political party. And, as Erich Weitz has pointed out, their experience of the terror and purges had accustomed many 'to the notion that political opponents could be dealt with by arbitrary arrest, physical intimidation, and execution'.[14] They had also participated in the intensive ideological and political training at the Comintern's famous Lenin School for foreign cadres. The courses were intended to produce qualified party functionaries who would serve the Soviet-dominated communist movement under all conditions. Among top Stasi officials who were trained at the Lenin School and also spent some time in Soviet exile were Erich Mielke, Richard Stahlmann, Markus Wolf, Wilhelm Zaisser and Ernst Wollweber. Wolf, who had fled with his family to Moscow in 1934, became a Soviet citizen and adopted a Russian name.

But many KPD leaders had been tried and tested in other arenas – the battles on the streets of Weimar Germany, the Spanish Civil War, Nazi concentration camps, the resistance in Western Europe. Violence, repression and a stark friend–foe image were intrinsic to their way of life. Take, for example, Wilhelm Zaisser and Ernst Wollweber, the first two ministers of state security. They both joined the KPD in 1919, worked for Soviet military intelligence and served short terms of imprisonment during the Weimar Republic. Zaisser, like Mielke and Ulbricht, participated in the Spanish Civil War, serving as head of the Thirteenth International Brigade under the name of General Gomez. Wollweber, on instructions from Moscow, set up a maritime sabotage unit which conducted operations against Nazi shipping.

In summary, by the end of the Second World War, the Soviet Union had at its disposal a corpus of experienced functionaries who were totally committed to the communist cause, experienced in Stalinist modes of repression and ready to assist the Soviets in the establishment of a new order in Germany and in the administration of the Soviet zone of occupation.

THE FORMATION OF A SECRET POLICE:
THE SOVIET ROLE

The history of the KPD before 1945 and the following examination of the emergence of the GDR from the chrysalis of Soviet occupation thereafter

---

[14] Weitz E. D. 1997: 300.

reinforce Naimark's claim that after 1945: '... the Soviets and the SED did not create the Stasi as an afterthought for securing the East German state structure and protecting its accomplishments. Rather, from the very beginning, security concerns within the German party and the Soviet military government helped to create an East German state that was inseparable from its internal police functions'.[15] Unquestionably, the Soviet Union played the decisive role in the formation of an East German security organisation in its zone of occupation. Appointments and dismissals required Soviet approval; senior officers were obliged to report directly to Soviet intelligence agents; and much of the police force's budget was financed by the Soviets.

The Allied Control Council enacted measures to confine the German police force to the maintenance of law and order and it explicitly proscribed the formation of any political police. However, these provisions were contravened in the Soviet zone of occupation, where from the outset the construction of secret police structures took on an important function in the consolidation of communist power.[16] Developments in the period 1945–50 occurred against the background of the outbreak of the Cold War, which the Soviets believed was potentially only the period of international tension preceding a conflict between East and West. The importance the Soviets attached to the role of intelligence operations in future warfare, combined with Moscow's narrow ideological definition of its enemies, ensured that an early emphasis was placed on building up secret police structures in East Germany.[17]

The Soviet Military Administration in Germany (SMAD) was set up immediately after the arrival of the Red Army in Berlin to oversee the everyday practicalities of occupation. SMAD and other Soviet agencies conducted their own independent security operations in the zone as well as exercising firm control over the German political police. One of the most influential officials was Lieutenant General Ivan Serov, who, though a top SMAD officer, was responsible in his capacity as a NKVD/MVD officer only to his superiors in Moscow. One of Serov's basic jobs was to create a virtually independent system of operations groups consisting of Soviet officers, troops and interpreters which drew on Germans as informers and *agents provocateurs*. The main Soviet security agencies, with offices in every district and *Land*, were the NKVD (People's Commissariat of Internal Affairs) and the NKGB (People's Commissariat of State Security), both renamed in 1946 as the MVD (Ministry of Internal Affairs) and the MGB (Ministry of State Security) respectively. In January 1946, there were 2,230 NKVD and 399 NKGB officers in the zone and 2,304 Germans who spied for the Soviets.[18]

---

[15] Naimark N. M. 1995: 354–5.
[16] Tantzscher M. 1998: 48.
[17] Childs D. and Popplewell R. 1999: 40–42.
[18] Gieseke J. 1998: 6; Foitzik J. 1998: 121, 131.

Fundamental to the development of an East German security force was the formation in August 1946 of the German Administration of the Interior (DVdI). In order to achieve the wide-ranging demands of consolidating Communist control, the localised structures of the special Criminal Police branches for political affairs were reorganised and brought under central control. At the same time, it unified the political police departments under DVdI Kommissariat-5 (K-5) of the Criminal Police department (Kripo). K-5 of the Saxon police force had been established, on Soviet orders, in the summer of 1945; other K-5 agencies soon followed in other police administrations. Their functions included protecting the new economic order, combating fascist gangs, uncovering ex-Nazi functionaries, the surveillance of Interior Ministry personnel and providing support for the KPD/SED.

The issue of SMAD's command no. 201 for the deNazification of the zone in August 1947 signalled an increase in K-5's political tasks, adding to them a range of judicial functions, and extended its regional organisations. Two months later, at a DVdI conference, Mielke informed K-5 personnel that they would take over the implementation of tasks previously reserved for the occupying power and that these actions were part of the 'struggle for political power'.[19] Later, in 1948, K-5 was separated from other Criminal Police activities and became the core of a centralised political police with additional powers for crushing political opponents.[20]

At leadership level, SMAD control over the DVdI was ensured by co-opting long-serving and trusted individuals from the pre-war KPD into the decisive positions of the administration. For example, Kurt Fischer, who became DVdI's president in mid-1948, had received military training in Moscow before fighting in the Spanish Civil War; he had already demonstrated his abilities in the centralisation of the police system in Saxony. The same principle also applied to K-5, where Soviet instructors were present throughout the apparatus. In reality, K-5 was only nominally housed in the People's Police; in practice, it was a Communist cadre organisation rather than part of the state system. This facilitated its deployment as a party police force, which, until October 1989, was trained in the canons of Marxism-Leninism at party schools. Already performing a range of tasks associated with the later MfS, K-5 acted as an auxiliary of the Soviet Union's MGB units. Under the cover of deNazification, this involved not only the arbitrary arrest and detention of all actual and alleged Nazis, but also acting against opponents of Communist control in the zone. In the late 1940s, thousands of Social Democrats and politicians of the parties of the middle classes were rounded up, frequently finding themselves sentenced by Soviet military tribunals to years in Soviet labour camps as well as to incarceration in the 11 Soviet 'special camps' located in the zone. These internment camps, such as Sachsenhausen,

---

[19] See the document in Tantzscher M. 1998: 50.
[20] Wegmann B. 1997: 17.

Berlin-Hohenschönhausen, Buchenwald and Torgau, were modelled on the Gulag Archipelago and most had served a similar purpose during the Third Reich. At least 154,000 Germans and about 35,000 non-Germans were interned and about 43,000 Germans died in the camps.[21] While the Soviet camps were not analogous to the Nazi extermination camps, the high death toll, mainly from malnutrition and disease, was in part the result of grievous neglect by the Soviet authorities.

Another crucial structural element in the zonal security system was the Main Division for Intelligence and Information under Erich Mielke. Officially constituted as an organ of the DVdI in November 1947, the new body was flanked by the existing regional offices; it carried out counterintelligence, controlled the media, and collected and disseminated information. Informers and confidants were recruited to meet Mielke's aim 'to know everything and to report on everything worth knowing',[22] a principle which Mielke would seek to apply throughout his long career. Measures were introduced in the DVdI to improve the political indoctrination and reliability of security staff, notably the launching of the Main Department Political Culture in the autumn of 1948. The department's highly trained political cultural officers – with a ratio of one to every 100 to 110 police officers by mid-1948 – conducted regular political training courses for members of the security organs and sought to ensure that appointments conformed with SED priorities.[23]

FROM K-5 TO MfS

The SED delegation to Moscow in December 1948, comprising Pieck, Ulbricht and other top officials, was informed by Stalin that the Soviet Politbüro had decided that the East German security apparatus should be organisationally separated from the People's Police on account of the extensive range of tasks it had to execute.[24] Such a development was not to the liking of the Soviet Minister of State Security, Victor Abakumov, who harboured reservations with respect to the limited number of suitable East German cadres and preferred security matters to remain in Soviet hands.[25] In May 1949, a series of organisational changes were put in train, culminating in the formation of the MfS in February 1950. As part of a general overhaul of security, the protection of the economy was transferred in the first half of 1949 into the hands of the Main Administration for the Protection of the National Economy (*Hauptverwaltung zum Schutz der Volkswirtschaft*, or HVzSV) in the Ministry of the Interior. This department also assumed many of the

---

[21] Dennis M. 2000: 38–9.
[22] Naimark N. M. 1995: 366.
[23] Wegmann B. 1997: 21.
[24] Badstübner R. and Loth W. 1994: 252, 269.
[25] Otto W. 2000: 113.

police functions of K-5 and enjoyed wide-ranging powers for combating the class enemy. Yet more organisational changes led to the dissolution of K-5 in August 1949 and the transfer of numerous functions to Department D of the Criminal Police. The new ministry, whose creation was approved unanimously by what was still the provisional parliament or *Volkskammer* in February 1950, consisted of the HVzSV, sections of the former Department for Intelligence and Information, the Criminal Police and the Main Department Political Culture. The new Ministry of State Security was not subject to control or supervision by the GDR parliament and, although an organ of the Council of Ministers, its true masters were the officers of the KGB. Each head of a Stasi service unit was responsible to Soviet instructors who kept an eye on activities and stepped in when necessary.[26] In the early 1950s, the KGB employed 2,200 staff who performed the latter tasks as well as their own secret service work. After Stalin's death, Beria reduced the number to 328, only for the target figure to be increased to 458 after his own fall from power.[27]

---

[26] Gieseke J. 1998: 12.
[27] Gieseke J. 2001: 58; Otto W. 2000: 128.

Chapter 2

THE MINISTRY OF STATE
SECURITY, 1950–71

THE SHARP SWORD

The law on the Ministry of State Security was terse and deliberately uninformative, its two short paragraphs amounting to little more than an announcement of the formation of the new body. On the other hand, the Minister of the Interior, Karl Steinhoff, was a little more forthcoming when he told the *Volkskammer*, on 8 February 1950, that the ministry's main task was: 'to protect the people's own enterprises and works, transport and the people's own property against the plots of criminal elements as well as against all attacks, to conduct a decisive fight against the activity of enemy agents, subversives, saboteurs and spies, to conduct an energetic fight against bandits, to protect our democratic development and to ensure uninterrupted fulfilment of the economic plans of our peace economy'.[1]

Although Steinhoff had once been a Social Democrat, his speech resonated with the militancy of the old KPD. The address also underscored the Stasi's role as one of the SED's key instruments in the Stalinisation of East German politics and society, a process which had been set in motion in 1947–48. This entailed the emasculation of the other political parties, notably the CDU and the LDPD, the subjugation of the large mass organisations such as the Free German Youth and the Confederation of Free German Trade Unions (FDGB), the transformation of the SED into a monolithic, hierarchical body on the model of the CPSU, and the assertion of the party's dominance over an increasingly centralised economy and administration. Nor were SED members spared the pain of the party's transition into a Marxist-Leninist party. A series of expulsions and purges which lasted between 1948 and 1953 turned the SED into a more disciplined and 'ideologically pure' party and strengthened the position of those Communists such as Ulbricht and Pieck who had spent much of the Nazi era in Moscow. The main targets for expulsion from the party were former SPD members and non-conformist Communists. The

---

[1] Cited in Gieseke J. 1998: 9–10. Our translation.

MfS was active in the purging of the SED and the other political parties as well as in securing the state from hostile groups in the West and their helpers in the GDR. The Western bodies included RIAS, the Organisation of Independent Lawyers and the Eastern Bureau of political parties such as the SPD and the CDU.[2] The paranoia ran so deep that inside the GDR even the small community of Jehovah's Witnesses was banned in 1950 on the absurd pretext that they were associated with Western secret services (see Chapter 10).

The reconstruction of the political system, together with the restructuring of the economy and society, had made sufficient progress from the point of view of the SED leaders for Ulbricht, with Soviet approval, to announce at the 1952 party conference that the GDR could now proceed with the 'planned construction of socialism'. Whereas the economy had come increasingly under central control by means of an elaborate planning mechanism and through the nationalisation of many sectors of the economy,[3] the SED had been reluctant to press ahead with the collectivisation of agriculture as it was so closely associated in people's minds with the millions of victims during the famine in the Soviet Union in 1932–33. Nevertheless, shortly after its party conference, the SED decided to accelerate its controversial collectivisation programme in agriculture at the same time as it introduced artisans' production cooperatives. Many farmers and artisans were summoned before the courts on trumped-up charges of committing crimes against the economy.[4] All this was part of a general campaign against the old social order, which also encompassed an intensification of pressure against the Protestant churches and the education sector. In addition, in 1952, a 5-kilometre-wide prohibited zone was created between the GDR and the FRG, the armed forces entered on a period of rapid expansion, the development of heavy industry was accelerated and the five *Länder* were dissolved and replaced by 15 Regional Administrations (*Bezirke*). In order to pay for this ambitious programme, deep cuts were made in the social budgets in early 1953 and, in May, wages were squeezed and ration cards withdrawn from 2 million people. In June, a sharp increase in work norms was announced for implementation at the end of the month, a measure which was tantamount to cuts in the real wages of workers of between 25 per cent and 30 per cent. So strong was popular discontent that the GDR stood on the verge of implosion.

The Stasi had made its own distinctive contribution to the 'construction of socialism' at a time, according to Ulbricht, of a sharpening of the class struggle. As yet, the SED Central Committee apparatus and the SED organisation in the Stasi were too underdeveloped to keep a firm grip on the MfS; however, the ministry worked closely with the Central Party Control

---

[2] Mählert U. 1998: 351–424.

[3] In 1948, the publicly-owned sector of the economy already accounted for 61 per cent of the gross product of the Soviet zone.

[4] Gieseke J. 2001: 51.

Commission in the purges of the party membership. The most notable victim was the former Politbüro member, Paul Merker, who was arrested by the MfS in 1952 after being mentioned in the so-called confession of Rudolf Slansky, the ex-General Secretary of the Czech Communist Party. Although Merker was not a Jew, his advocacy of Jewish interests and his solidarity with the Jewish victims of Nazism had brought him into conflict with the party at a time when anti-semitism was gathering momentum in the Soviet Union after the discovery of an alleged plot by predominantly Jewish doctors. The preparations for Merker's trial in the GDR had strong anti-semitic tones. During the interrogations conducted by the Stasi, Merker was mocked as the 'King of the Jews' and as a 'slave of the Jews'. He was spared a show trial by Stalin's timely death and was released in 1956.[5] The Stasi cast a long shadow: between August and December 1952, 1,476 persons were arrested in arbitrary fashion; and confessions were forced by means of constant interrogation and other brutal methods.[6]

Despite its active role in enforcing the rapid transformation of society, the MfS was far from being the omnipresent conglomerate of the GDR's final two decades. While the ministry's full-time staff had grown quickly from about 1,100 in 1950 to 8,800 in 1952 and it acquired ever more powers, staffing problems were legion. Not only was staff turnover high, but many officers were ill-equipped for the demands of secret police work. Most were recruited from among young members of the SED and the FDJ who came from a proletarian and unprivileged background. Flight to the West was not uncommon.[7]

THE JUNE 1953 UPRISING

The popular uprising, which erupted on the streets of East Berlin on 17 June 1953 and quickly spread to most other cities of the GDR, was a traumatic shock for both the SED and the MfS, even though they had been aware of the widespread dissatisfaction with the Communist attack on the old order. Stasi District Service Unit buildings were occupied by demonstrators in Bitterfeld, Görlitz, Jena, Merseburg and Nisky, and prisoners released from jail. The uprising was soon crushed by the Soviet forces. In their wake, the MfS hunted down demonstrators; by 7 July, it had arrested 4,816 persons.[8] Although Communist rule survived and Ulbricht managed to outmanoeuvre his critics on the Politbüro and the Central Committee, the Stasi had a high

---

[5] Gieseke J. 2001: 52–3.
[6] Gieseke J. 1998: 11–12.
[7] About 400 existing and ex-staff fled to the West before the building of the Berlin Wall in 1961: 108 returned through the use of force and trickery; seven of them were executed and the others received long jail sentences. See Gieseke J. 2001: 55.
[8] Ibid., 60–61.

price to pay for what Minister President Otto Grotewohl referred to as its failure to protect the state against enemy subversion and agents and its ignorance of the planned putsch.[9] It was downgraded to a State Secretariat and, on 18 July, Zaisser fell victim to the political infighting.

Zaisser's replacement was Ernst Wollweber, whom the Soviets favoured over Ulbricht's preferred choice, Erich Mielke. Wollweber (1898–1967)[10] was a KPD activist, having joined the party in 1919, served as one of its regional M-Leaders and had been imprisoned in 1924–26. His period as a Reichstag deputy was cut short by Hitler's accession to power. During the Third Reich, he organised sabotage operations against German, Italian and Japanese shipping. Arrested in Sweden in 1940, he spent the next four years in custody. After his release, he became a Soviet citizen and resided in the Soviet Union until his return to Germany in 1946. Before his appointment as State Secretary of the Stasi, he held high office in maritime and transport agencies and in the Ministry of the Interior.

Despite the setbacks of 1953, the Stasi's role as a spearhead of the socialist revolution remained intact and it recovered its ministerial status two years later. In the first of a series of actions against Western agencies such as the Gehlen Organisation and the Eastern Bureau of the SPD, 'Action Firework', launched in October 1953, led to the arrest of several hundred alleged agents. Soviet instructors played a key role in the planning and implementation of these measures. As a result of 'Action Firework' and similar campaigns, an estimated 600 to 700 persons were abducted from the West, including 120 of the 400 or so MfS staff who had fled the GDR. One of the Stasi's victims was the journalist Karl Wilhelm Fricke, who was seized in West Berlin in 1955.[11] After his release from prison, he would become West Germany's leading expert on the Stasi.

DESTALINISATION

Wielding the sword in this manner became less appropriate when, in February 1956, the Soviet leader Nikita Khrushchev initiated a process of deStalinisation with his denunciation of the personality cult and the terroristic methods of Stalin. Although Ulbricht attempted to limit the damage inflicted by these revelations on his own political position and the fragile GDR, he failed to halt the spread of revisionist ideas among students and intellectuals such as the philosopher Wolfgang Harich and the head of the *Aufbau* publishing house, Walter Janka. The political temperature was also raised by the spread of revisionist ideas from neighbouring Poland and Hungary. Wollweber,

---

[9] Otto W. 2000: 198.

[10] Ibid., 200–201. For a good biographical sketch of Wollweber, see Childs D. and Popplewell R. 1999: 28–32.

[11] Gieseke J. 2001: 63–4; Otto W. 2000: 214.

though no liberal in Stasi clothing, regarded Ulbricht's line as tactically mis-guided and introduced a milder regime in the Stasi prisons. He also aimed to reduce staffing levels by 10 to 20 per cent. Not only did he disagree with Ulbricht over how to approach deStalinisation and over Harich's treatment as a counterrevolutionary but they also clashed bitterly over Wollweber's inten-tion to restrict the SED leadership's access to Stasi internal data, including confidential Stasi reports on popular discontent. Wollweber, it seems, feared another uprising unless the party took action.[12] Ulbricht gradually reduced Wollweber's influence, adroitly using the KGB's dislike of the minister and of the seismic shock of the Hungarian Uprising in November 1956 to brand as revisionists Wollweber and critics of the First Secretary such as Karl Schirdewan. Wollweber was dismissed on 1 November 1957 and ejected from the SED Central Committee in January 1958. For the next decade, Ulbricht was the unchallenged leader of the SED, supported by a loyal, highly ambi-tious lieutenant and arch-Stalinist, the new Minister of State Security, Erich Mielke. The latter's Stalinist mode of thinking and language permeates his many speeches. Take his address in June 1951 to MfS colleagues regarding the establishment of the MfS: 'The GDR created the sword of the revolution, as comrade Lenin called the organs of the Stasi in the USSR, for repelling spies, saboteurs, subversives, terrorists and other enemies'.[13]

PEN, SWORD AND SHIELD

Over the next decade, Mielke, who was both arch-bureaucrat and Com-munist bruiser, presided over the Stasi's evolution from an already extensive instrument of Stalinist persecution into a vast apparatus of surveillance and repression. It was not, however, the highly intrusive body of later decades; for instance, in 1957, it did not even possess its own telephone network.[14] Although Ulbricht undoubtedly was Mielke's superior and although Mielke never tired of stressing the Stasi's role as the sword and shield of the SED, the minister was allergic to what he deemed to be unwarranted interference in his domain (see Chapter 3). An incident in 1959 illustrates the delicacy of SED–MfS relations in operational matters. When Schulz, the SED Party Secretary of the MfS Guard Regiment, informed a member of Honecker's Central Committee Department for Security Questions of an incident in the regiment, Mielke was furious. Insisting that he should have been informed first, he stressed that security matters were managed by him personally and the First Secretary (Ulbricht) and, massaging his own ego, he asked: 'Am I

---

[12] von Flocken J. and Scholz M. F. 1994: 182–98; Grieder P. 1999: 133–4; Otto W. 2000: 232–3.
[13] Cited in Otto W. 2000: 150. Our translation.
[14] Ibid., 260.

not a member of the Party? I am an elected member of the CC'.[15] He conveniently forget to mention his failure to enter the Politbüro, although in 1960 he did become one of the founder members of the National Defence Council, the umbrella organisation for the GDR's defence and security forces.

Opportunities abounded for the MfS to extend its influence, especially as the SED leadership began to switch the emphasis from surveillance of Western secret services and underground groups towards oppositional forces at home. Influenced by the ideas and agents of imperialism, the latter were allegedly undermining and subverting the GDR and other members of the socialist camp as well as striving to get rid of the SED's self-designated role as the leading force in society. The MfS referred to this method as political-ideological diversion. Among the ministry's main responsibilities were the liquidation of revisionist groups, the protection of military installations and industrial plant, the enforcement of the collectivisation of the land and stemming the mass exodus from the republic: 143,917 fled to the West in 1959, 199,188 in 1960 and 155,402 by 12 August 1961. With the GDR in danger of imploding, a reluctant Khrushchev agreed to Ulbricht's demands for the sectoral borders in Berlin to be closed by the building of the Berlin Wall, an event welcomed by Mielke.[16] The construction of the Wall was followed by a wave of repression to force the East German population to accept the new political realities. A sharp rise in the number of arrests and sentences was one of the consequences of the terror campaign. The MfS and the People's Police, it is estimated, were responsible for 6,041 arrests between the building of the Wall and 4 September 1961. In the second half of the year, 18,297 persons were sentenced for crimes against the state.[17]

THE PRAGUE SPRING

The next major wave of repression occurred during the Prague Spring in 1968. In the eyes of Ulbricht and the Soviet leader, Brezhnev, the reforms were not simply a matter for the Czechs and Slovaks but also posed a serious threat to their own rule as well as to the Communist power monopoly. As early as May 1968, Mielke was attacking what he regarded as counterrevolutionary events and insisting that the socialist camp would never allow Czechoslovakia to defect.[18] The SED leaders' fears were quickened by the positive reception of the Prague reforms among broad sections of the East German population. Although the GDR National People's Army did not participate in the Warsaw Pact's invasion in August 1968, the troops helped to seal the Czech–East German border. After the invasion, the Stasi assisted its

---

[15] Otto W. 2000: 284.
[16] Ibid., 299.
[17] Figures in Gieseke J. 2001: 75; Werkentin F. 1995: 268.
[18] Otto W. 2000: 331.

Czechoslovak counterparts in purging reformers from among their ranks. Within the GDR itself, the MfS was actively involved in the suppression of demonstrations and protests against the invasion. Harsh disciplinary measures were imposed on the protesters and the number of sentences imposed by the courts increased sharply.

THE MfS AS SOCIETAL CONTROLLER

Yet, as is apparent from a speech in December 1961, even Mielke appreciated that the high level of arrests after the erection of the Berlin Wall could not continue without jeopardising SED rule.[19] A second bout of deStalinisation launched by Khrushchev in October 1961 reinforced this conclusion, as did the SED's efforts to reach a rapprochement with the population now that the escape route via Berlin had been closed. As part of Ulbricht's search for a consensus with the population, a controlled reform of the command economy was introduced in 1963 under the banner of the New Economic System of Planning and Management. Not only were higher living standards promised but mass and top-level sport was promoted and the family and youth were wooed through new concessions. The result of these and other developments was, somewhat perversely, an increase in the range of areas which the Stasi was called upon to tackle, an opportunity which Mielke was only too happy to seize. The network of Stasi agents, including Officers on Special Assignments (OibEs), was expanded and the Stasi assumed responsibility for passport control at the GDR borders. In 1958, the MfS had issued its second guidelines on work with spies on the home front. They were defined as the 'main means' (*Hauptmittel*) for waging the struggle against a broad spectrum of enemies, including foreign secret services, 'demagogic elements and persons with the lowest qualities of character'.[20] The various types of informers mentioned in the document – for example, secret co-workers, secret informers on special assignments and occupants of apartments used for conspiratorial meetings – anticipated similar categories in later guidelines and underscored the fact that the MfS was already a long way along the path towards a comprehensive surveillance of society.

Wollweber's aspiration to reduce staffing levels fell victim to his successor's ambitions to enlarge his secret police and security empire. At the same time, the KGB reduced its direct involvement in MfS affairs. In 1958, its advisers were cut back to 32 contact officers, although it did retain its foreign intelligence branch in Berlin-Karlshorst until 1990.[21] The ministry's full-time staff rose from 17,400 in 1957 to 45,500 in 1971; the central departments were the main beneficiaries. Contributions from the state budget soared to feed

---

[19] Werkentin F. 1995: 271.
[20] Müller-Enbergs H. 1996: 197, 199.
[21] Gieseke J. 1998: 20.

this expansion and existing departments were merged and fresh ones materi-
alised to cope with the volume of work. Growth occurred not only in new
areas such as passport control but also in branches with the classic functions
of observation and interrogation – Main Departments VIII and IX. Main
Department XX was expanded in 1969 when Department 7 was created for
cultural policy, a reflection of the SED's concern over the appeal of the
Prague Spring for the East German cultural intelligentsia.[22] The expansion
did not go unchallenged. In 1962, as part of the SED's search for a milder
approach, the head of the SED Central Control Commission, Hermann
Matern, advocated a contraction of the ministry on the grounds that it was
exceeding its brief and fomenting popular unrest by its illegal arrests and
house searches. Coming from the SED's inquisitor-general, this was the
height of hypocrisy.[23]

A NEW LEADER

When Erich Honecker became First Secretary in 1971, he inherited from his
predecessor a vast apparatus of repression. He also inherited Mielke, with
whom he had conspired to overthrow the veteran Ulbricht. Ulbricht's grip
on power had been slackening since the late 1960s as a result of his faltering
economic reform programme, his ill-health and disagreements with Brezhnev
over the East German leader's criticism of Moscow's failure to assert what in
Ulbricht's eyes were the GDR's vital interests in negotiations with the USA
and the FRG. Ulbricht's highly conservative critics in the Politbüro, notably
the ambitious crown prince, Honecker, conspired, with Brezhnev's somewhat reluctant approval, to pension off Ulbricht. Mielke, appreciating in
which direction the political wind was blowing and also fearful that Ulbricht's
pursuit of an agreement with the FRG threatened the stability of the GDR,
threw in his lot with Honecker. His reward would be promotion to the
Politbüro.[24]

The new party leader was born in the Saarland in 1912 and stemmed from
a working-class family with strong KPD associations. The young Honecker
joined the KPD in 1929, soon developed a reputation as an activist, and spent
a training year at Moscow's Young Communist International School in the
early 1930s. After the Nazis came to power, he was involved in underground
activities in Berlin, the Ruhr and the Saarland. Arrested by the Nazis in 1935,
Honecker was sentenced in 1937 to ten years' imprisonment in the
Brandenburg-Görlen jail. His early political experiences convinced him of
the iniquities of the capitalist system and reinforced his belief in Soviet-style

[22] Gieseke J. 2001: 80–82; Otto W. 2000: 341.
[23] Gieseke J. 2001: 77–8; Otto W. 2000: 310–12.
[24] Dennis M. 2000: 127, 134–8; Otto W. 2000: 347–9.

socialism as the society of the future, a belief to which, like Mielke, he stubbornly adhered throughout his political life. After the end of the Third Reich, he soon ascended the political ladder, becoming chairman of the Free German Youth Organisation in 1946, entering the SED Politbüro as a candidate member in 1950, and occupying the key post of Central Committee Secretary for Security between 1958 and 1971.

Honecker's early years as leader of state and party were associated with the West's diplomatic recognition of the GDR and a more sustained attempt than under Ulbricht to woo the East German population by higher living standards and heavy state subsidies for rents, housing construction, transportation, basic foodstuffs and pre-school care. The period of relative prosperity and political stability began to fade towards the end of the 1970s under the twin pressures of the onset of a new ice-age in relations between the USA and the USSR and of the international economic turbulence arising from the oil crisis. However, Honecker was able to contain political dissent at home – thanks in no small part to the Stasi – and, through careful negotiations with Chancellors Helmut Schmidt and Helmut Kohl, to establish a mini-détente in German–German relations. Although the warmer relationship between the two Germanies aroused the ire of the Soviet leadership, it had the advantage of facilitating West German financial injections to help prop up the ailing East German economy and it enabled Honecker to play the role of international statesman. The culmination of this process was his visit to the Federal Republic in September 1987. While the visit appeared to be a clear demonstration of the independence and sovereignty of the GDR, both Honecker and his party would soon be swept from power. Gorbachev's accession to the post of General Secretary of the CPSU in 1985 was a last chance for the communist world to arrest the economic and political decay into which it had fallen, but his reforms and his rethinking of relations with the West, which called into question the continuation of the GDR as a separate state, encountered only obstruction from dogmatic and ageing rulers like Honecker and Ceauçescu. A combination of Soviet weakness, the conservatives' opposition to fundamental change and the allure of the West precipitated the fall of the Berlin Wall and the collapse of communist rule in East Germany in 1989. The Stasi and Mielke would not be spared the fate of the party and its leader.

Part II

THE SWORD AND THE COMPASS

Chapter 3

THE PARTY AND ITS SWORD

This chapter examines the organisational structure of the MfS, the political influence of the minister, and the Stasi's role as the SED's junior ally during Honecker's years in power. Although the Stasi was a vast bureaucratic apparatus enjoying a considerable latitude over operational tasks, it remained tied to the overall political and ideological control of the SED, which it served as an agent of repression against a perceived omnipresent enemy, as a source of intelligence and as a firefighter against the burgeoning symptoms of crisis in society. In retrospect, some MfS officers, Mielke not excluded, have come to rue the myriad burdens borne by the ministry and its staff.[1] When interviewed by the German weekly magazine *Der Spiegel*, the ex-minister protested, without any sense of irony, that the Stasi had been a 'maid of all work' and that it had to deal with 'trivialities'. 'If we had a supply problem, if for example rain was coming through a hole in the roof of a hospital, then they turned to us. And we tried to put things right'.[2]

ERICH MIELKE:
HONECKER'S LOYAL MACHIAVELLI

Before examining the organisational structure of the ministry, first a word about its autocratic boss.[3] Erich Mielke was born in the Wedding district of Berlin in December 1907 into a working-class family of six children. His father, Emil, a cartwright and a member of the KPD, was sentenced in 1923 to 18 months' imprisonment for his involvement in a clash with the Berlin police. Mielke's mother, a seamstress, died in 1910. Although Mielke won a scholarship to a grammar school in 1923, the family's financial difficulties required him to leave school at 16 to work as a despatch clerk. He acquired an

---

[1] See, for example, the comments in Schwarz J. 1994: 44.
[2] Interview with Mielke in *Der Spiegel*, no. 36, 1992, p. 480. Our translation.
[3] For the biographical details, see in particular Schwan H. 1997: 50–1, 65–6, 72–5, 276–9, 287–93; Otto W. 2000: 18, 33–7, 60–91.

impeccable pedigree as a Communist militant. In 1921, he joined the Communist party's youth organisation and the KPD itself a few years later. He was also a member of the Revolutionary Trade Union Opposition and took charge of a street cell. While he was unemployed in 1931, he worked for the KPD newspaper *The Red Flag*. As Germany's political and social crisis intensified in the aftermath of the great depression, a state of virtual civil war existed on the streets of Berlin. Mielke and a colleague, Erich Ziemer, who both belonged to a para-military formation, the KPD Self Defence Group, killed two police constables on 9 August 1931 in the vicinity of party headquarters during one of the many clashes between the KPD and the security forces. Mielke would be sentenced in 1993 to six years' imprisonment for this action, only to be released after two years on account of his senility.

Soon after the murder, Mielke fled to Moscow, where, under the alias 'Paul Bach', he trained for a short time at a military-political school headed by Wilhelm Zaisser and then at the Comintern's Lenin School for Cadres between late 1932 and 1936. He observed at first hand the denunciations, trials and purges of the Stalinist era. Although Mielke was not a target of persecution, the experience left its imprint on him and steeled him in the arts of survival and repression. In the words of one biographer: 'Jesuitical adherence to the faith and the principle: "The end justifies the means" became the political and ideological maxim pervading his life'.[4] At the end of his training, he signed a declaration that he would work for the Central Committee of the CPSU in an exemplary and obedient manner. Towards the close of 1936, he went to Spain and served there until 1939 in various divisions of the International Brigade. After Franco's victory in the civil war, Mielke was despatched by KPD central office in Moscow to Belgium where, from May 1939 onwards, under yet another cover name, this time 'Gaston', he co-edited the *Neue Rheinische Zeitung* and was active in the underground. His next destination was France where, as 'Richard Heller', he helped to build up an illegal KPD organisation in Toulouse. He worked for a while as a woodchopper before being interned and handed over to the Nazi Todt Organisation in January 1944. When the Germans retreated from France, he probably remained with the organisation until it crossed the Rhine in December 1944. By June 1945, he was in Berlin. Throughout the GDR era, Mielke shrouded his time in Belgium and France in secrecy, preferring his comrades to believe the official line that he had been in Moscow, making a vital contribution to the defeat of the Third Reich as a member of the National Committee for a Free Germany and other strategic groups.

Mielke was instrumental in setting up a security force in the Soviet zone and the GDR. He occupied the important position as State Secretary in the ministry between 1950 and 1953 and, for a second spell between 1955 and 1957 before his appointment as minister in the latter year. He owed his

---

[4] Otto W. 2000: 60. Our translation.

promotion not only to his Soviet connections but also to Ulbricht's desire for a loyal and politically reliable assistant after the upheavals under Zaisser and Wollweber, a wish that, given his customary obsequiousness to his superiors, Mielke was well able to fulfil. Mielke was also admirably qualified for the task of transforming the Stasi into a security colossus. Though not an intellectual like Markus Wolf, he was intelligent, a highly talented organiser, devious, ruthless and a true believer. His ruthlessness is evident from his comments on the execution by shooting in 1981 of a Stasi officer, Dr Werner Teske, suspected of spying for the Federal Republic:

> We are not immune against scoundrels in our own ranks. If I knew about this now he would not be alive tomorrow! Over and done with fast! Because I'm a humanist, that's why I take such a view. All this waffle about not executing, not sentencing to death – all nonsense, comrades. Execution, if necessary without a court verdict![5]

A fitness fanatic, Mielke swam every morning before work, abstained from drinking and smoking and was fond of hunting. Among the regular guests at his hunting lodge were the MfS generals Markus Wolf, Rudi Mittig and Gerhard Neiber. Brezhnev, Khrushchev and top KGB officers also joined him in the hunt. Sport was an abiding passion, second only to police work. From 1953 onwards, he was the chairman of the Dynamo Sports Association and from 1957 a member of the executive of the German Gymnastics and Sports Association (DTSB). Mielke used his influence in these positions to help transform the GDR into one of the world's leading sports nations. This was not done simply for love of sport but was also motivated by the drive to gain diplomatic recognition for the GDR and to demonstrate the superiority of socialism in the international class struggle. He was dedicated to the Berlin Football Club Dynamo, which was part of the Dynamo Sports Association. He attended most home games, and was unscrupulous in the search for success. When refereeing decisions went against his club, one high-ranking Stasi officer with Dynamo described a choleric Mielke shrieking: 'The referee is a bandit. He is against Dynamo. He is an enemy. The man must be sorted out, we must lock him up'.[6]

His determination to impose a strict disciplinary code on the ministry can be seen in his comments on the execution in 1960 of Manfred Smolka, a former East German border guard, for espionage and treason:

1. This order on the crime and punishment of Smolka is to be made known to all members of the Ministry of State Security.
2. The contents of this order, together with the 10 commandments of our socialist ethics and morality, are to form the topic of thorough discussion and instruction

---

[5] Cited in Fricke K. W. 1992: 158.
[6] Cited in Schwan H. 1997: 278. Our translation.

in service units in order to heighten their vigilance and solidarity and further to strengthen the political-moral unity and team-spirit in our ranks.

3. All colleagues in the Ministry are to be trained to hate treachery, to work as Chekists towards overcoming political-moral weakness, and to improve their technical qualifications so that they will place their whole strength at the service of the successful implementation of the political-operational tasks which are entrusted to them.[7]

Mielke did not deny himself some of the fruits of power. He and his wife, Gertrud, lived in the luxury Wandlitz compound reserved for the Council of Gods, that is, the members of the Politbüro. The veteran minister's vanity and addiction to military attire are well caught in Anne McElvoy's description of him as 'an ageing Cadillo', weighed down with ribbons and medals 'like a teddy bear in military fancy dress'.[8] The former *Financial Times* correspondent in East Berlin, Leslie Colitt, was even less flattering in his comparison of Mielke and Markus Wolf:

> The two men were exact opposites in almost every way. Wolf was extroverted, urbane, and towered over the dumpy and paranoically suspicious Mielke. Wolf's vastly superior learning automatically tagged him as a member of the intelligentsia, which Mielke instinctively mistrusted. Wolf was a cosmopolitan, part of an extended family that had been dispersed around the globe from Moscow to New York, whereas Mielke's horizon ended at the sector border of East Berlin.[9]

After the collapse of the GDR, former MfS generals like Wolfgang Schwanitz and Rudi Mittig and leading SED functionaries such as Dr Wolfgang Herger of the Central Committee Department for Security Questions all testified to Mielke's overweening self-confidence and his utter conviction of the superiority of the socialist cause. His generals held him in high regard for his anti-fascist past and for his devotion to duty, even though their relationship with the authoritarian Mielke seems to have been lacking in personal warmth.[10] According to Werner Großmann, the last head of foreign intelligence, Mielke laboured under the illusion that the stability of the GDR could be preserved only if one could know everything and everyone. This mania for omniscience was rooted in the traditional Communist International's perception of the class struggle and in the belief that internal opposition forces were influenced and steered from outside.[11] Großmann's criticism of Mielke's passion for minutiae was apt. Even after German unification and from his hospital ward in the Berlin-Plötzensee prison, Mielke insisted that the opposition forces in the GDR had been conducted from the West and that the critical

---

[7] Cited in Evans R. J. 1997: 852.

[8] McElvoy A. 1993: 94–5.

[9] Colitt L. 1996: 63.

[10] Interview with Mittig in Rieckert A., Schwarz A. and Schneider D. 1990: 177 and with Schwanitz in Villain J. 1990: 135–6.

[11] Großman W. 2001: 159, 177–8.

situation in the GDR had made it essential to expand the MfS and to collect information so that 'we soon noticed if anyone attempted to lead us up the garden path'.[12] Großmann's predecessor, Markus Wolf, is the only general to strike a significant discordant note, contemptuously referring to Mielke as a 'warped personality even by the peculiar standards that apply in the espionage world'.[13] However, while serving as one of his deputies, Wolf did not fail to pay fulsome tribute to Mielke in public and had fed his insatiable appetite for flattery.

SED AND MfS

The Stasi was first and foremost the agent of the hegemonic SED and repeatedly and unhesitatingly endorsed the party's leading role in society, as enshrined in the GDR Constitution. Broadly speaking, the party set the political and ideological compass and the MfS acted as its shield and sword. Declarations to this effect abound in top secret documents and in speeches by ministers. At the 1954 SED Party Congress, Wollweber described the MfS as the 'sharp sword' with which the party mercilessly beats the enemy;[14] and the 1979 guidelines to the Stasi's work with informers emphasised that: 'The reliable protection of societal development, the all-round guarantee of the internal security of the GDR and the strengthening of the socialist community of states require the further intensification of work against the enemy as well as damage prevention. It is therefore necessary to contribute effectively to the unflagging implementation of the policy of the party and state leadership'.[15] This function as servant of the party was underscored by the taboo, imposed in 1954 by a decision of the Security Commission of the SED Politbüro, on the Stasi's surveillance of the SED. The SED apparatus, unlike that of the bloc parties, could not be spied upon by the informers of the MfS, except when its assistance was required by the SED leadership in investigating deviationists within its own ranks.[16]

Another indicator of the role of the Stasi within the normative and institutional framework of the SED state can be found in the ministry's second statute, issued in 1969. The statute defined the MfS as an organ of the Council of Ministers and the basis of its work as the SED programme, the decisions of the Politbüro, the Central Committee and the National Defence Council and the laws of the People's Chamber. On the other hand, it should be noted that the statute recognised the ministry as a legal entity and laid down the principle of the individual management of the MfS by the minister,

---

[12] Interview with Mielke in *Der Spiegel*, no. 36, 1992, p. 44. Our translation.
[13] Wolf M. 1997: 66.
[14] Fricke K. W. 1991: 11.
[15] Cited in Gill D. and Schröter U. 1991: 417. Our translation.
[16] Süß W. 1995: 85; Fricke K. W. 1991: 14.

who was empowered to issue legally binding service instructions, orders and regulations.[17] These powers were adroitly utilised by the ambitious Mielke to boost his own position and that of his ministry.

The Stasi was not directly subordinate to the party as a corporate body, which encompassed 2.3 million members in 1988, but was rather the instrument of the political elites and the leading organs, notably the Politbüro and the Central Committee Secretariat. Erich Honecker, as General Secretary of the Central Committee, was *primus inter pares*. Despite all the professions of fealty, relations between the MfS and the SED elites were not always harmonious. As mentioned in Chapter 2, the early to mid-1950s had witnessed a struggle over the political and operational autonomy of the ministry between Ulbricht and the first two ministers, Zaisser and Wollweber. Direct party control was also very much limited by the presence of Soviet advisers; not until their number was reduced from 76 to 32 in 1958 was Soviet influence significantly curtailed and Ulbricht able to tighten SED control.[18] Although Mielke proved to be more amenable than his predecessors, disputes broke out in the 1960s over appointments and, as in 1962, over charges that the ministry was exceeding its brief. Although the controversy soon subsided, it did reveal an underlying tension at that time between the SED's steering function and what has been referred to as the Stasi's understanding of itself as the party's societal monitoring and control agency.[19]

Conscious that the ruling party's power had been undermined in other dictatorships by over-mighty police chiefs and by the security services' mania for empire building and conspiratorial methods, the SED was assiduous in spreading an organisational net over the Stasi. At the apex of party political control stood the Central Committee Secretary for Security Questions; he was responsible for the party's military and security policy and for the political monitoring of the National People's Army (NVA), the MfS and other armed forces. This post was occupied by Paul Verner from 1971 to 1983 and then by Egon Krenz until October 1989. Their influence over the Stasi should not be exaggerated, partly because their remit did not extend to operational activities and partly because Mielke's experience and political stature enabled him to keep them at arm's length. Krenz, who anyhow was stretched by his other responsibilities for youth and sport, was not held in high regard by the older and more experienced Mielke. Even when Honecker was in charge of the Department between 1958 and 1971, the office was far from being an omnipotent instrument of direction and control. Both Verner and Krenz were very much dependent on the next tier below them in the hierarchy, that is, on Herbert Scheibe's Department for Security Questions in the Central Committee apparatus for the armed forces. Scheibe who came from the

---

[17] Otto W. 2000: 345–6.
[18] Engelmann R. 1997: 52, 54, 70–71.
[19] See Suckut S. 1997: 166.

NVA in 1972 was replaced by a civilian, Dr Wolfgang Herger, in 1985. Within his department, the Section for State Security under Major General Fritz Bengelsdorf was directly responsible for the MfS.[20]

So much for the pyramidal structure and the leading officials of the SED's steering unit. What were its main duties and how did it seek to exercise control? In the first place, Herger's Department for Security Questions had a say in the selection and appointment of the Stasi's top officials, a task which it undertook in conjunction with the head of the ministry's own Main Department for Cadres and Training. Joint recommendations were submitted to Mielke before a final decision was reached after yet further consultation with other bodies. The process was a tortuous one and territorial disputes were frequent as Mielke was determined to limit undue interference by external agencies and to manipulate the nomenklatura system to his own advantage. In 1986, the nomenklatura of the Politbüro covered appointments to the post of minister as well as of the top generals of the Stasi and that of the National Defence Council included the heads of several key Main Departments and all the Regional Administrations. Among other SED bodies with a say in appointments to the MfS, the Department for Security Questions was responsible for the deputy heads of Main Departments. The nomenklatura, a Soviet practice, was designed to facilitate party control over appointments to key positions throughout politics and society, but, as regards the MfS, the process was far from transparent and awaits further investigation.[21]

The various organs of Krenz's Central Committee Secretariat for Security Questions implemented their control function first and foremost by means of the SED groups within the MfS. Their work was facilitated by the fact that virtually all full-time MfS staff belonged to the SED. The latter's main control organ within the Stasi, the Central Party Organisation of the MfS, operated on the basis of directives from the Central Committee and enjoyed the elevated status of a Party District Organisation.[22] In 1989, its apparatus consisted of 159 full-time MfS employees. Major General Dr Horst Felber, the head of the organisation and a member of the minister's Collegium, described the function of his unit in typical ministry jargon as: 'to expound on the decisions of the Central Committee and its Politbüro as well as the general orientations derived from them for carrying out the work of the MfS; to motivate and mobilise the party members politically for the solution of their tasks; and, drawing on the strength of the party, to overcome obstacles and deficiencies in our own ranks'.[23]

Below the Central District Party Organisation, the SED was further embedded in the MfS by means of a plethora of party organisations and party groups at central, regional, district and 'object' level. This kind of intricate

---

[20] Fricke F. W. 1991: 16.
[21] Süß W. 1997: 221.
[22] Schumann S. 1998: 6–7.
[23] Cited in Fricke K. W. 1991: 17–18. Our translation.

organisational network was to be found in other ministries and was instrumental in the political socialisation and disciplining of members. With regard to the latter, the SED District Party Control Commission in the MfS could impose penalties for a variety of offences, such as if staff neglected political training, deviated from the party's ideological norms and drank to excess. It did not operate independently as it was obliged to work closely with the disciplinary arm of the ministry's Main Department for Cadres and Training (see Chapter 6).[24]

The basic task common to all party organisations – although the language changed slightly over the years – was outlined in a Politbüro directive issued in 1954: 'To train the co-workers of the State Secretary of State Security in patriotism as well as in love for and devotion to the GDR and its government, to the SED, to the conscientious fulfilment of duties and to the uncompromising fight against agents, spies, saboteurs and all enemies of the workers' and peasants' power'.[25] Meetings of Party Groups, on the lowest tier of the ministry, were supposed to be convened twice a month and seminars were held within the framework of the Party Teaching Year and after important meetings of the Central Committee.[26] Through these and other means, including the elaborate system of training and military discipline discussed in Chapter 6, the SED organs within the MfS contributed to the inculcation of the official image of the enemy and to ensuring that the MfS was a politically and ideologically reliable aide of the SED.

A STATE WITHIN A STATE?

While the party organs were crucial for the political and ideological steeling of the MfS, Silke Schumann, an expert on SED–MfS relations, has shown that the Central Party District Organisation of Dr Felber did not have the same level of involvement in overseeing operational work and did not carry out surveillance of the service units.[27] This raises a central question, that is, the degree of autonomy and influence which the ministry exercised over its own internal affairs and on policymaking generally. It is not an easy question to answer, nor is it only applicable to the Stasi as historians similarly debate the issue with regard to the KGB and secret police forces in other countries, seeking to establish how the party or the government exercised political control over such clandestine organisations.

After the fall of the GDR, party big-wigs rushed to put as much distance as possible between themselves and the vilified Stasi in a largely vain attempt to rehabilitate their own reputation and that of the 'moral' party. Egon

---

[24] Fricke F. W. 1991: 17; Schumann S. 1998: 16–17, 21.
[25] Cited in Süß W. 1997: 224. Our translation.
[26] Fricke K. W. 1991: 17; also Villain J. 1990: 120.
[27] Schumann S. 1998: 3–4, 12.

Krenz, the ex-Central Committee Secretary for Security Questions, asserted in his statement to the Central Round Table in 1990, that he was powerless when confronted by the MfS 'state within a state', an interpretation of the role of the Stasi with which Honecker was only too happy to concur.[28] According to Krenz: 'In reality, the MfS developed increasingly into a state within a state, screened off from the outside world and even exercising control over members of the party. Without paying heed to democratic principles, questions of state security and the concrete operational work of the Ministry of State Security were, with the exception of cadre appointments and investments, discussed and decided between the Chairman of the National Defence Council [Honecker] and the Minister of State Security'.[29] Not surprisingly, this view has been fiercely contested by ex-Stasi officers. Werner Großmann, the last head of HV A, retorted that Krenz and other members of the SED elite have deliberately set out to distort the role of the Stasi as the loyal shield and sword of the ruling party.[30] This accords with his former chief's insistence that the ministry followed the party line, was under SED control until the very end and did not enjoy 'an independent existence'.[31]

The dispute over the degree of autonomy enjoyed by the MfS very much centres around the ministry's control over operational work. In an interview in February 1990, Wolfgang Herger, a close associate of Egon Krenz and head of the Central Committee Department for Security Questions between 1985 and 1989, insisted that a clear line of demarcation was drawn between political and operational work. His department, Herger contended, was authorised by the Politbüro, the Central Committee and the Central Committee Secretariat to carry out the political management and control of party work within the MfS, and although political-ideological questions were discussed at MfS party meetings, special service matters were off the agenda. Mielke put this with characteristic bluntness in a telephone conversation shortly after Herger's appointment: 'And furthermore – you do not need to worry yourself about operational matters. Your field is party work'.[32] Herger also asserted, correctly, that the Stasi's impulse to insulate itself was, in part, a consequence of the strict enforcement of the principle of conspiracy, which was applied not only to relations with the outside world but also within the MfS itself, where even full-time staff were often unaware of internal operational matters outside their own remit.[33] As for the political work of his own department, Herger saw it primarily as ensuring that MfS staff were faithful to the SED and to the implementation of the general decisions of the party.[34]

---

[28] Andert R. and Herzberg W. 1991: 367.
[29] Cited in Gieseke J. 2001: 92. Our translation.
[30] Großmann W. 2001: 171.
[31] Interview with Mielke in *Der Spiegel*, no. 36, 1992, p. 48.
[32] Interview in Villain J. 1990: 112. Our translation.
[33] Ibid., 112.
[34] Ibid., 111.

Before looking at the crucial area of SED–MfS relations, the Honecker–Mielke axis, a few methodological issues need to be borne in mind. In the first place, relations between the two bodies fluctuated over the four decades of SED rule and what was true of the era of stability under Honecker was not necessarily applicable to the period of close KGB control and to the crisis decade of the 1950s when SED and MfS leaders often clashed sharply. Secondly, research is needed into the ways in which the MfS used intelligence data to shape, consciously or otherwise, the direction of SED policy and into how Mielke exerted his influence on the SED elites. Thirdly, further research is urgently required into the relationship between the SED and the MfS at the local and regional level. Until this area is clarified, it is difficult to reach any overall judgement, especially as the SED was not reliant on the MfS alone for intelligence about developments in the enterprises and society as data were also provided by the members and organs of the party. Fourthly, personalities did matter in state socialism. Thus powerful autocrats like Günter Mittag in the economy and Mielke in state security were able to advance the interests of their own respective blocs, not least through their personal access to the party leader, who in his turn used the relationship to retain a grip over key groups and individuals.

Finally, it should be stressed that while a range of groups played some role in the political process, autonomous interest or pressure groups, such as those within the alternative political culture, were usually deemed to be both illegal and illegitimate. Even though it is difficult to identify boundaries and to delineate cleavages and the decision-making process both between and within the organs of party and state, it is nevertheless clear that core insider groups such as the central party apparatus and the military and security organs enjoyed primacy over many ministries and that they were in a qualitatively different category of influence from occupational groups like lawyers, writers and teachers. As regards the MfS, while its leaders harboured many reservations about détente and Honecker's Western policy, in the final analysis it toed the party line and remained a loyal servant of state socialism, a system which also guaranteed the ministry's expansion and influence.[35]

THE HONECKER–MIELKE AXIS

The relationship between the Minister of State Security and the SED party leader was crucial both for the ministry's performance of its functions and its political leverage in the overall political system. Under Ulbricht, Mielke was deliberately kept from the inner sanctum, but with Honecker's accession to power in 1971 Mielke entered the Politbüro as a candidate member and was appointed as a full member five years later. This was testimony to Honecker's

---

[35] On the influence of groups within state socialism, see Gieseke J. 2001: 94–101, 106–7.

recognition of the significance of the Stasi in the age of détente, to Mielke's assistance in engineering Ulbricht's political downfall, and to their long-standing cooperation in security and political matters. Despite their subsequent differences over Honecker's policy towards West Germany, both Honecker and Mielke were in fundamental agreement with regard to the need to maintain SED hegemony and the socialist order. In retrospect, Mielke describes their working relationship as a good one and that any other interpretation is 'twaddle'.[36]

After the end of communist rule, former members of the SED leadership corps became embroiled in conflicting assessments of their involvement in and knowledge of the scope of the Stasi's activities. The claim by top Politbüro members such as Kurt Hager and Günter Schabowski that the Politbüro was not provided with a full picture of the Stasi's activities and numerical strength was rejected by Mielke, who insisted that his colleagues were kept informed about the methods and the extent of the Stasi's work.[37] Yet even Honecker contended, in 1990, that he too had been kept in the dark with regard to the number of full-time personnel and informers on the Stasi's books. His best guess had been 35,000 full-time staff, including the Guard Regiment.[38] The candidate member of the Politbüro and long-serving Chairman of the State Planning Commission, Gerhard Schürer, found this hard to swallow. He argued that, even if Honecker's statement were true, he could have arrived at a reasonably accurate estimate by examining the materials of the State Planning Commission and the Finance Ministry relating to the Stasi's requirements for salaries and materials.[39] Although it is difficult to establish the truth of the matter, Politbüro records and statements by Egon Krenz[40] indicate that only selected members received information relating to the MfS,[41] a procedure which accords with the way in which Honecker ran the Politbüro in the 1970s and 1980s. He kept a tight grip on the management of business; open discussion was inhibited by the administrative *modus operandi*; and agreement was usually reached without a formal vote and on the basis of the position adopted in draft papers which had already received the General Secretary's seal of approval. Furthermore, most members were ill-equipped to deal with matters which were not directly related to their own functional sphere and they hesitated to disturb the smooth flow of team business.

---

[36] Interview with Mielke in *Der Spiegel*, no. 36, 1992.

[37] Ibid.

[38] Andert R. and Herzberg W. 1991: 369. Mielke, while conceding in the *Spiegel* interview (p. 48) that Honecker may not have known exactly how many IMs worked for the Stasi, insisted that he must have been aware of the number of full-time staff and of the full range of Stasi activities.

[39] Schürer G. 1996: 145.

[40] Krenz E. 1990: 124.

[41] Otto W. 2000: 353–4.

Another method favoured by Honecker was to deal with sensitive issues behind closed doors and in small groups. In the case of the Stasi, the Politbüro, according to Schabowski, failed to exercise control over the ministry as it did not act as a collective decision-making body.[42] At least one thing is certain: Honecker preferred to discuss matters of domestic and foreign security on a one-to-one basis with Mielke after the weekly Politbüro meeting on a Tuesday as well as after sessions of the National Defence Council (which met two to three times per year). Business was also conducted between them during car journeys and by telephone.[43] This form of contact suited Mielke,[44] who was suspicious of Honecker's intimates, such as the Minister of Defence, Heinz Keßler, and he was determined to keep at bay those Politbüro comrades whose position entitled them to have some say in Stasi and security matters. This was particularly true of Egon Krenz, Horst Dohlus, the Central Committee Secretary for Party Organs, and Erich Mückenberger, the head of the Party Central Control Commission.[45] As no records exist of the highly confidential talks between Honecker and Mielke, their content is open to different inter- pretations based on the selective memory of the participants. During his questioning by the military public prosecutor in June 1990, Mielke claimed that he had been a loyal servant of party and state and that: 'I could decide nothing. I submitted ideas and had my decisions confirmed'.[46] Honecker rejected Mielke's claim that he kept him fully informed and sought to transfer much of the blame on to the shoulders of Egon Krenz, the man who had been instrumental in his overthrow as General Secretary. As Krenz was in charge of the Central Committee Department for Security Questions for most of the 1980s, he was, therefore, according to Honecker, the official who was responsible for the political control and operational activities of the MfS.[47] Predictably, Krenz lobbed the ball back into Honecker's court, insist- ing that he was not the GDR's security chief, that he was kept in the dark as regards the contents of the Honecker–Mielke discussions, and that Mielke was responsible to Honecker as head of the SED and the National Defence Council.[48]

Although the Honecker–Mielke axis obviously requires further study, some documentary evidence has been unearthed which shows them cooperating closely on important matters of state security.[49] MfS materials from the year

---

[42] Schabowski G. 1990: 44.

[43] Interview with Herger in Villain J. 1990: 105.

[44] Wolf M. 1991: 27.

[45] Schwan H. 1997: 297.

[46] von Lang J. 1991: 271. Mielke in *Der Spiegel*, no. 36, 1992, p. 44 – our translation.

[47] Andert R. and Herzberg W. 1991: 363, 366–8.

[48] Krenz E. 1990: 123–4. Childs D. and Popplewell R. 1999: 67–8. Also Schabowski G. 1990: 41–2, 44.

[49] On the following, see Vollnhals C. 1999: 230–31, 251.

1979 reveal that the two leaders collaborated in the planning of criminal proceedings against Robert Havemann, one of the GDR's leading Marxist dissidents, a plan which also involved the partipation of the State Prosecutor, the Supreme Court and the Ministry of Justice. A similar linkage between the Stasi, the SED and judicial bodies is also apparent in the sentencing in 1978 of another major dissident, Rudolf Bahro, to eight years' imprisonment and in the preparation of the Third Amendment to the Criminal Code of 1979. In the latter case, Johannes Raschka has shown that both Honecker and Mielke were active in drafting the legislation.[50]

A provisional assessment of the influence of Mielke is that both he and the General Secretary operated on the basis of a broad consensus on means and ends but where disagreement occurred, Mielke had to bite his lip or use other channels. Mielke had serious reservations concerning détente with the West, the influx of visitors from the FRG and the growing dependence of the GDR on the hard currency infusions from West Germany, which were a corollary of détente and a consequence of the growing economic weakness of the GDR. However, although Mielke and Politbüro critics of Honecker's line, such as Werner Krolokowski and Willi Stoph, used their Soviet contacts to try and put the brakes on rapprochement between East and West Germany, they were unable to achieve their goal, partly because of Moscow's own economic enfeeblement and its gradual retreat from empire.[51]

---

[50] Raschka J. 2000: 158; for details of the process, see Raschka J. 1999: 290–98.
[51] See, for example, Werner Krolikowski's note on a conversation between Stoph and Mielke on 13 November 1980 printed in Przybylski P. 1991: 345–8, and the interview with Mielke in *Der Spiegel*, no. 36, 1992, p. 41.

Chapter 4

THE SECURITY COLOSSUS

THE ORGANISATIONAL STRUCTURE

While this chapter concentrates on the Stasi security conglomerate on the eve of the collapse of communist rule, it should be stressed that the structure had evolved and changed significantly over several decades in response to developments in the political, security, economic and foreign policy environment. The exhaustive internal survey of the organisational structure of the ministry, which has been published by the Gauck Authority under the editorship of Roland Wiedmann and extends to 362 pages, represents the main empirical source for this section of the chapter. In 1989, the 91,105 full-time staff of the ministry were spread across the central apparatus in East Berlin, the 15 Regional Administrations (*Bezirksverwaltungen* – BVs), the 211 District Service Units (*Kreisdienststellen* – KDs) and 7 'objects' (*Objekte*), that is, major complexes such as the nuclear power station in the Greifswald region and Dresden's technical university. The breakdown into regions and districts corresponded with the territorial structure of the SED and the GDR. Just under half of MfS staff worked in East Berlin and most of the remainder in the territorial organs. To what extent rivalries existed over status and operational boundaries are difficult to assess but, according to Werner Großmann, HV A officers felt that they constituted the ministry's elite troops and internal intelligence organs such as Main Department II were anxious to keep HV A off their operational patch.[1] Although there were also perceptible differences in the status of, and the salaries attached to, functions within departments, the cleavages should not be exaggerated for a high level of operational coordination existed between the various branches in the pursuit of enemies of the republic and, as will be seen in Chapter 6, the officers constituted an ideologically and politically cohesive corps.

---

[1] Großmann W. 2001: 28, 136.

THE CENTRAL APPARATUS

MfS headquarters were located in the Lichtenberg district of East Berlin. Although the official address was Normannenstrasse 22, the vast complex of ugly buildings, all protected by cameras, extended across several square kilometres from the Frankfurter Allee to the Gotlindestrasse. Other buildings were situated in the Hohenschönhausen, Niederschöneweide and Johannistal districts of the capital. The heart of the complex in the Normannenstrasse, where Mielke worked, now contains a museum dedicated to the history of the State Security apparatus. With the furnishings frozen in time, visitors can appreciate the iconography of power and the plain tastes of the minister and his associates. Tina Rosenberg describes these as:

> Downstairs in the lobby are statues of Lenin and Felix Dzerzhinsky. On the third floor Erich Mielke's office is preserved as he left it, his calendar turned to December 1989. Mielke's office has blue chairs, red rugs, wood panelings, and white polyester lace curtains. The furniture is the cheap fifties style found all over the East Bloc. On his desk are plastic ashtrays on doilies, a plaster bust of Lenin, a document shredder, and four telephones.[2]

But, as Rosenberg acknowledges, appearances are deceptive for this was the centre of 'the most extensive spy organization in world history'.[3] In 1989, the central apparatus in East Berlin encompassed 13 Main Departments and 20 Departments, sometimes with no clear rationale for the division or for the nomenclature. The top leadership groups, which were centred on Mielke, consisted of an executive committee of 13 generals called the Collegium, the Working Group of the Minister (*Arbeitsgruppe des Ministers*) and the Office of the Leadership (*Büro der Leitung*). The Collegium, which in theory was empowered to take decisions on major issues, had, certainly since the beginning of the 1970s, lost much of its political bite.[4] Wolfgang Schwanitz, one of the deputy ministers, has stated that while he was a member of the Collegium, it never discussed fundamental questions concerning the development of the MfS and that it met irregularly.[5] Other generals recall that they had to sit through tedious and lengthy monologues by the minister and that discussions rarely dealt with anything other than the trivial and superfluous; in other words, the Collegium was little more than a collective figleaf to cover up Mielke's authoritarian style.[6]

The four deputy ministers belonged to the Collegium and, like Mielke, each presided over a mini-empire of Main Departments and Working Groups. They were all members of the pioneer generation which had built the GDR

---

[2] Rosenberg T. 1995: 289.
[3] Ibid.
[4] Fricke K. W. 1991: 22; Otto W. 2000: 346.
[5] Interview with Schwanitz in Villain J. 1990: 133.
[6] Wolf M. 1997: 342; Großmann W. 2001: 115.

and had demonstrated their loyalty and aptitude during long years of service. After the departure of Markus Wolf in 1986, Rudi Mittig was the senior member of this inner circle. Born in 1925 in Czechoslovakia, he served in the Wehrmacht in the later stages of the Second World War and was imprisoned by the Soviets between 1945 and 1949. He joined the SED in 1951 and the Stasi two years later. He was appointed head of the Potsdam Regional Administration in 1955 and Main Department XVIII nine years later; in 1975, he attained the position of deputy minister,[7] one year before Wolfgang Schwanitz. The latter, five years younger than Mittig, was recruited by the MfS in 1951 and three years later became leader of the Pankow District Service Unit. He graduated as Doctor of Law at the Stasi's Law School in 1973 for his work on youth crime in the GDR. He was the head of East Berlin's Regional Administration between 1974 and 1986. After the fall of Mielke, he served for a few weeks as chief of the Office for National Security.[8] Gerhard Neiber, born in 1929 in Czechoslovakia into a working-class family, worked for the police in the immediate post-war period. He joined the Weimar District Service Unit in 1950, became leader of the Frankfurt/ Oder Regional Administration ten years later, graduated as Doctor of Law in 1970, and was appointed deputy minister in 1980.[9] Finally, Werner Großmann, born in 1929, carved out a career from the early 1950s in the foreign intelligence arm. After succeeding Markus Wolf as head of HV A, he was promoted to deputy minister.[10] The other nine members of the Collegium, all of whom were born between 1929 and 1934, included Dr Günther Kratsch, Dr Alfred Kleine and Dr Werner Irmler, who presided over Main Departments II and XVIII and ZAIG respectively.

THE EMPIRE OF THE GENERALS

This section will look schematically at the Main Departments, Working Groups and other units which comprised the security empire of Mielke and his four deputies. Table 4.1 provides an overview of the five-fold division of responsibilities; the figures on staff numbers refer to those working in the ministry's central apparatus in East Berlin. As the unassailable dictator of the MfS, Mielke's domain contained by far the largest number of units. He presided over the Working Group of the Minister, the Office of the Leadership, four Main Departments covering Cadres and Training, Counterespionage, Criminal and Political Investigation, and the Protection of Individuals as

---

[7] http://www.bstu.de. Also see his interview in Rieckert A., Schwarz A. and Schneider D. 1990: 164–70.
[8] Interview with Schwanitz in Villain J. 1990: 150; http://www.bstu.de.
[9] Ibid.
[10] Ibid.

Table 4.1 Organisational structure and numerical strength of the central organs of the MfS, 1 October 1989

Minister Erich Mielke	Minister of State Security — Minister Erich Mielke	Deputy Minister Rudi Mittig	Deputy Minister Gerhard Neiber	Deputy Minister Wolfgang Schwanitz	Deputy Minister and Head of HV A Werner Großmann (total staff: 3,819)
Collegium (14)	Secretariat of Minister (8)	Maintenance and General Services Administration (3,279)	HA I: Protection of NVA and Border Guards (2,319)	HA III: Radio Surveillance and Counterintelligence (2,361)	Political Espionage I (FRG)
Minister's Working Group (689)	Heads of Regional Administrations (BVs)	HA XVIII: Protection of Domestic Economy (674)	HA VI: Protection and Control of Borders and Holiday Traffic (2,025)	OTS: Operational Technological Sector (1,131)	Political Espionage II (EU, NATO, Western countries)
ZAIG: Central Assessment and Information Group (423)	Guard Regiment (11,203)	HA XIX: Security of Transportation, Postal and Telegram System (251)	HA VII: Protection of Interior Ministry Agencies (357)	Department Intelligence and Communications (1,599)	Scientific-technical Espionage
Office of the Leadership (324)	Department XII: Central Archives and Registry (344)	HA XX: Political Underground (461)	HA VIII: Enquiries and Observation (1,618)	Department XI: Cryptology (513)	Secret Services/ Operational Documentation
HA Cadres and Training (1,047)	Department XIII: Computer Centre (440)	ZAGG: Central Working Group for the Protection of Secrets (58)	HA XXII: Political Extremism and Terrorism (878)	BCD: Weapons and Chemical Service (176)	Maintenance and General Services

Table 4.1 (cont'd)

		Minister of State Security		
HA II: Counterintelligence (1,432)	Legal Office (12)	KoKo (120)	Central Coordinating Group (192)	Department 26: Telephone Control (436)
HA IX: Criminal Investigation and Interrogation (484)	Central Medical Service (1,161)	ZOS: Central Operational Staff (64)	AG XVII: Working Group West Berlin Visitors' Bureau (308)	
Department X: Liaison to other Eastern Bloc Security Services (46)	Law School (*Juristische Hochschule*) (758)			
Department XIV: Penal and Interrogation Institutions (255)	Department M: Post Control (530)			
Finance Department (177)				
HA Protection of Individuals (3,762)				
Office of the Central Board of the Dynamo Sports Association (about 1,400, of which 420 were MfS staff)				

HA = *Hauptabteilung* or Main Department.

Source: Fricke K. W. 1991: 26–7; Wiedmann R. 1996: *passim.*

well as seven Departments and ZAIG. Other important organs, such as the Guard Regiment, will be examined later in the chapter.

Of the three administrative organs which served the minister, the small Secretariat of seven operatives under Major General Carlsohn acted as a kind of staff office with responsibility for the personal care of the minister, the distribution of petitions or *Eingaben* and other postal communications.[11] The Working Group of the Minister, with 689 employees, was numerically the strongest of the three units. It prepared and dealt with documents relating to Mielke's work on the National Defence Council and, like the Working Groups of the Deputy Ministers, was involved in the planning of measures in the event of a national emergency. These plans included the arrest of about 3,000 hostile-negative persons and the transfer of a further 11,000 to designated internment camps.[12] Finally, the Office of the Leadership, under the command of Major General Egon Ludwig, coordinated the work on the petitions which were sent to the minister, processed documents and organised the guarding of the MfS complex in the Normannenstrasse.[13]

The largest Main Department under Mielke's direct control was that for the Protection of Individuals, followed by the Main Departments for Counterintelligence, Cadres and Training, and Criminal Investigation. The first dealt with the safety of leading party and state representatives and with guarding important buildings, such as the Palace of the Republic, the official residence of the Chairman of the Council of State and the Wandlitz compound for members of the SED elite. Wandlitz was set in a wooded area 30 kilometres north of Berlin, where the top leaders enjoyed a pampered existence. Special facilities were laid on for the keen hunters, notably Erich Honecker, Erich Mielke and Günter Mittag. While hardly luxurious by Western standards, within the context of the GDR's 'shortage economy' revelations in the media about the complex during the autumn of 1989 triggered off widespread anger and protests among East Germans. Some insiders were also critical. Andreas K., one of the MfS guards in the Main Department for the Protection of Individuals, became disenchanted with the MfS when he experienced at first hand the privileges of the elite and the artificiality of the hunt. He observed that Mittag was not allowed to shoot more deer than Honecker and that Mielke was not to exceed Mittag's score. Should this ranking be upset, then the Stasi officers had to join in the shoot in order to restore the pecking order.[14]

Lieutenant General Dr Günter Kratsch's Main Department for Counterintelligence was one of the main beneficiaries of the expansion of the MfS. It increased almost four-fold in strength between 1968 and 1982, primarily as a

---

[11] Wiedmann R. 1996: 15.
[12] Gieseke J. 1998: 41.
[13] Wiedmann R. 1996: 64–5.
[14] Interview with Andreas K. in Karau G. 1995: 161.

consequence of the party and Stasi leadership's anxiety to combat the negative elements of détente. When interviewed in the later 1990s, Kratsch was highly critical of what he regarded as the leaders' contradictory efforts to preserve communist rule at the same time as the country opened up to the West.[15] The numerous departments and operative desks of the Main Department for Counterintelligence were delegated to protect the social, economic and political spheres of the GDR against the machinations of the imperialists, whether Western journalists and intelligence services or Western citizens resident in the GDR. In addition, its remit extended to the political-operational protection of GDR embassies in the socialist states as well as combating Western intelligence agencies in what the MfS called the 'Operation Area', primarily the FRG. As it also infiltrated those enemy secret services who ran agents, notably West Germany's, its units cooperated closely with HV A.[16] Department M, which dealt with the interception, censorship, control and assessment of mail, had a staff of 530 operatives and was under the command of Major General Rudi Strobel. The Main Department for Cadres and Training, which grew by about 500 per cent between 1968 and 1982,[17] was a vital cog in the Stasi's administrative machinery. Under its head, Dr Günter Möller, it was concerned with the recruitment and training of full-time employees, the observation and disciplining of staff, and the organisation and supervision of the Stasi's own training establishments. The Main Department for Criminal Investigation and Interrogation and Department XIV are discussed in Chapter 5.

The Central Assessment and Information Group (*Zentrale Auswertungs- und Informationsgruppe* – ZAIG) of Dr Werner Irmler was the brains trust of the Stasi. Its relatively small staff of 422 operatives belied its significance. Not only did it gather and analyse external and internal sources of intelligence which were regarded as vital for the preservation of SED rule, but it also prepared materials for service conferences and statements by the minister. Its regular reports on the mood of the population, which provide an invaluable insight into the popular culture of East Germany, were transmitted by Mielke to selected state and party leaders, even though the higher the level of the Stasi and party, the more likely the dilution of criticism.[18] In addition, ZAIG fed information into SOUD, that is, the computerised data storage system of the socialist states administered by the KGB.

The Guard Regiment 'Feliks E. Dzerzhinsky', named after the founder of the Cheka, had 11,203 troops, of which 8,735 were conscripts performing military service. Conscripts normally served for three years and provided an

---

[15] Ash T. G. 1997: 159.
[16] Wiedmann R. 1996: 117; Labrenz-Weiß H. 1998: 6–7, 63–4.
[17] Gieseke J. 1998: 41.
[18] See the reflections in the interview with 'Klaus', a former member of ZAIG, in Wilkening C. 1990: 24–5.

important recruiting ground for full-time MfS personnel. The core of the regiment consisted of five units with four motorised rifle battalions, ten rifle battalions and four rifle companies. The regiment's tasks were to provide a guard of honour on ceremonial occasions, to protect important state and party buildings and to provide security at major events. The troops were quartered in Berlin-Treptow, Glieneke, Ahrensfeld, Erkner, and in the Potsdam Administrative Region (*Bezirk*), Teupitz. The regiment could also be called upon in the event of an emergency, as on 7 and 8 October 1989 when demonstrators in East Berlin were physically assaulted by its troops. Most of the Stasi's large arsenal was in the hands of the Guard Regiment. At the time of the Stasi's dissolution, the ministry possessed 124,593 pistols, 76,592 light machine-guns, 3,611 rifles, 766 heavy machine-guns, 3,537 anti-tank weapons and 3,303 flare pistols.

The domains of the four deputy ministers were much smaller than that of Mielke. The HV A of Großmann, a self-proclaimed 'pragmatist',[19] is examined in Chapters 12 and 13. Rudi Mittig's empire included a large Maintenance and Service Department, which carried out vehicle repairs and construction work and provided a series of services for staff, ranging from the allocation of kindergarten places and holidays to hairdressing and retail outlets. Two other Main Departments in Mittig's empire, HA XVIII and HA XX, were of vital importance once the country's problems began to mount both externally and internally from the mid-1970s onwards. Given its centrality to the struggle against the political underground and political-ideological diversion, HA XX had a surprisingly small staff of 461 operatives. It carried out surveillance of the mass organisations, the mass media, the four bloc parties and the churches, and it provided protection for major sports installations and the education sector. It cooperated closely with other units. This is exemplified by its liaison with HA VIII in the hounding of Wolfgang Templin, a leading member of the small opposition group Initiative for Peace and Human Rights. An observation report dated 26 January 1988 provides an insight into the kind of comprehensive and unremitting surveillance which so many others also had to endure. The document, signed by two officers in HA VIII, records the results of the monitoring of Templin's activities three days earlier. Observation began at 13.15 hours in Weimar. The document notes that Templin travelled by train from there to Erfurt, where he left the main station at 14.28 hours, took a tram to Cathedral Square, and entered the house of the Protestant Student Community at 14.42 hours. After a meeting in the house with eight to ten persons, Templin departed with three men in a car for Weimar at 19.18 hours. The number and owner of the vehicle were recorded.[20]

---

[19] Großmann W. 2001: 120.
[20] For these details and the full document, see *Stasi-Akte 'Verräter'* 1993: 109–11.

Dr Alfred Kleine's Main Department XVIII, which was also part of Mittig's sphere of interest, was entrusted with the safeguarding of the state economy and foreign trade relations, especially with the non-socialist countries. Finally, 120 staff were assigned to secure Alexander Schalck-Golodkowski's Koko (*Kommerzielle Koordinierung*), the shadowy organisation which raised hard currency outside the confines of the planned economy. As head of KoKo and a high-ranking Stasi officer, the burly, extrovert Schalck-Golodkowski was responsible in his own words: 'for guaranteeing a high level of security and order in the organisation, for achieving the fundamental and specific security politicy requirements in the selection, deployment and class training of cadres as well as utilising the opportunities of the organisation for the ministry's political-operational work, including the prevention of disruptive influences'.[21]

Dr Gerhard Neiber, friendly and a good host according to Markus Wolf,[22] was in charge of five Main Departments as well as Working Group XVII. The latter ran the GDR passport office in West Berlin, which processed visa applications for visits to the GDR. A Central Coordinating Group (*Zentrale Koordinierungsgruppe* – ZKG) was set up in 1976 to help tackle the problem of flight from the republic and, from 1977 onwards, the flood of applications to emigrate to the FRG. Its 192 operatives were under the command of Major General Dr Gerhard Niebling. Fricke refers to Niebling as 'a man who as an interrogating officer used psychological torture to drive to despair prisoners handed over to him . . .'.[23] The strength of Neiber's Main Departments ranged from the 2,319 operatives of HA I, which conducted counterintelligence work in the East German armed forces and the border guards, to the 357 of HA VII, which was involved in securing the Ministry of the Interior, its prisons and the German People's Police. Finally, Main Department XXII was responsible for combating the activities of left and right extremists, above all from West Germany, against the GDR.[24]

Dr Wolfgang Schwanitz, 'sharp and ambitious',[25] presided over the technological and electronic communications sphere. The staff in his only Main Department, HA III, monitored all Western radio broadcasts reaching the GDR and the shortwave bands inside the country. The Intelligence Department focused on the organisation and the safeguarding of the ministry's own intelligence work and the operatives of the notorious Department 26 monitored telephone conversations and set up optical and acoustic equipment such as cameras and bugs. Together, Departments 26 and M constituted a highly

---

[21] Cited in Schalck-Golodkowski A. 2000: 231. Our translation.
[22] Wolf M. 1997: 272.
[23] Fricke K. W. 2001: 561. Our translation. Niebling, born in 1932, joined HA IX in 1953 and was its deputy head between 1979 and 1983.
[24] Wiedmann R. 1996: 264.
[25] Wolf M. 1997: 272.

refined and comprehensive system of postal and telephone monitoring.[26] MfS staff in special secure rooms intercepted suspicious mail as well as post from persons already under investigation. In the 1980s, each of M's 15 sections opened about 6,000 letters a day. Not content with opening post, the MfS also falsified letters as part of its dirty tricks strategy. All cross-border packages – about 4,000 per day in each of the country's postal areas – were controlled by special parcel investigators. The MfS, it is estimated, seized valuables worth about 32.8 million DM between January 1984 to November 1989. Telephones were tapped in private homes as well as at places of work. In 1983, about 2,300 telegrams were read each day and a further 510 from abroad in the Stasi's Magdeburg Regional Administration. In East Berlin, 25 telephone stations enabled Stasi personnel to tap 20,000 connections simultaneously. From intercepted mail and phone calls, the Stasi was able to assess popular attitudes towards the FRG, the unsatisfactory supply situation in the GDR, and plans to flee the republic; it sometimes used the information to blackmail people into becoming informers. The Berlin Wall was strictly taboo: postcards showing the Wall were destroyed and printed materials referring to it were confiscated. While the extent of surveillance of post and telephone conversations was greater than anyone had suspected, East Germans nevertheless knew that they were being monitored and sought to outwit the Stasi.

THE TERRITORIAL STRUCTURE

Soon after the dissolution of the old *Länder* in 1952, the territorial structure of the MfS was brought into line with the country's administrative division into 14 Regional Administrations (*Bezirke*) and their subdivision into 211 Districts (*Kreise*). With respect to the four-power status of Berlin, the Stasi's East Berlin Regional Administration (*Bezirksverwaltung* – BV) was called the 'Administration for State Security Greater-Berlin' until 1976. Shortly before the fall of the Berlin Wall, the strength of a BV varied from the 3,926 full-time operatives of Major General Helmut Schickart's BV Potsdam to the 1,739 of Major General Gerhard Lange's BV Suhl. The capital's Regional Administration (2,775) occupied a middle position. The total strength of the BVs more than doubled to 43,168 between 1971 and 1989.[27] Their organisational structure followed the pattern of the central apparatus and the executive usually consisted of a leader and his four deputies. Several of the so-called lines (*Linien*) of the central apparatus ran downwards into the regional units, notably the lines of Main Departments II, III, VI–VIII, XVIII–XX as well as of Departments M and 26.[28]

---

[26] For these and other details, see Kallinich J. and de Pasquale S. 2002: 58–9, 63, 66–9, 71–2, 87.

[27] Gieseke J. 1995: 100–101.

[28] Fricke K. W. 1991: 32–4.

The much smaller District Service Units (*Kreisdienststellen* – KDs) had a less elaborate organisational structure, with activities tending to be bundled together rather than being disaggregated according to the line principle. The large BV Halle had 23 KDs and three 'objects' with a combined total of 1,539 employees, whereas Suhl only had 8 KDs and 340 personnel.[29] Several BVs were also responsible for major 'objects' such as the Leuna-Works 'Walter Ulbricht' in Halle, which had the status of an Object Service Unit (*Objektdienststelle* – OD).[30] The officers in the districts were the footsoldiers of the ministry who operated within the parameters of the guidelines and service instructions issued by Mielke and on the basis of orders from their regional headquarters. The District and Object Service Units employed a staff of over 11,000, varying considerably from one unit to another. Whereas the KD Leipzig had about 200 and the KD Dresden about 180 employees, some rural units had no more than between 25 and 40 full-time staff. About 7,000 full-time staff were directly engaged in operational work, about 2,800 with operational-technical and administrative tasks and over 1,000 with protecting the 'objects'.[31] The officers in the districts bore a heavy workload, as can be seen from the catalogue of responsibilities listed in an internal document of October 1988: to prevent flight from the GDR and to secure the country's borders; to monitor all forms of dissent; to guard against sabotage; to provide security for government installations; and to instigate investigations and recruit IMs.[32] As part of their comprehensive surveillance of society in their area, they targeted, among many others, foreign journalists and the churches, cooperated with leading functionaries in government and industry, reported regularly to the SED organs and ran a large army of informers. It is not surprising that many KD officers considered themselves to be overworked. As John Schmeidel has pointed out, the KDs ran about half of the ministry's IMs and whereas an officer in a BV had about eight IMs, a KD case officer was in charge of 13 to 40. The informers of the KDs were in general not of the highest quality and turnover was more rapid than among those run by the central organs and the BVs.[33] Although he must have known better, Mielke, not convinced that the districts were overloaded, objected in 1988 to the claim that one of the main causes was the sheer volume of trivial tasks.[34]

---

[29] Gill D. and Schröter U. 1991: 56.
[30] Fricke F. W. 1991: 33–4.
[31] Gill D. and Schröter U. 1991: 57.
[32] Schmeidel J. 1995: 27.
[33] Ibid., 28, 43–4. For further details on the ratio of IMs to officers, see Gill D. and Schröter U. 1991: 63.
[34] Gieseke J. 2001: 134.

Chapter 5

POLITICAL JUSTICE IN A DICTATORSHIP

LAW AS AN INSTRUMENT OF POLITICS

The MfS was deeply embedded in the GDR's system of political justice, a feature which one former ZAIG officer has described as a cancer in that political police measures were applied to problems which the MfS was in no position to solve.[1] The nature of the interaction between secret police and justice will be explored in this chapter with reference to the collaboration of SED and Stasi, the ministry's penetration of the legal profession and, above all, the repressive elements of a state which remained a post-totalitarian dictatorship despite an amelioration in conditions during Honecker's rule. Before examining the ministry's role, especially that of Main Department IX, several aspects of the judicial and the legal system deserve comment. As Klaus Marxen, Professor for Criminal Law at the Humboldt University, has argued, the SED treated law as an instrument of politics.[2] The undoubted primacy of politics over law was asserted by Mielke in uncompromising terms at a service conference in July 1979: 'Power is the most important position from which to fulfil the historical mission of the working class, to establish Communist society . . . Socialist law is an important instrument of exercising, enhancing and consolidating power'.[3]

Mielke's comments reflect the ruling elite's instrumentalisation of the legal system and the judiciary for the maintenance of the hegemony of the SED, even though officials attempted in public, with their domestic and international audience in mind, to give the impression of being supportive of legal reform and of adhering to due legal procedures. The SED leaders made no secret, however, of their disdain for so-called 'bourgeois' notions of the *Rechtsstaat*, that is, a state based on a transparent legal system. According to state socialist theory, 'bourgeois' law and the concept of the separation of

---

[1] Interview with Franz in Wilkening C. 1990: 155.
[2] Marxen K. 1999: 16.
[3] Cited in Vollnhals C. 1999: 227. Our translation.

powers served to protect the hegemony of the bourgeoisie in a sham democracy like that of West Germany, whereas 'socialist legality' was an expression of the will of the working class and its Marxist-Leninist party in alliance with the farmers, the intelligentsia and other working people. This ideologically driven idea of a unitary will of the whole society also functioned as a cloak for obscuring arbitrary practices. Indeed, the manipulation of the GDR's legal system in the interests of the SED justify applying the term *Unrechtsstaat* to the GDR in the sense that it lacked many of the fundamentals of a *Rechtsstaat* in its ideal form, such as the separation of powers, the protection of inalienable human rights, equality before the law, the subordination of the administration to the law and the independence of the judiciary. Without wishing to underestimate the flaws of the *Rechtsstaat* – the political use and the overriding of the law having been demonstrated by many commentators – the GDR *Unrechtsstaat* was undoubtedly less transparent, the space for non-conformist and various forms of oppositional political behaviour far more constrained and the secret police and security forces more insidious and pervasive than in liberal democracies such as the FRG. One example of the arbitrary exercise of power can be given here. In 1978, a court in the Karl-Marx-Stadt *Bezirk* sentenced a 27-year-old student of theology to imprisonment for 28 months on account of 'incitement hostile to the state'. His offence had been to obtain a copy of Orwell's book *1984* from a West German acquaintance and to lend it to some GDR friends. The court's judgment was:

> This trash [*1984*] is objectively a text that discriminates against the conditions created by the state and the political and economic situation in socialist society. The fact that, in the context of ideological diversion, the GDR has been deliberately targeted by this trash in the last few years proves that the enemies of socialism will make use of any means that serves their purpose of undermining the socialist order.[4]

THE NORMATIVE AND THE PREROGATIVE STATE

Despite widespread coercion, especially in the early decades, the GDR should not be equated with a criminal state (*Verbrechensstaat*). It did not pursue the barbaric Nazi policies of the mass annihilation of Jews and gypsies nor the selective murder of those deemed to be physically and mentally disabled. In practice, the SED dictatorship was a complex mix of lawfulness (*Gesetzlichkeit*) and para-legal party and state bodies,[5] which, in many respects, is encapsulated in the term 'dual state'. Ernst Fraenkel applied this term to the Third Reich in order to demonstrate that a partially dismantled traditional and rational 'normative state' continued to exist alongside an arbitrary 'prerogative state'

---

[4] Cited in Grasemann H-J. 1996: 202. Our translation.
[5] Rottleuthner H. 1994: 64.

comprising the NSDAP, SS, Gestapo and other Nazi organisations. The 'normative state' was essentially an administrative body with powers for safe-guarding the legal order and which was in constant friction with the agents of the 'prerogative state'. By 1936, however, the former had been substantially weakened by, and was undoubtedly inferior to, the forces of radicalism and lawlessness.

While recognising the many fundamental differences between the GDR and the Third Reich, Falko Werkentin has put forward a persuasive case for applying the model to the GDR's socialist system, especially in the area of criminal legislation.[6] In the GDR, the 'normative state' can be said to have encompassed the Department of State Prosecutors and a series of military, regional, district and lay courts, of which the Supreme Court was the highest organ of justice. In addition, an elaborate corpus of civil, family, labour and sections of criminal legislation provided the legal and regulatory framework for everyday transactions in the 'normative state' and the Constitution allowed for citizens' participation in the administration of justice. These guarantees and rights, however, were qualified and often undermined by political imperatives. 'Socialist legality' was not intended to impose constraints on the regime, but to promote the building of socialist society as defined by the hegemonic party. In keeping with this notion of the function of law, and in spite of the assertion in the Constitution of the independence of the courts, judicial and legal bodies were subordinated to the political authorities and were infiltrated by the MfS, as part of what Vollnhals has dubbed the 'state-police prerogative state'.[7]

The ways in which the 'prerogative state' subverted the 'normative state' were legion; one will be mentioned here: SED control over appointments. With the Central Committee Department for Organs of State and Legal Questions at the top of the pyramid of controls over the legal system, the SED monopolised appointments to key positions in a variety of ways. The Minister of Justice and his Secretary of State belonged to the nomenklatura of the Politbüro, as did the President and Vice-President of the Supreme Court and the State Prosecutor.[8] Main Department XX/I was central to the kind of intrusive control and surveillance of the legal system which is fundamental to the achievement of political and security goals in other dictatorships. Security checks were carried out to ensure that only politically and ideologically reliable comrades occupied key posts. Being an IM reinforced conformity, especially in the field of criminal justice. Vollnhals calculates that out of 307 judges and public prosecutors from Mecklenburg-West Pomerania who, after

---

[6] Werkentin F. 1995: 396–7, 402–3.
[7] Vollnhals C. 1999: 268. It should be noted, however, that in the less politicised areas, such as civil and labour law, many judges did in fact regard themselves as independent; see Werkentin F. 1995: 402.
[8] Vollnhals C. 1999: 232–4.

German unification, applied for a position in the legal system of the FRG, 25 had served as IMs. In Saxony, at least 23 judges and 20 state prosecutors (6 per cent and 9 per cent of applicants respectively) had worked for the MfS.[9] The Stasi also vetted lawyers and, it is estimated, recruited about 6 per cent of the profession as IMs in the Honecker era.[10] In such circumstances, working for the MfS created an inherent tension between a lawyer's duty to maintain professional secrecy when working with clients and a desire for professional advancement.

THE CODE OF CRIMINAL PROCEDURE

The entwining of the 'normative' and the 'prerogative' states can be traced in the framing and implementation of the Code of Criminal Procedure. The original code of 1968, which was revised three times during the 1970s, followed the State Prosecutor Act of 1963 in designating the MfS, the Ministry of the Interior and the Customs Administration as the three investigating organs. The responsibilities of the Stasi were not restricted, as GDR official commentaries were wont to claim, to acts defined as penal offences of a political nature in the Criminal Code but extended to a series of trumped-up charges of crimes against the socialist state.[11] In carrying out this broad task, the MfS and the other investigating organs could draw on the powers invested in them by section 101 of the Code of Criminal Procedure to conduct a preliminary criminal proceeding (*Ermittlungsverfahren* – EV) to 'uncover any action suspected to be an offence'.[12] A proceeding could be instituted in various ways, for example on the basis of initial observations made by the investigating organs themselves or on the instructions of the prosecutor. The latter was authorised by section 89 to supervise all inquiries conducted by the investigators, including the right to countermand any unlawful instructions. A preliminary proceeding had to be completed within three months; any extension required the consent of the prosecutor. Before the start of an interrogation, the accused had to be informed about the charge and their various rights. They were entitled to obtain counsel and to be informed of the evidence against them. Finally, the investigating organ was obliged to submit the proceedings to the prosecutor together with a final report summarising the results of the inquiry. The prosecutor could then decide on whether or not to proceed to a trial.

So much for the theory, practice was different: justice had to be unseen to be undone. The MfS controlled the prosecutors rather than vice versa; the

---

[9] Vollnhals C. 1999: 235.
[10] Eisenfeld B. 1999: 362, 367.
[11] Reinke H. 1996: 240.
[12] For the details on the conduct of a preliminary proceeding, see Documentation 1980: 38, 46, 50–51, 65.

judiciary and legal profession was thoroughly penetrated by Stasi informers; the right to see evidence was often infringed; and the MfS rather than the prosecutor decided whether or not to proceed to a trial. Indeed, the State Prosecutor often did not even know if the MfS intended to make an arrest.[13] This kind of blatant infringement of the law and human rights is fundamental to the operations of a secret police force. If detainees refused to sign the final record of their interrogation, then the period in custody could be extended well beyond the three months allowed for in the Code of Criminal Procedure. The ministry also influenced sentencing, as in the case of the mathematician Dr Horst Hiller. When he refused the offer of release from a Stasi pre-trial detention centre and complete immunity from imprisonment in return for becoming an informer, he was charged with espionage instead of the less serious offence of illegal crossing of the border. He was sentenced to eight-and-a-half years' imprisonment in 1978.[14]

INVESTIGATIVE PROCEDURES

A preliminary criminal proceeding was but one of the Stasi's modes of investigation.[15] Among the most flexible forms of inquiry using conspiratorial methods were the inelegantly named *Vorkommnisuntersuchungen* (VKUs – inquiries into incidents of a suspicious nature) and *Sachverhaltsprüfungen* (SVPs – checks on the facts of a case). These two types of investigation were free from even the weak constraints imposed by the Code of Criminal Procedure and were used by Stasi officers to carry out checks for evidence of a crime in connection with suspicious incidents such as accidents at the border or fires at the workplace. During the 1980s, they were frequently used to investigate and combat flight from the republic and the emigration movement. If evidence of a crime was detected, then either the Stasi or the Criminal Police could move to the next stage and launch the more formal preliminary criminal investigation.

Although far more complex than a VKU, an operational case (*Operativer Vorgang* – OV) was yet another flexible instrument of repression which obviated the need for even a preliminary criminal proceeding or, more significantly, for a court trial which might damage the international reputation of the GDR. Of course, if an offence could not be averted – prevention being one of the objectives of an OV – then a preliminary criminal proceeding could be instigated. Of the 1,750 operational cases which were concluded in 1988, 28 per cent led to a preliminary criminal proceeding. In that same year, the Stasi instituted 3,669 criminal proceedings against individuals suspected of

---

[13] Behlert W. 1994: 335.

[14] Fricke K. W. 1991: 62.

[15] The assessment in this paragraph of the system of operational checks and surveillance is based on the findings in Joestel F. 1999: 304–12.

committing a crime against the economy and the state and of an infringement of public order. Just over 90 per cent of the completed proceedings were transferred to the State Prosecutor and the courts passed sentence on virtually the same proportion of the 2,860 offenders who were prosecuted.[16] The final trial in the courts was usually held *in camera* and all documents relating to a trial had to be transferred to the MfS archives without the courts being allowed to retain copies.

The Criminal Code underwent a series of changes during the 1970s which sharpened its penal claws and empowered the MfS to investigate a series of activities which, in flagrant breach of human rights, it deemed to be criminal. This was particularly true of East Germans who sought to leave their country either by flight or by applying to emigrate. They could be charged with a variety of offences allowed for in the Criminal Code, such as an act of subversion and undermining public order by 'anti-social' activity.[17] From 1979 onwards, between 73 and 87 per cent of all preliminary criminal proceedings were instituted against East Germans who tried to flee or submitted an application to leave the GDR. In terms of the length of a sentence, the highest proportion of sentences in 1971 – over 40 per cent – ranged between two and five years, whereas in 1986 over half were sentenced for between one and two years.[18] Although sentences were therefore shorter, the number of political prisoners remained constant at about 3,100 to 3,300 per annum from the mid-1970s to 1989, thus persuading one expert, Clemens Vollnhals, that no significant liberalisation or normalisation occurred under Honecker.[19]

While 'attempted flight from the republic' was by far the most important offence dealt with by Main Department IX as part of a preliminary proceeding, the Stasi did not hesitate to pursue GDR citizens for offences such as 'contact with enemies of the state', 'incitement hostile to the state', 'public vilification' and 'hindering state or social activity'. Among the other elastic categories were 'rowdyism' and espionage.[20] What this meant in human terms can be seen from the following cases.[21] Article 215 of the Criminal Code allowed for imprisonment for participation in a riotous assembly which threatened or caused gross annoyance to people or malicious damage. Ines Meichsner, a book-binder from Karl-Marx-Stadt, ran foul of the law and was sentenced to ten months' imprisonment for causing gross annoyance. The 'offence' was her involvement in the activities of the unofficial peace movement. A second case concerns Uwe Kroker, who was sentenced to two years and six months' imprisonment in 1983 for 'rowdiness' and 'treasonable activity as an agent'.

[16] The statistics on the inquiries and prosecutions are to be found in Vollnhals C. 1994: 511.
[17] Dennis M. 2000: 229.
[18] Joestel F. 1999: 320, 322–3.
[19] Vollnhals C. 1999: 268, 270.
[20] Ibid., 244–5.
[21] See Amnesty International 1989: 31–3.

The charge of rowdy behaviour was based on peace slogans which he had sprayed on a wall. Also in 1983, article 222 – the misuse of state or social symbols – was applied against Roland Jahn, a leading activist in Jena's peace movement, for riding on his bicycle through the city with a Polish flag bearing the words 'Solidarity with the Polish people'.

HA IX: THE CENTRE OF THE INQUISITION

Mielke's understanding of the role of Main Department IX was determined by his crude Marxist-Leninist perception of the enemy. In 1979, he stated: 'Members of line IX are expected to do their work filled with hatred of the class enemy, constantly to adopt a clear class position. In so doing, they must preserve a lack of bias in their investigative work, which means adopting a clear position vis-à-vis the enemy, the lawbreakers – but with the approach and treatment corresponding to our principles of law'. 'An indispensable principle of investigative work', he continued, 'is always detecting comprehensively the hostile activities of subversive elements'.[22]

The investigative and interrogating activities of the MfS were brought under one roof in 1959 when the two units responsible for this work, Main Department IX and Department I/9, were merged. Colonel Dr Rolf Fister was appointed head of Main Department IX in 1973; he was later promoted to major general. In 1989, Main Department IX, which belonged directly to Mielke's own empire, had a staff of about 1,700, of which 484 worked at headquarters in East Berlin.[23] During the 1970s and 1980s, 12 departments were established in Main Department IX for investigating espionage and high treason, political underground activity, criminal acts against the state economy, crimes committed by members of the NVA, flight from the republic, political-operational offences such as arson, and Nazi and war crimes. In 1982, two of the departments were incorporated into Main Department IX's Assessment and Control Group.[24] In addition, Main Department IX had several separate desks, one of which, the 'Special Tasks of the Minister', was primarily concerned with the buying out of prisoners by the Federal Republic. This was a lucrative business: in the early 1970s, buying a prisoner free normally cost the West German government 40,000 DM. The Working Group Coordination planted cell informers in the ministry's own prisons and detention centres. In 1980, these informers accounted for an average of 17 per cent of all prisoners.

From the mid-1950s onwards, the MfS had its own pre-trial detention centres (*Untersuchungshaftanstalten*), the two central ones in Berlin-Hohenschönhausen and in the Magdalenenstraße in Berlin-Lichtenberg, and one each in the 15 Administrative Regions (*Bezirke*) of the country. After the

---

[22] Cited in Bundesministerium der Justiz 1994: 200. Our translation.
[23] Vollnhals C. 1999: 248; Weinke A. 2000: 146.
[24] Vollnhals C. 1999: 247–9, 255; Weinke A. 2000: 146; Wiedmann R. 1996: 131–5.

closure or transformation of prison labour camps into penal institutions in 1976, an additional 70 detention centres were placed in the hands of the Ministry of the Interior during the 1980s.[25] The running of these institutions was in the hands of Department XIV of the Stasi and its regional units. In 1989, this Department had a staff of 255 and worked closely with the Administration for Prisons in the Ministry of the Interior.[26] Relations between Main Department IX and Department XIV, including their respective regional units, were often strained as the latter's staff regarded themselves as merely a service arm of line IX, whose employees were more highly qualified on account of the more demanding nature of their investigative work. Difficult staff tended to be shunted into Department XIV, where job fluctuation was high, and drink was a greater problem than the class enemy.[27] The declassified material relating to the work of Main Department IX indicates that after 1970 more than 30,000 persons spent several weeks, sometimes years, in the Stasi's pre-trial centres and that for many of the primarily political prisoners this was usually the prelude to sentencing and incarceration in the prisons of the GDR. In the Honecker era, most of the Stasi's detainees simply wished to leave the country, whereas the proportion of those detained on account of a violent offence or who had been involved in actual intelligence or oppositional activities was probably lower than 10 per cent.[28]

A series of ministerial guidelines, rules and service instructions constituted the normative framework for preliminary criminal investigations, arrests and conditions in custody. For example, service instruction number 2708 issued by the Secretariat for State Security in 1955 defined the main aim of custody as the isolation of prisoners as 'criminals and enemies of peace and progress'.[29] This characterisation of the prisoner as an enemy would remain unchanged until the collapse of the GDR. The same service instruction also detailed how prisoners should be treated while in custody and it regulated matters such as discipline and contacts with lawyers.[30] In contrast to the immediate post-war period, conditions were better under Honecker for all categories of prisoners. For example, the use of physical torture declined and the provision of medical supplies increased. In general, medical supplies and hygiene were worse in the jails of the Ministry of the Interior than in those of the MfS, even though inmates' criticisms of conditions in the latter serve as a warning against too positive a picture.[31] Finally, although the Code of Criminal Procedure of 1968 provided the prisoner with certain basic rights, these could be circumvented by the Stasi. If an inquiry lasted more than three months, the

---

[25] Wunschik T. 1999: 468.
[26] Wiedmann R. 1996: 138–43.
[27] Beleites J. 1999: 451, 455–6.
[28] Ibid., 433, 455.
[29] Reinke H. 1996: 243.
[30] Ibid., 243–4.
[31] Müller K-D. 1997: 64, 83.

MfS was obliged by law to obtain the approval of the public prosecutor for an extension. What this meant in practice, however, can be judged by the case of the writer Jürgen Fuchs who was detained for over ten months between November 1976 and August 1977. His investigating officer told him: 'Your case is complicated, three months are not enough. A slip of paper is all it takes for the state prosecutor to agree to an extension. We are the people with power'.[32] The law had become the continuation of politics by secret police means.

PRISON CONDITIONS

Despite improvements, conditions remained harsh in the Stasi's prisons and the specially trained interrogators utilised a variety of psychological techniques. This can be illustrated in numerous ways. When an arrest was made, usually without warning, an individual was immediately disoriented. In the early decades, prisoners were neither allowed to see the route along which they were taken by car to prison, nor were they informed of their destination.[33] Arrest was a traumatic experience, whether it occurred at home or at work and whether it was expected or not. In the 1970s, it was common practice for the children of parents under arrest to be placed initially in one of the state's children's homes rather than in the care of relatives.[34] Wolfgang Hinkeldey, an electrician, was arrested by the Stasi on 11 December 1976 at his home in Jena, imprisoned in Berlin-Hohenschönhausen and proceedings initiated against him for incitement hostile to the state and for forming associations hostile to the state. Hinkeldey was deported to West Berlin on 2 September 1977 without a trial having been held. He describes what happened after he opened the door at 7.30 on the morning of his arrest:

> Three characters are standing outside.
> 'You are Herr Hinkeldey?'
> 'Yes.'
> 'Get dressed. You are coming with us to clear something up.'
> That is how it is. How often have I gone through this moment in my mind. It still frightens me now. I get dressed . . .
>
> A Stasi official stays in the flat. The other two take me out to a car. In front is the driver, with me in the middle behind him. My last journey through Jena ends at the Stasi building Am Anger. I have to wait. A young man watches me over his ND [*Neues Deutschland*]. Then they put handcuffs on me. I am driven away again in a car and taken to the State Security regional headquarters in Gera.[35]

---

[32] Cited in Fricke K. W. 1984: 135. Our translation.

[33] Beleites J. 1999: 457.

[34] Raschka J. 2001: 50.

[35] Cited in Fricke K. W. 1984: 123. *Neues Deutschland* was the SED daily organ. Our translation.

Although it was impossible to keep all prisoners in solitary confinement, every effort was made to reduce contact between prisoners other than with a cell inmate. The prison guards of Department XIV had to ensure that prisoners did not listen accidentally into conversations or radio and television programmes.[36] The surveillance of prisoners was remorseless. Guards kept regular watch over prisoners inside the cells, usually by means of the peephole in the door, and lights might be flashed on and off during the night.[37] Prison rooms were monitored by cameras and conversations with lawyers recorded. Defence lawyers had limited access to the relevant documentation.[38] From the 1970s onwards, greater use was made of bugging devices. In 1987, a joint Main Department IX and Department XIV report revealed that 30,959 hours of prisoners' conversations had been recorded in that year, the first time that the 30,000 mark had been exceeded![39] Bugging devices were complemented by the widespread use of cell informers. In 1985, there were two prisoners for every one informer in the Stasi's two pre-trial detention centres in East Berlin; in the regions, the ratio was between 3:1 and 10:1.[40] Among the main incentives for spying on fellow-prisoners were better conditions in cells, the prospect of an early release and 'atonement' for a misdemeanour.[41]

The treatment of prisoners gives the lie to the depiction of interrogations by a former Main Department IX officer with many years of service: 'Every prisoner under investigation had his defence lawyer, everyone was able to receive visits by relatives, so if anything untoward had happened, they would not have kept it to themselves'.[42] And while he acknowledged that imprisonment was a serious encroachment on a prisoner's life, he insisted that interrogations were stressful for both parties. Contrasting personal experience of conditions and treatment in Stasi custody are recalled by a political prisoner, Gerhard J., who was eventually sentenced to imprisonment in Cottbus in the late 1970s for would-be emigration. He recalled his first impressions of the MfS detention centre in the Otto-Nuschke-Straße in Potsdam, where he spent seven months. It was known as the Lindenhotel because of the lime trees which stood in the street outside; it had been used by the Nazis as a jail for political prisoners.

> I was led through a labyrinth of dark corridors and stairs. An eerie lack of space, hemmed in by ropes, red lights in every section, windows you could not see through. Then bars and more bars. Frightened and cowed I put my hands behind my back without being asked . . . Somehow I then arrived in the cell wing, was led to the room where prisoners' property was stored, taken to the partitioned-off

---

[36] Beleites J. 1999: 460–61.
[37] Fricke K. W. 1984: 129.
[38] Eisenfeld B. 1999: 371–2.
[39] Beleites J. 1999: 461; Müller K-D. 1997: 76–7.
[40] Beleites J. 1999: 462.
[41] Fricke K. W. 1984: 114.
[42] Interview with Manfred L. in Karau G. 1995: 71. Our translation.

space at the back and had to take off all my clothes again. I now had to come out of this partition completely naked and undergo a body search once more, but this time more thorough and extensive than on the previous occasions.

Since I was already familiar with this 'striptease', I was not unduly shocked or embarrassed. But I was still rather irritated by the people standing around me and gawping. And so I had to get into all the positions they wanted, bend down and move my limbs on command. That was not the end of it; I even had to push my penis to one side. My things were packed in a cardboard box and I was given the usual institution clothing.[43]

Gerhard J. was then led to his solitary cell and acquainted with prison rules by an officer:

He said: 'The day has 15 hours, very long hours, as you will see! When the siren sounds, your day is finished. Then it is time to sleep. Not until this moment are you allowed to get your bed ready and lie down. You are strictly forbidden to lie down during the day' . . . I was pleased to hear that I did not have to clasp my hands behind my back, a practice demanded in Hungary. But to make up for that, it was explained to me that I had to get up and stand to attention when the door opened. Then it was made clear to me that I was no longer Herr J. but number 53! . . . Being given a number was justified as follows: 'A personal number is solely for your security and to preserve your anonymity. In this way we are ensuring that other inmates cannot later hold your stay against you and turn it to your disadvantage!'[44]

Although the crude physical maltreatment of prisoners which characterised the Stalin era became the exception rather than the rule, the MfS refined its psychological techniques.[45] Prisoners were confronted with a range of penalties such as the withdrawal of leisure time and of the right to receive visitors, reading materials and cigarettes. Sleep deprivation, various types of threat and disinformation were used and a feeling of isolation and disorientation was cultivated. Deaths and suicide were not uncommon, although unexplained deaths were rare as the MfS was sensitive to possible adverse international reaction. One of the most notorious cases concerned Matthias Domaschk, who had belonged to the church's *Junge Gemeinde* in Jena since the early 1970s. It remains unclear whether his death in the MfS pre-trial detention centre in Gera in April 1981 was the result of suicide or of his harsh treatment by MfS interrogators. Elsewhere acts of defiance were punished severely, thereby reinforcing the conformity of most prisoners to prison rules and regulations. Siegmar Faust, for example, received 24 months in solitary confinement in the MfS detention centre in Cottbus for complaining to the prison authorities on behalf of his fellow-prisoners.

---

[43] Wernicke T. 1992: 35. Our translation.
[44] Ibid., 35. Our translation.
[45] Fricke F. W. 1984: 129; Raschka J. 2001: 64; Müller K-D. 1997: 50, 53, 103; Beleites J. 1999: 463.

An interrogation was a fundamental part of any detention. It was designed to clarify the nature of the alleged offence, obtain a confession and prepare the ground, where appropriate, for a prosecution in the courts. As Fricke points out, the interrogator's objective was usually to prove guilt, whatever the cost in time.[46] The *Erlebnisbericht*, a form of record of the hearing, reflected the conception of the interrogator, even though it was signed by the prisoner.[47] The ways in which the better-trained interrogators of the Honecker era preyed on prisoners' vulnerability and their sense of disorientation are recalled by Gerhard J. with regard to his main interrogator, a major, in the Stasi pre-trial detention centre in Potsdam:

> To me he seemed like a combatant of the old guard. An old-style Communist, then. He was not in the least hurried and to my surprise not in a bad mood but polite and obliging . . . His manner was conciliatory and unexpectedly displayed the characteristics of a normal human being.
>
> The image created by this man did not belong in this building according to my expectations and ideas at that time and did not correspond to the frightening image of the Stasi. In my state of anxiety I had expected a certain roughness and brutality and now I was being greeted in a friendly and polite way. Not only did it surprise me but also it threw me . . . In the following interrogations, approaches or tactics this major was, at least in my case, positively avuncular . . . The major spoke calmly to me and came across almost like a father.[48]

Gerhard J. discovered, however, that the kind uncle rapidly transformed himself into a strict disciplinarian when he refused to comply with the interrogator's wishes. Interrogators were skilled at playing on the fears of their charges. In the case of families who had tried to flee the GDR together, the partners and children were frequently imprisoned and separated immediately afterwards. Confessions were often extracted from parents afraid that their children would be sent to a home, and interrogators sometimes sowed so much distrust between partners that a divorce ensued.[49] A prisoner in Berlin-Hohenschönhausen in the early 1970s recalled that forged letters were presented to him during the interrogations, from which he formed the impression that his fiancée had left him.[50] In general, interrogators were adept at threatening prisoners – especially women with children – with repercussions for family members. A female prisoner, Christina Müller, writes of her time in custody in the MfS prison in Leipzig in the early 1980s:

> The investigating officer showed no sign of human emotions – on the contrary. When he had found the vulnerable spot he exploited it in order to put me under

---

[46] Fricke K. W. 1991: 62.

[47] Fricke K. W. 1984: 132.

[48] Wernicke T. 1992: 39. Our translation.

[49] Müller K-D. 1997: 57.

[50] Cited from a statement by Horst Schumm at a press conference in West Berlin in 1981: Fricke F. W. 1984: 130.

pressure. They used any means they could to destroy people's morale and to make them compliant, even with lies. They went so far as destroying the trust between married people. I myself suffered especially from being separated from my son and I worried about how he was coping with suddenly being alone.[51]

The damage to their health suffered by so many prisoners at the hands of the Stasi is described by Rudolf Piseur, who was kept in custody for over six months in the late 1970s:

> The never-ending, nerve-shattering interrogations last more than six months. My psychological and physical decline is being accelerated by the well thought-out and cunning interrogation methods that are pre-programmed again every day and deliberately use lies, slander, false statements and blackmail in abundance. So I can expect fifteen years to life in prison. At every conceivable opportunity the Stasi threaten me with this punishment. Gradually I come to believe it. Any contact with the outside world, even with my family is strictly prohibited. I do not receive any news from outside . . . Impotent rage, apathy take possession of me. I suffer a chronic nervous breakdown. Fortunately, I survived a heart attack, and the inter-rogations continue.[52]

THE LEGACY

Interviews conducted after German unification with 360 persons who had been imprisoned during the Honecker era reveal that many were still suffer-ing from psychological disturbances and long-term physical injury. Sleep disturbances, anxiety, psychosomatic illness, nightmares and depression were common. Among the main physical illnesses were heart and circulation dif-ficulties and teeth, stomach and eye problems, all of which can be linked to the unacceptable hygiene conditions and the labour system in the prisons of the Ministries of State Security and the Interior and to maltreatment by guards and other inmates; 60 per cent had been subjected to threats and blackmail and 80 per cent had been forced to endure solitary confinement.[53] Another study conducted in 1990 and 1991 among 16 men and 39 women aged between 20 and 62 also underlines the nature of the repressive prison regime. They had been imprisoned in the GDR for political reasons for periods ranging from six weeks to 12 years during the later 1970s and the 1980s. During their imprisonment, the inmates had been severely affected by feelings of helplessness when confronted by solitary confinement, the intrigues of fellow prisoners, the rejection of their innocence and the lack of contact with the outside world.[54] For these individuals, even in the new Germany, the arm of the Stasi and the police was still long.

---

[51] Cited in Müller K-D. 1997: 80. Our translation.
[52] Cited in ibid., 73. Our translation.
[53] Müller K-D. 1997: 122–4.
[54] Bauer M. and Priebe S. 1996: 35–8.

Part III

THE FIRM AND ITS SERVANTS

Chapter 6

SERVING THE CAUSE – THE OFFICER CLASS

RAPID GROWTH IN THE LONG 1970S

The full-time staff in the central, regional and district units, which formed the core of the 'multi-functional super apparatus',[1] had been transformed during the 1960s into a functional elite within the 'socialist service class' of the East German state.[2] This development had taken place without the abandonment of the Stasi's perception of itself as a militant defender of Marxist-Leninist ideology and of the 'workers' and peasants' state'. There was, however, an inherent tension between the professional ethos and the traditional Chekist ideal, a tension which would become more acute with the generational changing of the guard in the course of the 1970s and in particular after the advent to power of Gorbachev in 1985.

Under Mielke's direction, the full-time staff experienced a rapid expansion of about 147 per cent between 1967 and 1982, that is, from 32,912 to 81,495, with annual growth rates varying from 10.8 per cent in the former year to 3.8 per cent in the latter.[3] Although an all-time peak of 91,105 was reached in October 1989, the rate of growth slowed down appreciably from 1982 onwards. Table 6.1, which is based on Jens Gieseke's combing of the files of the Main Department for Cadres and Training, provides a detailed statistical picture. The explosion in numbers can be attributed to the paranoia which was endemic in the GDR service and political elites and which was quickened by the onset of détente and West Germany's *Ostpolitik*. Closer personal contacts between East and West German citizens and the GDR's signing of the 1975 Helsinki Accords, including the declaration on human rights, aroused fears among the elites of an imperialist Trojan horse. In their view, the Prague Spring served as a warning against the acute danger posed by opening up the communist world to Western influences and notions of democratisation and liberalisation.

---

[1] Villain J. 1990: 134.

[2] Gieseke J. 2000: 288.

[3] Ibid., 293–4.

Table 6.1 The numerical strength of the MfS full-time staff, 1950–89

	1950	1960*	1967	1969	1970	1971	1975	1979	1982	1986†	1988	1989‡
Total staff	2,700	22,843	32,912	40,328	45,580	48,786	59,514	75,138	81,495	90,577	90,257	91,015
% increase over previous year	135	12.3	7.1	10.3	7.4	5.2	6.7	3.8	3.8	6.2	–0.3	0.8
Women (%), excl. Guard Regiment until 1962	–	–	14.2	14.4	–	15.8	16.2	16.4	16.1	15.8	15.6	15.7
Territorial distribution												
MfS Berlin	–	6,151	11,238	13,269	14,331	15,661	22,312	29,407	34,481	37,698	37,665	36,421
Guard Regiment	–	4,372	5,705	7,351	7,924	7,980	9,245	9,952	10,437	10,306	9,861	11,526
Regional Administrations, incl. districts	–	12,320	16,269	19,708	21,056	21,939	27,957	32,868	36,577	42,573	42,731	43,168
Regions as % of all staff		55.9	49.4	48.9	48.6	47.5	47.0	45.5	44.9	47.0	47.3	47.4

* from 1958 includes HV A
† from 1986 includes HIMs
‡ until 31 October

Source: Gieseke J. 2000: 552–7.

Détente, in Mielke's view, provided the imperialists with an opportunity to subvert and liquidate the GDR's socialist system and thus demanded the utmost vigilance and protection by an ever larger security force.[4] While Mielke's scare-mongering was undoubtedly a calculated strategy to expand his empire, his deep-rooted ideological aversion to the West was equally important in turning the MfS, per head of domestic population, into the largest secret police and secret security apparatus in the Soviet empire and probably in world history. According to Gieseke, the ratio of full-time secret service personnel to population was 1:180 in the GDR (MfS), 1:595 in the USSR (KGB), 1:1,553–82 in Romania (*Securitate*) and 1:1,574 in Poland in 1989–90. These figures exclude the even larger number of unofficial collaborators.[5] The rapid growth of East Germany's vast secret service organisation, which was financed from the state budget, was challenged by the cost-conscious Gerhard Schürer, the head of the State Planning Commission, and by several other ministries.[6] However, the MfS emerged unscathed until the early 1980s, partly because of its vital role in the protection of the GDR and partly because of the close collaboration on security matters between Honecker and Mielke. While the financial burden of the MfS was not in itself sufficient to ruin the GDR economically, the combined costs of the security and defence organs and the heavy state subsidies for basic consumer goods and a variety of social welfare benefits meant that the GDR was living well beyond its means in its final decade.

WHO WERE THE OFFICERS?

The full-time MfS officers in the Honecker era were overwhelmingly male and tended to have a lower level of formal educational qualification than their peers in the party and the other state organs. They were committed both ideologically and politically to 'real existing socialism', did not eschew the material benefits of their position, and were recruited primarily from families with roots in the SED, the MfS and the other security forces. While significant variations existed in individual social profiles, the general pattern was that of a relatively self-contained, self-recruiting and exclusive elite.

The average age of MfS full-time staff increased gradually over the decades from 28.0 years in 1950 to 35.7 years in 1983,[7] although, as a result of the expansion of the ministry, there was a steady replenishment by younger cadres. The generation which entered the MfS in the 1950s gradually took over the key posts in the ministry. By 1982, two-thirds of staff came from

---

[4] Müller-Enbergs H. 1996: 52–4.
[5] Gieseke J. 2000: 538.
[6] Pirker T., Lepsius M. R., Weinert R. and Hertle H-H. 1995: 107.
[7] Gieseke J. 1995: 49–50.

this group, as opposed to 22 per cent in 1969. After the death in 1982 of his First Deputy Minister, Bruno Beater, Mielke was the sole survivor of the older generation of KPD cadres at the summit of the MfS.

Although the proportion of female staff in the MfS was a relatively high 25 per cent in 1954, this declined gradually to 15.8 per cent in 1971.[8] Changing little throughout the Honecker era, women's participation in the MfS was 15.7 per cent in 1989 or, in numerical terms, 14,259. Women were relatively well represented in services and administration, for example, the Medical Service, the Finance Department and the Main Department Cadres and Training, as well as in operational units such as the Central Coordinating Group and ZAIG. They were, however, less prominent in those units which were directly engaged in work with IMs, where their share was only between one-sixth and one-fifth. There was a perceptible gender differentiation, with women concentrated in secretarial and typing posts. In general terms, the nearer the top of the ministerial hierarchy, the less visible were women. They achieved a peak in 1978 of 4.5 per cent of all MfS leadership cadres, only for this to fall to 3.8 per cent ten years later. No woman ever became head of a Main Department and in 1988 only 1.8 per cent were in charge of a department.[9] In an interview given in 1993, a former MfS officer and mother of three recalled that: 'The functions which were associated with a lot of work but little honour were always filled by women. Because they had children, women were not put in functions which were really important'.[10]

The low participation of women in leadership positions as well as the distribution of jobs by gender can be explained in part by the numerous burdens typically borne by GDR women in the home and at work. A former secretary and an assistant in an intelligence evaluation group stated, in an interview in July 1990, that women with children were regarded as an element of 'instability' in the MfS and that they felt guilty when they had to take time off work to look after sick children.[11] As many were married to MfS staff, this added to rather than provided relief from their countless burdens. Moreover, in the militaristic Stasi, a veritable bastion of male chauvinism, women were deemed to be too 'gossipy' for the conspiratorial work of a Chekist.[12]

Data compiled by the Stasi on the occupational, educational and family profile of the full-time personnel have to be treated with caution as they were often manipulated to demonstrate the preponderance of 'workers' in an organisation which prided itself on being the sword and shield of the SED, the self-appointed representative of what was defined in ideological terms as

---

[8] Until 1962, the data on women did not include the Guard Regiment.
[9] Gieseke J. 2000: 432; Gieseke J. 1995: 54–5.
[10] Cited in Schmole A. 2001: 17. Our translation.
[11] Rieckert A., Schwarz A. and Schneider D. 1990: 134–5.
[12] Gieseke J. 2000: 352; Gieseke J. 1995: 56–7.

the most progressive force, that is, the working class. According to Stasi materials,[13] the working-class origins of personnel fell from 92.3 per cent in 1962 to 78.9 per cent in 1988, while that of white-collar employees and the intelligentsia rose from 3.9 per cent to 10.6 per cent and from 0.6 per cent to 6.6 per cent respectively. However, an analysis of 400 doctoral candidates of the Law School probably provides a more realistic picture of distribution by social group. The proportion from working-class families declined markedly from 91.2 per cent in the early 1950s to 51.8 per cent in the later 1970s and, even more telling, immediately prior to joining the MfS, only 13.1 per cent were classified as workers. The majority were recruited from the SED and the state apparatus, from the armed forces and the mass organisations and from among pupils and students.

The declassified files of the Main Department Cadres and Training under-score the significance of the armed forces and the Guard Regiment as sources of recruitment. 20.7 per cent of MfS full-time personnel in 1988 came from the National People's Army, 2.7 per cent from the People's Police and as many as 39.6 per cent from the ministry's own regiment.[14] In the 1970s, as the children of Stasi personnel reached maturity, the ministry drew increas-ingly on these offspring to restock the ranks. Two former HV A officers confirm this process of self-reproduction:

> So in the HV A as well the practice became common of reducing the work to bring on the next generation to a kind of 'internal reproduction'. The department was particularly keen to recruit colleagues who were the children or at least the relatives of other members of the Ministry of State Security. Irrespective of the particular individual, that ensured 'quality' and it guaranteed that these candidates did not have any contact with the West.[15]

Predestination by family can be traced in the comments of Andreas K., a lieutenant in the Main Department Protection of Individuals, who joined the MfS in 1978:

> . . . and I got to know the MfS through my father. He was the leader of a District Service Unit and I have to say he had a work collective in which each person was there for everyone else. That impressed me and also motivated me even as a boy. The families were integrated, we children played together, you felt a sense of security even as a young man.[16]

Not only did the ministry recruit heavily from the security and armed forces, but the concentration of Stasi families in apartments in the Lichtenberg and Hohenschönhausen districts of East Berlin narrowed social and cultural

---

[13] The details are in Gieseke J. 1995: 46–8.

[14] Ibid., 48; Gieseke J. 2000: 334–5.

[15] Richter P. and Rösler K. 1992: 113. Our translation.

[16] Karau G. 1995: 155. Later, he became disillusioned with his work and the SED leadership and fell out with his father. Our translation.

horizons. Sample survey data from 1989 on the political affiliation of MfS staff and their parents underline this point and indicate why the ministry constituted a bedrock of loyalty to 'real existing socialism': 79.1 per cent of the fathers and 56.2 per cent of the mothers of MfS employees were members of the SED and only 9.3 per cent came from homes in which neither parent belonged to a political party. The ministry was one of the favoured destinations for the children of Politbüro and Central Committee members. In 1986, eight of the twenty-one full members and the five candidate members of the Politbüro had at least one child in the MfS.[17] This indicates that the political elites were able to use their influence to place their progeny in key positions at a time when social mobility was slowing down. With regard to MfS full-time staff, the survey also revealed that in 1988 over four-fifths were members of the SED and only 6.1 per cent were not affiliated to any party.[18] While this might have buttressed loyalty to the SED system, it undermined critical reflection and ideas on reform.

A marked improvement in qualifications occurred over the decades. Those with a higher education qualification rose rapidly in the 1960s before a slowdown in the growth rate from the mid- to late 1970s onwards. Whereas only 1.6 per cent had such a qualification in 1950, by 1975 the figure had risen to 9.1 per cent and to 11.9 per cent in 1988.[19] The general improvement in the formal educational qualifications of the officer corps, facilitated by a plethora of further educational and training programmes, reflected the Stasi's drive for a more professional and competent administrative staff, a development which was also observable elsewhere in GDR society. The contrast between the level and intensity of training at the beginning of the 1950s and the Honecker era is instructive. In the earlier period, short basic courses in German and Marxism-Leninism were introduced in an improvised manner to raise the low standards. By the time that Honecker came to power, not only were staff receiving a grounding in the arts of political policing as well as a thorough training in Marxism-Leninism, organised by the SED Party organ in the ministry, but they were also able to take advantage of an array of opportunities provided by residential, distance-learning and correspondence courses. In the first quinquennium of the 1970s, the latter was the mode of study of over three-quarters of all trainees.[20]

Several Main Departments had their own training institutions. HV A provided instruction in foreign intelligence work at its school in Belzig until 1986, and subsequently at Gosen. At the apex of the system stood the Law

---

[17] Gieseke J. 2000: 422.

[18] Ibid., 423.

[19] Gieseke J. 1995: 48–9. Despite the improvements, an internal survey in 1986–87 showed that the proportion of university and college graduates was much lower in the MfS than in non-producing areas such as education and state administration: Gieseke J. 2000: 425.

[20] Ibid., 340, 343.

School (*Juristische Hochschule*) in Potsdam-Eiche. In 1955, it changed in status from a college to a university (*Hochschule*); the term 'Law' or 'Juridical' was added ten years later. By the mid-1960s, it was running numerous initial and further training courses for leading cadres and in 1968 it was granted the right to award its own academic degrees.[21] While the professional and educational level of MfS staff undoubtedly improved, it remained lower than in other major organs and the programmes were intended to boost efficiency, not to create a critical reform potential. The dissertations written by Stasi officers as part of their university training illustrate this: they were task oriented and primarily concerned with the smoother functioning of security operations.

THE LIFE-STYLE AND THE MINDSET OF THE STASI SERVICE CLASS

Alexandra Richie has sought to capture the life-style of the Stasi officer class:

> If they were successful, they could rise high in the system, and by GDR standards the rewards were high. Employees earned OM2,000 per month (a very high wage); they had access to special shops; they could travel abroad; they could bring friends and relatives in from the west through a hidden door in Friedrichstrasse; they had access to western literature, magazines, newspapers and pornography; and they lived in the most luxurious apartments or villas. The Stasi could enjoy a vast entertainment and leisure network, which included twenty-three separate vacation spas, exclusive hospitals and sports complexes with swimming pools, modern gyms, tennis courts and saunas. Officials were given a Lada and a driver, while generals got sleek new Citroens for official and private use . . . Some had yachts and motorcycles and shopped at the *Leiterläden* (special shops) for western jewellery, champagne and *haute couture*.[22]

Although personnel undoubtedly enjoyed many perks, the officers' lifestyle was less uniform and often less privileged than that depicted by Richie. There were elites within elites, as can be seen from salary and bonus differentials.[23] Salary depended on length of service, function and rank. The ministry's top earner was Mielke, with 76,062 GDR Marks per annum. Members of the Guard Regiment and the East Berlin Regional Administration received a 'capital city' supplement. In 1983, the average monthly salary in GDR Marks of the officers in East Berlin was 1,541 and in the Regional Administrations 1,371. By 1988, this had risen to 1,818 and 1,700 respectively. In the latter year, the average for all GDR employees was 1,280. Given these differences, it is not surprising that many staff desired to move from the District Service Units where pay and status were inferior. Differentials in

---

[21] Gieseke J. 1995: 35–6.
[22] Richie A. 1998: 760. OM denotes Ost- or GDR Marks.
[23] For details on salaries and bonuses, see Gieseke J. 1995: 58–63; Gieseke J. 2000: 442; Karau G. 1995: 12; Richter H. 2001: 262.

supplementary payments according to rank were not inconsiderable: in 1987, a soldier received 220 GDR Marks, a sergeant 450, a captain 550, a colonel 800, a major general 1,000 and a senior general 1,400. Additional benefits included very low levels of taxation on income and generous pensions as well as the possibility of a new apartment and access to a range of consumer goods beyond the reach of most ordinary East Germans.[24]

Financial and other material considerations, while by no means insignificant in earlier decades, seem to have played an increasingly important role for service in the MfS during the 1980s. After the collapse of communism, one officer lamented that his original idealism was not shared by some colleagues, who were motivated only by their monthly salary.[25] However, material inducements were not the only motives but were usually linked, in varying degrees, to political conviction, the attractions of membership of a powerful and elitist organisation and the excitement of espionage.[26] The MfS, especially its Law School, devoted considerable effort to identifying these motives as well as to ways of strengthening the officers' belief in the ultimate victory of socialism and of fostering their hatred of the enemies of socialism.[27] Once in the employ of the ministry, officers were required, according to the cadre guidelines of 1964, to adhere to the rules of conspiracy, lead an exemplary private life, raise their children in the spirit of peace and socialism and conduct themselves in a disciplined manner.[28] Discipline was strictly enforced throughout the ministry and, as all staff from waitress to minister held a military rank, it was based on strict military principles. Officers were required to swear a solemn oath 'to be an honourable, brave, disciplined and alert soldier, to obey military superiors without question, to carry out orders with determination and never to reveal military and state secrets'.[29]

The memoirs of, and interviews with, former MfS officers provide an insight into motivation, albeit with the qualification that they are not free of the methodological problems inherent in any such personal reconstruction of the past. Motives and values covered a broad spectrum: the desire to preserve peace, to serve the honourable and worthy cause of socialism, to continue the anti-fascist struggle of the KPD and to pursue a chosen career in a dedicated manner.[30] Markus Wolf speaks for most of his former comrades in his stubborn defence of HV A as a 'normal' foreign intelligence service dedicated to

---

[24] Gieseke J. 1995: 61–3.
[25] Interview with Andreas K. in Karau G. 1995: 155.
[26] On the excitement of espionage work, see the article by a former officer in Peter R. 1992: 24.
[27] Gieseke J. 1995: 65.
[28] Gieseke J. 2000: 277–8.
[29] Cited from a 1972 regulation in Süß W. 1997: 229. Our translation.
[30] Interview with W. Hartmann. This paragraph also draws on interviews which were conducted in 1990 and published in Rieker A., Schwarz A. and Schneider D. 1990, as well as on articles in the journal Zwie-Gespräch.

peace and the protection of socialism from surprise attack and an atomic war launched by the West. He asserts that his own communist past and his intensive political and ideological training in Moscow, together with his Jewish origins and the prominence of ex-Nazis in the Federal Republic, bound him to the GDR and shaped his perception of his work in the MfS as a link in the country's anti-fascist chain both before and after 1945.[31]

One of Wolf's colleagues in the top echelons of the domestic arm of the Stasi's service class, Rudi Mittig, arrived in the MfS via a different route. He had served in the Wehrmacht during the Second World War and was, at that time, a believer in fascist ideology. Subsequently, he came to admire anti-fascist fighters such as Mielke and was determined to protect the GDR's socialist order against its Cold War enemies.[32] When he joined the MfS in 1952, he was perhaps performing an act of contrition for his fascist past. A later generation's values are reflected by a lower ranking-officer, a lieutenant who enlisted in 1975. His motivation, he claims, was not driven primarily by material considerations, but by American imperialism's aggression in Cuba and Vietnam and by his wish to prevent war and to protect the GDR.[33]

One fundamental criticism of these views is that they are too uncritical of the Stalinist past and the less than honourable East German present. Although Markus Wolf has admitted to having qualms about the excesses of Stalin, the methods pursued by the Stasi and the shortcomings of the GDR, he has sought to rationalise his position by reference to the grand ideals of communism. Wolf justifies the East German communists' resort to repressive practices as a defensive reaction to the imperialists' efforts to destroy the GDR's socialist experiment. And as for Stalin's crimes, he pleads that 'We German Communists had perhaps the most complete blind spots of all the foreigners in Moscow . . . since we had been rescued from death or imprisonment by the Soviet Union. Any other doubts about what was going on were overshadowed by events under Hitler's regime, and I was incapable of seeing our socialist system as a tyranny'.[34] Determined to ensure that 'Nazism would never infect the Germans again',[35] he appealed to the greater cause by quoting the lines from Bertolt Brecht's play *The Measure Taken*:

What baseness would you not commit,
To stamp out baseness?
If you could change the world,
What would you be too good for?[36]

---

[31] Wolf M. 1997: 36–42, 49.
[32] Rieker A., Schwarz A. and Schneider D. 1990: 167–9; also Bergmann G. 1993: 1.
[33] Karau G. 1995: 37–8.
[34] Wolf M. 1997: 37.
[35] Ibid., 40.
[36] Ibid., 233.

A STASI COP CULTURE

The statements by Wolf and his co-generals point to the prevalence of what might be termed a Stasi 'cop culture' of shared assumptions and values which shaped and determined behaviour.[37] The main elements of this sub-culture are, for the most part, not peculiar to the Stasi for they are to be found in the security and police forces of many other countries. But like other forces, differences existed within the ranks with respect to an individual's adherence to the organisation's core values and attitudes. The latter caveat aside, the constituent elements of the MfS 'cop culture' were: a sense of mission in that officers felt that they were doing a worthwhile job in safeguarding the state; an endemic suspicion arising not only from their job, training and indoc-trination but also from the political and geographical location of the GDR; a pragmatism which eschewed innovation and basic research; and a machismo which expressed itself in hard drinking and sexist attitudes. The machismo and the self-perception as defenders of state and society flowed into the stream of political and social conservatism which was challenged by deviants from convention, such as punks, homosexuals, ecologists and peace activists (see Chapters 10 and 11).

DISCIPLINARY PROBLEMS

The records of the Gauck Authority not only undermine Wolf's insistence that HV A was separate from the repressive activities of counterintelligence, they also provide evidence of a divergence from some of the ideals acclaimed by the generals, especially the deviation from the image of a dedicated and disciplined elite corps serving an honourable cause. From 1966 onwards, the ministry's annual reports indicate that about 3 per cent of employees were penalised for misdemeanours. This is only an indicator as the figure does not include those misdemeanours which went unpunished.[38] Of the 1,301 pen-alties imposed in 1989, 18.6 per cent were for violation of duty and orders, 10.7 per cent for a penal offence and 10.1 per cent for an overdrawn bank account. Other transgressions included verbal indiscretions, causing traffic accidents and immoral behaviour. In a case which was dealt with by the disciplinary arm of the Main Department for Cadres and Training in 1989, a doctor of law and staff officer at the Law School was transferred to the University of Economics in East Berlin on account of his homosexual affairs, including one with a would-be emigrant, which were deemed to constitute a security risk to the MfS. After examination by the ministry's Central Medical Service, his 'orientation' was deemed to be 'irreversible'.[39] Fraud is evident in

---

[37] On the concept of 'cop culture', see Reiner R. 1992: 111–37.
[38] Gieseke J. 1995: 74–6.
[39] MfS ZA, HA IX, no. 8755, 'Bericht', 30 March 1989, pp. 11–13.

the case of an officer in Department XX of the Regional Administration in Gera. He was disciplined in 1976 for having acquired 30,000 GDR Marks to help him purchase a car from one of the informers under his control, IM 'Albert', an official of the Jehovah's Witnesses.[40]

Alcohol lay at the root of many offences. The disciplinary office within the Main Department for Cadres and Training calculated that about 25 per cent of all penalties were drink related.[41] The growing concern among the ministry's leaders over the problem of alcoholism during the 1980s is reflected in a letter sent out by Major-General Möller, to all service units in March 1987:

> The analysis of disciplinary procedures and the incidences of poor personal relations frequently point to alcohol abuse. Alcohol dependence and the presence of alcohol disease are being diagnosed in members by the health care service. It is my estimation that we have not succeeded everywhere and throughout the membership in consistently fulfilling the tasks set by the minister of educating people in the MfS to possess strength of character, moral purity and to adopt a healthy life-style.[42]

Alcohol abuse was not restricted to the ranks; even top officials were discharged on account of alcoholism. One tragedy occurred in December 1984 when an inebriated MfS guard shot dead a drunken worker and wounded two others.[43] Another example of alcohol-related disciplinary offences concerned the head of a Mecklenburg unit who, it was revealed in 1984, indulged in heavy drinking bouts, sometimes in the company of the Chair of the District Council and the District police chief. Their pleasure was subsidised from funds designated for operational activities. In addition, he had, for many years, used the services of several IMs for work on his weekend house and his daughter's boathouse.[44] Josef Schwarz, the former head of the Erfurt Regional Administration, contends, however, that using their 'connections' to acquire building materials and spare parts was not without justification as this kind of practice was endemic in GDR society because of the nature of the 'shortage economy'.[45]

WORK-RELATED STRESS

According to the annual statistics which are available from 1964 to 1987, suicide was by no means rare. Together with alcoholism, it was an indicator

---

[40] MfS ZA, KuSch, no. 428/89 (II), pp. 27–31, 36–9. The caution for neglect of duties was lifted in 1978, and five years later the officer, Bergner, became head of Department XX/4 in the Regional Administration.

[41] Gieseke J. 1995: 75.

[42] Cited in Süß S. 1999: 726–7. Our translation. Möller was head of HA for Cadres and Training.

[43] Gieseke J. 2000: 439.

[44] Ibid., 443.

[45] Schwarz J. 1994: 40–41. He is not specifically defending MfS practices, but it is implied.

of deep-seated psychological pressures and conflicts arising from MfS work. These problems were examined in one MfS research project conducted between 1969 and 1973 in the Rostock and Erfurt Regional Administrations. The authors, Jörg Franke and Meinholt Hennig, calculated that unfitness for work arising from neuroses was well above the GDR average of 3.1 per cent in 1973.[46] The factors conducive to neuroses in Departments VIII and XV, which were held to be applicable in other spheres, included officers' neglect of their families as a result of the pressure of work. This was particularly true of conflicts between staff and their family which were generated by the conspiratorial nature of MfS activities and, so the researchers asserted, of the inner tension between the ministry's 'humanistic ideals' and the need to be firm and unyielding towards the 'enemy'.[47]

After the fall of the GDR, ex-Stasi personnel have provided personal insights into the pressures of their work, a burden which many also use to justify their former privileges. One HV A officer claims that he worked six days out of seven and spent more time on the train and in the car than at home. Given this kind of stress, it was not surprising in his opinion that many of his colleagues' marriages collapsed.[48] The head of the Leipzig Regional Administration recalls that he had no time for hobbies and did not possess a car. He left for work early in the morning and returned home late at night. His wife had to accept the situation or leave.[49] In 1976, a Stasi report found that the divorce rate among MfS employees was as high as in society generally and identified the main causes as excessive drinking, lack of empathy with a partner's work and her household burdens, extra-marital affairs, and the special nature of service in the ministry. The MfS was sometimes directly responsible, enforcing divorce if partners had Western contacts or other 'dubious' connections.[50]

Garton Ash's interview with a former Stasi major, Klaus Risse, sheds further light on how the 'firm' interfered not only in the private lives of its targets but also in the private sphere of its own officers: 'You couldn't marry without the Ministry's approval. If your wife's father or even uncle had been in the SS, you would have to choose between her and the job . . . Why, you weren't even allowed to grow a beard. I think of General Kratsch, clean shaven in the photograph on his personnel card but bearded now'.[51] In their 'insider report' on the GDR's foreign intelligence arm, two former HV A officers, Peter Richter and Klaus Rösler, underline the close surveillance to which the Main Department Cadres and Training subjected their colleagues:

[46] Süß S. 1999: 713–14.
[47] Ibid., 16–17.
[48] Rieker A., Schwarz A. and Schneider D. 1990: 79.
[49] Ibid., 220.
[50] Gieseke J. 2000: 358.
[51] Ash T. G. 1997: 174.

The objective was to prevent any unsupervised contact. For this reason, close relatives were not allowed to have any connection with Western countries. The authorisation of journeys was subject to severe restrictions; even holidays in socialist countries abroad had to be reported to the authorities and were subject to official approval in the case of an increasing number of countries. You could only travel in groups. Camping holidays or renting private accommodation were forbidden. Unauthorised contact – no matter how fortuitous – had to be reported immediately. To test the behaviour of colleagues contact situations were staged. Any suspicion could lead to secret enquiries and intelligence officers were as likely as any other GDR citizen to be bugged or to have mail opened. Bugs might be put in office telephones.[52]

Furthermore, even though married partners and other close family members might be aware that a relative worked for the ministry, they were not supposed to have a detailed knowledge of the nature of this work, at least not until the latter part of the Honecker era.[53] Some of the pressures endured by other family members are recalled poignantly by the daughter of a Stasi officer in the Department for Intelligence and Communications. Through an exaggerated sense of duty and zeal, he had, in her view, worn himself out. As a child, she was not allowed visitors and her father took little interest in her. Then, when she was in her mid-teens, they clashed over her boyfriends and her visit to a church meeting. The tension became so acute that her father beat her and, at the age of 16, she attempted suicide. When, after she had left home, she announced her intention to marry, he accused her of attempting to wreck his career.[54]

Although the value system of MfS officers remained stable due to the intensive training programmes, the relatively closed social and political networks, the ministry's strict disciplinary code, material incentives and so forth, cracks in the outer shield began to appear from the later 1970s onwards. The cracks, albeit of a minor nature until the advent of Gorbachev, were primarily the consequence of détente. Not only did the opening to the West raise questions about the viability of the ministry's traditional image of the enemy but the more frequent contacts between East and West Germans made it increasingly difficult for the MfS to insulate its employees from Western influences. The latter was particularly pertinent to the relatives of staff, above all their parents-in-law, who paid visits to or received visitors from the FRG. Various tensions arose in families as a result. For example, some relatives blamed the Stasi for the rejection by the authorities of their application to visit the West, and the growing contacts between East and West Germans created additional difficulties for MfS employees in finding a suitable partner.[55]

---

[52] Richter P. and Rösler K. 1992: 117. Our translation.
[53] Karau G. 1995: 123. Interview with an officer of HV A.
[54] Rieker A., Schwarz A. and Schneider D. 1990: 262–75.
[55] Gieseke J. 2000: 371–2.

Chapter 7

MIELKE'S UNOFFICIAL
COLLABORATORS

AN ARMY OF INFORMERS

Although the MfS kept monthly statistics on its army of informers, many of the materials have not survived and a full record is only available from 1985 onwards. However, the data for the Frankfurt/Oder region are probably a reliable indicator of the general trend: whereas in 1952 only 533 informers were in the service of the MfS in the region, 13 years later the number had increased to 2,986, reaching a peak of 4,977 in 1985.[1] The main expert on the topic, Helmut Müller-Enbergs, estimates that about 250,000 full-time staff and about 600,000 *Inoffizielle Mitarbeiter*, that is, unofficial collaborators or co-workers (IMs) worked for the ministry between 1950 and 1989.[2] Müller-Enbergs's figures do not, however, include the informers used by the Criminal Police.

Despite the many statistical uncertainties, the explosion in the numbers of IMs is beyond dispute. A peak of about 180,000 was probably reached in the mid-1970s before falling slightly to about 176,000 ten years later.[3] The figures include a large shadowy group – 32,282 in 1988 – of IMKs (*Inoffizielle Mitarbeiter zur Sicherung der Konspiration und des Verbindungswesens*), who, usually in return for money or gifts, put their telephone, address or apartment at the disposal of the Stasi for clandestine meetings between controllers and IMs.[4] Most IMs spied for the units in Main Departments II, VI, XVIII, XIX and XX, with high concentrations too in the Main Department/Administration in the National People's Army and Main Department VII.[5] Turnover was rapid in the 1980s. There may well have been a complete turnover of IMs over the short period of three to six years in the District Service Units

---

1 Müller-Enbergs H. 1995b: 1.
2 Müller-Enbergs H. 1999: 1338.
3 Müller-Enbergs H. 1996: 54, 59.
4 Müller-Enbergs H. 1993: 10.
5 Gieseke J. 2001: 114.

but probably between seven and ten years among those controlled by the Regional Administrations and by the central organs in East Berlin.[6]

The rapid expansion of the IM network, like that of the full-time staff, is explained by the Honecker regime's determination to combat the negative effects of détente and closer relations with the West and, from the later 1970s onwards, to control the alternative political culture and the growing desire for emigration among the East German population. A deteriorating economic performance, too, gave cause for concern and prompted action against alleged spies and saboteurs. As the Stasi's 'eyes and ears', the agents were regarded as the 'main weapon' in the struggle against the enemy, without whom the full-time officials could not achieve their goals. According to the ministry's 1979 guidelines on IMs, they 'play a key role in ensuring overall internal security in the area of operations. Their work is to a great extent preventive in nature and contributes to the early detection and implementation of new security requirements. Their work must serve the comprehensive and secure evaluation and control of the politically operative situation in their area of responsibility and provide further clarification of the question of "Who is who?"'[7] As the bread and butter of counterintelligence, not only were IMs deployed to combat and prevent subversion by an external enemy but also to protect socialist society against the disruption and harm caused by the 'hostile' and 'negative' actions and attitudes of East German citizens. Mielke referred to this latter task in his usual uncompromising fashion at a service conference in 1973:

> By means of political-operative work, in particular the work of IMs, greater efforts have to be made in the ministries, institutions, economic organisations and especially in the foreign trade enterprises to keep them free of bribery, corruption, petty bourgeois behaviour but above all from the impact of hostile corrupting influences.[8]

As the enemies of the socialist state were supposedly omnipresent, then the MfS, too, had to be omnipresent – as well as omniscient. This aim led, in the opinion of the former head of the Erfurt Regional Administration, Josef Schwarz, to the principle that the unexpected had to be eliminated at all times and everywhere.[9] The resulting scale and depth of the penetration of people's private lives as well as of the institutions of state and society, not the organisation's methods, is, according to Klaus-Dietmar Henke, the historically unique feature of the MfS.[10] The techniques of surveillance such as phone-tapping, the opening of mail and house searches and the deployment of agents and spies to gather information and to subvert groups who were seen

---

[6] Geiger H. 1993: 47.
[7] Müller-Enbergs H. 1996: 314. Our translation.
[8] Cited in Geiger H. 1993: 43. Our translation.
[9] Schwarz J. 1994: 86.
[10] Henke K-D. 1993: 586.

as a threat to the existing political and social order have been practised by
dictatorships, monarchies and parliamentary democracies alike.

A TYPOLOGY OF INFORMERS

Until 1968, unofficial collaborators were called GIs (*Geheime Informatoren*),
that is, secret informers; thereafter, IM became the generic term. The Stasi
was keen to avoid the term spy or *Spitzel* as this was associated with the
Gestapo; IMs, it was asserted, constituted an elite of dedicated defenders of
their socialist homeland.[11] The range of tasks performed by IMs required an
ever more esoteric and sometimes bewildering differentiation into IMS, IMB
and so forth which renders inadequate the definition in Federal German law
of an IM as someone who had declared their willingness to supply information to the Stasi. This definition excludes, for example, several hundred prison
cell informers, the foreign spies of HV A, and 15,200 informers (*Inoffizielle
Kriminalpolizeiliche Mitarbeiter*) attached to *Arbeitsgebiet* 1 or K1 of the Criminal
Police.[12] The Stasi could also draw on voluntary helpers as contact persons
(*Kontaktpersonen* – KPs), SED functionaries, cadre managers and employees'
superiors who submitted reports without the knowledge of the persons concerned. KPs, though sworn to secrecy, did not enter into a binding and
official commitment to the Stasi, but they did provide information about
neighbours, work colleagues and others, and were often recruited as IMs at a
later stage.[13]

Five ministerial major guidelines (*Richtlinien*) were issued concerning the
work of IMs, three in the 1950s, one in 1968 and the final set in 1979.[14]
These guidelines defined the functions of the many different categories of
IMs, their recruitment and motivation, and how controlling officers should
work with their charges, in particular the need for regular meetings and the
establishment of a relationship of trust. The 1979 guidelines have been described
as a bureaucratic document which fostered the illusion that a totally conformist society could be achieved by comprehensive series of administrative and
repressive regulations.[15]

The following 'spyclopedia' may not be easy for a reader to digest, but it
should be borne in mind that it reflects the quality monitors' obsession with
defining and assigning specific tasks to the ever changing panoply of agents.
Some IMs were classed as unofficial full-time agents (*Hauptamtliche Inoffizielle
Mitarbeiter*, HIMs) and others as societal collaborators for security (*Gesellschaftliche*

---

[11] Interview with Heinz K. in Karau G. 1995: 169.
[12] BStU 1994: 14–18, 31. The number of Criminal Police informers relates to the year
1985.
[13] Krone T., Kukutz I. and Leide H. 1997: 113.
[14] The guidelines are to be found in Müller-Enbergs H. 1996.
[15] Otto W. 2000: 410–11.

Mitarbeiter für Sicherheit, GMSs). Although HIMs usually had a part-time job as cover, they were in the pay of the Stasi and they belonged in effect to the ministry's full-time staff. There were 4,347 HIMs in 1983 and 32,000 GMSs in 1986.[16] The latter were a looser category of collaborator, normally functionaries loyal to the system, who were willing to cooperate with the Stasi in a range of political-operational tasks and formed a reservoir of potential IMs. They provided the Stasi with information and assisted in damage limitation and other pre-emptive activities.[17] IMEs (*Inoffizielle Mitarbeiter für einen besonderen Einsatz*), of whom there were 7,213 in 1988, were deployed for work on difficult assignments and held important positions in the state apparatus, the mass organisations, the economy and other spheres. They supplied specialist information and expert reports on the situation in their area of responsibility.

Officers on Special Duties (*Offiziere im besonderen Einsatz*, OibEs), like the ambitious Alexander Schalck-Golodkowski, the head of KoKo, constituted a higher category of elite informers than the IMEs; there were 2,232 OibEs in 1989. 'Big Alex' admits to being attracted by the career advantages, the salary and the prestige attached to serving as a Stasi officer.[18] FIMs (*Inoffizielle Mitarbeiter für Führung anderer Inoffizieller Mitarbeiter*), in addition to their own duties, helped to relieve the burden on full-time officers by recruiting and running other IMs who were usually employed in the same area of work.[19] The 'pearls' among the spies, the IMBs (*Inoffizielle Mitarbeiter zur unmittelbaren Bearbeitung im Verdacht der Feindtätigkeit stehender Personen*), were highly proactive agents; they infiltrated opposition groups and kept an eye on individuals suspected of hostility towards the state and were involved in coordinated campaigns to damage their targets' careers and lives. As they usually enjoyed the trust of such persons, they were in a favourable position to report on their plans and activities. Like Sascha Anderson (IMB 'Fritz Müller') and Reiner Schedlinski (IMB 'Gerhard'), they were integral to the operational subversion strategy.

In 1985, the most common type of agent involved in political-operational work was the IMS (*Inoffizieller Mitarbeiter zur politisch-operativen Durchdringung und Sicherung des Verantwortungsbereiches*). In that year, of the key IM categories, IMSs constituted 84.5 per cent, IMBs 3.3 per cent, IMEs 7.5 per cent and FIMs 4.7 per cent, or, in numerical terms, 112,115. The 30,301 IMKs should be added to this total. As the footsoldiers of the Stasi, the IMSs were expected to contribute towards the assessment and management of security problems in a specific area and to help in answering the fundamental question

---

[16] Krone T., Kukutz I. and Leide H. 1997: 113; Gieseke J. 2000: 394; Müller-Enbergs H. 1993: 10.

[17] Ibid., 5–6.

[18] Schalck-Golodkowski A. 2000: 229–30.

[19] Geiger H. 1993: 60.

'Who is who?'[20] In spite of the many differences between the IMs, their main task was to provide information on people's attitudes towards the socialist system, especially those suspected of having contact with 'negative-hostile' forces, and to operate in all areas of public life. Some idea of the comprehensive nature of MfS surveillance of society can be derived from the regional distribution of IMs. In the mid-1980s, there was an average of one IM per 120 inhabitants, ranging from 1 per 80 in the Cottbus Administrative Region (*Bezirk*) to 1 per 159 in the Halle area.[21] Although it is not easy to account for regional differences, the head of the BStU branch office in Frankfurt/Oder, Stephen Wolf, has attributed Cottbus's leading position to the location in Lusatia of the energy industry.[22]

Statistics relating to the proportion of women and young people working for the MfS can only be estimated on the basis of the data of a few Regional Administrations. Of the IMs recruited in 1989 by the Rostock Regional Administration, about 10 per cent were women – a reflection of the patriarchal power structures of the male-dominated ministry – and about 6 per cent were under 18 years of age. Between January and June 1986, 63.5 per cent of IMs in the Karl-Marx-Stadt Regional Administration were employed in the state economy, one in three belonged to the SED and about one in two was aged between 27 and 40 years.[23] Recruiting officers much preferred men to women for a variety of reasons: the heavy burdens already borne by women in the home and at work; women's alleged gossipiness; and the greater ease with which men were able to absent themselves from home for clandestine meetings. Furthermore, the MfS was concerned about controlling officers and female IMs entering into a sexual relationship.[24] On the other hand, intelligent and sociable women were perfectly acceptable as IMs if they were prepared to prostitute themselves as part of elaborate 'operational beds' campaigns which targeted foreign journalists, businessmen and conference participants staying at hotels.[25] Several dissertations on the use of prostitutes as IMs, especially in the Interhotels, were produced by MfS officers as part of their training at the Law School. Angela Schmole, a researcher at the Gauck Office, draws the conclusion that, given their various activities both as IMs and full-time officials, these women should be regarded as co-perpetrators (*Mittäterinnen*).[26]

---

[20] Müller-Enbergs H. 1993: 9–10.
[21] Vollnhals C. 1994: 510. These ratios apply to the IMS, IMB, IME, FIM, IMK and GMS categories in the Regions but not to the IMs and the GMSs in the Main Departments: Müller-Enbergs H. 1993: 10.
[22] 'Cottbus war Hochburg der Stasi-Mitarbeiter', *Der Tagesspiegel*, 25 August 2001, p. 15.
[23] Müller-Enbergs H. 1993: 13. According to Schmole, the percentage of female IMs in 1989 ranged from 10 to 16 per cent: Schmole A. 2001: 17.
[24] Ibid., 18.
[25] Schmole A. 1996: 518–20, 522, 525.
[26] Schmole A. 2001: 18–19.

MIELKE'S WILLING EAST GERMANS?

Why did so many East Germans become IMs? Was it the result of coercion, commitment to the state, or expectation of material gain and status enhancement? The MfS was interested in exploring the motivation of informants not as basic research *per se* but as a branch of 'operational psychology', with a view to controlling not only its own staff and informers but also the East German population in general. The ministry had its own psychology unit at the Law School in Golm-Eiche near Potsdam. It organised staff training courses and its graduates produced dissertations on the theory and practice of work with IMs.[27] The 1968 and 1979 ministerial guidelines contain an elaborate catalogue of norms for work with IMs and document the secret police's ceaseless but often fruitless and counterproductive search to create an IM system of matchless quality and efficiency. In pursuit of this goal, the guidelines stressed the need for surveillance to be both comprehensive and focused and for IMs to adhere to set targets, deliver accurate reports to their controllers and not to lose their cover.

The ministry was averse to voluntary denunciations. Although 'spite' denunciations constituted a relatively high proportion of information gathered by the Stasi during the 1950s, this declined sharply in the following decades. The MfS preferred to select its own IM candidates and familiarise them with the values and practices of the service in the belief that this would greatly improve the quality and reliability of their work. As early as 1952, one ministry guideline warned: 'Particular care should be taken with those individuals who volunteer their services',[28] partly because it feared that they might be imperialist agents. By contrast, the Gestapo was almost entirely dependent on spontaneous denunciations and meetings with informers were rare.[29] The difference is frequently attributed to the greater legitimacy enjoyed by the *Volksgemeinschaft* of the Third Reich than that commanded by the SED's form of state socialism. However, the MfS did not entirely ignore 'spite' information, especially in the early years before the ministry had perfected its machinery of surveillance.[30]

MfS recruiting officers were provided with a template for identifying the personality traits of the 'model' IM: the ability to assess situations, to judge human character, and to reproduce information on situations both quickly and accurately. These characteristics were assembled in so-called recruitment profiles. The utmost importance was attached to individuals who could fulfil

---

[27] Müller-Enbergs H. 1995b: 103–4; Behnke K. 1995: 12–27, 38–42.

[28] Cited in Müller-Enbergs H. 1996: 173.

[29] Diewald-Kerkmann G. 1995: 55–7.

[30] In 1965, according to Gieseke, about 30 to 50 per cent of OVs were based on spontaneous denunciations, whereas IM sources accounted for only 20 per cent. The remainder seem to have come from interrogations by full-time staff and from information supplied by the Soviets. See Gieseke J. 2001: 122–3.

the requirements of a specific task, a goal which, however, was easier to set than to achieve.[31] Prospective IMs were checked beforehand and information collected from a variety of sources – other IMs, close relatives, work colleagues, neighbours, friends – regarding their political views, personal characteristics and habits, membership of organisations, health, sexual behaviour, contacts in the West and so forth. If the preliminary check was satisfactory, then formal contact could be initiated. The whole process from the initial stage to the final recruitment could last a few weeks or, as was sometimes the case with individuals connected with the churches, five to seven years. The first contact with a recruiting officer might be through an appointment arranged by letter or telephone, directly at work or at home, or via a third party. A pretext was usually found for the first meeting so as not to frighten off the target. Once contact had been made, serious wooing could commence.[32] The MfS was anxious that its recruiting officers exuded competence, political commitment and empathy with the candidate, and even that they dressed appropriately. One officer, Reiner Blühel, in a dissertation on the recruitment of homosexuals, stressed the need for 'stylish, clean clothes as in general homosexuals pay a great deal of attention to their appearance and their approach to other people is often dependent on the way they dress'.[33]

Despite the elaborate preparations, the recruitment process often ended in failure. It is estimated that in the 1960s and 1970s only one in three to four attempts succeeded; this ratio improved during the 1980s, partly because SED members were pursued with greater vigour.[34] But while many potential informers resisted the recruiting officer, others agreed to cooperate and sign an official commitment – a form of licence to spy. The new recruit assumed a cover name, which might be suggested by the officer or the collaborator, and a personal file was opened. The IM's file was normally divided into three parts: the first contained the oath of commitment and an evaluation of the IM's work, the second the reports submitted by the IM, and, finally, any payments and awards.[35] The words of the oath of commitment varied. One example reads: 'I herewith pledge voluntarily to co-operate actively and with initiative with the Ministry of State Security of the German Democratic Republic. I have chosen the cover name of —'.[36] Another might acknowledge socialist norms: 'I herewith declare myself willing to support the MfS in its activities to secure our socialist state. I will report to the appropriate officer of the MfS all indications of hostile activity. I further declare myself willing to produce official assessments to the best of my ability. I pledge not to divulge to any person conversations and facts that I have become aware of.

---

[31] MfS ZA, JHS, no. 24069, 'Lehrmaterial', pp. 13, 17, 22–3, 50.
[32] Miller B. 1999: 35–7.
[33] MfS ZA, JHS, no. 878/85, 1986, p. 22. Our translation.
[34] Geiger H. 1993: 51.
[35] Miller B. 1999: 39–40; Krone T., Kukutz I. and Leide H. 1997: 115.
[36] Cited in Richie A. 1998: 763.

Cooperation is based on secrecy and for this reason I am choosing the pseudonym Pistol'.[37]

Not all IMs, especially members of the intelligentsia and the churches, committed themselves in writing. In some cases, like that of Robert Havemann, who served under the cover name 'Leitz' in the later 1950s, a written engagement was waived on account of his proven commitment to the communist cause.[38] The 1953 guidelines on IMs made allowance for this procedure if it aided recruitment and the establishment of a close bond.[39] Many IMs from the churches followed this route, and the absence of a written commitment is one of the props of Manfred Stolpe's argument that he was not aware of his registration as IM 'Sekretär' by the Stasi. While not denying regular contacts and discussions with Stasi officers over many years, Stolpe claims that as the top lay official in the Protestant churches, he was 'an equal partner in negotiations'.[40]

Why then did East Germans from all walks of life cooperate with the Stasi? The motives may be classed under five broad headings: political and ideological conviction; coercion and fear; personal advantage; emotional needs; and a desire to influence official policy. Given the diversity of motives, no uniform type of informant is apparent, an observation which also applies to the 'spite informers' of Nazi Germany. There are, however, some indications that, as far as young people are concerned, a feeling of insecurity rooted in a disturbed family milieu and a poor relationship with their parents made many vulnerable to the blandishments of the Stasi's recruitment officers.[41] It is, however, extremely difficult in retrospect to be categorical and precise with regard to the motives of IMs and to draw broad generalisations. One difficulty is that the memoirs of and the many interviews given by informers since the end of the GDR tend towards exculpation and deliberate deception, and suffer from the fragmentation of memory. Secondly, although the contemporary records may provide an antidote to the latter, any interpretation has to take account of the distortions arising from the prism of the ministry's Marxist-Leninist ideology. Furthermore, entries in an IM's files often contain little more than a brief and highly general reference to an individual's motives for cooperation,[42] and motivation might change over time, perhaps from one of idealism to a more materialistic outlook. As a rule of thumb, cooperation was not usually determined by a single motive; a complex or bundle of motives was usually in operation.

As 'true believers' were expected to be the most productive and the most committed workers, the Stasi was keen to recruit those who were well

---

[37] Cited in Geiger H. 1993: 56. Our translation.
[38] Miller B. 1999: 39.
[39] Müller-Enbergs H. 1996: 212.
[40] Cited in Miller B. 1999: 81.
[41] This argument is developed in Rieker P. 1998: 308–22.
[42] Müller-Enbergs H. 1995b: 106.

disposed to the GDR's brand of socialism or who, in Stasi jargon, held Marxist-Leninist convictions and had a scientifically founded image of the enemy. This might be expressed as a pride in the GDR as an anti-fascist, socialist state, supposedly committed to equality, peace and social progress. Even if prospective IMs did not fully subscribe to the GDR's political system and goals, the MfS appreciated that some could be enticed through appeals to their anti-fascist sentiments.[43] According to one internal report dating from 1968, political conviction was instrumental in the collaboration of 81 per cent of IMs in Karl-Marx-Stadt.[44] Given the above-average number of functionaries and SED members who served as IMs, it is perhaps not surprising that this kind of motivation was widespread. And, certainly, many ex-informers continue to stress their high level of support for the GDR system. One IM, Kerstin Kaiser-Nicht, born in 1960 into a family of SED parents, progressed through the Thälmann Pioneers and the FDJ and was recruited while she was a university student. After German unification, she entered the Bundestag as a member of the Party of Democratic Socialism, but stepped down under pressure from her own party when her collaboration became public. When interviewed in 1995, she admitted to regarding her activities on behalf of the Stasi as 'the most normal thing in the world'.[45] It should also be recalled that several committed communists, for example Robert Havemann and Wolfgang Templin, both of whom later became prominent dissidents, spied for the Stasi.

Whereas the Stasi liked to stress the high ideals of its IMs, it was coy in attributing a significant role to various forms of coercion – whether blackmail, bribery or fear. Internal documents avoided a term like blackmail, opting for euphemisms like 'atonement' for a transgression. The 1958 guidelines advised, in the case of 'negative and hostile' individuals, that coercion should be used only when there was no alternative, and the 1979 guidelines required recruiters to obtain approval from their superiors if they intended to recruit on the basis of 'atonement'.[46] However, internal materials show that the Stasi was not averse to taking advantage of human weaknesses such as envy, hatred and vanity in the recruitment process[47] and to recommending recruiters to take advantage of cases where a misdemeanour had not come to light.[48] So-called 'compromising materials', which were used, for example, in recruiting IMs from 'hostile-negative groups', included 'dependence on drugs, abnormal sexual inclinations and undetected crimes'.[49]

---

[43] MfS ZA, JHS, no. 24069, 'Lehrmaterial', p. 27. This material demonstrates clearly that the MfS readily utilised a range of predispositions, both positive and negative.
[44] Miller B. 1999: 41.
[45] Ibid., 32–3, 41–2.
[46] Müller-Enbergs H. 1996: 213, 349.
[47] Richter H. 2001: 273.
[48] See the training manual, MfS ZA, JHS, no. 24069, 'Lehrmaterial', p. 36.
[49] Cited in Richter H. 2001: 276. Our translation.

Most young IMs were recruited from among those with previous convictions or the ones who did conform to official norms.[50] An example of coercion concerns R., a young punk from Halle, who became IMS 'Klaus Müller'. He had received a suspended sentence of one-and-a-half years for trying to escape to the FRG via Czechoslovakia before a second encounter with the authorities after stealing a moped in 1984. Gradually he was drawn into the Stasi net. After an initial meeting with a recruiting officer, the Stasi intervened with the public prosecutor to secure a suspended sentence of two years' instead of seven months' imprisonment. After a period in which he submitted verbal reports on a religious community in Halle, which was a meeting point for punks, he agreed, in 1985, to present written reports under a cover name. In 1988, he became a skinhead, although this did not prevent him from continuing to spy on his friends. He fled to West Germany in September 1989.[51] In general, older people were not so easy to coerce as these younger East Germans as they felt less vulnerable to the failure to 'atone' for past misdemeanours.[52] The Stasi also preyed on other human frailties. Fear of the disclosure of an adulterous relationship left many vulnerable to blackmail, and jealousy of a neighbour or work colleague persuaded others to enlist.

How compelling were pecuniary rewards, career opportunities and a higher status? Some young people certainly derived a boost from the approaches of the MfS. 'Now I am really important', wrote IM Sandra in her diary.[53] Others derived personal satisfaction from their involvement in the state's apparatus of repression. The bait of a university place or a much coveted job tempted some young East Germans into promising to serve the Stasi later in their career. Material rewards, a variety of services, foreign travel and status enhancement appealed to others. Given the shortages endemic in GDR society, many candidates were lured by the promise of a car, an apartment, a telephone or a holiday place. Cash payments were not necessarily a powerful incentive and were frowned upon by the thrifty Stasi. In their 1973 dissertation, three Stasi researchers, Korth, Jonak and Scharbeth, were highly critical of material interests, which they denounced as an egoistic striving for advantage. A stable motivational framework could not be built, so they asserted, 'on such egoistic needs, since they must constantly be fed by ever new rewards'.[54] One officer, Dirk Kreklau, admitted that material incentives merely reinforced the impression among young football hooligans that 'snooping' was equivalent to 'doing the dirty' on their friends.[55]

---

[50] Gries S. and Voigt D. 1998: 117.

[51] Ahrberg E. 1998: 199–207.

[52] Ibid., 118.

[53] Rieker P. 1998: 315.

[54] Miller B. 1999: 45.

[55] MfS ZA, JHS, no. 21466, 1989, p. 31. This refers to the recruitment of IMs from among the hooligan element of the Lok Leipzig football club.

IM candidates received a small basic sum of about 20 GDR Marks in return for the use of their apartment for clandestine meetings. This kind of sum could be topped up by payments to IMs of 50, 100 or more Marks for good quality work and information. Considerably higher sums of between 700 and 900 Marks were handed over to some of the collaborators in the GDR opposition. Presents and awards were also forthcoming. Joachim Walther has undertaken a careful assessment of payments to IMs working for Main Department XX/7 in the cultural sphere. According to his findings, regular payments such as the salary of 400 GDR Marks for Reiner Schedlinski from 1985 onwards were not the norm but material rewards undoubtedly helped to reinforce cooperation. The total financial outlay by Main Department XX/7 on IMs in terms of salaries, bonuses, the costs of meetings, payments for the use of a safe house and so forth amounted to 62,100 GDR Marks in 1974. This was above average as the figure tended to hover around 40,000 GDR Marks per annum until 1989.[56]

Since the end of SED rule, some IMs connected with the churches, like Manfred Stolpe, and members of grassroots groups have contended that their dialogue with Stasi officers emanated from a genuine desire to 'prevent the worst', that is, to protect individuals, to promote reform and to improve church–state relations. From this perspective, the Stasi functioned as a substitute for an effective public system of communication feedback. Some former IMs also claim that they sought to use their Stasi contacts in order to alert the authorities to defects in the supply situation, environmental pollution, labour problems, and, in the later 1980s, public support for Gorbachev's reforms. While this blend of altruism and political calculation undoubtedly motivated some IMs, it was usually self-delusion. The Stasi was adept at encouraging IMs to believe that they could indeed influence policy. In fact, IMs who sought to instrumentalise the Stasi were involved in an unequal relationship; they, not the Stasi, were usually the manipulated. There was also the attendant risk of entering into a labyrinth of double allegiance in which friend and foe, as well as the private and the political, became inextricably entwined.

Finally, whereas some candidate IMs enjoyed the thrill of doing glamorous-sounding secret work, others were attracted by feelings of security and a sense of belonging. Once again, Stasi recruitment officers and handlers skilfully manipulated these needs, as Klaus Behnke has illustrated from the biography of a former IM, Renate. She was recruited at the age of 17 with the promise of help in obtaining a study place. Renate informed on the activities of an ecological group. Her work as an IM and the contacts with her MfS officer provided her, at first, with the emotional security which was missing in her family life. Her parents quarrelled frequently and she lacked a close emotional bond with them.[57] She had no positive role models and as a child was

---

[56] Walther J. 1996: 506.
[57] Fuchs J. 1998: 178–82.

afraid of coming into conflict with the authorities. As she stated in a post-1989 interview: 'I have always done what I was told'.[58] Analogous to Renate's experiences is the well-known case of Monika Haeger, who spied on the Initiative for Peace and Human Rights in East Berlin. An orphan with a disturbed childhood, she also found emotional security and recognition in the MfS. As she explained in an interview shortly after the collapse of the GDR: '. . . the Stasi gave me roots. It seemingly gave me security . . . Day and night I could ring and my contact officer Detlef always had time for me'.[59]

It is extremely difficult to determine the relative weighting of the various types of motives for becoming an agent whether from IM statements or from their own Stasi files. It is, however, clear that a combination of motives was usually behind collaboration and, secondly, that the Stasi's search for true believers enjoyed some success. Helmut Müller Enbergs, a member of the Gauck Authority's research team, has uncovered a 1967 dissertation which emanated from the Law School. The empirical work was based on what was claimed by the author, M. Hempel, to be a representative sample of IMs in the Stasi's Potsdam Regional Administration. A clear majority identified political-ideological factors as decisive for their collaboration. A 'recognition of societal needs' was mentioned by 60.5 per cent (83 per cent by those who were SED members), followed by a frequency of 49.1 per cent (68.5 per cent by SED members) for 'moral constraints and duty'. Only 27.4 per cent specified 'personal advantages' and 23.4 per cent 'experience of pressure and duress'. However, if one adds the 22.1 per cent who mentioned the latter as a secondary element in their motivation, then almost half were motivated by fear and pressure.[60] There are a number of comments and qualifications to be made about these findings: they refer to only one investigation in one region in the later 1960s and it is therefore difficult to draw generalisations for other areas and time periods; and the high rating for political motives accords perhaps too conveniently with official positions. However, the data are by no means an unvarnished replication of official norms and goals, as can be seen in the Stasi author's reference to 'experience of pressure and duress' as 'unexpectedly high'.[61]

Hempel's dissertation is also valuable for the attention it draws to the changes in motivation during the period of collaboration. At the time of the field study, the 'recognition of societal needs' had risen to 78 per cent and 'experience of pressure and duress' had fallen to 12.6 per cent as main elements of motivation since recruitment; and the number of IMs who originally had harboured reservations had fallen from 50 per cent to 28.6 per

---

[58] Fuchs J. 1998: 193.
[59] Cited in Dennis M. 2000: 220.
[60] Müller-Enbergs H. 1995b: 120–22.
[61] Ibid., 121.

cent.[62] Such positive results notwithstanding, the turnover of the ministry's stock of IMs was relatively high. Between 1985 and 1988, about 10 per cent of IMs ceased to work for the Stasi; they were, however, replaced by a similar proportion. Thus in 1985, 11,749 new IMs were recruited and 11,335 departed.[63] When an IM broke off contact with the Stasi, this did not automatically result in some form of punitive action but it did entail the loss of many advantages, whether the prospect of a flat, a better job or financial rewards.[64] During the 1980s, several investigations in Regional Administrations revealed that the Stasi itself was responsible for the majority of terminations. Of the recorded terminations in the Frankfurt/Oder Regional Administration between 1981 and 1985, an unofficial collaboration was broken off in 63 per cent of the cases because the IM was unsuitable for operational work on account of age, illness and similar reasons; 10 per cent of the terminations resulted from a loss of cover and 11 per cent from the agent's dishonesty or unreliability.[65] Poor quality intelligence was another major factor.

THE WORK OF AN IM

An IM could expect to meet his or her contact officer every few weeks; sometimes, this had to be more frequent. While most meetings took place in 'safe houses', restaurants and parks were also used. These clandestine meetings were the main form of communication between controller and IM. The officer prepared each meeting in advance and sought to steer the IM towards the relevant issues. Usually well versed in the arts of human management, the officer was often successful in establishing a relationship of trust and dependence on the part of the IM.[66] Time and again, MfS training materials and dissertations on work with IMs emphasise the importance of close and regular contacts between controller and agent for a productive collaboration. But too positive a picture should not be painted as contact between controller and IM was frequently disrupted by informers failing to keep appointments. Additional problems included controllers' lack of empathy with their charges on account of discrepancies in age and personality, the 'necessary evil' of a change of controller, and a failure to define tasks precisely.[67] IMs, too, fell foul of the GDR's elastic penal code, committing a variety of offences for which they were interrogated by the officers of Main Department IX.[68]

---

[62] Müller-Enbergs H. 1995b: 122.
[63] Ibid., 123; Müller-Enbergs H. 1993: 8. The 1985 figures relate to the IMS, IMB, IME and FIM categories.
[64] Müller-Enbergs H. 2000: 192–4; also Schröter U. 1994: 11.
[65] Müller-Enbergs H. 1995b: 124.
[66] Ibid.
[67] MfS ZA, JHS, no. 20113, 1984, pp. 17–19, 24, 28, 31, 33, 42, 47.
[68] MfS ZA, VVS JHS o0001–343/84, 1985, pp. 54, 75, 93–4.

The reports of the meeting or *Treff*[69] could be delivered in various forms, depending on the situation and the individuals concerned. Written reports were signed in the IM's cover name and put in his/her file. A second option, a tape-recorded document, could be used by the contact officer as the basis of his final report; the source is identified by the IM's cover name. A controller sometimes assembled information from various reports. Initially, if an IM provided information over the telephone, this was registered as a telephone report (*telephonische Mitschrift*). Reports on meetings compiled by controllers are not always reliable as the officer may have misunderstood the IM or simply compiled an inaccurate record. While the contents of reports were often banal, they could be highly damaging as they sometimes contained intimate details on individuals. Only a small number of IMs, perhaps 5 per cent in the later 1980s, were engaged in highly elaborate campaigns such as OVs and OPKs.[70] IMs were subject to stringent security checks. Their reports were compared with those of other IMs and should they be suspected of unreliability, then their mail might be opened and their apartments bugged.

The ratio of IMs[71] to control officers fluctuated between 11 in 1985 and 9 in 1988. The main burden of IM work fell on the shoulders of the Regional and District Service units. *In toto*, 12,000 Stasi officers controlled the ministry's IMs; about 50 per cent were run by the regions and districts, the remainder by the central departments in East Berlin. Considerable regional variations prevailed: in 1986, the ratio of IMs to controlling officers in the Regional Administrations was 13.4 in Cottbus, 10.1 in Erfurt and 7.4 in Gera.[72] How often did IMs and contact officers meet? No definitive answer can be given, but materials from the local units provide some idea. The District and Object Service Units in Jena had an average of 646 IMs/GMSs in January–September 1989 and 3,920 meetings are recorded. In the Jena District, an IM/GMS met with a contact officer once in every six weeks. Almost half of the meetings took place in a safe house. The Stasi judged that about 25 per cent of information supplied by informers was of operational significance.[73]

A SOCIETY OF SPIES AND INFORMERS?

With over 250,000 agents and officers working for the Stasi in any given year in the later 1980s and with many others cooperating at various times as informers not only for the ministry but also for the party and the Criminal

---

[69] For the following details, see Krone T., Kukutz I. and Leide H. 1997: 20 and Geiger H. 1993: 63–4.

[70] Ibid., 63.

[71] The sub-IM categories consist of IMS, IMB, IME and FIM.

[72] Müller-Enbergs H. 1993: 10–11; also Geiger H. 1993: 46.

[73] Müller-Enbergs H. 1993: 13–14.

Police, East Germans appeared to be a nation of spies. Whatever an individual's motives, the SED had created a system which was conducive to collaboration with the MfS as well as conformity in public by prioritising the collective over the individual, by the sanctioning of actions which violated certain basic moral codes and by fostering the belief that 'Big Brother was watching'. As long as the Soviet Union was determined to maintain its East German outpost and while the Western powers condoned Soviet hegemony there – as in 1953 and 1961 – then most East Germans had little option but to come to some kind of arrangement with the state. Indeed, most opted for outward conformity which, in the case of those like the biologist Jens Reich who were not conformists out of conviction, meant having to live with various forms of inner conflict.[74] But like Reich, most East Germans were not Mielke's willing operatives and many rejected the wooing of recruiting officers. For example, in the Neubrandenburg Regional Administration, out of 5,764 efforts to enlist new IMs between 1970 and 1980, 1,851 collapsed.[75] Unfortunately, it cannot be said how many East Germans were refuseniks (*Verweigerer*) as the MfS did not carry out any comprehensive statistical analyses. Where reliable records do exist, for example, for the preliminary stage of recruitment, some Regional Administrations registered minors as contact persons, not as IMs. Moreover, it is frequently difficult to determine the precise nature of the termination of a contact between an officer and a potential IM when an approach never went beyond the initial feelers.[76]

Numerous counterstrategies were implemented by potential IMs who had been targeted by the Stasi. The first example concerns an engineer who, in 1962, had been imprisoned as a student on account of an unauthorised visit to the West. When, 11 years later, he was imprisoned for his part in the collapse of a bridge, he refused to work as an informant in return for his release.[77] Although outright refusal to serve as an IM was not the norm, examples can be found in the Stasi files, such as the statement 'I will not work with the red Gestapo' recorded by a recruitment officer.[78] The Stasi records also reveal 'Tomzig' refusing to become an IM as he had devoted his life to God and 'Oswald' protesting he would never 'do the dirty on his mates'.[79] In the autumn of 1971, MfS officers sought to recruit a medical student by threatening him with the charge of incitement hostile to the state on account of his sympathy for the Prague Spring. He refused to collaborate: 'I cannot reconcile that with my conscience. They have got incriminating material against me. I have put it in writing myself and then they can do with

---

[74] Reich became one of the co-founders in 1989 of the opposition group New Forum.
[75] Müller-Enbergs H. 1995a: 9.
[76] Müller-Enbergs H. 2000: 167–71.
[77] Gauck J. 1998: 10.
[78] Müller-Enbergs H. 2000: 175.
[79] Ibid., 184.

me what they like, lock me up, that is better for me than cooperating with them'.[80] Political reasons have also been unearthed. A punk, 'Karl', made no secret of his negative attitude towards the state and the MfS.[81] However, as in the case of the engineer cited above, resisting the Stasi's embrace required courage, determination and deviousness and it often resulted in periods of acute stress. Refusal, even when outright, was normally couched in a guarded manner in order to avoid negative repercussions. Ill-health was a common pretext.[82]

Andreas Schmidt has uncovered other examples of IM candidates who told the recruiting officer that they had no interest in cooperating with the Stasi, found excuses for not keeping appointments, withheld confidential information, provided only positive reports about their contacts, or dragged things out.[83] Many simply did not want to 'snoop' or, as one candidate exclaimed, to grass on close friends and relatives. By refusing to collaborate with the Stasi, it has been argued by Jürgen Fuchs that some East Germans were unwilling to work with a traitor, that is, with themselves. Schmidt quotes from the report of a recruiting office on the cat-and-mouse game played by one potential recruit. In order to avoid collaboration, he invited his wife to sit in on the discussions, insisted that the officer leave the house when his cup of tea arrived, and claimed to have no worthwhile information.[84] A married couple, the 'Radebeuls' employed similar tactics when a recruiting officer sought to use their apartment for clandestine meetings. They pleaded that this was inappropriate as they were about to refurbish the apartment and their children were in the habit of visiting them unannounced.[85] A doctor, who had been observed while making preparations for flight to the West, was pressed into service in 1975 as IMS 'Wolf'. During his meetings with MfS controllers over the next two years, he spent most of the time trying to withdraw from collaboration. The ministry's final report in 1977 included a reference to these tactics as well as to his bourgeois views, his church connections and his questioning of the leading role of the SED.[86] Another tactic was to declare a willingness to cooperate formally but not to do so in a conspiratorial manner as, in the case of 'Hermann', this did not accord with his moral standards.[87]

One favourite method was to break the conspiracy and reveal the Stasi's overtures to parents, work colleagues, teachers and so forth. Sonia Süß has described conspiracy as 'the elixir of life' of an unofficial collaboration.[88] In

---

[80] Cited from the final report on OV 'Foto' by Süß S. 1999: 256. Our translation.
[81] Müller-Enbergs H. 2000: 188.
[82] Ibid., 176.
[83] Schmidt A. 1995: 170–73.
[84] Ibid., 175–6.
[85] Müller-Enbergs H. 2000: 177–8.
[86] Süß S. 1999: 255–6.
[87] Müller-Enbergs H. 2000: 182.
[88] Süß S. 1999: 256.

the case of the 16-year-old 'Igel', his mother went directly to the local District Service Unit to express her objections. The recruitment officer commented in his report that 'Igel's immaturity and the negative political influence of his parents meant that he would not be able to preserve the necessary secrecy and was therefore unsuitable as an IM'.[89] The failure to meet a candidate's needs can also be found in the sources as a reason for termination. 'Ernst' withdrew his offer to cooperate when he discovered that he would not be able to leave the GDR to spy in West Germany.[90]

Most of these cases demonstrate that East Germans had not surrendered their individuality and their moral scruples and that it was possible to frustrate the Stasi.[91] Refusing to work for the Stasi did not usually lead to transparent disadvantages, with the notable exception of cadres whose work required them to visit the West. However, there can be no doubt that targets were worried about the negative repercussions, a factor which recruiting officers sought to turn to their advantage, sometimes threatening their targets with the possibility of criminal prosecution. While this was rather of psychological than of practical significance after the erection of the Berlin Wall, IMs who, especially in the 1950s, broke their cover were charged with the betrayal of secrets. Moreover, since the disappearance of the GDR, some refuseniks believe that they were disadvantaged, even though this often cannot be substantiated by archival material.

---

[89] Müller-Enbergs H. 2000: 180–81. Our translation.
[90] Ibid., 190.
[91] See Geiger H. 1993: 55, Miller B. 1999: 48; Müller-Enbergs H. 2000: 180–82, 190, 194.

Part IV

HUNTING FOR THE ENEMY

Chapter 8

MONITOR AND FIREFIGHTER

A UBIQUITOUS ENEMY

Chapters 8 to 11 are designed to assess the Stasi's role on the home front as an organ of surveillance, repression and ideological policing as well as its function as an economic firefighter and moral guardian. Whereas Chapters 8 and 9 concentrate on the Stasi's surveillance and protection of spheres which come broadly under the umbrella of the public sector such as culture, sport and the economy, Chapters 10 and 11 focus on those areas and groups which lay outside the immediate domain of the party and state administration, notably the evangelical churches, the Jehovah's Witnesses, the peace movement and fringe youth sub-cultures. The linkage between the four chapters is the Stasi's tunnelling into all sectors of society and its ruthless determination to expose and, where necessary, thwart all enemies, whether potential or actual, of the socialist order. The Stasi dictionary of political-operational terms compiled for officers described this vital task as follows:

> As a whole, fulfilling the main task of the MfS must produce results to put strategic and tactical information at the disposal of the party, to expose the enemy in his bases in the Operation Area, to disrupt and combat him, to prevent hostile activities directed against the GDR, to unmask internal enemies and to ensure the security of the GDR in all situations and to prevent damage and actions hostile to the GDR by means of preventive measures, greater vigilance, discipline and order.[1]

The same source also provided staff with the authoritative definition of the enemy as:

> Persons who in groups or as individuals intentionally develop political-ideological attitudes and views that are alien to socialism and who strive to implement these attitudes and views in practice by deliberately creating occurrences and conditions that endanger or damage the socialist state and society generally or specifically.[2]

---

[1] Cited in Suckut S. 1996: 169. Our translation.
[2] Cited in ibid., 121. Our translation.

The lexicon's militant language was a legacy of the fierce struggle between the German Communists and National Socialists and of the imprint of Stalinist totalitarianism on the mentality of members of the East German service class. It was also a product of the titanic clash between communism and capitalism during the Cold War, at least until the onset of détente moderated the language of political conflict of the SED, if not of the Stasi.[3] On the border between the two antagonistic systems, the GDR was ultra-sensitive to shifts in East–West relations and, uncomfortably aware of the many attractions of the West German model for East Germans, its leaders were constantly looking for signs of infiltration by the West. Even in the later 1980s, the MfS was still adhering to a simplistic and outmoded explanation of the causes of opposition and widespread popular dissatisfaction, attributing it to deliberate targeting by the imperialists. While the Stasi lexicon and official guidelines were written in bureaucratic and soulless jargon, the language could be crude and emotional when the mask slipped. An off-the-record statement by Mielke at a service meeting in February 1988 illustrates this point. Putting his manuscript to one side, he denounced would-be emigrants as 'bandits';[4] 18 months later, he was even coarser, referring to them as 'filthy swine'.[5]

The image of the 'enemy' encompassed a wide range of non-conformist behaviour which was regarded by the ministry as having 'hostile-negative' potential but which in a less authoritarian society would be far less likely to attract the attention of the secret police state. The MfS understood by 'negative' persons all those who were 'deviants from the party line, held different views and were unreliable and uncommitted'.[6] Although a distinction was drawn between loosely structured 'negative groups' and the more tightly organised 'hostile groups', in practice it was difficult to keep them separate and the Stasi often used the hyphenated term 'hostile-negative'. 'Negative' groups were described in the dictionary as: 'loose associations of mostly young people with relatively similar interpretations of life and morals that deviate from the socialist way of life and also with views lacking clarity and conviction that are in part politically-ideologically negative'.[7] These groups were unstable and the youngsters belonging to them typically gathered together on street corners and in pubs, parks and clubs. In the eyes of the Stasi, their 'spontaneous' behaviour represented a danger for public order and safety which could rapidly develop into acts of terror and 'attacks on the state border'. A 'hostile' group, which was regarded by the Stasi as posing the greater threat, was defined as a 'number of people who aim to carry

---

[3] See Suckut's observations in Suckut S. 1996: 18–19.
[4] Bergmann C. 1997: 29.
[5] Mitter A. and Wolle S. 1990: 134.
[6] Bergmann C. 1997: 30–31.
[7] Suckut S. 1996: 166. Our translation.

out acts hostile to the Constitution or together plan, prepare, attempt or perpetrate one or more crimes against the state. Hostile groups are in direct communication with each other and, over time, develop a group structure'.[8]

Notions of the 'enemy', as internalised by MfS officers, reinforced stereotyping and served as an instrument of repression. A physicist at the University of Leipzig, Günter Fritzsch, was told by MfS prison staff: 'You are wrong, in here there is no democracy, dictatorship rules in our state, the dictatorship of the proletariat. This is irreconcilable class war. You are our class enemy'.[9] This kind of antagonism was upheld as one of the main characteristics of a Chekist. Hatred was described in the MfS dictionary as 'an essential determining component of Chekist feelings, one of the decisive bases for the passionate and irreconcilable struggle against the enemy', a struggle which was not just simply a matter of loathing but was bound up with the need to 'destroy' or to 'harm' him.[10]

The Stasi image of the enemy was grounded in the theory that psychological characteristics are determined by external conditions and influences rather than by internal or cognitive factors. While in accordance with the regime's Marxist-Leninist ideology in that socialist society allegedly provided the preconditions for the development of all-round and productive personalities, the MfS, like other state and party bodies, had to account for behaviour and attitudes which deviated from the norm and made people susceptible to the influence of the enemy. Among the factors identified by the Stasi as conducive to such actions and attitudes were petty bourgeois egoism and careerism, anti-social or criminal behaviour and grumbling.[11] Those conditions in the GDR which enabled the imperialists to conduct political-ideological subversion against socialist society were regarded primarily as the 'relics' of the exploitative capitalism of an earlier age. Although the MfS stubbornly persisted in this interpretation, it was, however, difficult to explain away the country's problems simply by reference to the capitalist legacy and to external steering by the imperialist enemy. A recognition of this dilemma can be seen in several dissertations written by officers during their studies at the Stasi Law School which tentatively acknowledged that GDR society produced a number of internal 'contradictions' which caused distortions in the development of personality. Among these contradictions were poor quality accommodation, restrictions on travel and inadequate services. Such contradictions were not deemed to be 'antagonistic' in Marxist-Leninist terms but as capable of being rectified within the parameters of the existing social and political order.

---

[8] Suckut S. 1996: 163. Our translation.
[9] Cited in Bergmann C. 1997: 33. Our translation.
[10] Suckut S. 1996: 168. Our translation.
[11] Richter H. 2001: 160–62, 165.

TACKLING THE ENEMY – QUIET REPRESSION AND PREVENTIVE DECOMPOSITION

In the age of détente, the Stasi's main method of combating subversive activity was 'operational decomposition' (*operative Zersetzung*), which was the central element in what Hubertus Knabe has called a system of 'quiet repression' (*lautlose Unterdrückung*).[12] This was not a new departure as 'dirty tricks' had been widely used in the 1950s and 1960s. The distinctive feature was the primacy of operational decomposition over other methods of repression in a system to which historians have attached labels such as post-totalitarianism and modern dictatorship. This form of rule emerged out of the Stalinist era and, although the methods of control were less brutal and repressive than in the late 1940s and the 1950s, the GDR of the Honecker years was nevertheless a dictatorship of the party elites in which coercion and injustice were endemic. The concentration on so-called 'softer forms' of control in the 1970s and 1980s can be attributed to a series of interrelated factors: the stabilisation of the GDR since the mid-1960s; the greater sensitivity of SED leaders to the population's needs, not least the desire for a higher standard of living; the counterproductive nature of terroristic methods; the frail legitimacy of the less prosperous 'other Germany' in the East; and the GDR's search for international recognition. Although the GDR succeeded in ending its diplomatic isolation in the first half of the 1970s, closer relations with the West were a mixed blessing as it produced a massive increase in Western visitors. Furthermore, the signing of the Helsinki Accords of 1975 committed the GDR leaders to tolerating even greater movement across borders as well as guarantees for human rights. In this context, arbitrary acts and open repression appeared to threaten the gains derived from détente. Even Mielke had to adapt to the need for a more flexible system of control. He put this in his usual blunt fashion in a speech delivered in 1985: 'You know that, for political as well as operational reasons, we cannot immediately arrest all enemies, although the purely legal prerequisites exist. We know these enemies, have them under control and know what they are planning'.[13] Operational decomposition was particularly appropriate for tackling those opposition groups who were associated with the churches or who had links with the West and therefore had a limited protection from more blatant forms of state repression.

The MfS dictionary summarised the goal of operational decomposition as 'splitting up, paralysing, disorganising and isolating hostile-negative forces in order, through preventive action, to foil, considerably reduce or stop completely hostile-negative actions and their consequences or, in a varying

---

[12] Knabe H. 2000: 92.
[13] Cited in Knabe H. 2000: 94. Our translation.

degree, to win them back both politically and ideologically'.[14] The kind of measures which the ministry employed can be found in documents such as the 1976 guidelines on operational cases,[15] and included: the systematic compromising and isolation of a target by means of rumour, disinformation and deception concerning alleged immorality, excessive drinking, an 'unclean past' and spying for the West; undermining their professional and personal reputation; creating fear and uncertainty through frequent telephone calls at night, inserting fictitious adverts in newspapers, sending anonymous letters, and burglary. Some victims have claimed that the MfS deliberately poisoned food and drove its 'targets' to contemplate suicide.[16] Other nefarious methods involved telephone tapping and the interception of mail, dangling the bait of travel to the West and promotion at work, provoking disagreements among opposition groups, and the criminalisation of offences such as alleged tax evasion and the disturbance of public order. Targets were also subjected to restrictions on their movement, the withdrawal of a driving licence and illegal house searches.

OPERATIONAL MEASURES

As discussed in Chapter 5, the search for more flexible and more efficient forms of control resulted in the widespread use of operational personal checks (*Operative Personenkontrollen* – OPKs) and integrated operational clandestine campaigns or, for short, operational cases (*Operative Vorgänge* – OVs). If initial enquiries revealed indications of hostile-negative attitudes or of a crime, an operational person check could be instigated. In 1988, the MfS carried out 19,169 such cases. Of some 8,000 which were concluded, 87.5 per cent failed to produce evidence of 'undesirable' attitudes or actions, 4 per cent formed the basis for the recruitment of an informer and 8.5 per cent led to an operational case.[17] Although the most important sources of information were IMs, the German People's Police, local authority departments and state enterprises also helped out. Lars Klinberg, a student at the Humboldt University in East Berlin, was the target of an operational personal check. IM reports revealed that he was opposed to the GDR election system and military training and an admirer of the West German Greens.[18] A check, initiated in 1986, sought to expose the nature of his contacts with the West, to ascertain whether he had committed a criminal offence, and to discover whether he was in possession of 'pseudo-pacifist' literature and fascist texts such as *Mein Kampf*. Although the Stasi was convinced that Klinberg held negative views,

---

[14] Suckut S. 1996: 422. Our translation.
[15] The relevant sections are printed in Gill D. and Schröter U. 1991: 390–91.
[16] Knabe H. 2000: 100.
[17] Vollnhals C. 1994: 510–11.
[18] See Raschka J. 2001: 22, 152–65.

the enquiry failed to produce evidence of a crime. Consequently, although the MfS Department XX/3 in East Berlin, which was responsible for Klinberg's case, was unable to implement measures designed to 'prevent' an offence, Klinberg was disciplined by his university department and forced to participate in a military training course.

If an operational personal check discovered evidence of hostile-negative actions or an intention to commit an offence which infringed the Criminal Code, then an operational case (OV) could be initiated to furnish proof. This was the most elaborately organised and comprehensive form of surveillance conducted by the ministry and was usually the culmination of a series of checks and enquiries. An operational case could also be set in motion even if the names of the persons who had committed an offence were unknown. Sometimes several cases were combined together in what the Stasi called a central operational case (*Zentraler Operativer Vorgang* – ZOV). As with an operational personal check, a detailed plan set out the goals of the OV, the measures to be implemented, the forms of cooperation with other organs of state, and how informers were to be used. Enemy intentions and actions, it was stressed, were to be identified and dealt with as quickly as possible.[19] Between 1985 and 1988, the Stasi conducted about 4,500 to 5,000 OVs per year.[20]

The MfS bureaucracy devoted its usual attention to detail in ministerial guidelines no. 1/76 on the 'Processing of Operational Cases'.[21] The guidelines stressed the need for smooth cooperation between controlling officers and IMs – the main instrument for carrying out a case – and for ensuring that the data gathered by informers shed light on the motives of persons under surveillance. Through bureaucratic precision, the ministry aimed to obtain 'value for money' from all the effort expended on accumulating the vast amount of information in an OV.

The decomposition measures referred to earlier were an essential ingredient of OVs and, according to the 1976 guidelines, were 'to be applied, extended and further developed in a creative and differentiated' manner according to the 'concrete conditions' of each case.[22] An OV was terminated either when proof of a crime was obtained or if an offence could be prevented. In the harsh language of a 1985 regulation relating to a central operational case, the criteria for termination included 'undermining, paralysing or rendering harmless the hostile forces in such a way that they only carry out their hostile activities at a low level of intensity and danger to society or they are not capable of any acute subversive activity so that they can be dealt with or controlled by different methods'.[23]

---

[19] Suckut S. 1996: 281.
[20] Raschka J. 2001: 23.
[21] See Fricke K. W. 1991: 114, 123, 127.
[22] Ibid., 127.
[23] Cited in Fuchs J. 1997: 12–13. Our translation.

The nature of the more sophisticated though insidious methods of the Honecker era can be appreciated from the final report compiled in 1984 on OV 'Kreuz' against pastor Dietmar Linke. The document, which was compiled by the Strausberg District Service Unit in the Frankfurt/Oder Regional Administration, listed some of the measures used against Linke and his wife:

> The Linkes lost their credibility as Christians and holders of Church office when they were targeted by measures to incriminate them. So recently there have been more and more rumours about selfishness, embezzlement and the venality of the Linkes . . . The proof of the hostile-negative activities of the Linkes was documented and prepared as decomposition and differentiation measures to stir up dissension within the Church . . .[24]

Although the MfS was unable to discredit Linke in the eyes of his congregation and it decided not to initiate criminal proceedings for fear of turning him into a martyr, the pressures exerted by the state and the Stasi's decomposition measures forced the Linkes into leaving the GDR. The report concluded, not without a note of sadistic satisfaction: 'Both are unemployed in West Berlin and have no fixed abode. They receive support only from the Church'.[25]

Like the Linkes, other victims of operational cases often had to cope for many years with surveillance and discrimination and frequently suffered from persecution mania and other symptoms which damaged their health. Among the many notable instances of this type of campaign were OV 'Lyrik' and OV 'Ecke' against the writers Reiner Kunze and Gabriele Eckart respectively. Kunze came into conflict with the SED over his positive attitude towards the Prague Spring and over his publications, notably *Die wunderbaren Jahre*. The latter, a collection of short stories and poems concerning the everyday problems of young East Germans, confirmed the Stasi in its view of Kunze as an enemy of the GDR. The publication of excerpts from his Stasi files in 1990 reveal that his phone had been tapped, his mail intercepted, his foreign contacts scrutinised, his movements observed by his neighbours and his wife's professional reputation besmirched.[26] Gabriele Eckart, who, ironically, had once spied on Kunze, became a Stasi target herself on account of her 'negative-hostile' attitude in association with a book published in West Germany – *So sehe ick die Sache* – which provided a realistic picture of GDR workers on a fruit farm. Before finally receiving permission to leave the GDR, she suffered several house searches and physical attack.[27]

---

[24] Cited in Raschka J. 2001: 173. Our translation.
[25] Ibid., 174. Our translation.
[26] See *Deckname 'Lyrik'* 1990.
[27] Walther J. 1996: 710–12.

WRITERS AND ARTISTS

The surveillance of culture and the mass media was the responsibility of four desks of Department 7 within Main Department HA XX, which worked together with regional units to combat political-ideological diversion and political underground activity. In the eyes of the Stasi – as well as of the party leadership – cultural and political issues were intertwined. SED leaders like Honecker fondly hoped that the cultural intelligentsia would be fervent protagonists of peace and socialism among the masses. The relationship between party and writers did not accord with this idyll and cultural policy fluctuated between periods of thaw and frost. Mielke and his Stasi colleagues regarded many of the GDR's writers as Trojan horses of 'counterrevolution', fearing that the enemies of the GDR might persuade the writers that socialism could be made 'more humane' by open criticism and by the formation of an internal opposition. The Hungarian Uprising of 1956 and the Prague Spring of 1968 were cited as examples of how 'hostile-negative forces' conducted political-ideological diversion among writers and artists in order to foster revisionism and counterrevolution.[28] Mielke's perception of the potential threat posed by critical GDR writers is reflected in a pronouncement made in 1966: 'If Heym and his ilk and artists were in power, then we would soon see the GDR gobbled up'.[29] It is not surprising that Stefan Heym, Christa Wolf and other critical writers and artists were treated as actual or potential enemies despite professions of loyalty to socialism and to the GDR. However, the MfS had to move cautiously as these writers were well known in the West and their work helped to boost the GDR's international reputation.

The MfS did not develop a special unit devoted to writers until Main Department XX/7 was founded in late 1969. The impact of détente and the furore surrounding the expatriation in 1976 of Wolf Biermann, a highly satirical writer and singer and a bête noire of the Stasi, culminated in the creation two years later of a special desk in the Main Department, which was responsible until 1982 for the key areas of publishing and the Writers' Union. During the 1980s, desk 4 of Main Department XX/7, desk 7 in the Regional Administrations and Main Department XX/9 investigated political underground activity in the literary sphere. In terms of numbers, the 27 full-time officials employed by Main Department XX/7 in 1980 rose to 40 in 1989, that is, from 8.7 per cent to 9.7 per cent of all officials in the department.[30] Joachim Walther has uncovered 379 IMs who worked for Main Department XX/7 in 1975 and about 600 IMs at regional level in 1968. To these should be added approximately 500 in the District Service Units. The estimated total of about 1,500 IMs in the cultural sphere probably changed little throughout

---

[28] Walther J. 1996: 33.
[29] Cited in ibid., 51. Our translation.
[30] Ibid., 179.

the Honecker era. The Stasi's thorough infiltration of the literary sphere can be illustrated in many ways. For example, in 1989, 49 out of the 123 members of the executive of the Writers' Union had been or still were Stasi collaborators, and 12 out of the 19 members of the Presidium were former or current IMs.[31] Hermann Kant, who was President of the Writers' Union from 1978 to 1990 and the writer of several highly-regarded novels, notably *Die Aula* (1965) and *Der Aufenthalt* (1976), served as a Stasi informer for many years.[32] IMs were installed in *belles lettres* publishing houses such as *Aufbau Verlag* and *Mitteldeutscher Verlag* in order to influence publishing programmes. One notable IM, Paul Wiens, was the editor-in-chief of the GDR's most important literary journal, *Sinn und Form*. As IM 'Dichter', he spied on fellow East German writers such as Christa Wolf, Volker Braun and Stephan Hermlin.

One of the most notorious informers, Sascha Anderson (IMB 'Fritz Müller'), belonged to the pearls among informers – the IMBs – whose various tasks accorded with the ministry's strategy of silent repression and operational decomposition. They were to paralyse, undermine and disrupt the structure of a particular group or individual. Anderson, a gifted poet, was groomed by the Stasi for his future role. In the early 1980s, he established contact with East Berlin's alternative sub-cultures and by about the middle of the decade had become one of the most influential figures among the writers and artists in the Prenzlauer Berg area. Anderson's main goal was the de-politicisation of this artistic community. He eventually moved to West Berlin where he spied on the city's colony of former GDR artists and opposition figures such as Roland Jahn and Jürgen Fuchs.

Not only did the MfS pursue writers in the public arena but the hetero-geneous alternative sub-cultural scene in the Prenzlauer Berg district of East Berlin and other cities of the GDR, notably Leipzig and Dresden, also attracted its attention. Artists, musicians and writers struggled to create a counter-public in private houses, galleries and churches for the production of ideas and forms of expression which did not conform to official concepts of culture and, in the eyes of the Stasi, represented a conduit for political-ideological diversion and political underground activity. According to Klaus Michael, an estimated 5 to 10 per cent of members of the sub-cultural scene worked for the ministry,[33] and in some cases the Stasi even created its own alternative groupings.

The cooperation of so many writers and cultural functionaries with the security forces is not peculiar to the GDR; Western agencies also covertly funded and co-opted writers, painters and musicians, both at home and abroad. Why so many East German writers collaborated with the MfS can be ex-plained by reference to the complex of motives identified elsewhere in this

---

[31] Walther J. 1996: 557–8.
[32] Corino K. 1995.
[33] Kaiser P. and Petzold C. 1997: 84.

book, although it is extremely difficult to pinpoint the actual drives behind an individual's collaboration. For example, claims since 1990 by some writers that they were working, through their MfS contacts, for the higher goal of constructing socialism may be little more than an exercise in self-deception and self-justification. On the other hand, it seems that the GDR's most famous writer, Christa Wolf (IM 'Margarete'), collaborated for a brief period, between 1959 and 1962, out of a somewhat naïve ideological conviction and with little apparent benefit to the Stasi. Her thin IM file contrasts sharply with the voluminous files which the Stasi later kept on her and her husband Gerhard for over three decades as part of the ministry's OV 'Doppelzüngler'. Meetings with her controllers were infrequent and she was not implicated in any denigration or harassment of her fellow writers.[34] What does jar, however, is the belated recovery of her memory of her Stasi past after initial denials. Another well-known woman writer, Monika Maron, claims that her collaboration was prompted by a wish to construct a more humane socialism as an alternative to capitalism.[35] Working for the Stasi could bring material benefits: a visa for a journey to the West, a better apartment, a higher publishing run, loans, financial bonuses and presents. Regular payments such as the 400 GDR Marks to Rainer Schedlinski from 1985 onwards were not the norm but material rewards undoubtedly helped to reinforce cooperation. In 1974, the total financial outlay by Main Department XX/7 on IMs in terms of salaries, bonuses, the cost of meetings, payments for the use of an apartment and so forth amounted to 62,100 GDR Marks; the figure tended to hover around a lower total of about 40,000 GDR Marks per annum until 1989.[36]

SAFEGUARDING THE ECONOMY

The GDR's highly centralised economy was structured around an elaborate planning mechanism and public ownership of most of the means of production. If Honecker's SED were to sustain its paternalistic social welfare system and the informal social contract with the population, much would depend on the capacity of the economic system to deliver high rates of economic growth and labour productivity. Economic performance was also crucial to the legitimacy of the entire socialist system in view of the popular appeal of West Germany's social market economy. Thus, given the cardinal importance of the economy, the MfS was called upon to protect it against the GDR's enemies, whether internal or external. At first, the main responsibility for safeguarding the economy fell to Main Department III and then from 1964 onwards to the newly formed Main Department XVIII. However, especially

---

[34] Vinke H. 1993: 9–17, 111–40.
[35] Walther J. 1996: 515.
[36] Ibid., 506.

during the 1950s and 1960s, all the ministry's other counterintelligence units were engaged in the uncovering of sabotage and espionage in the economic sphere. The creation of Main Department XVIII boosted the Stasi's role in securing the economy in conjunction with the launching of the New Economic System of Planning and Management (NES) in 1963. The greater autonomy granted to the enterprises and the more sophisticated methods of economic management in the age of the scientific-technical revolution required, or so it was claimed, a more extensive system of surveillance.[37]

Main Department XVIII's relatively small staff constituted a mere 1.5 per cent of the Stasi's central administrative apparatus at the end of the 1980s. Its significance is better measured by other indicators, however. For example, 11 per cent of the 3,310 operatives of the Halle Regional Administration worked on security matters relating to the economy, as did 23 per cent of the 1,099 staff in the District Service Units and the 'objects'.[38] At the end of the 1960s, their main responsibilities were identified as the protection of the country's major economic structural projects, basic research, military production and foreign trade; the surveillance of Western businessmen; and unravelling the causes of serious economic crimes and of accidents at work. In institutional terms, this meant keeping watch over public enterprises, the central state organs and mass organisations such as the Confederation of Free Trade Unions (FDGB). In order to carry out these tasks, the network of IMs was expanded and Officers on Special Assignments or OibEs were created by a 1966 regulation. The most prominent OibE was Harry Möbis, the head of the Department of Inspection in the state economy.[39]

Despite the reassertion of central control of the economy after Honecker came to power in 1971, the perceived dangers of closer contacts with the West and the urgent need to fulfil productivity targets ensured that surveillance of the economy remained all-pervasive. And, as ever, the Stasi was on the lookout for signs of sabotage and economic espionage by the imperialist foe. As late as 1988, the paranoia endemic in the ministry is observable in the dissertation of a trainee officer, Marian Schöne, of Schwerin's Regional Administration. The enemy, he alleged, is making every effort to disrupt economic and social policy and, through political-ideological diversion, to demoralise researchers by trying to convince them of the superiority of the research capacity of capitalist firms.[40]

After several years of growth, the GDR's economic position began to deteriorate in the wake of the explosion of world raw material and energy prices after the Yom-Kippur war of 1973. However, it was not until the second price escalation of 1979 that the highly industrialised GDR felt the

---

[37] Haendke-Hoppe-Arndt M. 1997: 121.
[38] Hertle H-H. and Gilles F-O. 1995: 118–19.
[39] Haendke-Hoppe-Arndt M. 1997: 47–8, 50, 66.
[40] MfS ZA, JHS, no. 21188, 1988, pp. 10–11, 13.

full impact. Poorly endowed in raw materials, the GDR was also hit by the rising price of Soviet oil and Moscow's sharp reduction in oil supplies in 1982. With the terms of trade so unfavourable, the GDR soon ran into a deficit in its trade with the West and built up an appreciable hard currency debt. While the serious liquidity crisis of 1982 was overcome with the aid of credits from the FRG, the GDR was plagued by hard currency indebtedness for the remainder of the 1980s. The heavy investment in microelectronics and other key technologies, which overstretched the country's limited re-sources and also diverted investments from the necessary modernisation of the communications system, would be a significant factor in the collapse of SED rule.

Under these circumstances, the MfS, and in particular Main Department XVIII, was caught on the horns of a dilemma: the imperialist saboteur and enemy was also the capitalist sibling and neighbour whose financial assistance was crucial for the stability of the GDR at a time when fraternal help from the Soviet Union was declining. It was therefore called upon to perform a plethora of tasks as guardian of the economy: the safeguarding of vital areas such as microelectronics, the ailing energy sector, the chemical industry and foreign trade; the protection of key personnel and groups; the uncovering of enemy plans and activities in enterprises and institutions at home as well as those of enemy secret services in the Operation Area, especially the FRG; ensuring a stable balance of payments; comprehensive surveillance of would-be émigrés and East German citizens who had contacts with Westerners; monitoring the general political-operational and economic situation; and the prevention of unrest, strikes, fires and damage to plant and equipment.[41]

The sheer range and complexity of their duties often turned the Stasi's operatives into economic firefighters who, while they might douse the flames in some areas, were unable to tackle the basic causes of the conflagration. The latter can be illustrated quite literally by the ministry's investigations into fires and accidents at work. These checks usually revealed that faulty and out-of-date equipment was the cause, not 'hostile-enemy' forces. In November 1987, at a meeting of top officers of Main Department XVIII/3, which was responsible for metallurgy, power and light industry, it was concluded that 'accidents and disruption to the electricity supply are often attributable to out-of-date plant and, in part, to the over-utilisation of this technology'.[42] In 1989, in carrying out Main Department XVIII's host of tasks, including 17 operational cases, 157 top agents were assisted by 2,138 IMs and 509 other types of informers.[43] However, departmental leaders were by no means satis-fied with the operational 'value' obtained from the heavy investment in

---

[41] Haendke-Hoppe-Arndt M. 1997: 5, 80.
[42] MfS ZA, HA XVIII, no. 6886, 'Protokoll', 1978, p. 76.
[43] Haendke-Hoppe-Arndt M. 1997: 12, 1001–11. The IM figures relate to 1988.

IMs.[44] Among the improvements suggested was the replacement of older IMs by younger and more adaptable ones.[45]

HIGH TECHNOLOGY

As space does not permit an examination of all HA XVIII's activities, the remainder of this section will focus on the surveillance of the high-tech sector and the ministry's internal assessment of economic performance and popular reactions to SED social and economic policies. The research and development (R&D) sector was not immune to the general dissatisfaction with conditions in the GDR and researchers were among the would-be émigrés. From the point of view of the MfS, applications to leave the GDR, in conjunction with the increase in the number of exchange visits by scientists after the Helsinki Accords, represented a grave security risk and the loss of human capital and scientific intelligence. The ministry was also most concerned about GDR citizens who 'misused' officially approved visits to stay in the West. Out of the 1,299 who remained in the FRG in 1986, 215 were from the scientific-technical sector. Several of the defectors had worked for the Stasi as IMs or in a similar capacity.[46]

While SED leaders regarded microelectronics as the most important of all the new technologies, others such as biotechnology, industrial robots, nuclear energy research and electronic data processing were also necessary for economic progress and the financing of the social welfare and social security budgets. The significance of science and technology is reflected in the development of Departments 5 and 8 in HA XVIII. The former had most of the country's scientific and technical elites in its sights, and the latter was responsible for electronics. Both Departments cooperated closely and ensured that personal communications were shrouded in secrecy in the top research centres of combines like Carl Zeiss Jena and Robotron as well as the Central Institute for Cybernetics and Information Processes.[47]

Department 5, in conjunction with the local service units, was responsible for the political-operational protection of over 100 institutions and 30,000 employees in science and technology. East Berlin was the focal point as the Academy of Sciences of the GDR and the Ministry of Science and Technology were located there. In June 1989, Department 5 had at its disposal over 54 full-time staff and 15 OibEs and was subdivided into five desks. As one controlling officer had to run between 16 and 20 IMs, the Department

---

[44] MfS ZA, HA XVIII, no. 415, 'Protokoll', 1986, p. 16.
[45] MfS ZA, HA XVIII, no. 6400, 'Einschätzung', 1986, p. 13. This was recommended by Colonel Roigk in July 1986.
[46] Buthmann R. 2000: 31–4, 45–6.
[47] Ibid., 10.

regarded itself as seriously understaffed.[48] During the 1980s, microelectronics and optoelectronics were by far the Department's most important areas of operation, followed by space research and then, at a distance, by nuclear research and biotechnology. Departmental work was not confined to the home front as it gathered intelligence in the FRG in order to counter enemy threats to the GDR's nuclear energy programme, cosmos research and basic research in nuclear physics.

Department 8, officially established in 1970, was HA XVIII's largest unit and was responsible for security in 'objects' such as the Ministry of Electrical and Electronic Engineering, the Carl Zeiss Jena, Robotron Dresden and Erfurt Microelectronics combines and the cumbersomely named Trade Section 4 of the Foreign Trade Enterprise Electronics Export-Import. It also kept watch over the many cadres whose work required them to travel abroad; about half of the Department's informers came from this group. Contacts between East and West German scientists, firms and academic institutions were anathema as, in the eyes of the MfS, they provided the West with opportunities to disrupt and perhaps even destroy the GDR's research and development capacity. In 1981, the Department was responsible for about 25 per cent of the entire research and development potential of the GDR economy. As the GDR's economic problems mounted in the 1980s, the Department sought in vain for remedies. It was deployed to combat serious economic crimes, prevent the leaking of intelligence to the West and to help break the COCOM embargo on the export of high-tech goods and know-how to Eastern Europe.[49]

IMs were indispensable, with Department 5 deploying as many as 306 in 1986. While not all institutions were penetrated, some, like the Central Institute for Optics and Spectroscopy and Trade Section 4, were firmly in the grip of the ministry's 'hidden hands'. As the political and ideological reliability of the GDR's top researchers was a constant concern, IMs monitored them not only at work but also in their leisure time. Indicators of unreliability which were deemed to require vetting were a lack of 'revolutionary vigilance', Western contacts, belittling the achievements of the socialist countries in science and technology, a fondness for drink and women, and 'abnormalities in the sexual sphere'.[50]

Were the Stasi's efforts worthwhile? Official SED publications and statements in the later 1980s sought to give the impression that the GDR was in the vanguard of the scientific-technical revolution. The country's 1986–90 Economic Plan envisaged a tripling of production in biotechnology and the manufacture of 80,000 industrial robots. In 1986, a 16-bit microprocessor

---

[48] On Department 5, see Buthmann R. 2000: 40, 42–3, 126.

[49] Ibid., 60, 73, 81. COCOM, the Coordinating Committee for Multilateral Export Controls, was founded in Paris in 1949.

[50] MfS ZA, JHS, no. 2188, 1988, pp. 20, 55–62.

was first exhibited at the Leipzig trade fair and two years later the prototype of the 1-megabit chip was unveiled amid much ballyhoo. The SED leadership's efforts to achieve technological autarchy in selected components and products was determined by the urgent need to cope with rising energy prices, short-falls in Soviet oil supplies, over-dependence on the West, the Eastern bloc's lack of innovative stimuli and flagging regime legitimacy. However, the view of one former official on reactions to SED propaganda in the media is perhaps an accurate reflection of popular opinion: 'We have trouble filling our shopping baskets. Pretty soon they'll just give us all a microchip instead of something to eat'.[51]

The GDR was palpably unable to close the technological gap with lead-ing Western and Japanese firms. For example, NEC of Japan was already producing 2 million 1-megabit chips in mid-1988 and 4 million per month by the end of the year.[52] In order to overcome some of their problems, GDR enterprises turned to illegal imports and to copying Western soft-ware programmes such as the 32-bit computer of the American firm Digital Equipment Corporation. By 1987, it was anticipated that an overall invest-ment of 300 million GDR Marks and 85 million Valuta Marks would lead to the production of the computers from the initial pilot production. Al-though IMs with expertise in this area regarded the target date as unreal-istic, Department 8 was of a different opinion. By the close of 1985, security checks had been carried out on 170 of the 600 cadres who were to work on the project.[53]

Stasi intrusion was a millstone round the necks of researchers. The 45 volumes of one operational case – OV 'Molekül' – graphically illustrate how research potential could be undermined and destroyed by the imperatives of security. The case was initiated in 1965 against Professor Werner Hartmann, an expert in molecular electronics and a pioneer in microelectronics. While the MfS was unable to uncover any criminal offence, Hartmann's views on the inherent risks of innovation were not to the taste of Department 8. He was relieved of his post in 1974.[54] Hartmann's subsequent complaints failed to strike a sympathetic chord, Rudi Mittig denouncing him in May 1975 as 'a bourgeois scientist with an anti-Communist and anti-Soviet attitude'.[55] A clear statement of the primacy of politics over science!

The illegal procurement of know-how, which dated back to the 1950s, was a complex operation involving the Scientific and Technical Section (SWT) of HV A, Department 8 of Main Department XVIII, Commercial Coordination and Trade Section 4. Other partners were the special directorate

---

[51] Cited in Geipel G. L. 1999: 243.
[52] Dennis M. 1993: 38.
[53] Buthmann R. 2000: 202. One Valuta Mark was equivalent to one DM.
[54] Ibid., 67–9.
[55] Cited in ibid., 68.

in the Microelectronics combine and the Ministry of Electrotechnology and Electronics. SWT had an intelligence evaluation team and three operational Departments, which covered basic and applied research in atomic physics, microelectronics, electronics technology, armaments and economic espionage in banks. By the end of the 1970s, the acquisition of computer technology was one of the top priorities.[56] Embargoed computers and high-tech goods were also procured on the black market by Alexander Schalck-Golodkowski's pseudo-trading empire Commercial Coordination (*Kommerzielle Koordinierung* – KoKo), which had been set up in 1966 to procure hard currency. Schalck-Golodkowski, a Stasi Officer on Special Assignment and with a doctorate from the ministry's Law School, became known as the 'currency procurer' in recognition of the latter role. With an array of front companies extending throughout Western Europe, KoKo used its political and business contacts to generate legal trade, such as the sale of meat, but was also engaged in the illegal sale of arms and state-held art treasures to Western dealers in order to bankroll the economy. In 1983, it was Schalck-Golodkowski's political contacts in the FRG, notably the Bavarian leader Franz-Josef Strauß, who helped secure a massive loan to relieve the state debt.

Efforts to circumvent the West's embargo enjoyed only mixed success. A secret deal with Toshiba in 1986 to avoid the embargo on 256-kilobit chips ran into difficulties when the Japanese firm's links with Eastern bloc countries leaked out. Illegal imports became even more difficult from the mid-1980s onwards when COCOM tightened restrictions on technology transfers to the Soviet Union and Eastern Europe. There was, however, no alternative for the GDR but to pull out all the stops to break the embargo as, in the view of Department 8, the GDR was continuing to fall even further behind in the field of microelectronics.[57] The MfS managed to pepper the West German computer industry with well-placed spies such as Gerhard Arnold ('Sturm'). Arriving in the FRG as a 'refugee' in 1957, Arnold rapidly rose in the ranks of the German branch of IBM, passing research on computer systems and software to East Berlin throughout his career. Markus Wolf later commented that the GDR electronics combine Robotron was so dependent on IBM technology that 'it became a sort of illegal subsidiary'.[58]

Internal assessments indicated that both the Scientific and Technical Section and Trade Section 4 recorded a 'profit' on their transactions. On 3 November 1989, it was estimated that the annual value of Trade Section 4's imports was between 9 and 10 million Valuta Marks per member of staff.[59] While such figures are impressive – if they are reliable – and while the GDR was able to take advantage of its intelligence data to purchase atomic power

---

[56] Macrakis K. 1999: 85–6, 94–6.
[57] Ibid., 115–16; Buthmann R. 2000: 275, 277.
[58] Wolf M. 1997: 187.
[59] Buthmann R. 2000: 286.

plant and gas pipelines at below world prices,[60] the full costs of the operations have to be taken into account and the illegal imports did not necessarily have a beneficial effect. In many enterprises new technologies were not fully integrated into the production process, bureaucratic procedures slowed down the diffusion of basic research, and the illegal imports from more highly developed countries and the isolation of so many GDR researchers reduced much of the GDR's research effort to imitation and redevelopment. One former SWT officer was scathing when interviewed about the scientific and technological espionage programme. In his opinion, its goal was to 'make gold out of shit'.[61] Furthermore, the security mania suffocated creativity and innovation. This was, as Förtsch points out, at the heart of the modernisation paradox:

> On the one hand, the political leadership proclaimed 'scientific and technological progress' as the watchword of social development, and propagated its advancement, without limits or alternatives . . . On the other hand, however, the political establishment continued to see itself as the supreme authority and to act accordingly, imposing limits on activities and creative processes. Whenever it saw its authority threatened (and that was most of the time), it interfered in and restricted efforts to modernize.[62]

There was yet another drawback: the GDR's ambitious microelectronics programme deprived other sectors of much-needed investments. Although the high-tech sphere was plagued by many problems, they were of a different quality and magnitude from those industries which had to stagger along with out-of-date equipment and plant. The chemical industry in the Halle region, a major economic development area in the 1950s and 1960s, is typical.[63] The Halle Regional Administration had three special service units at the giant Bitterfeld, Leuna and Buna combines. In 1989, 40 full-time officers and about 260 IMs kept watch over the Buna combine. As in the high-tech field, the MfS concentrated on securing the combine by carrying out security checks on employees and by keeping a tight control over cadres with the right to travel abroad. It also made strenuous efforts to prevent staff from disclosing information to Western agencies and to stem applications to leave the GDR. But the problems posed by Buna extended beyond normal operational work as its capital stock, with a few exceptions, dated back to the 1930s and 1940s. In 1987, a Stasi report judged the technical equipment in elastometers, carbides and thermoplastics to be almost unworkable and that the high pollution level endangered the health of many of the workers. This kind of insight notwithstanding, the Stasi's Buna unit continued to use its IMs in obsolete areas of production as part of the campaign against underfulfilled

---

[60] Stokes R. G. 2000: 170.
[61] Cited in Macrakis K. 1999: 82.
[62] Förtsch E. 1999: 42.
[63] See Hertle H-H. and Gilles F-O. 1995: 123–4, 129–30.

plan targets, breaches of factory regulations and management failure to implement order and security. Over 100 IMs were used to help discipline those
responsible for breaches of security. But, as Hertle and Gilles have pointed
out, the real enemy was an inefficient economic system, not the external foe.
The MfS could only paper over the cracks; it could not compensate for
underinvestment and the lack of modernisation of worn-out stock.[64]

ECONOMIC PROBLEMS

Stasi evaluation groups, such as the Central Assessment and Information
Group (ZAIG), were fully aware of widespread popular dissatisfaction with
work organisation, wage levels, poor quality housing, the numerous shortages
typical of a highly centralised economy and the restrictions on travel to the
West. The chronic state of the economy in the summer of 1989 is captured
vividly in a Stasi report on the Elbe dockyard at Boizenburg. The problems
at the dockyard were legion: the inadequate coordination of work planning
and the provision of materials; a shortage of urgently needed parts and work
standstills of two to three days; the manipulation of work performance data;
and foremen's indifference towards 'negative' behaviour among the workforce,
such as deliberately failing to meet performance targets and leaving the dockyard early. Other frequent misdemeanours included drinking and falling asleep
at work. Foremen were reluctant to take action for fear that the workers
would simply walk out![65]

In summary, there is good reason to regard the Stasi as omniscient in the
economic arena. Departments 5 and 8 were au fait with the country's technological gap with the West and Japan. The hard currency foreign trade deficit,
production shortfalls and popular dissatisfaction with working and living conditions are also well documented in the Stasi files. However, even though the
Stasi might try and shape decisions through the transmission of selected data
to the party leaders and by virtue of Mielke's membership of the SED
Politbüro, the Stasi was not an economic decision-making body. The limitations of the Stasi's influence in the economic field, as well as of a general
failure to reflect critically on its own role, can be gauged by the fate of a
report drawn up in the early 1980s by four members of Department 4 of HA
XVIII. On the basis of materials of the State Planning Commission and
discussions with economic experts, they concluded that not only was the
hard currency deficit running out of control but that the GDR was on the
verge of economic collapse in 1980. Reprimanded by Mielke, they resorted
to more guarded comments, thus disappointing those economic functionaries
who had hoped to utilise the MfS to help solve the pressing problems in the

---

[64] Hertle H-H. and Gilles F-O. 1995: 131–2.
[65] MfS ZA, ZAIG, no. 17253, 'Information', 1989, pp. 5–9.

enterprises.[66] In the final analysis, the Stasi's 'safeguarding' of the economy served primarily to prop up the SED's political power monopoly and the avoidance of risky reforms, thereby blocking, as the East German sociologist Detlev Pollack has observed, the autonomy of the individual sub-systems such as the economy and science which was essential for a competitive economy and the modernisation of society.[67]

FOREIGN WORKERS AS SECURITY RISKS

Main Department XVIII was not only responsible for securing the economy but was also in charge of coordinating operations relating to foreign workers in the GDR. A 1982 service instruction defined the department's tasks in typical ministerial jargon as the frustration of enemy plans to utilise foreign workers for subversive activities, the detection and prevention of hostile-negative acts by foreign workers, and the clearing up of offences committed by GDR citizens against foreigners.[68] Although foreign workers as a proportion of the total East German population was a low 0.65 per cent in 1989, it was nevertheless the highest among COMECON member states.[69] The 380,000 members of the Group of Soviet armed forces and their 120,000 family dependants formed the largest contingent of foreigners in the GDR. In addition to this group, the records of the State Secretariat for Labour and Wages indicate that, in June 1989, about 154,000 foreign workers were resident in the country, most of them on fixed contracts. Numbers had risen sharply since the middle of the 1980s: from about 83,900 in 1986 to about 128,500 in 1988. In 1989, some 85,020 foreigners had the status of contract workers (*Vertragsarbeiter*) whose terms of employment and residence were regulated by intergovernmental agreements. Most contract workers were from Vietnam (52,130), Mozambique (15,300) and Cuba (9,600). Others stemmed from Angola, China, Mongolia and elsewhere. In addition to the contract workers, over 32,000 workers, mainly Poles, were engaged in the building and assembly trades as a result of arrangements between firms. Finally, another group, about 19,130, mainly from Poland, Hungary and other East European socialist countries, had the right of permanent residence in the GDR.[70]

The recruitment of foreign labour from the 'fraternal countries' commenced in the mid-1950s and from 1966 onwards was based on bilateral

---

[66] Haendke-Hoppe-Arndt M. 1997: 75–6; Haendke-Hoppe-Arndt M. 1995: 125–6; and the interview with Roigk in Karau G. 1995: 26–8.

[67] Pollack D. 1999: 30–31.

[68] MfS ZA, HA XVIII, no. 13130, '5. Durchführungsbestimmung', 1983, pp. 97–8.

[69] Spennemann N. 1997: 8.

[70] MfS ZA, ZAIG, no. 20646, 'Jahreseinschätzung', 1989, pp. 20–21. Although these statistics may slightly underestimate the actual numbers, they do provide a reliable record of the general trend.

agreements between states. In these early years, the emphasis was on education and training programmes. An acceleration in the numbers of the contract
workers occurred in the 1970s and 1980s, increasing rapidly from 1985–86
onwards as the SED sought desperately to alleviate the severe and growing
labour shortage in the GDR. Most contract workers were relatively young
males who were assigned to shift work in heavily industrialised regions like
Karl-Marx-Stadt (now Chemnitz), Dresden, Halle, Leipzig, East Berlin, Cottbus
and Erfurt; however, they were poorly represented in the predominantly
agricultural areas of Schwerin and Neubrandenburg.[71] The Vietnamese and
the Mozambicans were employed primarily in light industry, especially tex-
tiles, machine construction and heavy industry.[72]

The contract workers from Vietnam, Cuba, Mozambique and Angola
were employed on four-year contracts, although there were limited opportunities for a short extension and, in 1987, the Vietnamese were granted the
right to remain for an additional year.[73] A contract could be terminated
prematurely if a contract worker committed an offence or failed to fulfil
work norms. Until the beginning of 1989, if a female worker became preg-
nant, she either had to undergo an abortion or face deportation. Workers
enjoyed the right to send money and goods back to their homeland. The
Vietnamese and the Cubans were allowed to transfer 60 per cent of their net
income above the sum of 350 GDR Marks, although they had to pay for
transfers into the currency of their own country. This was one reason why
many workers opted to despatch goods instead. While the Vietnamese preferred to send clothing, electrical appliances and household goods to meet the
needs of their families, the Cubans, Angolans and Mozambicans despatched
larger items such as refrigerators, television sets or motor bikes. A former
Vietnamese contract worker and engineer explained the importance of his
work in an interview in 2001: 'When I returned to Haiphong after my first
two year contract my family begged me to go back to the GDR again . . . They
were dependent on my wages to live. My mother was ill and needed my
earnings to buy medicines. There was very little money for food'.[74]

Although the contract workers did enjoy a number of other guarantees,
such as that of equal pay to East Germans for the same job, their situation has
been likened to that of modern wage slaves.[75] They were concentrated in
multi-shift systems and performed low-level tasks on the assembly line and
old equipment. The warden-controlled hostels provided by enterprises and
local authorities were, in relative terms, more expensive and less spacious
than the apartments of East Germans, rooms were often overcrowded and
access by visitors was severely restricted, leading to ghettoisation and

---

[71] Müggenberg A. 1996: 5; MfS ZA, ZAIG, no. 20646, 'Jahreseinschätzung', 1989, p. 21.
[72] Elsner E-M. and Elsner L. 1992: 58.
[73] On the terms of the contracts, see Müggenberg A. 1996: 9, 16, 21, 25–7.
[74] Interview in the *Financial Times*, 22 September 2001, p. 24.
[75] Schüle A. 2002: 92.

marginalisation. Sometimes, workers were able to circumvent the restrictions because the janitors were unable to distinguish one Vietnamese from another.[76] In 1991, a Mozambican worker reflected on some of the problems:

> Our life in the workers' hostel was to a large extent governed by the hostel rules. As a result, for example, we could only have visitors from 6.00 to 22.00. The visitors had to prove their identity to the porter and they had to be at least 18 years old. In practice this is what happened: between 22.00 and 6.00 checks were carried out by the staff in the hostel. If a German woman was found in the room of an African man after 22.00, he got a first warning from his firm. If it happened a second time he was sometimes even sent home. The woman was forbidden to enter the hostel again or she was taken straightaway to the police. Naturally, this regulation deterred many Germans from visiting us at all.[77]

Stasi records from the 1960s and 1970s reveal considerable popular animosity towards foreign workers. Violence occasionally erupted between East German youths and the foreigners, whether Mozambicans, Poles or Algerians, at pubs, discos and in the vicinity of hostels. In the town of Stollberg in the Karl-Marx-Stadt region, a series of clashes between Mozambicans and East Germans culminated, in June 1988, in the death of an East German youth as a result of injuries suffered after a dance.[78] In the following year, violent clashes between GDR citizens and Mozambique workers caused such an uproar among the public in eastern Saxony that the Mozambicans were moved to other regions and replaced by Vietnamese.[79] Although the number of incidents escalated at the end of the 1970s, for example against Algerian workers,[80] it was not until the later 1980s that the Stasi noted, with a degree of alarm, a rise in xenophobia. This was partly related to the greater numbers of workers from Vietnam and Mozambique and to what East Germans regarded as an exacerbation of the poor supply situation in the south of the country. Foreign workers were accused of hoarding and buying up goods, either legally or illegally, and Polish and Vietnamese workers, in particular, were criticised for stripping shops bare.[81] In 1989, the Stasi Central Assessment and Information Group referred to popular perceptions of the Vietnamese as leading a parasitical life-style and as glorifying capitalism; their living quarters were likened to warehouses.[82] In addition to problems in the leisure sphere and consumer envy, the contract workers represented, according to the Stasi materials, a disruptive influence at work. Some East German workers

---

[76] Schüle A. 2002: 98.

[77] Cited in Schmidt I. 1992: 68–9. Our translation.

[78] MfS ZA, HA XX, no. 3035, 'Information', 1988, p. 77.

[79] MfS ZA, ZAIG, no. 20646, 'Jahreseinschätzung', 1989, p. 30.

[80] Müggenberg A. 1996: 30. The Algerian government withdrew its workers from the GDR as a result of the mistreatment of its workers: Spennemann N. 1997: 9.

[81] Müggenberg A. 1996: 27.

[82] MfS ZA, ZAIG, no. 20646, 'Jahreseinschätzung', 1989, pp. 26–7.

accused the Vietnamese and Mozambicans of poor work discipline and un-reasonable wage demands.[83] In a shortage economy like that of the GDR, labour migrants, although from countries with even greater economic problems, were not welcome. At the same time, it should be remembered, East Germans were moving to West Germany, partly in search of a higher standard of living and better jobs.

Although the MfS was fully aware of the Vietnamese workers' right in accordance with their contracts to send goods home and that these goods and their wages were crucial for their families and the Vietnamese economy, the ministry was more anxious to appease East Germans by increasing the supply of consumer goods than to improve the lot of contract workers who were perceived primarily as a security problem.[84] While the SED leaders were unwilling to open a public debate on the complexities of the situation and on the details of the contractual arrangements and they most certainly did not wish to provide Western critics with ammunition,[85] the problems of the contract workers could not be concealed. In the late 1970s, but especially towards the end of the 1980s, the matter was raised at church synods and in newspapers such as *Die Kirche* as well as by Second/Third World groups within the alternative political culture. Although the SED did eventually allow the media to broach the issue of violence against foreigners, it lacked the nerve to prepare East Germans in advance for the arrival of foreign workers. The official line continued to laud the employment of foreign labour as part of the GDR's solidarity with foreign citizens and its friendship with the fraternal socialist countries.

Some idea of the general level of popular antipathy can be gleaned from studies conducted soon after the end of SED rule. One investigation carried out on behalf of the German Ministry for Labour and Social Affairs revealed that 'only one quarter of foreigners in the sample had not been insulted or sworn at' and one-fifth reported that they had been 'physically attacked' by East Germans.[86] At the extreme end of the attitudinal spectrum stood the visceral hostility of the extreme skinheads who not only regarded foreigners as parasites on the social welfare system but, above all, as a threat to a German ethnic identity.[87] Chauvinism and negative perceptions of the 'exotic for-eigner' as the 'other' were not just an individual problem and restricted to militant skinheads, but they were reinforced by the authorities' 'demarcation' policy which sought to wall off the GDR from the undesirable influences of the external world, whether saboteurs and enemy agents or Western political-ideological diversion. As Marianne Krüger-Potratz has observed,[88]

---

[83] MfS ZA, ZAIG, no. 20646, 'Jahreseinschätzung', 1989, pp. 26, 28.
[84] Ibid., 27.
[85] MfS ZA, HA XX, no. 3035, 'Information', 1988, p. 95; also Kolinsky E. 2000: 150.
[86] Ross G. C. 2000: 165.
[87] Müggenberg A. 1996: 18.
[88] Krüger-Potratz M. 1991: 59–60.

'the exclusion of everything "alien," or more precisely, of everything defined as alien' was one of the means whereby GDR society sought to sustain its identity. This is particularly pertinent to the Stasi, which inculcated a sharp friend–foe image and deployed its agents in the relentless search for hostile-negative forces and incidents, thereby precluding a culture of tolerance.

Chapter 9

SECURING SPORT – OLYMPIANS AND SOCCER HOOLIGANS

SAFEGUARDING THE ELITE

G iven the importance attached to top-level sport in securing the international recognition of the GDR and in demonstrating the alleged superiority of socialism over capitalism, it is not surprising to find the MfS and
its informers in all areas of elite sport. The GDR was a world power in sport:
at the Olympic Games in Mexico City in 1968, the GDR team gained 25
medals (9 golds) and attained the unofficial third place behind the USA and
the Soviet Union, a remarkable achievement for the 'diplomats in tracksuits'
of such a small country. Twenty years later, its team won 102 medals,
including 37 golds.

The GDR's successes owed much to the state drug programme and the
concentration on those sports which were likely to reap a harvest of medals.
An intricate organisational network was created in support of the state's goals.
The German Gymnastics and Sports Association of the GDR (DTSB) was
the key body for the integration of sport into the SED's central planning
system and for the production of world-class athletes. Manfred Ewald, its
president between 1961 and 1988, was the mastermind behind East Germany's achievements. Other organisations which had a vital role to play were
the State Secretariat for Culture and Sport, the SED's Central Committee
Department for Sport, the Research Institute for Physical Culture and Sport
in Leipzig (FKS), the German College of Higher Education for Physical
Culture (DHfK), also in Leipzig, and the Central Institute of the Sports
Medical Service (SMD). The DHfK, founded in 1950, became famous for its
systematic training of thousands of top coaches and instructors. Powerful
incentives were on offer to the elite: foreign travel, payments in Western
currency, bonuses and good career opportunities. As part of the tightly controlled system, highly gifted children were selected early in their school life
for development at one of the GDR's 25 elite sports schools for children and
youth (1989 figure) and talented performers were concentrated in about 30
well-endowed sports clubs and in the sports associations of the Stasi and the
armed forces (*Dynamo* and *Vorwärts* respectively).

The role of the MfS in the sports system was to prevent sports stars from defecting to the West; to protect the secrets of the state doping programme; to ensure the smooth running of major sports events; to collect information on the opinions and behaviour of leading sports personalities; to maintain the GDR's position as a top sports nation; and to ensure success for the Dynamo Sports Association. The MfS used several Main Departments and set up numerous working groups and sections at regional and district level for sport but the main body for the organisation and coordination of sport was Main Department XX/3. Founded in 1964, it was relieved of other responsibilities in 1981 in order to concentrate solely on sport. In 1989, 30 officers were employed in its four desks.[1]

IMs were the Stasi's 'main weapon' and were recruited primarily from the world of sport itself, for example, trainers, masseurs, journalists, functionaries, scientists and top athletes. During the 1970s and 1980s, about 3,000 IMs were employed each year in top-level sport.[2] Informers infiltrated the leading sports clubs and bodies such as the FKS and the executive of the DTSB. In 1978, about 20 per cent of the staff of the FKS worked for the Stasi as informers.[3] An analysis of the files of 172 out of 320 informers who are known to have been involved in top-level sport in Leipzig since the foundation of the Stasi unearthed 25 trainers, 20 sports scientists (including lecturers) and 46 sportsmen/women or DHfK students. Among this group were seven Olympic, world or European champions, ten professors and a chairman of Leipzig's leading football team, Lok Leipzig.[4] Professor Dr Hans Schüster, the Vice-Chancellor of the DHfK between 1964 and 1967 and director of the FKS between 1969 and 1990 was recruited as an informer in the mid-1960s. Unbeknown to the Stasi's Leipzig Regional Administration, he was controlled from the ministry's headquarters in East Berlin and was able to carry out his responsibilities in the state doping programme secure in the knowledge that he enjoyed Stasi protection.[5]

Informers were regularly deployed, especially during the 1980s, to stem the rising number of sportsmen and women applying to leave the GDR or defecting while abroad. An application was tantamount to ending a person's career. Between 1950 and 1989, 615 East German sport stars fled the republic (including 431 since 1961, mainly athletes, footballers and rowers).[6] The highly delicate question of the temptation of the West was addressed at a central service conference in June 1981 where it was stated that:

---

[1] MfS und Leistungssport 1994: 59–60.
[2] Spitzer G. 1998b: 190.
[3] MfS und Leistungssport 1994: 10.
[4] Spitzer G. 1998b: 190–92.
[5] Ibid., 199.
[6] MfS und Leistungssport 1994: 31.

The young sportsmen and sportswomen are the biggest group of young GDR citizens who, on account of their visits to capitalist countries for training and competition, are sometimes exposed for a lengthy period to targeted systematic influence by the enemy. Not infrequently these young cadres are 'impressed' by the targeted measures to influence them. Thorough investigation and analysis of just such reactions and behaviour and then the evaluation for further political-operational security work coordinated with official measures are central to security checks.[7]

Those who fled were designated 'sports traitors' and their flight could trigger the kind of investigation launched against the rowing trainer Richard Wecke. He defected while in the Netherlands in 1977. 'Operation Ring' was designed to prevent his wife and son from following him, to destroy his marriage by smear tactics and to discover why he had defected. Not until December 1984 were his wife and son allowed to leave the GDR.[8]

Elaborate precautions were taken to control GDR sports delegations abroad. At the 1980 Winter Olympics held in Lake Placid, out of a party of 176 athletes, officials and journalists 35 were IMs (10 of them sportsmen and sportswomen). Their tasks included the detection and prevention of attempts to encourage East Germans to defect, to safeguard sports equipment and medicines, and to uncover hostile actions against the GDR, the Soviet Union and other socialist countries.[9] The level of surveillance was also high at international sports events in the GDR, like the prestigious Leipzig Gymnastics and Sport Festival, in order to prevent close contacts between Westerners and GDR citizens, including those women who were described in official parlance as 'persons who frequently change their sexual partners'.[10]

FOOTBALL HOOLIGANISM

The monitoring of football games between teams from the GDR and the FRG was planned meticulously, partly because the Stasi was anxious to prevent any damage to the GDR's international reputation from the kind of football hooliganism which plagued games between premier league (*Oberliga*) teams such as Lok Leipzig and FC Union Berlin. Premiership football attracted over 2 million spectators per annum in the mid-1980s.[11] Incidents abounded and the MfS was perplexed throughout the entire decade by the failure to curb the problem. The disturbances were committed primarily by young people aged between 14 and 22 years of age. Incidents included insulting spectators, members of the armed organs and passers-by; causing damage to train coaches

---

[7] Cited in MfS und Leistungssport 1994: 16. Our translation.

[8] Ibid., 33.

[9] Ibid., 24–6.

[10] Ibid., 21, 23–4.

[11] MfS ZA, BdL, no. 3122, 'Information', p. 11. This report stems from the Department for Sport of the SED Central Committee for Security Affairs.

and not paying fares; and penal offences such as physical assaults and damage to property.[12] The football hooligans were referred to as 'rowdies' by the MfS and, like punks and skinheads, were classified as 'negative-decadent'.

In a Stasi report dated July 1981, FC Union Berlin was identified as a focal point of much of the violence committed by youths and young adults. The club, situated in the Köpenick district of East Berlin, was popularly regarded as a 'genuine' football club in contrast to the Stasi-sponsored BFC Dynamo. In the period 23 February to 7 December 1980, of the 472 registered arrests, just over half occurred at matches involving FC Union.[13] Although incidents were less frequent at BFC matches as security measures were much tighter,[14] the Stasi was particularly concerned about the fan clubs which had a violent and right-extremist element like the club's 'Anale Berlin', which was founded at the start of the 1987–88 season. Some of these 'hard-core hools' linked up with the 'rowdies' of FC Union in the East and Hertha Berlin in the West. The following extract from a Stasi report is not untypical. It concerns six young men who met in the Mitropa restaurant in Leipzig's main station prior to leaving by train for Lok Leipzig's away game against BFC:

> Under the influence of alcohol they decide to travel without paying and to use the money for alcohol. Having got themselves worked up, the word goes round: we'll smash the rival fans. On the train they go on drinking and bawl obscenities to rhyme with the other team and to show their superiority over them. At the Berlin-Schönefeld station they insult transport policemen. At the Planterwald station they try to break open a stamp machine and a food kiosk but without success. A statue is in their way and it is promptly knocked off its base. They are in this frenzied state of mind when two men come towards them. They block the way for no reason, hit them in the face and kick them in the back and stomach. The men try to defend themselves but this only causes one of the drunken hooligans to use his knife in a frenzied attack. Shortly afterwards the two men are found unconscious and bleeding on the ground.
>
> In the meantime, the gang moves on, waving flags, and trashes three summer houses where they intended to sleep. The culmination of their trail of violence was not the football stadium but a police cell.[15]

Despite a variety of countermeasures coordinated between the various interested parties, among them the clubs, the police and the Stasi, football hooliganism persisted throughout the 1980s. The MfS was keen to recruit IMs among the so-called 'negative-decadents', which included the hard core of violent fans. It was recognised that this was a difficult task as group norms and feelings of solidarity formed a barrier to snitching on pals, as did their mistreatment by the police.[16] The recruiting officers preferred to concentrate

---

[12] MfS ZA, BdL, no. 3122, 'Information', pp. 11–12.

[13] MfS ZA, BdL, no. 1684, p. 12.

[14] Ibid., 13.

[15] Ibid., 13–14. Our translation.

[16] MfS ZA, JHS, no. 21466, 1989, pp. 16, 26.

on those youths who were not already integrated into a 'negative-decadent' football group and who, potentially, had some respect for law and order. Material incentives and offers of 'atonement' were also on offer.[17]

The failure to stamp out football hooliganism, together with its awareness of the activities of militant skinheads in the soccer scene, prompted the MfS to seek an explanation of its prevalence in the GDR. Some of the factors identified by MfS officers and groups like the Office of the Leadership could have been found in Western analyses of the problem – drunkenness, provocative behaviour by players, the hooligans' search for excitement and their desire to provoke the security forces.[18] However, official ideology dictated that the emphasis be placed on Western political-ideological diversion in the form of foreign media reports and personal contacts between East and West German fans. The receptive Eastern hooligans were labelled as unstable and negative-decadent persons who adopted Western habits uncritically and glorified the Western style of life and football.[19]

Referees' controversial decisions, another trigger for hooliganism, also caused arguments in the upper echelons of party and state, especially over matches involving BFC Dynamo. The Stasi team, which dominated GDR football in the 1980s to an even greater degree than did Sir Alex Ferguson's Manchester United the English Premiership in the following decade, was widely believed to enjoy preferential treatment by referees. On one occasion, during the 1985 FDGB cup final between BFC and Dynamo Dresden, Harry Tisch, the trade union boss and a member of the Politbüro, was so incensed by the performance of the referee that he protested to Mielke that such referees were ruining the reputation of the FDGB cup.[20] Even the SED-controlled daily newspapers such as *Neues Deutschland* and the specialist football press were sometimes critical of referees for their bias towards Mielke's favourite team.[21] A report in this vein appeared in March 1986 on the game between Lok Leipzig and BFC in the Free German Youth's organ, *Junge Welt*. The referee, Bernd Stumpf, had controversially sent off Liebers, one of the Leipzig players, and awarded a disputed penalty to BFC in the 95th minute. The report demanded referees who do not 'provide doubtful justice which does harm to our champion team BFC, its reputation acquired by continuous high performance, indeed to each and every player in this team'.[22] This report and the performance of referees generally were discussed soon afterwards at a meeting

---

[17] MfS ZA, JHS, no. 21466, 1989, pp. 21, 23–4.
[18] MfS ZA, BdL, no. 1684, 1981, pp. 4–6.
[19] Ibid., 10–12.
[20] MfS ZA, HA XX, no. 2701, 'Information', p. 15. This is from the meeting of IM 'Harald' with his controlling officer on 28 June 1985.
[21] See MfS ZA, ZAIG, no. 4331, 'Einschätzung', 1971, pp. 57–77. The assessment covers the second half of the 1968–89 season to the end of the first half of the 1970–71 season.
[22] Article in *Junge Welt* on 24 March 1986, p. 5, cited in Reinartz K. 1999: 382. Our translation.

between Mielke, Ewald and Hellmann, the head of the Central Committee Department for Sport and a BFC supporter. Although it was agreed by all concerned that the standard of refereeing in the GDR left much to be desired, Mielke complained: 'What is the point of all this scribbling in *Junge Welt* about Liebers? What's it all about? Why was this scribbler from *Junge Welt* given this job? Why? Both BFC and the standing of the Dynamo Sports Association are harmed by this kind of reporting'.[23] Like any football fanatic, he insisted that the penalty had been awarded just before the end of the match and that there are 'some people who can't accept the position, the leading role of BFC in the top league. On top of that there are poor refereeing decisions that increase hostility to BFC even more'.[24]

DOPING IN SPORT

Perhaps the Stasi's most important task in sport was to secure the GDR's illegal doping programme. Indeed, without the records of the Stasi, it would be extremely difficult to reconstruct the history of doping in GDR sport. The significance of the Stasi's role in the programme can hardly be over-estimated as the systematic use of anabolic steroids was crucial for the GDR's achievements and for its international reputation in sport. Leakage of vital scientific information, as in the case of Dr Alois Mader who fled in 1974,[25] would, it was feared, help its rivals boost their own standards but, as the programme was illegal and a health risk, also discredit the GDR and cause parents to stop their children from entering the elite sports schools. Hence, IMs, whether athletes or top officials like Schüster and Höppner, were planted in the leading clubs and scientific organisations. Performance-enhancing drugs were first used in 1964 in the Dynamo Sports Association and were specifically authorised by Mielke. Dynamo's successes in sport encouraged the DTSB and the army's own *Vorwärts* Sports Association to follow its example.[26] The early attempts to coordinate drug research and applications, such as the formation of a Sports Commission under Ewald in 1967–68,[27] culminated in the State Research Plan 14.25 of November 1974. An integral element of this plan was the Research Project 'Additional Performance Reserves/Complex 08-Additional Performance'; the latter term was the euphemism for drugs.

The scientific centre of the whole programme was Leipzig's Research Institute for Physical Culture and Sport, which was founded in 1969 and was

---

[23] MfS und Leistungssport 1994: 105. Our translation.

[24] Ibid., 103. Our translation.

[25] Franke W. W. 1995: 914. Mader was co-responsible for the doping programme in the Halle *Bezirk*.

[26] Spitzer G. 1998a: 19, 21–4, 221, 409.

[27] Ibid., 54, 408.

attached to the State Secretariat for Physical Culture and Sport. The key group which was responsible at the institute for the Research Project 'Additional Performance' was directed by Professor Alfons Lehnert. It cooperated closely with trainers and partner institutions such as the Academy of Sciences and the Central Institute for Microbiology and Experimental Therapy.[28] Another pivotal body, the Central Research Institute of the Sports Medical Service Kreischa, served as a doping control laboratory. Not only were thousands of leading athletes, such as the shotputter Margitta Gummel and the sprinters Renate Neufeld, Marita Koch and Marlies Göhr, caught up in the doping programme but so were many talented children. Cases are well documented of the systematic administering of drugs to minors, especially swimmers and athletes, without their parents' consent. Recent investigations indicate that from 1972 onwards at least 2,000 top sportsmen/women were doped each year and that between 1,500 and 2,000 doctors, trainers, functionaries and others were involved in the distribution of drugs.[29]

Dr Manfred Höppner, the deputy director of the GDR Sports Medical Service and head of the Research Group 'Additional Performance', was the senior figure in the doping programme. He was also IMB 'Technik' – a case of 'Vorsprung durch Technik'? – who reported in detail to Ewald on the programme's successes and problems, thus giving the lie to Ewald's later protestations of ignorance.[30] Indeed, at one meeting with Höppner in 1975 on the development of the state doping research programme, Ewald stated:

> . . . that for me the performance levels are crucial and every possible means must be fully exploited to achieve them. He emphasised to the IMV (Höppner) that sports medicine had to make its contribution to achieve this goal and, going into some incidents regarding the health of sportsmen, he commented that communists don't kill people.[31]

At the time, some medical practitioners were unhappy about the damage to the health of the athletes. One Dynamo doctor referred to the concern among some of his colleagues after the Olympic Games of 1976:

> Some sports doctors have made comments to the effect that measures taken, especially in the case of sportswomen, are to a certain extent criminal. It raises the question to what extent the sports leadership in the GDR is at all interested in sport being clean.[32]

At least 500 of the 10,000 East Germans who were doped are expected to develop cancer, gynaecological damage and heart and liver problems.[33]

---

[28] Spitzer G. 1998a: 409.
[29] Ibid., 411–12.
[30] MfS und Leistungssport 1994: 142, 160–62.
[31] Ibid., 147. Our translation.
[32] Cited in Spitzer G. 1998a: 172. Our translation.
[33] Ibid., 412.

Despite the success of the doping programme in enhancing performance, the country's sports functionaries and the MfS had much to worry about: the introduction of tighter international tests, the defection to the West of sports stars and medical personnel, and the practice of 'wild doping', especially in weightlifting. Cases are also documented of athletes selling anabolic steroids in the form of tablets to other sportsmen.[34] After a cutback in the use of anabolic steroids under the impact of more rigorous international controls in the later 1980s, a report dated May 1989 warned that: '. . . with a consistent application of the ban, the previous performance levels, mainly in swimming and weightlifting and in some winter sport disciplines, can no longer be achieved'.[35] Although it was decided to terminate the doping of junior athletes, the same report noted that doping would continue for a smaller circle of about 600 athletes in various sports and that efforts would be stepped up to devise more effective ways and means of managing to avoid positive testing.[36] When informed by Ewald in 1986 of the failure to attain targets in some winter sports disciplines such as ski jumping and reminded of the country's relatively poor performance in that year's Winter Olympic Games, Mielke urged an improvement in the quality of trainers and in the political commitment of sports functionaries.[37] Although the former would obviously have helped, the GDR's standing as a leading sports nation was under serious threat. Under these circumstances, the Stasi's activities in elite sport were not dissimilar to its function in the securing of the economy: it could collect endless data, mobilise its IMs, try and prevent defections, investigate contraventions of regulations and guard state secrets, but it could not overcome problems of a systemic nature.

---

[34] See the MfS report on Höppner's meeting with Ewald in 1985 in MfS und Leistungssport 1994: 198–9.

[35] Cited in ibid., 205. Our translation.

[36] Ibid., 206.

[37] Ibid., 88–91.

Part V

CREATING AN ENEMY

Chapter 10

THE RELIGIOUS
COMMUNITIES

C hapters 10 and 11 focus on the Stasi's ultimately unsuccessful battle against groups and organisations which, unlike the state-run enterprises, the mass media and the sports organisations, lay essentially outside the immediate domain of party and state. These ranged from the Protestant churches and the Jewish communities to punks and skinheads. All were penetrated by IMs and controlled or held in check throughout most of the Honecker era. Some, like the alternative peace and ecological groups and right-wing extremists, might be undermined, splintered and broken up but the process often resembled cutting off the head of the hydra. There were, of course, many fundamental differences separating the groups. For example, the Protestant churches enjoyed a significant degree of control over their internal affairs and represented an alternative belief system to the prevailing Marxism-Leninism. By contrast, the kaleidoscopic autonomous peace, ecological, gay, human rights and women's groups, many of whom depended on the church for shelter, constituted a variegated counter-culture which was engaged in a constant struggle to obtain space for the articulation of alternative views and styles of life to those propagated by the SED. Whereas many of these groups aspired to the creation of a reformed, democratic socialism – a kind of third way between SED-style socialism and capitalism – the punk, heavy metal and skinhead sub-cultures of the 1980s veered between the anarchic nihilism of many of the punks and the xenophobia and pan-Germanism of the extreme skinheads and 'fascos'. Finally, the emigration 'movement' posed perhaps the greatest challenge to SED rule for not only did the numbers of those wishing to leave the GDR escalate from the mid-1970s onwards but they were a clear demonstration of the failure of the SED to devise an attractive and viable alternative to the social market economy and political pluralism of the Federal Republic. In politicising and treating all these groups in a blanket fashion as 'negative' (albeit with differences according to their perceived 'decadence' and 'hostility'), the MfS and the SED marginalised and subverted some of the groups which might have contributed to the recasting of the GDR, and, just possibly, its survival as a separate political entity.

THE PROTESTANT CHURCHES:
COMPLIANCE AND CONTROL

By their very presence both the Protestant and Catholic churches, as well as the Jewish communities and Jehovah's Witnesses, posed a challenge to the SED's ideological primacy and to its aspiration to erode autonomous organisational tendencies. This section will concentrate on the largest group, the Protestant churches which, in 1989, had a membership of 5.1 million, that is, about 30 per cent of the total population, albeit much lower than the 80.4 per cent in 1950. The secularisation of society partly accounts for this drop, as well as the much lower proportion of the population who actually attended a church service.[1] The Roman Catholic church played a less active role in the GDR than its Protestant counterpart, partly because it lacked the latter's numerical strength. Situated above all in the Eichsfeld, Upper Lusatia and in some of the larger cities, it attracted 11 per cent of the total population in 1950, a figure which had halved by 1989.[2] Although smaller and playing a less conspicuous role in politics than the Protestant churches, it was unable to keep the Stasi at bay. Individuals were officially authorised by their bishops to enter into contact with the MfS. Others did so without formal permission and a few priests and laymen served as IMs.[3]

The fierce battle which the SED waged against the allegedly counter-revolutionary Protestant churches reached its peak in 1953. Although the churches continued to face accusations of being a centre of imperialism, the struggle eventually abated in the later Ulbricht years, as signalled by Ulbricht's statement in 1960 that 'Christianity and the humanist goals of socialism are not irreconcilable'.[4] The regime's new policy was essentially to co-opt or incorporate the churches into the socialist order. This policy was facilitated when, in 1969, the GDR churches withdrew from the all-German umbrella organisation, the Protestant Church of Germany, and established its own separate League of Protestant Churches in the GDR. The separation was not complete as, for example, one-third of the East German churches' total budget came from West German subsidies. By the late 1970s, the more harmonious relationship between the SED and the churches was underpinned by an informal accord at a meeting in 1978 between Honecker and Bishop Schönherr, the chair of the League of Protestant Churches, which confirmed earlier and new concessions such as the construction of church buildings in new towns and a modest amount of TV time. It had been Schönherr who in 1971, at the synod of the League of Protestant Churches in the GDR, had made a considerable personal contribution to laying the

---

[1] Dennis M. 2000: 246.
[2] Wolle S. 1998: 248.
[3] Grande D. and Schäfer B. 1996: 395–404.
[4] Dennis M. 2000: 246.

groundwork for a compromise by issuing the carefully crafted and ambivalent statement that they do not want to be a church against or alongside but to be a church within socialism.

As far as the regime was concerned, the arrangement had a number of advantages in that the churches, due to their links with the West, were regarded as a useful ally in Honecker's efforts to influence Western political leaders and peace movements. Moreover, the churches were supportive in other respects as they opposed NATO's nuclear build-up in the 1980s and advocated recognition of GDR citizenship in 1985. However, the SED was still not satisfied: it was determined to bind conservative elements in the churches ever more closely to the regime and, according to a circular from Mielke to Stasi officers on 19 April 1978, to subvert, divide and paralyse hostile-negative persons and groups associated with the churches.[5] This approach was underlined by Mielke in a speech in 1976: 'We must support with our Chekist means and methods the efforts of our party and of our state to strengthen progressive church circles and forces, to promote the differentiation process, to induce church groups to act with mature reflection and to marginalise reactionary forces'.[6]

The decomposition measures against the churches, though not uncommon before the 1960s, were pursued with greater vigour in the era of détente and lend weight to Clemens Vollnhals's argument that while the SED's methods might have changed over 40 years, its long-term goal remained constant even in periods of relative political liberalisation: that is, it wished to eliminate the churches as an association with a high level of internal autonomy.[7] The perception of the churches as an alien body in real existing socialism was reflected in Rudi Mittig's statement in 1983 that 'Religion is and remains a type of bourgeois ideology and is incompatible with Marxism-Leninism. At this particular time, such an assessment cannot be the subject of public discussion but it must always co-determine the political as well as the basic political-operative conception'.[8]

Within church circles numerous conflicts and disagreements erupted over relations with the regime and over the position of the autonomous peace and other groups in the church. With regard to the former, a considerable division existed between those ministers and officials who, like Bishop Schönherr, preferred to avoid confrontation and others, notably Bishop Gottfried Forck, who were prepared to take greater risks, for example, in aiding the basic groups. In general terms, the church hierarchy sought to embrace the autonomous groups without jeopardising the fragile compact with the state. It had no intention of becoming an overt political opposition against state and party.

---

[5] Wagner H. 1993: 111.
[6] Cited in Besier G. and Wolf S. 1992: 299. Our translation.
[7] Cited in Vollnhals C. 1996a: 80. Our translation.
[8] Ibid., 80. Our translation.

This balancing act left church leaders open to the charge of expediency from the more impatient peace and human rights activists. Tension also arose within the churches over the extent to which the groups should be incorporated more firmly into the organisational framework of the religious community. The MfS was most concerned that the groups, especially the peace groups, threatened to disrupt the more harmonious relationship between state and church. According to an internal report compiled in 1983 by several MfS officers, 'opponents were seeking, under the guise of pacifism, to unite all hostile-negative forces and to set in motion a counterrevolutionary process'.[9] The MfS, in other words, regarded independent activities as part of a political underground activity under the roof of the churches which, to quote the officers once more, was characterised by:

> The creation or adoption and propagation of anti-socialist ideas and platforms, in particular written materials, objects and symbols by hostile-negative forces within and outside the churches, working together with enemy organisations in non-socialist countries abroad and gathering together hostile-negative individuals in the GDR by using the opportunities afforded by the churches, attempts to form an ostensibly legal opposition movement and the reshaping of hostile organisations.[10]

THE MONITORING AND CONTROL OF THE CHURCHES

The Stasi made deep inroads.[11] Although unofficial agents were planted in the church at all levels, the ministry concentrated its efforts on the leading bodies. High-ranking officials such as the East Berlin Superintendent Günter Krusche and Bishop Horst Gienke in Greifswald served as informers. The personal secretary to Bishop Schönherr, Anita Steinmetzger, worked for many years as an IM, supplying the MfS with highly confidential documents on church policy. As the church was only able to train a few of its own lawyers and therefore had to recruit from state institutions, the Stasi succeeded in placing lawyers as IMs in important positions. At some church synods as many as 25 out of 100 synod members and assistants might be operating as informers. Many top officials, who were not officially agents, engaged in highly secretive conversations with party and state bodies such as the State Secretariat for Church Questions – itself deeply penetrated by the Stasi[12] – and were frequently indiscreet in disclosing information on church policy and individual members. The body with major responsibility for the churches was

---

[9] Cited in Besier G. and Wolf S. 1992: 39.
[10] Ibid., 44. Our translation.
[11] See in particular Neubert E. 1993.
[12] Even the State Secretary for Church Questions, Klaus Gysi, was a Stasi informer between 1956 and 1964: Vollnhals C. 1996a: 96.

the relatively small Department 4 of Main Department XX, which employed 43 staff at central level and about 120 full-time officers at regional level in 1988.[13] Its similarly named predecessor, between 1953 and 1964, had been located in Main Department V and it worked closely with the State Secretary for Church Questions and the more important Working Party for Church Questions of the SED Central Committee. The number of IMs is difficult to assess. Although there were at least 800 working for the central and regional organs in 1988, it is not clear how many were run by the District Service Units, perhaps 200.[14]

The ministry's goal, in accordance with the general decomposition strategy, was to depoliticise, neutralise and, where possible, 'coordinate' the churches and to use its agents, especially those in key positions, to influence policy and appointments. Critical individuals and groups were to be contained and, where necessary, silenced by the insidious methods employed elsewhere in society. Bishops and prelates were caught up in this net: campaigns were organised to isolate and discredit them and their private life was subjected to close scrutiny. Pastor Eppelmann was for many years 'dealt with' in OV 'Blues' and Main Department XX/4 nurtured church organisations and circles loyal to the SED in order to promote opposition to the church leadership. These groups included the Weißensee Study Group and the Evangelical Pastors' Association.[15] Even though Main Department XX/4 had only 1 per cent of all the ministry's IMs, running the network was an expensive business. In 1987, the cost amounted to 23 per cent of the department's total expenditure and was considerably higher per capita than was spent on the larger networks in those units which dealt with sport, culture and the media.[16]

As in other spheres, the Stasi recruited agents by taking advantage of human frailties and needs such as the desire for personal security, material goods, career advancement, trips abroad and university places for their children. Payments could be high, such as to the 24 IMs who received over 2,000 GDR Marks, including the 14 top earners with over 5,000 Marks in 1988.[17] But as many informers received nothing or only small sums, controllers had to be adept at encouraging IMs to believe that they were helping to modify some of the state's more repressive characteristics. Most church IMs do not seem to have believed that working for the Stasi was tantamount to changing sides; indeed, many who betrayed friends managed to convince themselves that they were working in the interests of the church and in furthering its relationship with the SED and the state. Neubert has referred to

[13] Wiedmann R. 1996: 200.
[14] Vollnhals C. 1996a: 106.
[15] Roßberg K. 1996: 61.
[16] Vollnhals C. 1996a: 103, 119.
[17] Ibid., 104, 109–10.

this as a kind of dual loyalty, which is not easily classified into dichotomies of collaboration and refusal, resistance and accommodation, and which was under-pinned in church circles by the authoritarian structures of Protestantism, a utopian belief in a humane socialism as the preferred third way between capitalism and communism, and a pragmatic perception of the GDR's capacity for survival.[18]

THE DILEMMAS OF COLLABORATION

Manfred Stolpe's involvement with the MfS encapsulates the dilemmas of weaving, no matter how adroitly, between the two tracks of church and state. It also highlights the complexity of a retrospective reconstruction of the motivation of IMs. A church lawyer, Stolpe was the top lay official of the Protestant churches and later, between 1990 and 2002, served as the SPD Minister President of the *Land* Brandenburg. Although registered by the Stasi as an unofficial informer (IM 'Sekretär') in 1970, Stolpe has emphatic-ally denied that he worked as an agent. While there is no evidence that Stolpe entered into a contractual relationship with the MfS, he undoubtedly enjoyed close contacts with Stasi and party officials for almost 20 years. Stolpe went beyond his brief as he did not receive authorisation from or inform the church leaders of his MfS links. This kind of relationship was not untypical of church IMs as the Stasi, on occasions, deliberately refrained from asking officials in sensitive positions from entering into a formal con-tract.[19] Indeed, from the mid-1970s onwards, the recruitment of a full-time church official required, in some Regional Administrations, the prior approval of its leading officer.[20] The decisive factor was the value, the conspiratorial nature and the regularity of the contacts. Praised before 1989 as a skilled intermediary between East and West and as a protector of dissidents against the state, Stolpe stands accused of being the man of the state in the church. He informed his Stasi and party contacts on the political views of church leaders and he warned them of the danger of an alliance between the altern-ative political culture and Christians with so-called 'negative' political atti-tudes. He was also exceptionally indiscreet in his views on pastor Rainer Eppelmann and discussed ways and means of reining him in. Not sur-prisingly, some former dissidents have turned vehemently against their former 'protector'.

---

[18] Neubert E. 1993: 93–103; also Vollnhals C. 1996b: 438–46.

[19] Reuth R. G. 1992: 33–4, 42–3. Roßberg, the deputy head of HA XX/4, confirms in his autobiography that the MfS registered Stolpe as IM 'Sekretär' without his knowledge but contends that the crucial criterion was the frequency and the confidential nature of their contacts. Roßberg was Stolpe's MfS contact for about 20 years and regards him as an opportunist and a pragmatist. See Roßberg K. 1996: 85, 88–9.

[20] Vollnhals C. 1996a: 99.

In his defence, Stolpe has argued that he had been working in the best interests of the churches and had helped thousands of would-be émigrés.[21] Given that the GDR appeared to be a permanent feature, the pragmatist in Stolpe probably persuaded him that the churches' internal autonomy could be safeguarded and furthered through dialogue with the party and the state authorities while, hopefully, removing some of the regime's worst features. In a justification of this position after the collapse of communism, he claimed that the GDR 'was a dictatorship, but one which wore velvet gloves, and despite everything, it was possible to do a great deal'.[22]

For many, this kind of defence is unacceptable. In 1992, Joachim Gauck, a former pastor from Rostock and the first head of the Federal office responsible for the Stasi files, opined:

> The argument that the church or the opposition could only be effective because they were good 'diplomats' at work overlooks the danger that the 'diplomats' would set the norms for activities within the church, and that it was then child's play for the state to limit those activities. It also overlooks the fact that in church discussions of individuals and issues, the 'diplomats' had often internalized the ideas and behaviour of SED comrades.[23]

In retrospect, it is clear that the Stasi enjoyed considerable success in influencing church policy and in curtailing critical potential. This was certainly true throughout most of the 1960s and 1970s and it was not until the emergence of the peace and other small autonomous groups that the situation within the churches gave reason for concern and led to the formation in 1983 of a special desk in Main Department XX/4 for combating political underground activity.[24] However, the churches were not pliant and defenceless objects. The plurality of opinions and organisations, as well as the dedication of individuals and groups, ensured that critical voices were not silenced and policy was not a mere reflection of the ruling party's priorities. Even though church leaders might seek to distance themselves in public from Eppelmann and other critical pastors, they sought, in the course of discussions with state and party authorities, to ensure that Eppelmann remained at liberty.[25] And it was in no small part thanks to the protection of the churches that the basic groups, though infiltrated by the Stasi, constituted a countervoice to the SED in areas such as human rights and peace (see Chapter 11). Further evaluation of the impact of the Stasi on decision-making processes in, and the development of, the churches will, however, depend very much on further research, in particular on case studies based on oral testimonies and scrupulous documentary studies.

---

[21] Reuth R. G. 1992: 51.
[22] Cited in Sa'adah A. 1998: 191.
[23] Cited in ibid., 206.
[24] Vollnhals C. 1996a: 94.
[25] Besier G. and Wolf S. 1992: 85.

THE JEWISH COMMUNITY

In the later 1980s, the GDR's Jewish community comprised less than 400 registered members, about half of whom resided in East Berlin, and several thousand people of Jewish origin.[26] The anti-semitism of the early 1950s, economic difficulties and the regime's antagonism towards religion led to a sharp decline in membership of the official communities (*Gemeinden*) from about 8,000 in 1950 to about 1,500 in 1961. By the mid-1970s, more than 90 per cent of members were over 55 years of age. There were, of course, many other East Germans of Jewish descent who did not belong to the communities, some of them being deterred by the requirements of orthodoxy and by political considerations. Among those of Jewish descent were the Politbüro members Albert Norden and Hermann Axen, high-ranking state officials like the State Secretary for Religious Questions Klaus Gysi, the Minister of Culture Alexander Abusch, the playwright Friedrich Wolf, and the writers Stephan Hermlin and Stefan Heym. Wolf's two sons, Konrad and Markus, were a film director and the head of Stasi foreign intelligence respectively.

As the SED's claim to legitimacy was based, in part, on its anti-fascist credentials, the regime's treatment of the Jewish communities and the official interpretation of the Holocaust are important indicators of the regime's commitment to anti-fascism. While the bravery of many communists in the resistance to National Socialism cannot be denied, the GDR and Soviet adherence to the Comintern's 1935 interpretation of fascism as a class problem endemic in capitalist society made it extremely difficult to appreciate the Holocaust in terms of its ethnic-religious dimension and as part of the history of anti-semitism. For reasons of self-legitimation, the SED and East German historians depicted the communists as the most important victims of National Socialism, thereby marginalising the Jewish catastrophe, and by locating fascism in the capitalist system transferred the guilt and the responsibility for restitution to West Germany. Furthermore, the position of Jews in the GDR was damaged by the repercussions in the GDR of the Slansky trial in Czechoslovakia and the 'doctors' plot' in Moscow between 1952 and 1953. The purging of the SED apparat of Titoists, Trotskyites and Zionists resulted in the dismissal and flight of many Jewish citizens. Hundreds of Jews left the GDR, including the leaders of most of the communities.[27] Although persecution slackened and the enfeebled communities were able to devote themselves to socio-cultural and religious activities, anti-semitic tendencies were not eradicated and many East German Jews, including those in the MfS, remained sensitive to the ambiguities of Jewish identity in a communist state. A former Stasi officer, Herbert Brehmer, has recalled that his few fellow Jews

---

[26] MfS ZA, ZOS, no. 1164, p. 78.
[27] Timm A. 1993: 48–9.

in the ministry did not openly admit to their Jewish identity and it was rumoured that Markus Wolf's departure in 1986 was linked to his Jewish origins.[28]

Not until the mid-1980s did the SED adopt a more positive attitude to Jewish organisations and give the green light to a more nuanced understanding of National Socialist persecution of the Jews. This policy was closely linked to the SED's efforts to boost its international reputation, to improve relations with Israel and to attain Most Favoured Nation trading status with the USA. In 1988, the GDR went to great lengths to commemorate the 50th anniversary of Crystal Night and Honecker agreed with Heinz Galinski, the leader of the West German Jewish communities, to establish a Centrum Judaicum in the former synagogue in East Berlin's Oranienburger Strasse. However, when Jewish groups in West Germany and Israel sought to gain access to the archive of the Berlin Jewish community, which had been moved to Potsdam, neither the GDR authorities nor the MfS were keen to release sensitive documents on the expropriation of the Jews in the Third Reich lest they be used to support restitution claims against the GDR.[29]

Despite the relaxation of persecution and the greater toleration afforded the Jewish communities, Marxism-Leninism's aversion to religious denominations and organisational autonomy, the regime's friendship with Israel's Arab opponents and the links of the Jewish communities with Western organisations meant that the Jewish communities were regarded as a 'security issue' to be dealt with by the Secretariat for Religious Questions and by the Stasi. As with the Protestant and Catholic churches and the Jehovah's Witnesses, Main Department XX/4 was mainly responsible for the control and surveillance of the Jewish communities. Other Main Departments were also involved. HA II, for example, kept watch over Western visitors to the Jewish communities.[30] IMs were also recruited from among the latter in order to influence decisions and provide information for the ministry.[31] Among the leading officials in East Berlin who served the MfS for many years were Peter Kirchner, the chair of the capital's community since 1971, and two members of the Board of Directors, Werner Zarrach, and Irene Runge. Zarrach, who had worked for the Polish security service in the 1950s and subsequently as Stasi informer IM 'Rainer Buch', reported on the Polish opposition and on the East Berlin Jewish community. He belonged to the latter's Board of Directors from 1972 onwards. Kirchner, who was registered as IM 'Burg' in 1977 and then as a higher category (IMB) in 1980, was still cooperating with the MfS as late as the autumn of 1989. Dr Peter Fischer ('René'), cooperated, though not unproblematically, for many years as an IM; he was appointed secretary of the East German Organisation of Jewish Communities in April

[28] Brehmer H. 1991: 25, 27.
[29] MfS ZA, HA IX/11, AV 15/87, 'Stellungnahme', 18 September 1989, pp. 2–3.
[30] Offenberg U. 1998: 152–3.
[31] For the details on IMs, see ibid., 160–63, and Wolfssohn M. 1997: 152–3.

1989 and became the leader of the Berlin branch of the Central Council of German Jews in 1990. Community officials and members elsewhere in the GDR were implicated too. In Dresden, Helmut Aris, the president of the community, was recruited in 1954 and Helmut Eschwege, the historian and a community member, was a long-serving informer ('Ferdinand'). Eschwege, one of the co-founders of the Social Democratic Party in Dresden in November 1989, overlooked his MfS links when he came to publish his autobiography in 1991. With a minuscule and senescent membership and a high level of politically reliable SED members among the executives, the communities led a largely quiescent and marginalised existence in the Honecker era.

JEHOVAH'S WITNESSES

Whereas the Jewish communities, the Mormons, the Baptists and the Protestant churches enjoyed a limited space and legal recognition, the Jehovah's Witnesses were beyond the pale and their organisation was banned from 1950 onwards. The society had also been proscribed and Witnesses dismissed from their jobs during the Third Reich. After 1939 most active congregation members were incarcerated in prisons and concentration camps such as Sachsenhausen and Buchenwald, where between 2,500 and 5,000 died. Although after the end of the Second World War the Witnesses had been officially recognised as 'victims of fascism', they soon came into conflict with the SED because of their distinctive doctrine and their links with the society's headquarters in Brooklyn and its Eastern Bureau in Wiesbaden, West Germany, where a special GDR branch was located. The SED and MfS were convinced that the Witnesses were agents of American imperialists and warmongers. The brethren vigorously denied the charge. They saw themselves as citizens of God's Kingdom, firmly believed that the end of the present order was nigh and predicted that destruction loomed for the nations under the sway of Satan. Although Witnesses accepted that they should obey the law of the land – except where it was in conflict with the law of God – they remained politically neutral, resolutely refusing to swear allegiance to any state other than that of God and to take part in elections. They also declined to bear arms, not through pacifism, but because they perceived themselves to be soldiers in God's army.

While the consolidation of SED rule in the later 1960s and détente brought some relief to the Witnesses, both party and Stasi clung to the view that the brethren were engaged in pseudo-religious, anti-communist subversion as lackeys of American imperialism. Allegedly steered from Brooklyn and Wiesbaden, they were thus part of the imperialist strategy to undermine and liquidate the socialist order of the GDR[32] through political-ideological diversionary methods such as:

---

[32] MfS ZA, JHS, no. 901175, 1975, p. 6; MfS ZA, JHS, no. 123/79, 1978, pp. 4, 8.

... hindering or preventing the formation of a socialist consciousness in children and young people, opposing German-Soviet friendship ... propagating superstition and hostility to science ... and spreading in socialist society the anxiety, uncertainty and fear in their daily lives and for the future such as is found in bourgeois capitalism.[33]

As harsh repression had failed to destroy the society, preventive decomposition, first used against the Witnesses in the 1950s, became more prominent from about the mid-1960s and was the main plank in the struggle against the society.[34] Information was gathered according to the customary 'Who is who?' principle and the main targets were the organisation's functionaries, the training schools, study groups, the Eastern Bureau in West Germany, members who refused to do military service, and the courier system. It was generally recognised that the Witnesses' doctrinal and missionary arteries could be severed by preventing the distribution by secret courier of tracts such as *Watch Tower* and *Awake!* from Brooklyn and Wiesbaden.[35] Despite the emphasis on softer forms of control, punitive measures were not abandoned, especially against young male Witnesses who refused military call-up on the grounds of conscience. As the movement's doctrine did not require total conscientious objection, an unknown number opted for service in a construction unit, the GDR alternative to formal military service. Many refused, however, to take advantage of this provision and between 1964 and 1974, about 1,000 were imprisoned, usually for terms of up to 18 months. Although the GDR authorities became less draconian in the course of the 1980s, 100 Jehovah's Witnesses out of a total of 150 conscientious objectors were imprisoned in 1985. Yet even before they were incarcerated, many members had already experienced discrimination at school and had been deprived of an apprenticeship for refusing to take part in pre-military training.[36]

From the late 1960s onwards, the authorities frequently imposed penalties in accordance with the 1968 Decree on Minor Offences and the 1975 Decree on the Formation of Associations. Fines of 10 to 300 Marks, and on occasions even 1,000 Marks, were imposed for infringements relating to these decrees.[37] Proselytising was punished: in 1983, one Witness was fined 300 Marks for calling on citizens in their apartments in Angermünde and another of the brethren had to pay 50 Marks for approaching people in a cemetery in Hoyerswerda.[38] Such penalties were justified on the grounds that the Witnesses were an illegal organisation. The number of proceedings relating to minor infringements of the law rose sharply in the early 1980s, from 96 in

---

[33] MfS ZA, HA IX, no. 51, 'Kurzauskunft', 1984, p. 71. Our translation.
[34] Dirksen H-H. 2000: 19–20.
[35] MfS ZA, JHS, no. 135/80, 1980, pp. 5–6.
[36] Hacke G. 2000: 85–6, 88–9, 103.
[37] Ibid., 80.
[38] MfS ZA, HA IX, no. 51, p. 47.

1983 to 269 in 1984.[39] Partly because the Witnesses appealed against the penalties and contested the whole procedure, Main Department XX/4 was most anxious that operations be coordinated smoothly with the People's Police.[40]

The Stasi deployed its usual repertoire of dirty tricks in order to control and, ultimately, to liquidate the Jehovah's Witnesses' organisation. In a thesis devoted to decomposition operations against Jehovah's Witnesses, Lieutenant Bergner of Department XX/4 of the Gera Regional Administration identified a number of measures which could be used to undermine their organisational network: 'defamation of officials', 'denigrating the intellectual and psychological capabilities of group members', 'blaming them for criminal offences', and 'spreading malicious rumours about marital infidelity'.[41] He described one distasteful but successful operation in 1965 concerning a Jehovah's Witness functionary who, while out walking with the wife and four-year-old daughter of an imprisoned Witness, touched the child's genitals. After an IM had discovered the story from the girl's mother, he launched a letter campaign which resulted in the dismissal of the Witness from his function.[42] The thesis received the rating 'very good' from the Stasi assessor, who commended it for its scientific quality and its contribution to practical work.[43] As with other groups and individuals, Witnesses were subject to intensive surveillance in operational cases. As part of OV 'Thurm', the Karl-Marx-Stadt Regional Administration reported in 1972 that the apartment of a Witness district official, Werner Oertel, had been broken into and searched on the basis of information supplied by an informer. A neighbour had helped with the search.[44]

IMs were central to all such operations. For example, Willy Müller, the founder and long-time leader of Christian Responsibility and a Witness official, was recruited as an informer in 1959 after succumbing to psychological pressures and health problems as a result of imprisonment. Christian Responsibility, a special study group of ex-brethren, had been founded in 1952 with the aim of sowing dissension among practising Witnesses.[45] As early as 1951, a service instruction issued by Mielke in his capacity as Secretary of State in the ministry stated that: 'It is only possible to uncover the top functionaries and most dangerous agents of the Witnesses' sect through targeting our work and recruiting GMs and informers with the right potential'.[46]

---

[39] MfS ZA, HA IX, no. 51, p. 77.
[40] MfS ZA, HA IX, no. 51, 8 April 1985, p. 83. This is a circular from Major General Kienberg to heads of Departments XX.
[41] MfS ZA, JHS, no. 23540, 1976, pp. 31–2, 34.
[42] Ibid., 31–2.
[43] Ibid., 48–50.
[44] MfS Außenstelle Chemnitz, no. XIV 864/62, pp. 1–3.
[45] Hacke G. 2000: 71–5.
[46] MfS ZA, Allgemeine Sachablage, no. 940/67, no page. Our translation.

The recruitment of IMs, whether congregation members or outsiders, was a complicated and lengthy process because of what the Stasi referred to as the organisation's conspiratorial practices and also because the Eastern Bureau and the functionaries in the GDR were always on guard against MfS spies, carrying out checks on the least suspicion.[47]

Many Witnesses collaborated with the MfS in the belief that they could somehow exert a positive influence on state policies.[48] Given the sensibilities of Witnesses, recruiters were prepared to overlook a written commitment to cooperate.[49] Signs of human weakness were seized upon. In the case of IM candidate 'Blumenberg', the recruiter sought to take advantage of his interest in pornography and alcohol and his aim to purchase an apartment in 1973, ironically two years before the end of the world predicted by the society.[50] Those IMs whom the MfS smuggled into the congregations had to adapt to the Witnesses' belief system and to make fundamental adjustments in their life-style. They were expected to withdraw from politics, retreat into the closed circles of the congregations, possibly forgo watching TV and, if they had children, raise them in the Witnesses' faith. As the process of adjustment was so difficult, the Stasi preferred to recruit IMs from among former or practising Witnesses, including elders. On the other hand, it was recognised that while functionaries might be able to provide invaluable 'insider' information, they were unlikely to have a firm ideological commitment to GDR-style socialism, therefore increasing the chances of being uncovered.[51] Those who were active within the congregations and districts were often initially approached during interrogation after an arrest.[52] The Stasi preferred to recruit single young males, partly to avoid the conflicts of conscience and other problems arising from married life and partly because women did not play a central role in the Witnesses' organisation. Women, however, could be useful as informers on the so-called 'periphery', where agents carried out control and surveillance activities in the neighbourhoods as well as at the workplace. If an IM was married, then the Stasi, aware of the close family ties among Witnesses, considered it advisable that a wife be informed about her husband's work and even attend some of the meetings between the IM and his controller.[53]

Despite the intensity of surveillance and the frequency of arrests, the Jehovah's Witnesses managed to survive and rebuild their networks, although, as the Stasi knew from its agents, the disruption of the courier links between West and East Germany and the decline in the number of new members

---

[47] MfS ZA, JHS, no. 23501, 1976, p. 10.
[48] Hacke G. 2000: 78.
[49] MfS ZA, JHS, no. 263159, 'Auszüge aus der Lektion HA V/4', 1951, pp. 3–4.
[50] MfS ZA, JHS, no. 138176, 1976, pp. 21–2.
[51] MfS ZA, JHS, no. 23504, 1976, pp. 22–5.
[52] Hacke G. 2000: 78–9.
[53] MfS ZA, JHS, no. 23501, 1976, pp. 6–7, 11, 17.

were causing concern in Brooklyn and Wiesbaden in the early 1980s.[54] In some respects, the final quinquennium of SED rule was a period of hope for the Witnesses in the face of continuing discrimination. Missionary activities were stepped up and, sensitive to external criticism and pressure, the SED was less draconian in its treatment of those refusing to do military service. Developments elsewhere raised spirits in the GDR. In Poland, small congresses were allowed from the early 1980s onwards and the final legalisation of the Witnesses occurred in May 1989. Disturbed by these trends, the MfS attempted to prevent East German Witnesses from meeting their Polish brethren. This was not always successful: in the summer of 1989, 150 Witnesses from the Karl-Marx-Stadt region attended international congresses in Poland.[55] However, the sect was not legalised in the GDR until March 1990 as the Witnesses lacked the political leverage of the Jewish communities and in the eyes of the SED and MfS, the sect was still too much of an exotic outsider and too closely linked to foreign agencies for recognition to be granted.

---

[54] MfS ZA, HA XX/AKG, no. 5495, pp. 28–30. The organisation calculated that membership had dropped slightly from 21,450 in 1975 to 20,000 in 1983. In January 1989, the Stasi estimated membership at around 21,700, half of whom lived in the Dresden and Karl-Marx-Stadt areas. On the numerical strength of the Witnesses, see Hacke G. 2000: 84 and MfS ZA, ZAIG, no. 3733, 17 January 1989, p. 5.

[55] Hacke G. 2000: 92–3.

Chapter 11

ALTERNATIVE SUB-CULTURES

THE DEVELOPMENT OF AN ALTERNATIVE POLITICAL CULTURE

Of greater concern to the Stasi than the small religious communities and sects was the emergence towards the close of the 1970s of what can broadly be described as an alternative political culture which managed to find a relatively safe haven in the Protestant churches. Many emerged from existing circles and they recruited heavily from among the so-called GDR generation which had grown up in the shadow of the Berlin Wall. Members of this generation had been influenced by emancipatory tendencies in the West since the mid-1960s and by the democratic socialism of the Prague Spring. The autonomous groups constituted an 'alternative political culture' in that they articulated outside official channels a series of peace, ecological, women's, human rights, gay and Second/Third World issues. Because of the severe restrictions imposed by the SED and implemented, among other bodies, by the Stasi, autonomous activities in the public sphere were largely confined to the protected space afforded by the Protestant churches.

The autonomous groups tended to have a collective rather than a power-political orientation, to be reactive rather than proactive and to favour grass-roots democracy over parliamentary forms.[1] The thrust of their activities and programmes was for a reform of the existing system, not its overthrow. They wanted a democratic socialism which respected civil liberties but, with the exception of individuals such as the Naumburg theologian Edelbert Richter, little attempt was made to develop a theoretical framework. The Naumburg peace circle around Richter was one of the few groups to thematise the German question. Others who did so were the East Berlin pastor Rainer Eppelmann and Robert Havemann. In 1982, they issued the Berlin Appeal, in which they proposed the overcoming of the division of Germany as a prerequisite to the safeguarding of peace. However, the opposition groups

---

[1] Knabe H. 1990: 23.

were circumspect with respect to the German question as many had had no direct experience of the other part of Germany and the division of Germany into two states was by no means perceived in negative terms. A Europe without frontiers and some form of reformed socialism rather than a capitalist Germany had a more positive ring.[2]

Central to the alternative political culture was the issue of peace. Since 1978, when the introduction of compulsory pre-military education in schools for pupils aged 14–16 triggered off widespread protests on the part of the clergy and parents, the autonomous peace groups became more outspoken and peace initiatives attracted considerable popular interest.[3] The growth in activities and interest can be attributed not only to GDR-specific conditions such as the growing militarisation of life at school and in mass organisations such as the Society for Sport and Technology but also to the advent of a new ice age in East–West relations. Among the most significant initiatives for peace were the annual Dresden Peace Forum, which since 1982 attracted several thousand people, Peace Weeks and Peace Workshops. These events were not confined to peace groups: the Peace Workshop held at East Berlin's Church of the Redeemer in July 1983 was attended by women's, gay and ecology groups. Conscription was another controversial issue. Although con-scripts were entitled by law to serve in a construction unit instead of per-forming formal military service, in 1981 a group in Dresden proposed the more radical idea of a community peace service as a truly civilian alternative to military service. This envisaged employment in homes for children, old people and the physically handicapped. The idea of a community peace service was part of an attempt to thematise political conditions in the GDR and indicate how conflicts could be overcome through various mechanisms, including peace education and the responsibility of individuals for peace. Another development was the establishment of small women's peace groups in several cities, notably the Women for Peace Group in East Berlin. The decisive impetus to the women's peace movement was given by the 1982 Military Service Law which provided for the conscription of women aged 18–50 in the event of an emergency.

Issues of peace fed into the broader stream of the denial of human rights, which included the highly sensitive matter of popular discontent with restric-tions on travel. From about the mid-1980s, human and civil rights issues came to occupy a more prominent place within the alternative political culture and to attain a dynamic quality lacked by the single issue movements. The accession to power of Gorbachev in the Soviet Union in 1985 and efforts in Hungary and Poland to establish the roots of a civil society encouraged human rights activists in the GDR. A key role was played by the Initiative for Peace and Human Rights (IFM). Formed in late 1985, it numbered no

---

[2] Meckel M. and Gutzeit M. 1994: 69.
[3] See Sandford J. 1983.

more than 30 participants before the autumn of 1989.[4] However, the IFM, like so many of the other autonomous groups, was both small and largely isolated from society. A Stasi report of June 1989, indicated that there were only about 350 so-called opposition groups associated with the Protestant churches and an additional ten groups, such as the Church from Below, which performed a coordinating function. The Stasi reckoned with about 2,500 activists in these groups, 60 of whom were described as the hard core 'fanatical enemies' of socialism. This is probably too low a figure. Insider calculations suggest that the number of activists may have been between 10,000 and 15,000 but that the total number of groups was lower, around 320.[5] The limited appeal of the groups may be attributed in part to their relatively underdeveloped institutional and communication networks. This remained a serious problem despite the boost to networking in the 1980s by the formation of the Church from Below, the ecological network *Arche* and the environmental libraries in East Berlin, Leipzig and elsewhere.

THE STASI INTERVENES

Another reason for the groups' lack of popular support was the unwillingness of most citizens to involve themselves in such highly politicised issues as civil rights because of the risks to themselves, family members and their careers. Coercion, too, played its part: the MfS subjected the 'unpalatable' dissidents to regular surveillance, occasional detainment and expulsion, sometimes forcibly, to the West. Even by its own standards, MfS penetration of the groups was extremely thorough. Of the many examples which could be given, the following are typical. About 50 per cent of the IFM's members were IMs who sought to provoke unrest and dissension within the group as part of the decomposition strategy. Various members suffered arrest and expulsion from the GDR. Ibrahim Böhme and Wolfgang Schnur, two of the leading figures in the citizens' movements which in the autumn of 1989 helped to sweep the SED from power, were unveiled in 1990 as long-standing Stasi informers. One tragic case was the revelation after the East German revolution that Vera Wollenberger's husband, Knud (IM 'Donald'), the son of a distinguished Jewish academic, had been reporting not only on her peace and ecological activities but also on the details of their private life. Ironically, other Stasi agents, not knowing that IM 'Donald' was one of them, were describing him to their superiors as a 'negative, hostile element'. As with the IFM, Stasi agents sought to undermine the effectiveness of the groups by, for example, inciting divisive internal discussions and conflicts and by encouraging radical activities in order to provoke counteraction by the state authorities. Many groups collapsed because members suspected that the Stasi was 'among them'.

---

[4] Templin W. and Weißhuhn R. 1991: 150–51.
[5] Deutscher Bundestag VII/I 1995: 690–91.

From the point of view of the regime and the Stasi, the autonomous groups constituted a particularly threatening form of hostile-negative activity as part of the so-called political underground. Mielke had no doubt that they were 'sworn enemies of socialism' and that political police measures were required to deal with them.[6] Although the major responsibility for combating the groups was assigned to Main Department XX and its various territorial organs, other units were also enlisted according to their specific areas of operation. Thus Main Department I was empowered to uncover and prevent the spread of 'pacifist and pseudo-pacifist' views among the armed forces.[7] The Stasi perceived the groups, whether peace, ecological or human rights, as forming a counterculture to that of the monistic SED system, enjoying close contacts with like-minded organisations in the West and abusing the space afforded by the churches for internal activities. Yet, given the small size of the groups, their fragile relations with the Church and the high level of infiltration by the Stasi, they hardly posed an immediate threat to SED rule even though Stasi reports abounded with references to their allegedly deep-seated hostility to the GDR state.

YOUTH AS A SOCIETAL PROBLEM

Although public statements by the SED on East German youth were usually full of praise for their commitment to the GDR and its socialist system, young people were nevertheless regarded as a major problem by both party and Stasi. A service instruction issued by Mielke in 1966, which remained in force for the following two decades, bears telling testimony to the deep-lying distrust and suspicion of youth as well as shedding light on the reasons behind the ministry's apprehension. According to the document,[8] the 'lack of experience of life, ignorance of the capitalist system, desire for adventure, being easily influenced, excessive self-confidence' and other characteristics of some young East Germans made them vulnerable to the machinations of the imperialist enemy. The latter sought to sow mistrust between young people and the state, undermine their belief in the future of socialist society and spread decadent ideas through the illegal distribution of Western literature, personal contacts and West German television and radio programmes. These 'focused' activities by the enemy promoted, according to the Stasi, flight from the GDR, arson in the factories, disturbances of the peace, 'alcohol abuse at so-called parties' and 'the adoption of certain forms of Western decadence, clothing and behaviour of a range of young people'.

---

[6] Besier G. and Wolf S. 1992: 73.
[7] See Mielke's service instruction of February 1985, printed in Fricke K. W. 1991: 146–63.
[8] The following quotations in this paragraph are from Süß W. 1996: 55–8.

PUNKS – TURNING MIELKE'S HAIR WHITE

While Honecker's SED managed to keep the lid on the younger generation through a mixture of intensive political socialisation, the dense network of FDJ, GST and other state organisations, the enticement of apprenticeships and job opportunities as well as concessions in the pop music sphere, both the party and the Stasi looked aghast at the emergence in the early 1980s of unconventional fringe youth sub-cultures consisting of new romantics, poppers, punks, heavy metals, goths and skinheads. These developments in the GDR lagged slightly in time behind the Western fashions in dress, music and haircut which punks and skinheads sought to imitate. As one 15-year-old female punk stated in a 1982 interview: 'I got used to being a punk when I saw a few from over there [West Germany], I liked how they were dressed'.[9] The East German sub-cultures soon acquired typical characteristics: the 'no future' punks 'dropped out', goths dressed in black attire, engaged in the irrational, and shaven-head skinheads wore bomber jackets and combat boots. Whereas punks arrived on the scene shortly before the militant skinheads, the latter were more significant by the mid- to late 1980s and loathed the unkempt punks' life-style and alleged pacifism. In the early phase until about 1985–86, these sub-cultures, notably the punks, were essentially an unpolitical and uncoordinated form of protest against conformity, consumerism and restrictions on self-expression and individuality in a state which in the eyes of many of the younger generation was becoming increasingly anachronistic.[10]

According to a Stasi report in 1981, there were around 1,000 punks with about 10,000 sympathisers in the GDR. Three years later, the figure had dropped to about 900, of which 400 were to be found in East Berlin, 95 in Leipzig and 60 each in Magdeburg and Cottbus.[11] These are only estimates as the boundaries between punks, skinheads, heavy metals and others were fluid and turnover rapid. Many skinheads were recruited from among the punks and punk bands often used elements of ska music. Security officers intent on classifying punks must have scratched their heads at the diversity with which they were confronted: 'grimy' punks, Nazi punks and fashion punks as well as black eagles. The so-called 'grimy' punks recoiled against conventional standards of cleanliness and the black eagles were football fans who wore a black scarf to denote their anarchist inclinations. They attended the matches of BFC Dynamo and from about 1982–83 drifted into the violent elements associated with the rightist skinheads.[12] Punk began to lose its drive by the middle of the 1980s and in early 1989, the majority of Regional Administrations reported a continuing fall in numbers.[13]

---

[9] Interview in Furian G. and Becker N. 2000: 11. Our translation.
[10] Korfes G. 1990: 6; also Büscher W. and Wensierski P. 1984: 35–6.
[11] Michael K. 1999: 74; MfS ZA, ZAIG, no. 3326, 'Informationen', 1984, p. 4.
[12] Horschig M. 1999: 21–2.
[13] MfS Aussenstelle Halle, Abteilung XX, no. 774, 'Information', 1989, p. 20.

The MfS looked with revulsion on all punks. In MfS reports, they are usually associated with 'degeneracy' in their external appearance, with safety pins through noses, 'scruffy, sometimes torn, dirty or greasy clothes – conspicuous, usually dyed hair, conspicuous haircuts (Mohican cut, hair sticking out) and with an aggressive, provocative manner'.[14] A Mohican hairstyle was often sufficient for a punk to be hauled into custody by the police. The MfS also believed that Western political-ideological diversion had managed to turn many punks against the political and social order of the GDR, as allegedly exemplified by the punks' identification with bourgeois concepts of freedom and 'pseudo-pacifist' and left-radical ideas.[15] A further source of Stasi antipathy was punks' disdain for regular employment and their withdrawal from the Free German Youth and the Confederation of Free German Trade Unions (FDGB), thereby infringing the socialist work ethic as well as undermining the effectiveness of the workplace and the youth organisation as instruments of political control. Thomas Bautzer, a former punk, reckons that frustration with life and work was why he became a punk:

> I had to go to work, get up at 4.30 every day. 6 o'clock at the docks, every day the same idiots . . . and repulsive old men who I had to spend the whole day with. It made me feel sick.[16]

The punks were contemptuous of the aridity of GDR rock music and turned to the anti-dancing pogo and primitive unmelodic lines. They saw no future in either capitalism or, unlike many peace and human rights activists, any form of reformed socialism.[17] Lines like 'Observed, denounced, controlled. What has he done?' by the Dresden band *Letzte Diagnose* were a political provocation to the Stasi 'pigs'.[18] All of this does not mean, however, that punks were necessarily apathetic and resigned. Punks as outsiders and as provocateurs are fondly remembered by a former GDR punk, Mario Schulz:

> It started with me liking the music. I didn't understand the English lyrics but living the life of an outsider, the in-your-face existence – I liked that. I had always been a stroppy little yob. That's why I became a punk.[19]

Commenting on the politicisation of punk in the mid-1980s, for instance into left- and fasco-punks, he asserted:

> That did not mean anything. We would have stuck a picture of Adolf Hitler or Lenin on our jackets but only to shock people, not because we were outsiders, we were in the business of shocking people . . .[20]

---

[14] MfS ZA, ZAIG, no. 3366, 'Information', 1986, p. 8. Our translation.
[15] MfS ZA, ZAIG, no. 3366, 'Information', 1986, p. 5.
[16] Written statement in Furian G. and Becker N. 2000: 88. Our translation.
[17] Michael K. 1999: 72–3.
[18] MfS ZA, ZAIG, no. 3366, 'Information', 1986, p. 30.
[19] 1999 interview in Furian G. and Becker N. 2000: 85. Our translation.
[20] Ibid., 85. Our translation.

Until the skinhead problem became critical towards the end of the 1980s, Western political-ideological diversion provided the standard explanation – and alibi – for the troublesome youth sub-cultures. Accordingly, the MfS tracked with its usual diligence the links with the Operation Area, above all the impact of the electronic media and individual contacts between Eastern and Western punks in restaurants, clubs, parks and private apartments. Operational cases carried out by the Regional Administrations in Potsdam, Dresden and Leipzig in 1985 detected personal links between GDR punk bands such as *Paranoia*, *Schleim-keim* and *L'Attentat* and punks from West Germany. Records, cassettes and fanzines were exchanged.[21]

REPRESSION

The state authorities moved with alacrity against the punks. In 1981, a campaign of repression was launched by the Criminal Police, which failed, however, to stem their appeal. The campaign involved arrests, interrogations and harsh prison sentences.[22] One former punk describes a raid on an apartment in East Berlin, which was a meeting place for punks:

> The police stormed in, they locked us all in a room, then chose one and took him into the kitchen where he was beaten up by several pigs. They grabbed the next one and dragged him into the kitchen. By the time it was over they had beaten up and taken away everybody, including the girls. During the journey to the police station they were beaten on the back seats of the huge numbers of police vans that had turned up and then for half the night in the police station they were threatened and beaten. I came home late that day and found the flat in a catastrophic state. The whole kitchen, cupboards, curtains, cooker, walls, and even the ceilings, were spattered with blood . . . The people who had been beaten up were between 15 and 18 years of age. Taking legal proceedings against the police would have been a mockery.[23]

As part of the general offensive, the MfS, police and other state institutions were authorised in 1984 to keep a detailed record of the situation among negative-decadent young people; two years later, this brief was extended to include unregistered punk bands.[24] The MfS also began to ban those punk groups which it judged to be hostile to the Constitution and the social and political order of the GDR. Six bands were closed down in 1983, including the East Berlin band *namenlos*, which had been the target of an operational case. Its members were arrested in August 1983 and sentenced to between 12 and 18 months' imprisonment for disparaging the state.[25] Contacts with the Western

---

[21] MfS ZA, ZAIG, no. 3366, 'Information', 1986, pp. 15, 19.
[22] Horschig M. 1999: 23–4.
[23] Ibid., 24–5. Our translation.
[24] Michael K. 1999: 77.
[25] Ibid., 78.

media were severely punished. In his study of punks in the GDR, Klaus Michael has shown that punks were more likely to be punished according to the GDR's penal code than were members of the political opposition and the basic groups, mainly because the punks' plight received less attention in the Western media or support from the Protestant churches.[26] Relations between punks and the churches as well as with the peace and ecological groups ran far from smoothly. Punks were too strikingly different in appearance, attitude, language and behaviour, even though opposition to the state sometimes paved the way for joint actions like the laying of wreaths.[27] Towards the end of the 1980s, as punks came increasingly under attack from extremist skinheads, some punks became involved in the activities of the Church from Below and the alternative peace groups.[28] Much to the annoyance of the Stasi, punk bands like *Rosa Extra* and *L'Attentat* were allowed to perform on church premises and the Protestant churches provided some help for punks who were victimised by the state. However, many church officials, to say nothing of members of the congregation, were less than enthusiastic about having punks in their midst.[29]

The MfS actively sought to subvert the punks.[30] Not only were they hounded into leaving the country and frequently called up to serve in the NVA reserves but they were also recruited as IMs to report on other punks and the alternative cultural scene in general. Although the MfS appreciated that enlisting punks as informers was difficult on account of what the ministry described as their relatively close feeling of solidarity, it was able to catch two big fish, Frank Zappe and Iman Abdul-Majid. They collaborated with the MfS for several years during the 1980s. Abdul-Majid, the son of an Iraqi resident in Leipzig, was a key figure in the Leipzig punk bands *Wutanfall* and *L'Attentat* and was recruited in 1982 as a Criminal Police informer before registering as IM 'Dominique' four years later. By doing so, he hoped to speed up his application to leave the GDR. Although not a punk himself, Sören Naumann, the manager of the Dresden punk bands *Dresdner Musikbrigade* and *Fabrik*, was deployed as an IM in the city's alternative cultural scene. As was the case with some of the small human rights groups, one punk band in Jena consisted almost entirely of IMs. Taking advantage of help from the youth pastor, Ulrich Kasparick, who allowed them to use church rooms, they undermined his work with Dresden's peace and human rights groups. Their noise, drunkenness and damage to property led to so many complaints from the public that an exhausted Kasparick gave up his post.

While several punk bands were able to re-establish themselves after being banned, springing up like 'mushrooms from the ground'[31] and some East

---

[26] Michael K. 1999: 78–9.
[27] Horschig M. 1999: 28–9.
[28] Wagner B. 1995: 46.
[29] Horschig M. 1999: 30–32.
[30] On the Stasi's methods, see Michael K. 1999: 80–83.
[31] Interview in Furian G. and Becker N. 2000: 22.

German punk music found its way to the West on cassettes and records, by the mid-1980s punk was losing many of its innovative and subversive impulses. This can be attributed in part to MfS coercion. One former member of the punk band *namenlos*, Jana Schloßer, recalls that when she came out of prison in 1984 things had already changed as the Stasi had just about managed to smash punk.[32] But clashes over the direction of the punk 'movement' also contributed to the decline. Whereas some groups were tempted by new opportunities, albeit very limited, for officially tolerated but relatively harmless punk music, others adhered to Bert Papenfuß's insistence on maintaining their artistic autonomy and aggressive lyrics.[33]

SKINHEADS IN THE GDR

At the beginning of the 1980s, Western skinhead music, dress and militancy began to appeal to young East Germans among punks, heavy metal fans and soccer hooligans in East Berlin, Potsdam and some other cities. As with the punks, this was, at first, a cultural, not a conscious political tendency. GDR skinheads soon adopted the attire of their British and West German contemporaries: tight-fitting jeans, braces, a black, green or orange bomber jacket, a shaven head and highly polished Doc Marten boots. As many of the standard accessories could only be acquired via personal contacts in the West, youngsters often had to content themselves with more conventional sporting attire. Clashes between skinheads and what they denigrated as the smelly, dirty, lazy and pacifist punks were often fierce contests over hegemony in the alternative sub-cultures. By the later 1980s, the skinheads had undoubtedly gained the upper hand not only over the punks but also more easy targets such as the goths. The macho aggressiveness of the violent skinheads was encapsulated in the phrase 'Where words don't help, the fist will'.[34] Extremist incidents were not confined to the GDR's final decade. Ross and Waibel have also unearthed a wide range of offences which occurred in the first three decades of the GDR, albeit on a minor scale. These included the daubing of swastika graffiti on school and factory walls and the desecration of Jewish cemeteries in Potsdam, Dresden and East Berlin.[35] Nor were the NVA and the MfS right-extremist free zones. Between 1965 and 1980, over 700 right-extremist incidents were registered in the ranks of the Stasi and the army.[36] Some militants were imprisoned and several were deported to the West. In 1968, the West German government bought the 20-year-old Arnulf Winfried Priem

---

[32] Interview in Furian G. and Becker N. 2000: 106.
[33] Michael K. 1999: 90.
[34] Hockenos P. 1993: 74–5.
[35] Ross G. C. 2000: 86.
[36] Madloch N. 2000: 69–70.

out of his GDR prison. He would become one of Germany's most notorious militant extremists.[37]

During the 1980s, the incidence of right extremist violence and crime increased sharply. According to statistics of the Criminal Police, such offences rose five-fold between 1983 and 1987.[38] Another significant development was the evolution of a rudimentary organisational structure.[39] Relatively tightly organised and small militant groups such as the Lichtenberg Front, founded in 1986, were far less common, however, than the informal groupings and cliques which gathered in pubs, youth clubs and at discos and football grounds. The Lichtenberg Front, which was named after a working-class district in East Berlin, was constituted as a *Kameradschaft* or clandestine brotherhood. Later, in 1988, two prominent right-extremists, Ingo Hasselbach and André Riechert, founded 'The 30 January Movement', which, according to the former, was the first neo-Nazi party in the GDR. It was dissolved by the MfS in March 1989.

At the end of December 1987, the Stasi's Regional Administration in East Berlin reported that 17 IMs, together with informers attached to the Criminal Police, were involved in operations against skinheads and that, through closer cooperation between the Stasi and the police, the number of incidents had fallen at football matches in the capital during the 1987–88 season.[40] Eleven skinhead groupings were deemed to be operationally significant, ranging in size from a very loosely organised group of eight in Hellersdorf to the 17 members of the 'Sandow' group in the Lichtenberg district.[41] The skinheads' feeling of solidarity was reinforced by their distinctive attire and music as well as by their macho behaviour. Acts of violence were usually committed in a group where the pressure to conform was intense. Pumped up by alcohol, the skinheads chanted their battle cry 'Oi, Oi, Oi' and fascist-type slogans such as 'Heil Hitler!' and 'Germany Awake!'. One skinhead informer – IMS 'Diana Wolf' – told her controller in September 1986 that she became a skinhead in Hennigsdorf after her release from Bautzen prison in April because:

> . . . being a skin[head] means respect and recognition for me but also power and strength. I am respected in the group and I have a good feeling . . . Previously no one took the slightest notice of me, but now that I've got a bald head and the clothes they all look at me. That's brilliant and exciting.[42]

The MfS classified the skinheads as a 'negative-decadent force' and regarded them as 'under control' and, initially at least, as a less serious threat than the

---

[37] Schmidt M. 1993: 61–2.
[38] Ross G. C. 2000: 89.
[39] Ibid., 76–8; Wagner B. 1995: 71–2; Süß W. 1996: 24–5.
[40] MfS ZA, HA XXII, no. 17625, 'Einschätzung', 1987, pp. 120–21.
[41] Ibid., 125–6.
[42] MfS ZA, JHS, no. 21598, 1989, p. 78. Our translation.

punks. The greater tolerance afforded the skinheads was determined in part by the overlap between the martial and authoritarian values of ministry staff and many of the skinheads. In a letter of 7 July 1986 to the leaders of service units, Mittig stressed that political-operational measures against negative-decadent young people should focus on punks.[43] Given the rudimentary organisation and the low number of skinheads – about 38 groupings and approximately 800 skinheads in December 1987[44] – the MfS and the Criminal Police were not unduly concerned about the skinhead problem. In an assessment of youth crime between 1984 and 1986, the Criminal Police reported little evidence of the spread of neo-Nazi ideas and the glorification of fascism.[45]

THE ZIONSKIRCHE INCIDENTS

The security forces' complacency would be shaken by the growing politicisation of sections of the skinhead scene and then shattered by the Zionskirche incidents on the night of 30 October 1987. About 30 well-inebriated skinhead extremists, after attending the FC Union and Lok Leipzig football match and the birthday celebrations of one of the GDR's most militant extremists, Ronny Busse, attacked visitors at an evening rock and punk concert at the run-down church in the Prenzlauer Berg district of East Berlin. One of their goals was to exact revenge on the punks for alleged insults on the previous day at a youth centre in the capital. Screaming 'Sieg Heil!', 'Jewish pigs!', 'Stasi bastards!' and 'skinhead power!' and singing the Horst Wessel song, the yobs attacked members of the audience with bottles and bicycle chains before, outnumbered, they were repulsed by punks. The police did not respond until several emergency calls alerted local police stations to the brawl. By the time the patrol cars arrived, the violence had ended and it was not deemed necessary for the police to take further action. Among the skinheads from West Berlin was André Riechert, whose father was a Stasi officer with responsibility for combating right extremism.[46] The clash at the Zionskirche was not an isolated incident. A few days later, skinheads from Veltin and Oranienburg demolished a restaurant in Veltin and beat up guests.[47] While the Stasi had been taking a keener interest in skinheads since 1986, their brutal behaviour at the Zionskirche finally prompted SED and Stasi leaders into a concerted campaign against skinheads. The authorities were most

---

[43] The letter is printed in Süß W. 1996: 69.

[44] MfS ZA, HA XXII, no. 17625, 'Einschätzung', 1987, p. 139. The Stasi estimated that there were 350 skinheads and 200 sympathisers in East Berlin in 1987 compared to 80 persons in 1986 and 50 in 1985.

[45] MfS ZA, HA IX, no. 772, 'Information', p. 89.

[46] See MfS ZA, HA IX, no. 1588, 'Urteil. In Namen des Volkes!', pp. 29–49; also Hockenos P. 1993: 79–80; Waibel H. 1996: 56–7.

[47] Madloch N. 2000: 74.

anxious, however, that the right extremist character of the militants was concealed under the cloak of charges of excessive hooliganism.

SMASHING THE SKINHEADS

The files of the MfS, the Criminal Police, the Ministry of the Interior and the SED amply demonstrate the authorities' determination to erase the skinhead problem. On 11 November 1987, all MfS Regional Administrations were instructed by Kienberg, the head of Main Department XX, to compile comprehensive reports on all known skinheads.[48] Main Departments IX and XX played a key role in coordinating the plethora of countermeasures: the identification of the ring leaders and the militant skins; the initiation of preliminary criminal proceedings; the deportation of skinheads to the West; and tighter restrictions on the entry into the GDR of Western skinheads and well-known neo-Nazis. Some of the main Zionskirche offenders were brought to trial before an invited audience in order to demonstrate the state's determination to deal with 'trouble-making yobs' and as a warning to others. In the case of the first four offenders tried before the district court in East Berlin, the original sentences of between one and two years imposed in December 1987 were increased to between one-and-a-half and four years' imprisonment. The decision to increase the sentences, especially that against Busse, was influenced by public indignation,[49] and was agreed between Krenz and the State Prosecutor, Günter Wendland. Permission to publish details of the harsher sentences in a press release was secured from Honecker.[50] A subsequent trial in January 1988 of a further eight perpetrators brought sentences of between one year and three months and three years.

The crackdown was tightened several notches with the Politbüro decision on 2 February 1988 to tackle 'anti-socialist manifestations' among the country's youth.[51] This was underlined by Mittig's highly confidential letter of the same day concerning further measures to suppress 'rowdiness' among young people with neo-fascist views.[52] The determination to stamp out skinhead violence and expressions of right extremism quickly led to the arrest of skinheads for the desecration of Jewish cemeteries in East Berlin and elsewhere, for assaults on African contract workers in Dresden and Halle and for painting graffiti on the walls of the Sachsenhausen concentration camp. Between late November 1987 and July 1988, 49 skinheads were sentenced in nine separate trials.[53]

---

[48] Kienberg's circular is printed in Süß W. 1996: 74–7.

[49] MfS ZA, HA IX, no. 1588, 1987, p. 12.

[50] See Wendland's letter to Krenz on 4 December 1987 in MfS ZA, HA IX, no. 9875, pp. 3, 5–6.

[51] MfS ZA, JHS, no. 21433, 1989, p. 13.

[52] Süß W. 1996: 87.

[53] Hockenos P. 1993: 84; Waibel H. 1996: 56–8; Ross G. C. 2000: 137–8.

The 'show trials' were accompanied by a media campaign, which the MfS had belatedly concluded was essential for combating right extremism. For example, the *Neue Berliner Illustrierte* magazine ran a lengthy feature on five teenagers who, between January and March 1988, had damaged 222 gravestones in the Jewish cemetery in East Berlin's Schönhauser Allee. They were sentenced to between two-and-a-half and six-and-a-half years' imprisonment. Following the regime's standard interpretation, their distorted ideology with its fascist-like elements was attributed to West German TV and radio programmes.[54] Despite the recognition of the need for an improved coverage in the media of the problem of skinhead militancy, this kind of reporting highlights the SED's reluctance to allow a frank public debate on the causes of right extremism. The party's preferred line was to depict it as a form of serious rowdiness committed by anti-social elements. The Stasi, too, adhered to this line. In an appendix to Mittig's letter of 2 February 1988 reference is made to the need for public campaigns, like the show trials, to demonstrate that: 'instances of neo-fascism and nationalism are alien to socialism and the causes are rooted in the imperialist system and it is the influence on individuals of neo-fascist elements from the FRG that give rise to these phenomena in the GDR'.[55] The sooner the militant skinheads were knocked out, so the MfS and the SED calculated, the less would be the damage to the GDR's reputation as a socialist society where the preconditions for the revival of the swastika had been eliminated.

IMs were integral to the battle against right extremism. In December 1987, the MfS East Berlin Regional Administration used 17 agents in operations against skinheads; 60 per cent had been recruited in 1986 and 1987.[56] Their tasks were to identify right extremists and to provide information relating to their links with like-minded persons in the West, their meeting places as well as their organisational structure, goals and actions. Youthful extremists provided the main source of IMs, although the Stasi was averse to recruiting those with firm neo-fascist views. Several dissertations written by Stasi officers as part of their programme of studies at the Stasi Law School in Potsdam provide an invaluable insight into MfS thinking on the recruitment and deployment of 'negative-decadent' IMs.[57] Experience had shown that the young IMs, preferably aged 17 to 25 years, could be recruited by playing on their sense of adventure, expectations of material advantage and the ministry's intervention on their behalf in the courts of law or at work. Commitment to the socialist cause was not expected to be a significant motive, although an appeal to what skinheads regarded as typical German virtues, such as a sense

---

[54] *Neue Berliner Illustrierte*, no. 29, 1988, pp. 28–9.
[55] Süß W. 1996: 96. Our translation.
[56] MfS ZA, HA XXII, no. 17625, 'Einschätzung', 1987, p. 147.
[57] See, for example, MfS ZA, VVS JHS, no. 689/70, 1979, pp. 7–9, 21–2 and MfS ZA, VVS 001/105/79, 1979, p. 21.

of duty, steadfastness and loyalty, was seen as an effective lever. Although some 'negative-decadent' IMs were recruited while in prison, the Stasi was not keen on this route as many terminated the contact after their release. As 'negative-decadent' IMs were regarded as highly unstable and often lacking in self-confidence, good work was to be praised and every effort made to ensure that the IM trusted and respected the authority of the controller. In addition to the danger of the informers' cover being broken by indiscretions on the part of the IMs, the Stasi was also concerned about them becoming involved in violent actions. The IMs, it was appreciated, might be unable to withdraw from scenes of violence as it would attract suspicion and put them at risk. However, they were not expected to initiate violence and they could not be guaranteed blanket immunity from prosecution for certain types of acts, particularly if other members of the group were also imprisoned.

THE SKINHEADS AND RIGHT EXTREMISM

The right extremist potential was a cause for great concern, not only in terms of the rising numbers but also because the embryonic right-extremist ideo-logy threatened to undermine the GDR's self-legitimation as an anti-fascist state. With the quickening of the authorities' interest in skinheads, studies were conducted in the later 1980s by sociologists, the MfS and the Criminal Police which, together with records of interrogations and personal recollections, document the extremists' values and attitudes. By the time of the Zionskirche events, a hybrid of xenophobia, nationalism and anti-communism had begun to take shape. A Stasi internal report of February 1988 points to the centrality of a pronounced German nationalism among skinheads as an antidote to Communism. Germanness (*Deutschtum*) was associated with being strong as well as being productive and disciplined at work. In parenthesis, it should be noted that in East Berlin Germanness sometimes manifested itself in the form of a Prussianism which targeted not only foreigners but Saxons and Mecklenburgers too. Skinheads were highly critical of the poor work dis-cipline and wastage in the state socialist economy as can be seen in the statement by one skinhead that: 'I go to work regularly and am of the opinion that I am industrious and do good work. That is the thing which marks out a genuine skin[head]. I belong to a group where every member acts just like that. On the whole, we are industrious and cannot stand shirkers and parasites at work'.[58] On the other hand, not all skinheads were dedicated workers. The report of the Criminal Police in the Cottbus region noted, as part of a preliminary criminal investigation involving eight skinheads, that most missed shifts and performed badly at work and in their apprentice collectives.[59] As one skinhead stated:

---

[58] Cited in Kinner K. and Richter R. 2000: 280–81.
[59] MfS ZA, HA IX, no. 1278, 'Auswertungsbericht', 6 May 1988, p. 2.

I didn't like going to work. In November/December 1987 I didn't turn up for work for about two weeks. I usually slept at [name blacked out]'s house and he didn't have an alarm clock and didn't go to work either. So I stayed in bed like him.[60]

While some skinheads acknowleged that life in the GDR was relatively secure, the Stasi realised that most of them supported German unification and the restoration of a powerful German Reich within the borders of 1937. They admired the discipline, order and national pride allegedly prevalent in the Third Reich as well as the heroism of German soldiers during the Second World War. The skinheads' views were by no means uniform: whereas some glorified fascism and the concentration camps, others rejected the crimes of fascism and the launching of world war.[61] One 21-year-old skinhead hailed Hitler and Goebbels as 'great personalities' but criticised the Second World War as 'senseless'.[62]

The militant skinheads' feverish nationalism was combined with a visceral dislike of foreigners, who were accused of bringing AIDS into the GDR, living comfortably at the expense of East Germans, treating German women as prostitutes and depriving the local people of consumer items. The escalation of the number of contract workers from 1986 onwards fuelled the extremists' prejudices and prompted brutal attacks like that on a Mozambican in Halle, for which five youths were sentenced in April 1988.[63] One skinhead told the Cottbus police that:

There is a whole housing complex with negroes and a house full of Poles in Hoyerswerda. If these people weren't there everybody in Hoyerswerda would have a flat, which is not the case just now. I am in favour of violence against foreigners. Somebody has just got to chuck them out. We skinheads feel it is our job to do it.[64]

An apprentice at the lignite works in Jänschwalde was equally extreme in his views: 'And what's more, negroes rape our girls and women and the Poles buy everything there is in our shops'.[65] Homosexuals and Jews were rejected as 'non-German'. Under police cross-examination, one skinhead claimed that during the Third Reich communists and socialists should have been gassed or shot like the Jews.[66] However, while not all skinheads approved of the mass

---

[60] MfS ZA, HA IX, no. 1278, 'Vernehmungsprotokoll', 18 February 1988, p. 78. Our translation.
[61] MfS ZA, HA XXII, no. 17625, 'Einschätzung', 1987, p. 142 and MfS ZA, HA IX, no. 1278, 'Auswertungsbericht', 1988, p. 3.
[62] MfS ZA, HA IX, no. 1278, 'Befragungsprotokoll', 30 December 1987, p. 83.
[63] Madloch N. 2000: 86.
[64] MfS ZA, HA IX, no. 1278, 'Befragungsprotokoll', 7 April 1988, p. 118. Our translation.
[65] MfS ZA, HA IX, no. 1278, 'Befragungsprotokoll', 3 March 1988, p. 106. Our translation.
[66] MfS ZA, HA IX, no. 1278, 'Auswertung', 6 May 1988, p. 4.

murder and persecution of Jews, the antipathy towards homosexuals was widespread among the eight Cottbus skinheads interrogated by the police. Prejudices abounded: 'cannot stand such people', 'an affront to the honour of a German', and 'make little attempt to practise normal sexuality and have female mannerisms'.[67]

A SOCIAL PROFILE

Who were the right extremists? As skinhead violence escalated from the mid-1980s onwards, the SED, the MfS and other authorities drew on a variety of sources, including materials emanating from the Criminal Police, the Central Institute for Youth Research and the Humboldt University, in order to obtain a differentiated social profile of the skinheads, punks and other negative groups. Of particular importance are the reports drawn up by two sociologists at the Humboldt University, Loni Niederländer and Gunhild Korfes. The reports were commissioned by the head of the Main Department of the Criminal Police, Nedwig, with the knowledge of the Stasi.[68] Although the findings were not GDR representative, they do at least provide some indications of the age, gender, educational attainment, occupation and family background of the extremists. Gordon Ross's judgement that the right-wing groups largely consisted of 'children of the regime' and that they did not come from a deprived family background[69] seems to be borne out by the Criminal Police and Humboldt data.

The project for the Criminal Police and the Stasi was based on 596 persons who had been involved in criminal proceedings as well as almost 2,000 transcripts of the questioning of the accused and witnesses in the period October 1987 to November 1989.[70] Based on data from several regions, the social profile of the militants reads (in per cent): pupils 4, apprentices 24, partly qualified skilled workers 4, skilled workers 50, technical college students 2, and those without an occupation 14. The conclusion reached by the researchers in 1989 was that all strata and classes in society were represented and that the level of qualification, family status and general circumstances corresponded to a cross-section of society. If it also recalled that the skinheads were usually held in high regard by their work collectives, advocated a 'German' work ethic and believed that service in the National People's Army was integral to 'Germanness',[71] then the thesis that they were children of the GDR has much to commend it.

---

[67] See the various documents in MfS ZA, HA IX, no. 1278, March–April 1988, pp. 106, 138, 149.

[68] See Süß W. 1996: 34, 52 and MfS ZA, HA XXII, no. 18438, p. 52.

[69] Ross G. C. 2000: 106.

[70] Kinner K. and Richter R. 2000: 273, 279–80.

[71] Süß W. 1996: 24.

The Stasi and the SED were unhappy with the notion of 'normality'. After all, what should not exist in an anti-fascist state could not exist. This is apparent from a report compiled by an officer of Main Department XXII shortly after the Zionskirche incident: 'The occurrence of skinheads in the GDR is the result of the increased attention given to their behaviour in the Western media. This is done mainly with the aim of turning young people against socialist society'.[72] MfS materials – Law School theses, transcripts of interrogations, operational case records and situation analyses – searched for a scapegoat in the lack of positive parental influence. An assessment in 1989 by Main Department IX referred to the break-up of families and inadequate upbringing at home as one of the main factors behind a 'flawed development'.[73] Indeed, if the empirical data on the biographies of skinheads who came into conflict with the authorities and were subject to a Stasi preliminary enquiry are taken into account, there is reason to qualify the 'our children' thesis which emerges from the Niederländer and Korfes data. Likewise, the Stasi assessment mentioned above asserted that many skinheads stayed in a job in order to avoid possible penal measures regarding unsocial behaviour and that therefore they were merely keeping up the pretence of working.[74]

THE STASI FRUSTRATED

The repression launched after the Zionskirche events was only a partial success. Militants were forced to go underground and into the security of their own apartments.[75] However, this was only a tactical retreat and numbers began to rise once more. In October 1988, the MfS estimated that there were 1,067 skinheads. Of these, 42.7 per cent were located in East Berlin, 11.5 per cent in Potsdam and 8.4 per cent in Leipzig.[76] The militants devised their own countertactics. They placed more of their followers in organisations like the Society for Sport and Technology and a radicalisation of the scene was marked by the emergence of the fascos, a term first coined in 1986.[77] The fascos, a strand of the more extremists skinheads, operated in small, highly disciplined clandestine groups of between six and twelve members, imposed strict membership criteria and met several times per week to discuss aims and beliefs. As their name suggests, they were committed to National Socialist ideology. Hitler's *Mein Kampf* was one of their main texts and for some, like Hasselbach, prison constituted a training ground in fascist ideology under the

---

[72] MfS ZA, HA XXII, no. 17625, 'Referat', 1987, p. 16. Our translation.

[73] MfS ZA, HA IX, no. 10712, 'Thesen', 1989, p. 19.

[74] MfS ZA, HA XXII, no. 17625, 'Referat', 1987, p. 17.

[75] Süß W. 1996: 100.

[76] Kinner K. and Richter R. 2000: 78.

[77] On the fascos, see Hasselbach I. 1996: 60; Wagner B. 1995: 65–6; Ross G. C. 2000: 122; Madloch N. 2000: 76; Siegler B. 1991: 619; Hockenos P. 1993: 89.

guidance of fellow prisoners with National Socialist leanings. More ideologically focused than the skinheads, they advocated the establishment of Germany as a world power, the use of concentration camps for leftists, homosexuals, anti-social and subversive elements in general, punishment for sexual relations with 'non-Aryans', and the destruction of the 'unworthy life' of the physically and mentally 'handicapped'. Although they often aped Hitler by wearing their hair with a parting down the side, they were less conspicuous in outward appearance than the skinheads. The fascos were dedicated to the violent overthrow of the GDR and did not hesitate to impose harsh disciplinary measures against recalcitrant members.[78]

The MfS lamented that its societal partners, especially the schools and the Free German Youth organisation, had palpably failed to implement measures to stem the extremist problem,[79] a failure which was linked to the alienation of so many young people in the later 1980s. The Stasi, as a secret police and agent of coercion, was hardly in a position to act as an educator, and it could not compensate for deficiencies among the other agents of social control. This frustration was expressed by one MfS officer in East Berlin who was responsible for preliminary criminal proceedings: 'Combating this phenomenon cannot be the sole task of the investigative organisations. It is a task that can only be tackled by the whole of society and with the involvement of all education providers'.[80]

Why then did right extremism manifest itself in a state which claimed through the deNazification measures of the late 1940s and the early 1950s and through the establishment of a new socialist order to have removed the preconditions for fascism? The Stasi clung doggedly to the thesis that right extremism was inspired by the political-diversionary strategy of the Western adversary, especially among East Germany's negative and decadent elements. The Western mass media, together with personal contacts at major sports events in towns like East Berlin and Potsdam, were regarded as important channels of Nazi ideas. In accordance with this perception, the MfS kept a careful watch on actual and potential links between East German extremists and West German neo-Nazis, including groups like the Nationalist Front and the Viking Youth. It calculated that in 1987 131 skinheads paid visits to the GDR from West Berlin and mixed with their East German counterparts at football matches and in pubs.[81] However, by the beginning of 1988, the MfS had been unable to uncover anything other than loose contacts between East and West. One officer, Torsten Roß, in a detailed analysis of the activities of Western neo-Nazi and groups, such as the Viking Youth and the National Democratic Party, in 1986 and 1987, failed to find any elaborate network of

---

[78] Siegler B. 1991: 619; Hockenos P. 1993: 89.
[79] Süß W. 1996: 29–30.
[80] Cited in ibid., 49–50. Our translation.
[81] Madloch N. 2000: 81.

group and personal contacts in the GDR. Acts of militancy in the GDR, he concluded, stemmed primarily from imitating West German neo-Nazis via the Western mass media.[82]

The 'import' thesis – as applied to skinheads, punks and heavy metals – had already been undermined in the sociological report compiled by Niederländer. In her opinion, the thesis 'encourages the inclination to feel powerless in the face of the problem. It reduces the readiness to invest energy in tackling the problem'.[83] The Stasi made some minor amendments to the standard interpretation, in particular by developing the notion of 'negative-decadent' individuals whose chequered family, educational and occupational biographies made them responsive to Western political-ideological diversion. The sources of maladjustment of the socially 'deformed' youth were identified as 'relics' from Germany's imperialist past, deficiencies in the upbringing of children and the negative influence of peers.[84] Some Stasi officers expressed reservations about aspects of official paradigms. Torsten Gruhn, for example, regretted the failure to analyse the social and political character of the skinhead problem and drew attention in his dissertation to the failures of parents, teachers and police. Schools and parents were too passive, the Free German Youth was insensitive to the special needs of young people, the police were baffled as regards appropriate countermeasures, and the population at large was becoming increasingly fearful.[85]

But the MfS, too, was part of the problem for not only did the ministry's hostility to the alien and 'exotic other' feed prejudices but its own authoritarian structures and mentalities provided a normative underpinning for the very extremists it sought to destroy. As Süß has pointed out, while the approach developed by scholars such as Heitmeyer, which seeks to locate right extremism in the problems and risks associated with modernisation and individualisation, may not be salient for the less developed GDR, nevertheless his emphasis on an unscrupulous willingness to use force and the ideology of inequality as constituent elements of right extremism does seem to have some purchase.[86] Intolerance, repression, intimidation and force were part and parcel of the socialisation of young people in the GDR, as expressed in the paramilitary Society for Sport and Technology, the use of military toys, the friend–foe dichotomy and the segregation of foreign contract workers. Military service was also proclaimed as a duty and, as one skinhead stated, 'I was able to improve my physical fitness because during military service sport is one of the most important activities'.[87] Furthermore, while it cannot be denied that punitive deNazification measures in East Germany were

---

[82] MfS ZA, JHS, no. 21169, 1988, pp. 24–5, 76, 101.
[83] MfS ZA, HA XXII, no. 17625, 'Information', p. 62. Our translation.
[84] MfS ZA, HA IX no. 1278, 'Befragungsprotokoll', 30 December 1987, p. 82.
[85] MfS ZA, JHS, no. 21463, 1989, pp. 52–3; also Ross G. C. 2000: 27, footnote 3.
[86] Süß W. 1996: 5–7, 40–42.
[87] MfS ZA, HA IX, 'Befragungsprotokoll', 27 April 1988, p. 101. Our translation.

comprehensive and that the GDR's self-portrayal as an anti-fascist state enjoyed considerable popular resonance, the 'reckoning' with Nazism and nationalism remained highly flawed. The SED still clung to the 1935 Comintern's outmoded and economistic definition of fascism as 'the open terroristic dictatorship of the most reactionary, most chauvinistic and most imperialistic elements of finance capital'. And likewise the straitjacket of Marxism-Leninism impeded a searching analysis and open discussion of nationalism and nationality. The SED's propagation in the late 1980s of a 'socialism in the colours of the GDR' merely compounded the problem as it was primarily designed to ward off the reformist impulses emanating from the Soviet Union and Poland and was totally inadequate in its efforts to persuade East Germans of the superiority of GDR-style socialism over the capitalism of its West German sibling. In addition, as members of a relatively closed society, GDR citizens enjoyed limited opportunities to acquaint themselves with other nationalities and cultures and to develop a mutual tolerance and understanding.

Part VI

WOLF'S ESPIONAGE EMPIRE

Chapter 12

THE MISSION AND STRUCTURE OF FOREIGN INTELLIGENCE

INTRODUCTION

Thanks in part to the publicity skills of Markus Wolf and to its victories on the 'invisible front', the Main Administration for Reconnaissance (*Hauptverwaltung Aufklärung* – HV A) has been semi-heroicised as a remarkably efficient and professional espionage service. Its role in the fall of Chancellor Willy Brandt, the recruitment of Bonn's lonely 'secretaries' by 'Romeo' agents, and most significantly of all, its penetration of the highest levels of West German society and politics have aroused widespread public interest. However, HV A's aims and objectives were not confined to the procurement of intelligence.[1] As an arm of the omnipresent Ministry of State Security, HV A also coordinated its actions with the Stasi's 'domestic' departments in rooting out opposition to SED rule, both in the GDR and in West Germany. Not only did HV A organise its actions on both sides of the inter-German border with other MfS units, their common mission as the 'sword and shield' of the SED regime was also determined by the thesis of political-ideological diversion (PID). As discussed in Chapter 8, this posited that the origins of opposition to the communist system came essentially from beyond its own borders, not least from the alleged role of the Western secret services.

In recognition of HV A's key role in maintaining SED rule, foreign intelligence left its offices in the Ministry of Foreign Affairs in 1953, re-housing itself in the Ministry of State Security under the leadership of Markus Wolf, who would achieve notoriety as one of the Cold War's most successful spymasters. These observations are not in themselves new, although the subject tended to be avoided by 'serious' academics who saw the topic as a Cold War minefield best left to the realm of the media and a number of specialist journalists. What has changed is the access to the documentation, which can support an investigation of HV A's structure, function and methods. This

---

[1] HV A's role in the circumvention of the West's embargo on high technology is examined in Chapter 8.

chapter will look at the role of HV A in both its intelligence and state security capacities, while the focus in the following chapter is on operations against West Germany, the subject of the SED's greatest fears for its continued survival as an independent state. Before looking at the latter, however, it is necessary to assess HV A's methods of working, location within the SED's power structures and relations with the parent service, the KGB.

THE STRUCTURE AND STRATEGY OF EAST GERMAN ESPIONAGE

HV A's full-time personnel represented a handpicked elite, carefully selected on account of proven political loyalty and, especially by the 1960s, a higher level of education than their domestic MfS counterparts. In numerical terms, HV A employed 4,744 staff in its central office in East Berlin and its Departments XV in the Regional Administrations in 1989.[2] This constituted an above-average increase of 151 per cent since 1982, when the total strength was 2,973.[3] In addition, there were the officers in the District Service Units, bringing the 1989 total up to about 5,000, of which almost 80 per cent were in HV A itself. The latter's number had grown rapidly since the 500 or so officers in the 1950s and the 1,425 HV A and Department XV staff in 1972. As other sections of the MfS were also involved in intelligence work, then there may have been a grand total of 9,000 to 10,000 MfS staff engaged in foreign espionage related activities. Not only did this exceed the 7,500 staff in West Germany's BND in 1989 but per head of population the foreign intelligence of the GDR easily outstripped the 20,000 employees of America's Central Intelligence Agency (CIA) in the Reagan era.

HV A's mission statement during the Honecker years was set out in two Stasi guidelines, issued in 1968 and 1979, which concur in all crucial areas. In theory, HV A's first priority was to impede the 'imperialist' role of the USA, and its security service the CIA, from endangering the security of the GDR and the Eastern bloc. This meant that HV A's area of operations, known as the *Operationsgebiet*, stretched across the globe from the United States and other NATO countries to the Near East and southern Africa. In practice, however, three-quarters of HV A's foreign operations were conducted against West Germany. Throughout the history of the GDR, the Bonn Republic was constantly regarded as the principal threat to SED rule. In 1973, Wolf informed fellow officers that the FRG was the main operational area as it was 'the centre of almost all hostile activities against the GDR'.[4] And as a KGB directive four years later revealed, the FRG was a major target for all Eastern bloc intelligence activities as it was NATO's main strategic bridgehead and

---

[2] For most of the figures in this paragraph, see Gieseke J. 2001: 201–2.
[3] Gieseke J. 2000: 396.
[4] Cited in Knabe H. 1999: 39.

the leading West European capitalist country both economically and militarily.[5] If the means of ideologically underpinning the legitimacy of communist rule changed from Ulbricht to Honecker, then the principle that secret service activity inside both East and West Germany were inseparably interrelated remained constant. HV A's intelligence gathering had the objective of preventing East Berlin being confronted by threatening surprise developments in West German political, economic and military life. Importantly, the guidelines issued in 1979 also indicate that HV A would work both in the West and in the GDR to 'uncover and expose enemy bases'. In addition, HV A was a key instrument in avoiding the West's embargo on high technology goods. So important was this task that by the late 1980s, economic espionage accounted for a higher proportion of top IMs (39 per cent) than any other area of activity.[6] To achieve these broad objectives, HV A coordinated an extensive network of several thousand IMs in the FRG, which ensured an eastward flow of information from the government in Bonn, its security services and the military, the economy, research centres and grassroots political life. In the Stasi's militaristic jargon the network of IMs in the West was regarded as the 'main weapon' in the fight on the 'invisible front' against communism's adversaries.

Considerable confusion surrounds the number of agents, especially West German citizens, who worked for the Stasi. Hubertus Knabe, a former researcher in the Gauck Authority, estimates that 20,000 to 30,000 worked in the FRG in the period after the founding of the MfS in 1950, not simply as casual sources of information but as fully fledged agents.[7] This is not easy to verify as HV A records are incomplete on account of the shredding and destruction of most HV A files in late 1989 and early 1990. Indeed, Christopher Andrew has pointed out that historians remain ignorant of what they do not know.[8] However, data on HV A can be found in the files of other Main Departments of the MfS. These materials, together with information from HV A's own SIRA (System der Informationsrecherche der Aufklärung) data bank and the availability, albeit restricted, of the 'Rosewood' materials, provide a relatively accurate picture of the activities and structures of HV A. The SIRA records were decoded painstakingly by employees at the Gauck Authority and contain short reports on the work of HV A's foreign agents between 1969 and 1987.[9] The 'Rosewood' materials contain the cover and the true names of HV A's Western agents which the CIA acquired in 1990 as part of a top secret coup named 'Operation Rosewood' and passed on in CD-ROM format to Germany in 2000–2002. The 'Rosewood' data indicate that at the end of 1988 1,553 West Germans were working for HV A. Other sources,

---

[5] Andrew C. and Gordievsky O. 1992: 39.
[6] Müller-Enbergs H. 1998: 196.
[7] Knabe H. 2000: 10.
[8] Andrew C. 1997: 23.
[9] http://www.trend.partisan.net/trd7889/t077899.html

such as the investigations of the Federal Public Prosecutor, point to roughly the same number of agents in the West who worked for the Stasi's domestic units and the army's military intelligence arm.[10] A sample of about 500 Western IMs who have been prosecuted since 1990 reveals that about one-third had a university qualification, that they had served the MfS for about 15 years and that the average age at the time of recruitment was 31 years.[11] Of the 1,533 West Germans who worked as IMs for HV A in December 1988, men outnumbered women by 72 per cent to 28 per cent.[12] In addition to its Western agents, HV A may have used approximately 10,000 GDR citizens as IMs.[13]

At the time of the collapse of SED rule, HV A's leadership was headed by Werner Großmann and a staff of four major generals and a colonel, who took responsibility for formulating and coordinating working methods.[14] HV A's functions were divided across its Department XV in each of the Regional Administrations with responsibility for special targets in the West German *Länder*, and the 21 Departments at the centre, each of which subdivided into desks (*Referate*) dealing with the procurement and evaluation of intelligence, logistics and administration. A number of working groups were also used to coordinate specific tasks, such as securing IM networks in West Germany. The main role of these desks can be given in overview according to the following categories. HV A's 'political' operations against the West German government, the state apparatus, the political parties and related organisations were conducted by Departments I and II. The *Zersetzung* or decomposition of organisations and individuals hostile to SED rule by means of disinformation was the task of Department X. Among its many activities were the efforts to undermine the public reputation of politicians such as Rainer Barzel of the CDU and Herbert Wehner of the SPD. Economic and technical espionage was conducted by the Scientific and Technical Section (SWT) and Departments V and XIII to XV. Military espionage in the FRG was carried out by Department IV, with specific operations against NATO and the European Community coming under Department XII.[15] Counterespionage operations against the West German and other states' security and intelligence agencies, such as the BND and the CIA, were undertaken by the large Department IX. The intelligence materials obtained by HV A were evaluated by Department VII, while the technological development of the equipment used in espionage was the role of Department VIII.

---

[10] Gieseke J. 2001: 202–3; Müller-Enbergs H. 1998: 39–40.

[11] Frank R. 2002: 123.

[12] Müller-Enbergs H. 1998: 152.

[13] Ibid., 142.

[14] On the organisational structure of HV A, see Wiedmann R. 1995: 364–71, and Fricke K. W. 1997: 19–20.

[15] On military intelligence carried out by the National People's Army which was subordinate to that of the MfS, see Kabus A. 1993.

The only branches concentrating on intelligence operations in the wider world were Departments X and III. The former dealt with the USA, Canada and Mexico and while it targeted the White House and the Pentagon for infiltration by its agents, American installations and forces in West Germany were its primary focus. Department III, which concentrated on residents in the Third World and Western countries other than the FRG and the USA, ran its own IMs in these states, including three academics in the UK.[16] HV A had its own training school, in Gosen, which as an autonomous branch of the Law School in Potsdam had the right to award degrees. Its head was Colonel Professor Dr Bernd Kaufmann. HV A was also organisationally anchored at regional level in the MfS's administrative structure. Department XV in the Regional Administrations were responsible for penetrating a West German region, carrying out in total some one-third of all HV A operations in the field. They were able to take decisions relating to the recruitment and running of IM networks in the FRG.[17] The Regional Administrations used liaison officers to coordinate work from the Stasi's local branches as and when required. What this organisational structure primarily indicates is the concentration of HV A's operations against 'them over there', the 'other' German state.

WHO DID WHAT?

Some 70 per cent of HV A officers were primarily 'desk soldiers', who concerned themselves with the planning and organisation of intelligence operations proper. The remaining 30 per cent were involved in carrying out missions and running agents.[18] Although HV A's official guidelines placed most of its agents under the general category of IM, it remains possible to delineate a basic classification of types and a hierarchy from the organisation's elite troops of full-time staff in positions of extensive responsibility down to those on the periphery of the organisation. At the apex of the agent hierarchy stood the classic moles, the 'O-sources' (*Objektquellen*) and 'A-sources' (*Abschöpfenquellen*).[19] The former, who included Dr Gabriele Gast and Günter Guillaume, were the top-flight sources or agents who had access to classified information in key areas of West German politics and society and numbered 449 in December 1988. A-sources were directed to 'cream off' information from key personages without their knowledge. One example is the cultivation of the then up-and-coming politician Helmut Kohl by

---

[16] Müller-Enbergs H. 1998: 209–10.
[17] See the document from the Leipzig Regional Administration of 6 September 1989 in Sélitrenny R. and Weichert T. 1991: 261–4.
[18] Fricke K. W. 1997: 19.
[19] On the classification and functions of these two types, see Müller-Enbergs H. 1998: 39–47.

the long-serving agent Hans-Adolf Kanter ('Fichtel'). There were 133 such IMs in 1988. Some, but not all, of these top agents were also Officers on a Special Assignment (OibEs). These were individuals who had to be resistant to the overtures of 'enemy' agents on whose territory they operated. For this reason, OibEs were selected on the basis of strict political as well as professional qualities. Politically, they had to have 'proven loyalty' to the SED and 'solidarity' with the Stasi; professionally, they had to be capable of operating independently abroad, in the so-called area of operations. About 50 per cent of the ministry's OibEs in the 1960s and about 33 per cent in the late 1980s were run by HV A.[20] Their operational importance is reflected in the fact that either Mielke or Wolf had to sanction their use. Furthermore, they remained secret even within the ranks of the Stasi's wider staff; to ensure this, they were run directly by the relevant heads of a Department. These were lone-wolf fighters of singular importance to East German espionage. However, in order to moderate any 'male vices', which may have drawn unwanted attention, they often worked as part of a married couple espionage unit.[21] These elite agents were above all found in East German institutions, which cultivated political, diplomatic or trade relations with West Germany. Their 'special missions' included long-range operations, such as working their way into positions of importance in West German political and economic life; perhaps the classic example of an OibE who was also an 'O-source' is Günter Guillaume, the spy in Chancellor Willy Brandt's Federal Chancellery.

SUB-CATEGORIES OF IMs

The following four sub-categories of IMs were in reality intelligence service professionals, a term beloved by the Stasi, with important functions in the espionage apparatus.[22] Residents, as the name suggests, had legal residence in the Operation Area either as an employee of the East German quasi-diplomatic missions, a cultural institution or a trading company based there. In 1988, HV A and its Departments XV had over 32 residents in the FRG. Residents were capable of independently running agent networks and evaluating the intelligence obtained. They often worked with trainees, who carried out technical measures and maintained contacts with an agent. Secondly, the role of FIMs or controlling IMs was similar, in that they also had legal residence in the Operation Area; however, they supervised only individual IMs or sources. Efforts to extend the agent network were undertaken by

---

[20] Müller-Enbergs H. 1998: 100.
[21] Schlomann F. W. 1984: 11–13.
[22] See Müller-Enbergs H. 1998: 48–102; Schmeidel J. 1995: 141–3; Schell M. and Kalinka W. 1991: 180–81; Gill D. and Schröter U. 1991: 86–7.

recruitment IMs who identified and recruited suitable persons. In universities, for example, recruitment was done by an IM whose objective was to gain a foothold among the rising generation of the West German elite, who might later become politicians and journalists. Finally, West German citizens recruited with the ultimate aim of moving them into useful positions were known as long-range agents. The Stasi's headquarters in Berlin's Normannenstrasse also dispatched controllers to relay their directives and to ensure they were carried out. These agents crossed the border as East German citizens, but once conducting their mission they could also assume false identities, working as so-called 'illegals'. In their dealings with important IMs, whom Stasi headquarters wanted to run directly, it was essential that they were capable of making decisions on the spot.

The HV A apparatus was supplemented by a wide range of IMs who were recruited from either East or West German citizens. Some were involved in the support networks which facilitated the intelligence work proper. These included: couriers, who passed on information, technical equipment and money; so-called border IMs, who smuggled persons and materials over the border; radio operators, who transmitted information between headquarters and the active operatives; and investigators, who placed persons under observation or obtained information essential for particular operations. This support network was reinforced by other collaborators, who provided addresses for mail, the use of telephones, 'safe houses', and pick-up points for collecting information and materials. Contact persons were defined as persons who were not officially registered as IMs, but were receptive to the overtures of an officer or an 'A-source' who was in regular contact with them. Frequently, they were motivated by a belief that their discussions played a small part in reducing international tensions. Often on the political left, a classic area for approaching and using contact-persons was in the West German peace movement of the early 1980s.[23] 'Influence agents', who used their political or social position to disseminate pro-Eastern bloc propaganda, also belonged to the Stasi's wider work in the West; they ranged from university lecturers to the broader reach of media commentators and politicians. A final category of IM remains to be mentioned: the so-called 'sleeper'. As part of the Stasi's intentions to conduct acts of sabotage behind enemy lines in the event of an East-West crisis, most probably a war, these 'sleepers' would be reactivated as a fifth column to break 'enemy' resistance and conduct sabotage. The role of the last two categories has recently been further detailed by the revelations of the Mitrokhin archive, a collection of top-secret KGB records smuggled out of Russia by the eponymous archivist.[24]

---

[23] On the use of contact persons in the peace movement, see Sélitrenny R. and Weichert T. 1991: 196–200.
[24] Andrew C. and Mitrokhin V. 1999.

RECRUITMENT AND TRAINING OF INTELLIGENCE OFFICERS

HV A's full-time staff were selected and approached by officers; it was not possible to offer one's services. In order to ensure the loyalty of HV A agents, the second generation of intelligence personnel was increasingly drawn from the families of the SED apparatus, and this was reinforced by the stipulation that they had no contact with any relatives in the West.[25] Nevertheless, the probationary period remained protracted. Prospective operatives were frequently identified in their final years at school, serving a spell in the Stasi's Guard Regiment after the higher education which most officers received, before entering HV A. During this trial period, it was normal for the candidate to act as an IM on the home front with steadily increasing responsibilities. Certain former HV A personnel point to how the creation of a secret service social elite reinforced the narrow ideological worldview that opposition to SED rule derived from external influences, and how this prevented the reforms that may have saved the system from collapse.[26] However, the narrow selection criteria among individuals who had a strong ideological affinity with the SED did greatly limit the number of defections to the West.

The qualities looked for in an agent were a belief in espionage's positive role in the 'international class war' and an intellectual flexibility to entice the 'capitalists' who were of interest to HV A. Agents were trained in the craft of espionage in a process lasting up to two years. This could take place either at HV A's training school in Gosen, or on an individual basis in 'safe houses'; some former agents also claim that, instead of formal training, they brought their own experience of life to the intelligence service.[27] The training taught agents how to recognise if they were under observation, how to send radio messages, to arrange clandestine meetings and make dead letter drops, how to respond to arrest and, if necessary, how to live under an assumed identity. Agents were also taught that as few persons as possible should participate in an operation. An important psychological preparation for work in the West was the so-called 'operational regime study', which familiarised agents with everyday life and culture in the country where they were to operate. For agents who crossed the inter-German border, it was also necessary to familiarise them with the border checks so that they showed no fear of apprehension.

The methods used to smuggle agents into West Germany also went through certain identifiable phases. In accordance with the long-term strategy conceived

---

[25] Runge I. and Stellbrink U. 1990: 20.

[26] According to this view, Wolf had come to realise that all opposition did not derive from external influences and that reform was essential. On the other hand, his successor, Großmann, adhered to the ideologically narrow perspective.

[27] Interview with Wolfgang Hartmann on 3 September 1999.

by Markus Wolf, until the construction of the Berlin Wall in 1961, long-range agents, who gradually wormed their way into important positions, were floated in on the tide of refugees from East to West. Thereafter, HV A increasingly smuggled in agents through Austria and other third countries; this process involved the adoption of a false identity, using techniques which also changed over time. During the 1950s and 1960s, agents adopted the identity of another living person, perhaps a German living abroad. It was the introduction of computer traces in the mid-1970s, uncovering important East German spy networks, which necessitated a change of approach. The response was to use the so-called 'doppelgänger combination', whereby West Germans citizen who wanted to live in the GDR, normally for personal reasons, were permitted entry on condition that they re-registered with the police in a city where they were unknown; an HV A agent then assumed their identity. The 1980s also brought a return to the use of agents posing as 'refugees'.[28]

RECRUITMENT AND TRAINING OF WEST GERMAN CITIZENS AS IMs

Identifying and recruiting moles belonged to an intensive and protracted official process. All agents were obliged to identify individuals regarded as potential recruits. If HV A was interested in someone, a number of researchers, acting independently of each other, were set to work uncovering the potential recruit's professional and personal life and any problems (such as debts, discontentment or debauchery) which might facilitate recruitment. As the risk of failure was high, recruits were never drawn from an existing mole's immediate environment; it was not unusual for the whole process to take in excess of two years. Around half of all recruitment pitches among West Germans were made during a visit to the GDR. Potential recruits were approached by undercover agents who posed as kindred spirits, using this as a springboard to sanction some form of cooperation in an area of 'mutual' interest. An effort was made to gain their support, or indeed entrap them, by setting a small, manageable task to be carried out in West Germany. The classic case was purchasing books that were unavailable in East Germany. If these tasks were carried out, and even better if a receipt was signed, the recruitment pitch was made.[29] As a rule, recruits were selected by HV A. However, there was also a small, if occasionally important, number of 'walk in' offers of cooperation. The motivation of 'walk ins' ranged from hostility to West German rearmament and the hopes of reunification during the 1950s

---

[28] Schlomann F. W. 1984: 105, 120; van Bergh H. 1965: 317; Gill D. and Schröter U. 1991: 89.
[29] Schlomann F. W. 1984: 79–81; and for a failure to recruit a British student at Leipzig University, see the *Guardian*, 21 September 1999.

to the more frequent desire for cash payments. Although some of these 'walk ins' proved to be useful, they were rightly treated as unreliable for a number of reasons, such as their materialistic motivation or the risk that they were double agents.[30] One of the more surprising recruiting grounds for IMs was among political prisoners in East German jails. Recruitment was based on providing an opportunity to 'make good' the particular offence 'committed' by working for the intelligence service; an incentive was the prisoner's early release. Although some of these unlikely recruits did work for HV A after being 'bought free' by West Germany, most did not; some even reported what had happened to the authorities in the FRG.[31]

Perhaps the best-known method of recruiting IMs by deception was the use of 'Romeo' agents who seduced secretaries with access to classified materials in Bonn. However, it has become apparent that the use of female 'love commandos' was higher than once thought. Recruitment took place among secretaries and students, often by lavishing attention on the lonely and insecure, dressed up as an appeal to assist 'fatherland and world peace'; many of these women resisted these state-sanctioned calls to join the world's two oldest professions at a stroke.[32] Recruitment by deception was also used in so-called 'false flag' operations in order to obtain information from persons who would otherwise have had no interest in cooperation. Depending on the case, secret service operatives posed as either members of a 'friendly', Western secret service, as politicians of an allied country, or, in economic espionage, as representatives of a rival company. If a potential recruit was of enough importance, an elaborate web of deception could be spun over a lengthy period, sometimes using other moles who had already been recruited in this manner. Perhaps the crudest, but not ineffective, method was blackmail. This form of coercion was applied to both politicians and secret service men, whose unwanted ties to the Stasi were cemented by inducing them to provide information which could incriminate them if they tried to break free from their ties to East Berlin. At least when IMs such as secretaries and researchers were required to copy and pass on classified documents, some training in the ways and means of espionage was given.[33]

Markus Wolf continues to emphasise that HV A was successful in its intelligence operations because it used agents recruited on the basis of ideological commitment to the Communist cause.[34] However, although HV A, at least in the early years, did recruit among Western Marxists and fellow travelling leftists, for example among West German students, this declined along with the Eastern bloc's image in the West. The danger of war in the later

---

[30] Knabe H. 1999: 559; Müller-Enbergs H. 1998: 121–2.
[31] Schlomann F. W. 1984: 72–4.
[32] See *Scotland on Sunday*, 26 September 1999.
[33] For the case of secretaries, see Quoirin M. 1999: 9–12, 79–84.
[34] Wolf interview in *International Herald Tribune*, 22 November 1989.

1970s and early 1980s was another powerful motive. An analysis by the West German intelligence authorities in the early 1990s stressed that economic incentives were much more prominent and ideological motivation much less prevalent than HV A believed to be the case. Already by the 1960s, the pattern of recruitment began to change from ideological motivation to 'false flag' entrapment.[35] It is, however, difficult, as with IMs who worked in the GDR for other departments, to compartmentalise the various motives. As was recognised by HV A, motives were 'bundled together' and subject to fluctuation.[36]

TO CATCH A SPY: HV A IN THE EAST GERMAN POWER STRUCTURES

Since the collapse of the GDR, HV A's former leaders, Wolf and Großmann, along with several more minor figures, have insisted that they belonged to a foreign intelligence service like any other, free from association with the Stasi's domestic repression.[37] These claims, it should be noted, were made against a backdrop of legal proceedings against former HV A officers' role in suppressing domestic opposition to the SED regime and having supplied the KGB with materials endangering the security of the former West German state. The most high-profile of these cases was brought against Markus Wolf. However, a December 1993 conviction for high treason and espionage was overturned by a ruling of the Federal Constitutional Court in May 1995 that former HV A intelligence officers could only be prosecuted for acts committed under West German jurisdiction.[38] In 1990, the protracted public debate and legal preparation that would have been required to ensure a legal basis for conviction were sacrificed to the immediate objective of rapid reunification. Although this became clear to observers at the time, it did not end the Federal Prosecution Service's efforts to prosecute Wolf. A second trial took place in 1997, this time centring on the criminal acts, which accompanied the espionage activities *per se*. As the influential news magazine *Der Spiegel* pointed out, there was now a search for 'blood on Wolf's hands' in order to facilitate his conviction as a 'common criminal' for acts of bribery, corruption, wrongful deprivation of liberty and causing physical injury.[39] Although Wolf received a two-year suspended sentence in May 1997, the ruling largely gave some credence to his claims that these trials were about a 'victors' justice' imposed on the losers in the Cold War.[40] Wolf and his subalterns escaped

---

[35] Schmeidel J. 1995: 135; Sélitrenny R. and Weichert T. 1991: 45.

[36] Müller-Enbergs H. 1998: 134.

[37] Bohnsack G. 1997; Eltgen H. 1995: 8.

[38] Colitt L. 1995: 274.

[39] See the interview with Federal Prosecutor Kay Nehm in *Der Spiegel*, no. 43, 1997, pp. 34–5.

[40] See the interview with Wolf in *Der Spiegel*, no. 18, 1993, pp. 40–54.

imprisonment because the Federal Prosecutors could not prove that he had committed a crime under West German jurisdiction or according to East German law.

RELATIONS WITH THE KGB

The East German foreign intelligence service was set up in 1951 as a carbon copy of the KGB's foreign intelligence wing. However, although all roads to decision making ran through Moscow, the relationship between the KGB and HV A changed from one of strict subordination to a measure of cooperation.[41] Between 1951 and 1952, the fledgling intelligence service was run by a staff of omnipresent Soviet 'instructors'; then, from 1952, a so-called apparatus of 'advisers' was installed throughout the MfS hierarchy. The change was largely symbolic, since the former 'instructors' enjoyed a broadly similar remit. At least until the later 1950s, these 'advisers' regulated the work of all operational departments, even in matters of everyday routine, and trained the apparatus functionaries. Looking back on HV A's relationship with the KGB, Markus Wolf later wrote of the 'domineering role' played by Moscow:

> At first our section chiefs drew up all their plans for work under the watchful eye of these [Soviet] advisers, who followed extremely bureaucratic Soviet methods, which drove us crazy. Besides copying regulations and other papers by hand, we had to spend hours binding them neatly into file folders, a procedure introduced by the Czar's secret police before the Revolution. No one knew the rationale for this procedure, and no one questioned it either.[42]

By around 1960, a landmark stage in this transformation was the dramatic scaling down of the apparatus of 'advisers' to a system run by 32 'liaison officers' in the leadership of the individual sections.[43] With the reduction in the direct Soviet presence, the borders between the Eastern bloc's intelligence services also receded. From the mid-1960s, the Soviet bloc exchanged intelligence information at bi- and multilateral conferences. When the SOUD database came on line in 1979, HV A also benefited from access to information on the international connections between the growing human rights and peace movements, which transcended the East–West and inter-Eastern bloc political divides. However, while Moscow had unlimited access to this information, HV A's use of it was regulated by the KGB.[44] Although the HV A leadership comprised Soviet-trained, communist stalwarts, the relationship was never truly one of trust. The KGB laced the East German security and

---

[41] Important sources for the relationship between the MfS and the KGB include Marquardt B. 1995: 297–331 and Fricke K. W. 1984: 37–46.
[42] Wolf M. 1997: 46.
[43] Engelmann R. 1997: 71.
[44] Schmeidel J. 1995: 129.

intelligence services with 'informal sources', which kept Moscow informed behind their colleagues' backs: this form of spying on 'friends', as the KGB referred to their German counterparts, made this the system of panopticism *par excellence*.

HV A, MfS AND SED

Since 1953, when the foreign intelligence service was organisationally integrated into the MfS, HV A had worked closely with the 'domestic' wing of the Stasi, even though there are indications of resentment and internal boundary disputes, for example, on the part of Main Department II against HV A's growing responsibilities in the 1970s for counterespionage in the GDR.[45] Along with Erich Mielke and the head of the party organisations in the state security services, Wolf and, after his departure in 1986, Großmann sat on the MfS central Collegium. Not only did the guidelines and instructions issued by this body stress HV A's integral role in guaranteeing the security of SED rule but Wolf himself also constantly stressed to his officers the need to work in tandem with the relevant domestic MfS units.[46] This cooperation took the form of a direct involvement in domestic operations and in supplying information gathered by HV A's network of agents in the West on political opposition in the GDR and their external links. The other units of the MfS provided intelligence obtained by post controls, telephone taps and radio signals intercepts.[47] Documentation discovered in Leipzig following the fall of the Berlin Wall also details the activities of HV A's Regional Department XV against the local peace and church-based opposition movements.[48] During the 1980s, foreign intelligence was increasingly called upon in the ultimately vain effort to stem the emigration movement.[49]

Markus Wolf's close personal and political ties, as well as his aptitude and intelligence, made him Moscow's ideal spymaster. Wolf's earliest political socialisation had been in the communist movement. After his father, Friedrich, joined the German Communist Party in 1928, Markus and his younger brother, the eminent East German filmmaker Konrad Wolf, joined the Young Pioneers. The intellectual credentials of the family – Wolf's father was a playwright and doctor – contrasted sharply with the humble origins of Mielke, as did the spymaster's cosmopolitanism with the coarse personality of the minister: beauty and the beast. The Wolf family's commitment to communism was reinforced by their Jewish origins. Wolf has frequently stressed that without the Soviet Union granting his family asylum, they too would have

---

[45] Richter P. and Rösler K. 1992: 69–70.
[46] Fricke F. W. 1997: 22, 25.
[47] Knabe H. 1997: 7–8.
[48] Sélitrenny R. and Weichert T. 1991: 126–32, 218–20.
[49] For details, see Chapter 14.

died in the Holocaust, as other relations did. Having arrived in Moscow in 1934, aged ten, and taking on citizenship five years later, Wolf became one of the few bilingual functionaries of German extraction. In 1943, Wolf was chosen to attend the Comintern's training school, which was engaged in the formation of a small group of top KPD functionaries to run Germany after the defeat of the Third Reich. Wolf's adoption of the Stalinist tenets of unquestioning discipline, undeterred by the purges of the mid-1930s or the Nazi-Soviet Pact of 1939, and his identity as a socialist 'true believer' made him precisely the type of loyal *apparatchik* Moscow required after 1945 to serve in the Eastern European satellite states. Appointed to the nascent East German foreign intelligence service in 1951, Wolf headed HV A from 1956 until his departure in 1986; thereafter, his links with leading KGB figures remained close. If Wolf's reform-communist face of the later 1980s is widely regarded as a mask, then his success as its head goes largely unquestioned. There can, however, be little doubt that Wolf knew precisely what his functions in the communist system required: to act in any manner along with the MfS to preserve SED rule. While the highly urbane and intellectual Wolf stresses the high degree of personal antipathy between himself and Mielke, there is absolutely no reason to believe that their working relationship suffered from this. Wolf's successor, Großmann, a long-serving officer in HV A, was less creative and a more compliant partner for Mielke.[50]

---

[50] Richter P. and Rösler K. 1992: 133–4.

Chapter 13

IN THE OPERATION AREA

PARALLELS BETWEEN THE BND AND HV A

During the early 1990s, Wolf and his former officers claimed that HV A had acted no differently from the West German foreign intelligence service, the BND. Historians of the Stasi have tended to stress the differences while opting to omit the parallels between the actions of the BND and HV A. In contrast to HV A, the BND is presented as a foreign intelligence service protecting a democratic republic using secret service methods within the framework of legality and parliamentary accountability.[1] However, studies of the BND have drawn quite different conclusions, pointing to structural similarities with HV A. Particularly during the early years of the Bonn Republic, the BND's relationship with parliamentary democracy was at best ambivalent. The BND was the only West German authority to have an unbroken line of continuity with the Nazi era. Continuity was particularly pronounced during the Gehlen era (1942–68). Gehlen, the first head of the BND, had headed the Nazis' intelligence apparatus in the East and many of his personnel shared a similar past. The organisation's objectives also remained rooted in the Third Reich's pronounced anti-communism, substituting the organisation's constitutional duty to serve democracy with its own hostility to the West German mainstream left, the Social Democratic Party (SPD) and trade unions. Particularly before the reforms initiated in 1967, hundreds of files were built up on SPD and trade union leaders. Throughout the life of the old Federal Republic, West German citizens' postal correspondence and telephone conversations to and from the GDR, and more generally the Eastern bloc, were randomly monitored. During the 1970s, it is estimated that some 10,000 letters were sent each day for intelligence evaluation by the BND.[2] In theory, the BND had no West German 'unofficial collaborators' on their books; however, in practice, information flowed to the BND from as many as 5,000

---

[1] See, for example, Schell M. and Kalinka W. 1991: 220–22.
[2] Schmidt-Eenboom E. 1993: 59–60; *Der Stern*, no. 47, 1978.

sources, who functioned as *de facto* agents.[3] The extent of the BND's operations against West German citizens led one commentator on the West German foreign intelligence during the 1970s and 1980s to conclude that:

> Exerting influence on the trade-unions, directing the press, infiltrating research institutions, or secret co-operation with the church, was part of the BND's every day activities. In some important areas of society there are more agents employed than salaried staff. In this respect the BND's success is less that it proved itself an efficient foreign intelligence service, than it succeeded in establishing itself, largely undetected, as the fifth power in the state along with the three official state authorities and a genuinely free media.[4]

While there are evident and significant differences between the BND and HV A, especially in terms of the scale of surveillance of their own citizens, the attempt to make a distinction between 'good' spies, who defended democracy, and 'bad' spies, who served communist dictatorships, should not be allowed to go unchallenged.

ESPIONAGE AGAINST WEST GERMANY: THE IMPLICATIONS OF DÉTENTE

The early years of East German espionage against the FRG were conditioned by the Cold War era of open antagonism between the power blocs. In inter-German relations, this was symbolised by the building of the Berlin Wall and the adoption of the Hallstein Doctrine, according to which Bonn would break off diplomatic relations and financial aid with any country recognising the GDR as an independent state. The GDR's isolation from the West accorded well with the worldview of Mielke, who believed that contact with West Germany risked undermining the always fragile legitimacy accorded to SED rule. However, as discussed in earlier chapters, caught between Brezhnev's new direction in foreign policy and the West's desire to reduce international tensions, Ulbricht was ejected as SED leader. His replacement, Erich Honecker, was given the task of addressing détente in its specifically German incarnation: the *Ostpolitik* adopted by the SPD–FDP coalition under Chancellor Willy Brandt. The central tenet of foreign policy in the Honecker era was the achievement and consolidation of international recognition of the GDR, while maintaining sufficient distance from the Federal Republic to prevent a challenge to SED rule from within its own borders. The improvement in inter-German relations had its drawbacks for the SED as the rapid increase in personal contacts across the border was thought to entail the expansion of 'subversive' political contacts and the rise of anti-socialist social forces. In accordance with this East German interpretation of events, not only was HV A called upon to take advantage of official representation in West Germany

---

[3] Schmidt-Eenboom E. 1993: 345–6.
[4] Ibid., 363.

and closer inter-state contacts as a springboard to the further penetration of political and economic life there but its role in the struggle against critics of the SED in the two Germanies received a further boost.[5] The consequence was a stepping up of HV A operations against the FRG and the comprehensive infiltration of West German political and economic life, universities and research institutes, the peace movement and the churches, the military and GDR critics in West Berlin, thus making it one of the strongest foreign intelligence agencies in the world. MfS agents were placed in research units and university departments concerned with GDR research, such as Walter Völkel (IM 'Rosenow') of the GDR Archive of the Free University in West Berlin and Professor Dietrich Staritz (IM 'Erich') of the GDR research centre at the University of Mannheim, as well as in the broader context of East–West relations Peter Heilmann of the Evangelical Academy in West Berlin and Professor Hans-Dieter Jacobsen (IM 'Hoffmann') of the Otto Suhr Institute.[6] Although in the 1970s and 1980s the MfS pursued critics such as Wolf Biermann and Jürgen Fuchs who had found residence in the West, at least it did not carry out the kind of ruthless kidnappings which occurred in the 1950s of critics in West Berlin such as the lawyer Walter Linse and the author Karl Wilhelm Fricke.[7] However, as space does not permit an examination of all these areas, the focus will be on the penetration of nerve centres in the political, economic and security spheres.

PENETRATION OF WEST GERMAN POLITICS: THE GUILLAUME AFFAIR

In 1974, shortly after the Brandt administration's success in implementing its flagship *Ostpolitik*, the Chancellor's personal aid, Günter Guillaume, was exposed as an HV A agent.[8] Guillaume was the classic example of the Stasi-schooled agent, who had been floated into West Germany on the mid-1950s tide of refugees; he worked as part of a husband-and-wife team, which rose through the SPD's ranks from the local Frankfurt-am-Main branch to the Chancellor's inner circle. By 1972, Guillaume relayed detailed information from the Chancellor's Office to East Berlin on *Ostpolitik* and the foreign policy position of West Germany's allies. During Günter Guillaume's four years as a personal assistant to Brandt, his access to top secret domestic and foreign policy materials ensured that he was run directly by Wolf.[9] This was not the

---

[5] Siebenmorgen P. 1993: 125–6.

[6] Knabe H. 1999: 287–94, 344–8, 375–6, 399, 408–9.

[7] Ibid., 305–26.

[8] On the affair, see, among many other accounts, Childs D. and Popplewell R. 1999: 142–3 and Koehler J. O. 1999: 151–63.

[9] On the other hand, a recent examination of SIRA records indicates that the information provided by Guillaume and his wife may not have been as significant as hitherto assumed; see Frank R. 2002: 123.

first time that Brandt had come into the Stasi's gun sights. In the late 1950s, when Brandt was mayor of West Berlin, HV A had tried to bring about his 'political death' in a disinformation campaign labelling today's anti-communist cold warrior as yesterday's fellow travelling Nazi, who had cooperated in the occupation of Norway, where he had lived as an émigré since 1933. Unlike the events of 1974, the earlier attack failed to take out its political target, not least because Brandt's role as an anti-fascist was beyond question.[10]

There is much irony in the situation as MfS machinations in 1972 had helped thwart a CDU/CSU attempt to depose Brandt as chancellor by the constitutional device of a constructive vote of no confidence. A successful vote in the Bundestag would have enabled the CDU candidate, Rainer Barzel, to replace Brandt, and to overturn the social-liberal coalition's *Ostpolitik* and the Eastern Treaties which it was negotiating with the Soviet Union and its allies. At this juncture as Brandt was regarded as the lesser of two evils, the MfS intervened: the CDU deputy Julius Steiner received an advance payment of 50,000 DM via HV A Department II for his vote in favour of Brandt. His vote proved to be crucial as the chancellor only survived by a majority of two.[11] On balance, GDR interests dictated that Brandt was the lesser evil and that his *Ostpolitik* would help deliver international recognition of the GDR.

The fall of Brandt, who resigned after the spy scandal broke, did as much to make the reputation of East German espionage as it did to tarnish the name of West German counterespionage. However, Wolf has presented the un-covering of Guillaume as a significant setback for those 'moderates' in the SED who wanted to reduce East–West tension. According to this argument, top-level insider information on the position of a leadership divided over *Ostpolitik* helped persuade the SED's sceptics that Bonn was serious about the sea change in inter-German relations.[12] As ever, much remains unclear re-garding elite attitudes towards *Ostpolitik*; however, if hardliners in East Berlin welcomed the impact of the spy-scandal, then Moscow, which was a primary beneficiary in the transfer of intelligence, was clearly worried by the anti-spy mania unleashed by the Guillaume affair.[13] Perhaps of greater significance is that Guillaume merely sat on the tip of an espionage network which extended across Bonn and the West German party system.

WEST GERMAN POLITICAL PARTIES

East Berlin attached a high priority to infiltrating the West German federal and regional governments and the state machinery that drove them, as well as

---

[10] 'Suche nach Blut an den Händen', *Der Spiegel*, no. 2, 1997, pp. 32–5.
[11] Knabe H. 1999: 15–16; Richter P. and Rösler K. 1992: 68; Wolf M. 1997: 156.
[12] Wolf M. 1997: 155–6.
[13] Andrew C. and Gordievsky O. 1992: 38.

the parliamentarians, their research and support staff and the wider political parties themselves. HV A showed remarkable aptitude in maintaining a flow of information running eastwards. Although the SPD proved to be more porous than the other major political parties, HV A was able to infiltrate the entire spectrum of West German political life from high politics into the fringe groups. By the late 1990s, over 120 IMs had been identified who worked on behalf of the MfS in the political parties.[14]

A plethora of revelations of political espionage have hit the headlines since the fall of the Berlin Wall. A great blow to the SPD was the discovery that Karl Wienand, a former manager of the party's parliamentary group in Bonn, had spied for the Stasi for 13 years as IM 'Streit'. A long-serving senior party figure, he had been close to both Chancellors Brandt and Schmidt. Another revelation from the ranks of the SPD concerned Kurt Gröndahl, who had been recruited by the MfS as a radical left-wing law student in the mid-1960s, and went on to supply East Germany with a range of sensitive material from the Ministry of Inter-German Affairs. Between 1986 and 1988, his position as a political adviser to the West German permanent representation in East Berlin facilitated the supply of classified materials on Chancellor Kohl's policy towards the GDR.[15] Since 1975, the SPD's Bonn headquarters had also been infiltrated by the secretary Doris Biesenbaum, who, for four years, was privy to all of the party's parliamentary business because of her work in the chief whip's office. Along with her husband, who had recruited her in the early 1970s, she earned some 20,000 DM annually. If ideological inclination reinforced with cash payments helps to explain the motivation of these moles, then the case of Armin Hindrichs (IM 'Taler') is more complex. In 1960, after a long period of imprisonment in East Berlin, Hindrichs agreed to take up residence in West Germany and to infiltrate the SPD. By 1972, Hindrichs was an SPD speaker on foreign policy in the Bundestag, and in 1983 became head of the party's documentation centre. Hindrichs, who was close to Herbert Wehner, had worked for the deputy parliamentary group leaders Horst Ehmke and Norbert Gensel. In 1996, he was sentenced to three years' imprisonment. Both Biesenbaum and Hindrichs were in key positions, able to influence opinion formation and decision making in the party.

Access to the Stasi's files indicates that Hindrichs was not the only former dissident imprisoned in the GDR to collaborate with the Stasi. Wilhelm Borm, a high-profile FDP parliamentarian, similarly converted to communism during a nine-year stretch in Bautzen. After his release in 1960, Borm rapidly rose through the Free Democrats' hierarchy. From the 1960s until his death in 1987, he represented the party on committees dealing with domestic and foreign affairs as well as sitting on a highly selective committee comprising eight deputies who were kept informed of Bonn's treaty negotiations with

---

[14] Knabe H. 1999: 47.
[15] Koehler J. O. 1999: 188–9.

Moscow, Warsaw and East Berlin. Borm was a high profile 'influence agent' who openly advocated reconciliation with the GDR, making many parliamentary speeches and publishing newspaper articles, which had been written by HV A's Department X.[16] Another unlikely recruit by East German espionage was the 'millionaire Marxist' Hannsheinz Porst, who had made his money as an entrepreneur in the mass photography market. Until his unearthing in 1967, Porst used his position in the FDP to establish high-level political and business contacts. The Stasi also succeeded in penetrating the FDP's administrative headquarters in Bonn, the agent's identity, however, remains unknown.[17]

By the late 1980s, infiltration of the CDU/CSU had become a top priority in East Berlin. Although no new names among the Conservatives' senior figures have come to light, the Stasi had amassed materials such as defence committee reports, internal party papers and advance copies of parliamentary reports. Furthermore, a 'second Guillaume' was passing information out of the Federal Chancellery, including preparations for Honecker's visit to the FRG.[18] One interesting revelation is the role of IM 'Zady', who worked for the MfS in West Berlin between 1958 and 1989. 'Zady' had been recruited by the MfS Regional Administration in Dresden in 1954 before taking up his mission to infiltrate the CDU and a wide range of organisations which stood politically close to the party. 'Zady' did this with verve, joining some 25 organisations in addition to the West Berlin CDU; his reports filled 16 files and over 3,962 pages; the final file, from 1988 to 1989, was shredded. In addition to supplying membership lists, documents and situation reports, in 1975 'Zady' successfully penetrated a West Berlin group which planned to assist an engineer from Leipzig to defect; his efforts led to the East German's imprisonment for three years and nine months.[19] An example of 'long-range' agents used against the CDU is that of the Otto brothers. In the early 1970s, Rainer Otto had been recruited by the Stasi and charged with infiltrating the Ministry of Inter-German Affairs. However, failing to make the grade, Rainer recruited his brother, Reinhard, who was a CDU member and adviser on economic affairs to the party's parliamentary group in the North-Rhine Westphalian *Landtag*. In this instance, the Stasi gained access to classified information in addition to that originally intended.[20] The long-serving agent Hans-Adolf Kanter ('Fichtel') was personally acquainted with Kohl from their early days in regional politics and he later served on the political staff of the management of and, as a lobbyist in Bonn, for the vast Flick business conglomerate. The latter positions enabled him to penetrate the secrets of the Flick Affair which broke out in the 1982 over the group's laundering of

---

[16] Knabe H. 1999: 67–70.
[17] Schlomann F. W. 1993: 107, 130; Wolf M. 1997: 114–18; Koehler J. O. 1999: 189–90.
[18] Schlomann F. W. 1993: 108, 112–13, 128.
[19] Informations- und Dokumentationszentrum Berlin 1998: 4.
[20] Koehler J. O. 1999: 190.

contributions since the mid-1970s to the three major political parties in return for tax concessions and other favours.[21]

The rise of the Greens during the 1980s brought with it an increase in HV A's efforts to penetrate the anti-Communist radical left. Dirk Schneider, a member of the party's executive committee and media spokesperson for its Bundestag group in the mid-1980s, had been recruited by HV A in 1975. Schneider's efforts to suppress the Greens' efforts to highlight human rights abuses in the GDR pushed many West Berlin activists out of the party. More seriously still, his information about his party's links to the East German opposition assisted in the arrest of several individuals, including the leading peace movement activist, Bärbel Bohley.[22] Leaving no political stone unturned, HV A also penetrated right-wing extremist groups in West Germany.

THE SECRET SERVICES AND THE STATE BUREAUCRACY

Throughout the history of divided Germany, East Berlin succeeded in deeply penetrating the West German security services. The susceptibility of Stasi recruits to the overtures of a foreign secret service had its roots in a range of motives and pressures: vulnerability to blackmail and avarice, ideological idealism and 'operational' romances. The earliest infiltration of the West German intelligence service was the Soviets' recruitment of Heinz Felfe, who worked for the BND between 1951 and 1961, becoming head of the anti-Soviet section in 1958. For ten years, Moscow had top-level information from the nerve centre of West German intelligence. Although Felfe has stressed his motivation was anti-Americanism, it appears more likely that his past as an officer in the ranks of the Third Reich's intelligence service left him open to blackmail.[23] In keeping with the times, the recruitment of the BND officer Alfred Spuhler in 1968 derived from anti-militarism and socialist idealism. In the belief that West German rearmament was threatening to destabilise the power balance in Europe, Spuhler agreed to pass on material to East Berlin, including documentation on active agents working in the GDR. Alfred and his brother Ludwig, who had acted as a courier, were only finally found out following the defection of the same source who facilitated the exposure of the more famous Gabriele Gast.

The recruitment of Gast represented a major espionage success for HV A. She was recruited in 1970 by Department XV of the Karl-Marx-Stadt Regional Administration while researching for her doctoral thesis on the political role of women in the GDR. Her recruitment began after she fell in love with a

---

[21] Gieseke J. 2001: 207; Knabe H. 1999: 55–6.

[22] Sélitrenny R. and Weichert T. 1991: 46; Schlomann F. W. 1993: 109–10, 131–2; Knabe H. 2000: 73–9.

[23] Andrew C. and Gordievsky O. 1991: 452–3; Wolf M. 1997: 51.

Stasi agent called 'Karliszek'; however, something of a political transformation sealed this upper-middle-class student's support for communism. Gast
became a model 'long-range' agent, who, after graduating from the University of Aachen in 1972, rose rapidly in the BND. Having served at the Soviet
desk and acting as a West German intelligence service representative at meetings throughout the world from Washington to the Far East, in 1987 she was
promoted to deputy head of BND's research into the Eastern bloc. Gast went
on to write Chancellor Kohl's daily intelligence briefing, meaning nothing
less than that the Stasi was sharing this information. The importance of the
information Gast supplied is indicated by Markus Wolf's hands-on approach
to running her: they met personally on seven occasions.[24] She would serve six
years and nine months in prison.

The motivating power of avarice is exemplified in classic fashion by the
1980s penetration of the West German security service, the Office for the
Protection of the Constitution (*Bundesamt für Verfassungsschutz* – BfV). One
of Wolf's most important informants in the BfV was Klaus Kuron. Having
joined the BfV in 1962, Kuron became head of Department 4, which 'ran'
former HV A agents who had been 'turned', the so-called 'countermen'.
However, the lack of a degree-level education blocked his career path and
limited his salary scale. Kuron became increasingly resentful of younger, to
his mind less able, colleagues who passed him on the professional ladder. It
was this desire for greater financial reward and professional recognition that
precipitated his initial 'walk in' offer to East Berlin in September 1981. After
a series of mandatory security checks, Wolf, along with other senior HV A
staff, met Kuron in Austria in 1982 and accepted his financial demands,
which effectively doubled his remuneration by the BfV. HV A received a
high return on its investment, discovering which of their agents had been
'turned' as well as gaining information on the personal problems of BfV's
officers, such as debt, extra-marital affairs or alcoholism, greatly assisting the
Stasi's own counterespionage operations.[25] During Kuron's nine years in the
service of the Stasi, he 'betrayed' at least 18 GDR agents who had become
'doubles'. In order to ensure that HV A's detection of 'turned' agents did not
lead to Kuron coming under suspicion, Wolf agreed only to relocate these
'doubles' from sensitive positions to unimportant backwaters.[26] In 1990, when
Kuron gave himself up to the authorities, his role as an HV A agent took his
superiors completely by surprise. He was later sentenced to 12 years in
prison.

A further serious setback for West German counterespionage was the
defection of Hannsjoachim Tiedge in August 1985. Tiedge had worked for
the BfV since 1966, reaching the position of head of the counterintelligence
department. Tiedge's defection was motivated by a desire to wipe clean his

---

[24] Reichenbach A. 1992: 71–82; Gast G. 1999: 177–213, 273–5, 281–2.
[25] Reichenbach A. 1992: 82–5; Koehler J. O. 1999: 164.
[26] Schmeidel J. 1995: 141; Schlomann F. W. 1993: 142–5.

gambling debts and the offer of treatment for his escalating alcoholism. His recruitment handed East Germany highly sensitive intelligence information, including the nature of all ongoing West German operations inside the GDR, and the identity of East Germans working for the West. Tiedge also wrote an exposé of the BfV's counterespionage methods in the form of a 'doctoral thesis' for the Humboldt University. The very fact that an individual with alcohol and debt problems had undergone no security clearance update in 16 years points to serious lapses on the part of the BfV itself.[27] The *Landesamt für Verfassungsschutz* (LfV), the regional security service, which complemented the BfV's counterespionage activities and monitored domestic political extremism, was also infiltrated in each of its 11 branches. In addition to its officers' early inexperience, financial reasons and career frustrations provided the primary motivation for the 'walk in' offers of cooperation with East German intelligence. In this manner, HV A gained access to valuable information on which of their agents had been 'turned', West German counterespionage methods and ongoing operations; several double agents were imprisoned in East Germany as a direct result.[28]

Military counterintelligence also proved susceptible to East German penetration. After the fall of the GDR, the one-time deputy head of West German military intelligence (*Militärischer Abschirmdienst*), Joachim Krase, was unearthed as a mole; between 1973 and his death in 1988, Krase had passed top-secret intelligence information to the Stasi. Once again the motivation was thwarted career ambitions: Krase resented younger staff, with the formal educational requirements, stepping into the positions he felt should rightly be his own. As deputy head of counterespionage, Krase had coordinated all intelligence operations and knew the active personnel. Not only did Krase pass this information to East Berlin, but, more gravely still, Moscow received the coordinates pinpointing the secret location of the USA's Poseidon tactical nuclear weapons in West Germany.[29] This case also illustrates the interconnection of the 'domestic' arm of MfS with HV A in operations in the Federal Republic. Krase was not run by Wolf's organisation, but by the deputy head of Main Department II (counterespionage). This was no exception as it reflected Krase's importance to the Stasi; for example, the payroll of Main Department VIII included policemen and local government employees with access to computer data covering West German citizens' occupational and residential location.[30]

The West German state apparatus was also peppered with spies, who were often placed in strategically significant posts dealing with Bonn's foreign policy and NATO's defence strategies. East Berlin was able to gain valuable information on foreign relations through the work of moles in Bonn's diplomatic corps. Between 1961 and the fall of the Eastern bloc, Hagen Blau

---

[27] Childs D. and Popplewell R. 1999: 166–7.
[28] Koehler J. O. 1999: 192–3; Richter P. and Rösler K. 1992: 58–9.
[29] Koehler J. O. 1999: 171.
[30] Reichenbach A. 1992: 151.

rose through the ranks of the Foreign Ministry, passing on information which provided a valuable overview of foreign policy from his postings across the three continents of Europe, Asia and Latin America. Blau had been recruited on the basis of his support for socialism. However, Ludwig Pauli, another senior diplomat in the Foreign Ministry, is the only known agent who fell into a Stasi 'honey trap', being unable to resist the charms of a Yugoslavian during a posting to Belgrade. Until 1989, Pauli also supplied details of West German foreign policy from its embassies and consulates, including Edinburgh and Liverpool, as well as Bonn itself.

The Ministry of Defence was also penetrated by HV A. The most serious case was that of the agent couples Lutze and Weigel. The *spiritus rector*, Lothar Lutze, had spent his childhood years in the Young Pioneers in Thuringia before his parents moved to West Germany; an enduring ideological tie to East German communism had been forged. Lutze recruited his wife, Renate, who was employed as secretary to the director of social affairs, and Jürgen Weigel, another secretary.[31] Even more significant was the information travelling eastwards from NATO headquarters on the Western Allies' military strategy and planning. Not only did HV A manage to recruit multilingual secretaries who were relocated from Bonn, but a number of earlier recruits also found their way to Brussels. While working at the West German trade mission in 1968, Herbert Kemp was recruited by two HV A men who posed as representatives of the firm ITT. After this 'false flag' recruitment, Kemp supplied the Stasi with material from Bonn's permanent diplomatic representation in Brussels. Similarly, the 'walk-in' offer of cooperation from the navy cryptographer Heinz-Helmut Werner in 1974 took the Stasi from the Bundeswehr's command and control centre in Nuremberg to NATO headquarters. Werner supplied some 1,200 NATO documents, including materials on the debate among member states on the deployment of short-range nuclear weapons in Europe, the West's policy intentions concerning Germany, and its negotiating position in the arms race; he also provided Soviet military intelligence with technical and operational material on code breaking.

The most serious case of cold-war espionage against NATO came to light only in 1993, following the supply of information by the former HV A officer Heinz Busch. Rainer Rupp ('Topaz') had been recruited by HV A as a 'long-range IM' while he was involved in the 1960s student movement, and, on his handler's advice, sought to obtain a position in NATO. In 1972, Rupp recruited his British wife, Anne-Christine ('Türkis'), who then cooperated in supplying documents from her various desks in Brussels until the birth of their first child. From 1977, however, Rupp was himself employed by NATO, beginning 12 years of top-level espionage activity. Rupp not only supplied a vast quantity of high quality material, concerning the Western Allies' military planning and nuclear first strike policy, but put inaccessible

---

[31] Reichenbach A. 1992: 126; Richter P. and Rösler K. 1992: 58.

jargon into easily digestible reports; this material, which was passed to Moscow, had obvious implications in the event of an international crisis.

ROMEOS AND SECRETARIES

HV A's Romeo agents did not restrict their activities to Bonn's secretarial pool. However, according to Markus Wolf, it was his agents' success in this area that will probably secure his place in espionage history. Although the exact number of secretaries seduced into cooperating with the Stasi may never be accurately established, one informed estimate places the figure at some 60 'Juliets'.[32] Romeo agents were used throughout the history of the GDR, with their collection of intelligence peaking during the 1970s. At some point during the late 1950s the recruitment of Romeo agents was stepped up. The selection procedure, according to Wolf, was extremely rigorous: scouts working in the SED, its youth organisations and the universities identified possible agents, who were eliminated by background checks and interviews until some 1 per cent of the initial number remained. Those selected then underwent a training programme at the HV A training school, which included a dry-run mission in the West. The new 'graduates' were then sent to either Bonn, under an assumed identity, or to one of the holiday resorts in southern and eastern Europe, such as the Bulgarian Black Sea coast, which were known to attract single secretaries who were 'looking for love'. Both the initial pick-up and the escape route in the event of difficulties were planned in detail. Once the secretary had taken the bait and fallen for the agent, a back-up network of couriers and controllers was put in place to deliver the fruits of espionage to East Berlin. Wolf's denial that blackmail was used has a hollow ring.

The targeted secretaries corresponded to a given profile: they were entering middle age (the secretaries' average age was 38) and lacked strong links to their parents and wider families.[33] The significance attached to the recruitment and running of these women is exemplified by instructions from Wolf in 1970 that 'scientific' investigations be carried out into the process. The resulting dissertation compiled by two HV A colonels received the commendation 'magna cum laude'.[34] If it was necessary to retain a secretary who began to doubt either her romance or role in espionage, then all means were sanctioned by HV A from 'operational (that is, invalid) marriages' to a bogus priest taking confession. HV A showed great patience, slowly manoeuvring their recruits into positions with access to sensitive materials, waiting while they moved from the private to the public sector or underwent professional

---

[32] Reichenbach A. 1992: 103. Between 1965 and 1980, 15 secretaries were caught; their sentences were relatively light, amounting to up to five years' imprisonment: see Koehler J. O. 1999: 183.

[33] Reichenbach A. 1992: 103–4.

[34] Knabe H. 1999: 58.

retraining. Interestingly, however, the West German authorities' contemporary reports as well as the secretaries' later statements point to their voluntary co-operation motivated predominantly by love of a man over that of a country.[35]

The aim of this type of intelligence operation was to gain access to the state secrets of the West German government, the bureaucracies of the governing parties and the state apparatus. HV A had found a rich seam of information, with early successes including material fuelling the East German campaign against the chief of Chancellor Adenauer's office, Hans Globke, who resigned in 1963 amid a barrage of propaganda concerning his Nazi past. However, if the 1960s proved to be the period of successful recruitment, then the 1970s increasingly became the age of these agents' exposure. The arrest of agents was not new, the first 'Juliet' had been caught in 1958, but the scale of the West German campaigns against this form of espionage expanded rapidly in the late 1970s. The first case to hit the headlines was that of Dagmar Kahlig-Scheffer, recruited by HV A in 1973 while working as a journalist's researcher before starting work in Chancellor Schmidt's office. Her arrest followed the BfV's introduction of a system of computer-based name traces, which identified her controller in Düsseldorf as a Stasi officer. She subsequently discovered that her marriage to her Romeo was an 'operational marriage' as he was already married.[36] In the course of 1979, one disclosure of East German espionage followed another. The first arrest was that of Ingrid Garbe, a secretary in the West German mission to NATO, followed by the defection of Ursel Lorenz, another secretary based at NATO's headquarters in Brussels. Before the storm subsided, Ursula Hoefs, a secretary in the CDU's Bonn headquarters, was arrested. This triggered East Germany's withdrawal of Inge Goliath, an em-ployee of a CDU-funded research institute, and Christel Broszey, who had worked for four CDU party chairmen, fled to East Berlin. Helga Roediger, who had been an assistant to a senior civil servant in the foreign ministry, followed in their immediate train. According to Wolf himself, this represented only the tip of the iceberg: between 1972 and 1982, 30 agents were arrested and some 100 withdrawn as the BfV came close to identifying them.[37] It was a change in the BfV's tactics that had led to the spate of exposures, which, with such scope for public interest, ensured that the Western media had a field day retelling the spying-for-sex story with a modern twist.

COLD WAR PARTISANS AND INTERNATIONAL TERRORISM

The role of IMs in the West extended beyond the gathering of political and economic information to the assignment of a military function to suitable

---

[35] Wolf M. 1997: 124; Schmeidel J. 1995: 145–6.
[36] Koehler J. O. 1999: 183.
[37] Wolf M. 1997: 133.

members of their ranks. When an IM signed the official statement obliging him/her to work with the Stasi, notions of antimilitarism, patriotism and helping to preserve world peace were often prominent. However, even during the 1980s, when the Politbüro endlessly discussed the matter, the SED's so-called 'peace policy' was essentially a concomitant of its general search for international and domestic legitimacy. At home, the 'peace policy' was turned into campaigns in the factories for higher production, using slogans such as 'my workplace – the place from which I struggle for peace'.[38] In fact, throughout its existence HV A was involved in the Stasi's military preparations for the anticipated final conflict with the West. Despite his claims to the contrary, documentary evidence now identifies Markus Wolf as a leading figure in training these forces.[39]

The East German intelligence and security services were not only concerned with fighting battles on the 'invisible front' but along with the Central Committee and the NVA they also played a key role in organising a communist fighting force which was to function behind enemy lines. The number of Stasi officers involved in coordinating these activities was extensive. Since the 1950s but more systematically from 1964 onwards, the Stasi had trained special taskforces to function as partisan fighters, whose tasks included sabotaging the supply of essential services, such as gas and water, disrupting the public transport system and in particular playing a key role at the beginning of a war against the FRG.[40] Between 1964 and 1984, about 3,500 staff took part in such courses and the coordinating unit was eventually called the Working Group of the Minister/Special Questions (*Arbeitsgruppe des Ministers/Sonderfragen*). A secret military organisation in the West German Communist Party was set up in 1968–69; 20 years later, it had 200 members. From the mid-1970s, members were trained in camps in the GDR by MfS and NVA staff with the aim of creating a fifth column in the FRG. Under the leadership of the veteran Communist Harry Schmidt, the West Germans learned how to take up arms, conduct strategically planned acts of sabotage and liberate captured comrades.[41] It was also envisaged that certain carefully selected IMs in the West would take part in a future invasion force, particularly in West Berlin, which had been planned in detail by the SED leadership. For these purposes, arms dumps had been carefully hidden in strategic locations throughout Europe.[42]

The Stasi's campaign to assist the West German peace movement's protests against stationing NATO nuclear missile on German territory must be seen in

---

[38] This features strongly in the meetings of the Politbüro; see, for example, SAPMO DY 30/2218.

[39] Knabe H. 1997: 14.

[40] Fingerle S. and Gieseke J. 1996; Gieseke J. 2001: 216–17; Auerbach T. 1999: 10–11, 15–17, 22, 49.

[41] Gieseke J. 2001: 217; *Der Spiegel*, no. 1, 1990, pp. 65ff and no. 2, 1990, pp. 61ff.

[42] Knabe H. 1997: 17.

the light of these Eastern bloc military concerns. In order to influence Bonn's defence policy during the Second Cold War of the late 1970s and early 1980s, the Stasi set up a regional headquarters to direct a network of agents.[43] Its role included influencing grassroots members of the SPD, the Greens and the FDP against the West German government's decision to station nuclear weapons in the hope of affecting party policy. An attempt to influence the SPD's 1981 congress 'from below', however, had absolutely no impact.[44] The Stasi also funded organisations sympathetic to its objectives, such as 'Generals for Peace', which alone received some 100,000 DM.[45]

The Stasi's connections to the Red Army Faction (RAF), under Andreas Baader and Ulrike Meinhof, are also to be understood in terms of East German preparations for the final conflict with the West.[46] Declassified documentation confirms that the Stasi's support for the RAF and other 'international terrorists', which was coordinated by the Main Department XXII, was considerably greater than contemporary observers had ever suspected. However, their relationship was characterised by the maxim 'my enemy's enemy is my friend'. The RAF did not regard East Germany as a model society, but accepted military training and, after 1977, asylum in the GDR. The *quid pro quo* was that when the moment finally came to destabilise West Germany the RAF too would join the fifth column of the Cold War's communist partisans.

The Cold War's division of the Third World into zones of influence also characterised the Stasi's wider relationship with the 'international terrorism' of the 1970s and 1980s – a period in which the Soviets optimistically believed they were gaining the upper hand in a politically polarised international climate. Throughout these two decades, the Stasi had close relations with a number of Third World states, some of which, such as Iraq and Syria, sponsored terrorist groups. Despite the evident risks exposure would cause to East German foreign policy, a common hostility to the former Western colonial powers was reinforced by the involvement of the Stasi and the KGB in the formation of secret services in Cuba, Zanzibar, Tanzania, Ghana, Mozambique, Angola, Ethiopia, Sudan and South Yemen. Although the Soviet Union was the major player in the Third World, East Berlin also trained guerrilla fighters from South Africa (ANC), Namibia (SWAPO) and Rhodesia (ZAPU).[47] It should be remembered, however, that if conditions in the Third World seemed to favour the expansion of Eastern bloc influence, then relations within the Soviet world were at times severely strained. In the Honecker era, this was above all the case during the events in Poland during 1980–81, with the formation of the independent trade union Solidarity.

---

[43] Sélitrenny R. and Weichert T. 1991: 196–200.
[44] Knabe H. 1997: 12–13.
[45] Wolf M. 1998: 343.
[46] See Childs D. and Popplewell R. 1999: 138, 140–41; Koehler J. O. 1999: 387–401.
[47] Childs D. and Popplewell R. 1999: 140–41; Schleicher H-G. and Engel U. 1996.

Fearing that Poland was about to fall into the 'enemy camp', operative groups were active in Poland's main cities, while HV A's Department X (disinformation) was behind the propaganda and operational preparations which aimed to prevent strikes spreading to East Germany.[48]

HV A AND 'EXTERNAL DEFENCE'

The HV A's role in guaranteeing the security of the GDR against internal 'political-ideological subversion' and the activities of the 'political underground' amounted to a cross-border operation in close cooperation with Main Department XX, which had the specific task of rooting out individuals and groups critical of SED rule. Since the formation of the GDR, the organisations on the receiving end of HV A's measures of 'external defence' ranged from groups promoting political and human rights, such as the Alternative List for Democracy and Amnesty International, to environmental groups like Green Peace. By 1985, some 150 West German organisations stood on the Stasi's list of external enemies.[49] In 1987, as the church-based, inter-bloc peace movement of the 1980s grew in strength, HV A set up counterintelligence units to 'neutralise' activists in the GDR and reconnoitred their contacts with churches in West Germany.[50] East Berlin's ideologically driven interpretation of the influence of external forces in producing domestic opposition was highlighted in a Politbüro report from 1986 on the opinions and attitudes of youth in East Germany. The report stressed that the West was attempting to form a 'political opposition' in the GDR by exploiting these environmental and civil rights organisations.[51] With a worldview that attributed opposition to SED rule to subversive influences emanating from the West, it was axiomatic, at least in the SED's terms, that HV A should be involved against peace and civil rights activists in the GDR too. HV A's struggle in the Operation Area involved infiltrating IMs into these organisations in order to gather material for disinformation campaigns, including smear campaigns against individuals, and fomenting distrust and discontent within the organisations themselves. A case study of HV A's campaign against the International Society for Human Rights details the role of IMs in 61 'operational cases'.[52]

A typical example of the Stasi's methods of conducting an 'operational campaign' against an organisation involved in publicising its criticisms of the GDR is provided by the Society for Former Political Prisoners, which had several thousand members in the FRG. In the early 1980s, the election of a

---

[48] Tantzscher M. 1995: 2610–13, 2642, 2662–3, 2750–55.
[49] Wüst J. 1996: 37–53.
[50] Fricke K. W. 1997: 25; Sélitrenny R. and Weichert T. 1991: 214.
[51] SAPMO, DY 30/IV 2/2.039.
[52] Wüst J. 1996: 37–53.

new branch chairman in West Berlin was contested by a woman member, who claimed that the new chairman had 'touched her up' and repeatedly made obscene phone calls to her. Although the branch membership continued to support the new chairman until these allegations could be substantiated, he resigned in order to enable the organisation to resume its human rights activities. After 1989, it was discovered that the woman and her husband were IMs who had acted in accordance with instructions from their Stasi handlers.[53]

The full extent of West German citizens who were the target of Stasi's actions remains unknown. However, an indication of the numbers involved – about 1,400 persons – can be derived from an incomplete listing compiled by the Stasi's East Berlin organisation. The GDR security services were particularly involved against former East German citizens who had been expelled to West Germany in order to eliminate them from 'troublemaking' at home. One example is the harrassment of the author Jürgen Fuchs, a prominent GDR dissident who had been deported to West Germany. In September 1982 alone, he received intimidating anonymous phone calls, goods of a compromising nature were delivered to his home, home improvement companies frequently arrived expecting to carry out work, and taxis and the emergency services were called out in his name.[54] One of the leading authorities on the Stasi, Karl Wilhelm Fricke, uncovered an official communication from 1982 bearing Wolf's signature, which had been sent to the head of Main Department XX, Major General Paul Kienberg, providing information obtained by his intelligence service considered of value in the operational case against the prominent dissident Rainer Eppelmann.[55] Critics of communist rule living in West Berlin and active in groups hostile to the SED regime, especially former East German citizens, were also subjected to harassment campaigns such as 'telephone terror', whereby an anonymous voice, normally in the early hours of the morning, would announce: 'We will get you'.[56] The Stasi was also involved in actions against at least one Marxist group, which tried to set up organisational bases in East Germany. During the 1970s, one such 'enemy' organisation was the Maoist (later pro-Albanian) Marxist-Leninist German Communist Party (KPD/ML).[57]

CONCLUSION: SUCCESS IN ULTIMATE FAILURE

During the Honecker era, HV A was a highly effective intelligence service, running an extensive array of agents and informers in West Germany and not

---

[53] Interview with Jörg Drieselmann in Berlin on 26 August 1999.
[54] Knabe H. 1997: 13–14.
[55] Fricke K. W. 1997: 24.
[56] Interview with Jörg Drieselmann in Berlin on 26 August 1999.
[57] Wunschik T. 1997.

bound by the restraints on operations in democratic societies. Using a highly trained staff of professional officers and their IMs as well as the advantage of a common language, HV A was able to penetrate West German politics and society from its upper levels to areas of everyday life. In politics, East Berlin gained an important insight into Bonn's decision-making process, conflicts among the political elites, the function of the state apparatus which drove government in the Federal Republic, and its policy towards the GDR. In economic life too, the GDR economy benefited both financially and technically from the fruits of espionage. In military espionage, access to the secrets of the Western Allies' planning and intentions would certainly have meant a severe setback for any NATO-based military strategy. However, if HV A had been able to obtain information a mile wide, then the SED's evaluation of this intelligence data was often an inch deep. The SED's strict adherence to an ideologically-based interpretation of how the capitalist West would act meant that intelligence information which ran against the political grain was often ignored.[58] Ironically, the ideology, which helped integrate and motivate HV A's officers, ultimately clouded the party's assessment of the true significance of the intelligence material obtained. In distorting perceptions of the West, the Marxism-Leninism which underpinned the MfS led to an over-estimate of the steering influence of Western 'imperialists' as well as a failure to appreciate the GDR's lack of appeal for most West Germans.

Furthermore, care must be taken not to exaggerate the value of the information supplied by IMs. Wolf, for instance, has opined that much of Guillaume's data has been overrated and as has been observed by Leslie Colitt in his study of Wolf: 'As with so much espionage material, Guillaume's information had served largely to boost the ego and the budget of the HV A'.[59] The former HV A officers Richter and Rösler have argued that in later decades the decline in morale and the greater administrative load of HV A not only reduced efficiency but also resulted in data which, as elsewhere in the MfS, was world class only in its mediocrity.[60] And as discussed in Chapter 8, while the transfer of scientific and technological data was of significant value in the short term, one effect was to block much-needed economic reform while simultaneously reinforcing the GDR's dependence on Western know-how and failing to narrow the technological gap. Some of the data procured by HV A, GDR visitors to the West and the residents attached to GDR embassies in the West were of limited value. This was also often true of the information obtained by those cadres who visited the West from East Berlin's Institute for Politics and Economics, which cooperated closely with HV A. The academics' contacts with research institutes in the FRG elicited data which tended to be academic in nature rather than having a secret

---

[58] Fricke K. W. 1997: 22.
[59] Colitt L. 1995: 109.
[60] Richter P. and Rösler K. 1992: 108.

service content and of little more value than information gleaned from articles in a good weekly West German magazine like *Der Spiegel*.[61] Moreover, the HV A Regional Departments, as in Gera and Magdeburg, seriously questioned whether the heavy investment of resources in the recruitment and running of agents produced its equivalent in worthwhile information.[62]

It was the SED's ideology of the 'unity of reconnaissance and defence' which tied HV A to the Stasi's apparatus of domestic repression and to the belief that internal opposition was the work of foreign 'political-ideological subversion' of East German citizens. In the 1970s, HV A's role was primarily to supply the MfS's domestic units with relevant information concerning opposition to SED rule. However, with the rise of cross-border opposition movements in the aftermath of the events in Poland in the early 1980s and the inter-bloc peace and ecology movements, HV A's role became increasingly hands-on. Not only did HV A act against the 'external enemy' in the Operation Area, its regional branches also acted against the church-based opposition in East Germany. HV A's greater involvement in the work of the domestic apparatus is symbolised by its officers' participation in the efforts to suppress the demonstrators in East Berlin in October 1989 during the regime's 40th anniversary celebrations.[63] The fact that there has been a debate about the extent to which HV A played a part in the Stasi's domestic repression is a final testament to Wolf's, and his officers', adept use of their tradecraft. It represents no less than their final campaign of disinformation by one of the Cold War's most efficient intelligence services. In this respect we should not be overly surprised that Wolf has no wish to tell us the whole story of his role in sustaining the communist system; it was, after all, his job to prevaricate for a political purpose. However, as the researchers of the Gauck Authority uncovered the traces of HV A's actions, Wolf became the spy who had said too much, and one day's denial became the next day's reluctant admission.[64]

---

[61] Richter P. and Rösler K. 1992: 99–100.

[62] Müller-Enbergs H. 1998: 259, 281.

[63] Richter P. and Rösler K. 1992: 143–4.

[64] For example, compare Wolf's denial of any role in the imprisonment of Georg Angerer in an effort to extract information in the late 1950s to discredit Willy Brandt as a fellow-travelling Nazi with a subsequent admission to having played a central role; see *Der Spiegel*, no. 18, 1993 and no. 2, 1997.

Part VII

THE OCTOPUS LOSES ITS TENTACLES

Chapter 14

THE COLLAPSE OF COMMUNIST RULE

DÉNOUEMENT

At the beginning of 1989, Honecker had some good tidings for his sub-jects: the Berlin Wall would remain in place for another 50 to 100 years unless, he conceded, a change occurred in the conditions which had led to its construction.[1] In other words, at least for the ageing SED leader, the Cold War was not over. But by the summer of 1989, with popular protests breaking out on the streets of East Berlin, Leipzig, Dresden and elsewhere and the mass exodus gathering momentum, not only was the Wall looking obsolescent but the other foundations of SED power were also starting to crumble. At a conference with his top regional leaders at the end of August, an anxious Mielke asked if popular unrest was likely to lead to another 17 June 1953. He was reassured by Colonel Dangrieß, the head of the Gera Regional Administration, that this would not happen. Most of the other officers concurred with Dangrieß's view that the situation was stable and under control; after all, that was what the Stasi was there for.[2]

This proved to be a disastrous prediction: the 77-year-old Honecker was removed from power on 18 October in a palace coup and replaced as head of party and state by Egon Krenz; the Berlin Wall fell on the night of 9–10 November without the Soviet Union moving a muscle to protect its westernmost outpost; demonstrators became ever bolder; new parties and citizens' groups articulated in the public arena their ideas on a civil society free from the grip of the SED and Stasi; and 343,854 East Germans had left their country by the end of the year. Succumbing to the multiple pressures, an increasingly bewildered SED ejected Honecker and Mielke from its ranks, reluctantly decided to abandon its leadership role in society, and in February 1990 finally and after much hesitation adopted a completely new title, the Party of Democratic Socialism (PDS). The latter decision had been partly

---

[1] See Mitter A. and Wolle S. 1990: 125.
[2] Süß W. 1999: 181.

motivated by the need to refurbish its image for the forthcoming elections to the GDR Parliament, the *Volkskammer*, in March 1990. Although the PDS obtained a creditable 16.32 per cent of the vote, it was overshadowed by the astonishing 47.79 per cent scored by the Alliance for Germany of CDU, Democratic Awakening and German Social Union. The Alliance had been sponsored by the West German Chancellor, Helmut Kohl, as a vehicle for the rapid unification which he had been pursuing since early February. The conservatives' overwhelming victory was an endorsement of the fast track to unity: on 1 July, monetary, economic and social union was sealed by the introduction of the Deutschmark as the sole legal currency in the GDR, and on 3 October the GDR, now reconfigured as the five new states or *Länder*, was incorporated into the Federal Republic. Germany's political division and the Cold War had ended.

At some stage in this process, at least until early October 1989, the momentum might have been arrested by concerted force. Not only had SED leaders such as Krenz and Margot Honecker issued thinly veiled threats of a GDR version of the bloody suppression of the Chinese students' democratic movement in Tiananmen Square in June, but the SED had the military capability to do so. It had at its disposal the troops of the NVA, the workers' militia, the People's Police and, by no means least, the MfS. It had sanctioned gratuitous violence against protesters at the time of the GDR's macabre 40th anniversary either side of 7 October. And had not Mielke proclaimed to his officers only a few weeks before that it was better to die defending socialism than to live in servitude to the imperialists?[3] But when the crunch came on the night of 9 October in Leipzig, the emptiness of such boasts was plain for all to see. Before the customary Monday night demonstration, rumours were rife that armed troops and tanks were ready to move into the city and that hospital beds had been prepared for the wounded. However, the political struggle between Honecker and Krenz in East Berlin, the peaceful nature of the protests and the incalculable risks of civil war and international opprobium rendered the powerful powerless.

The feebleness of the communist leaders and the sheer rapidity of unification was beyond the imagination of even the most fervent Cold War warrior when Honecker had spoken of the survival of the Berlin Wall. And yet, Honecker had not spoken with confidence. His speech had been crafted as a response to mounting pressures on East Berlin to adjust to Gorbachev's more conciliatory line on reform and accommodation with the West. These pressures had been felt keenly by Honecker at the Vienna meeting of the Conference on Security and Cooperation in Europe in early January 1989 when the Soviet Union had forced the GDR to make concessions on human rights. Even more worrying was the statement by the Soviet Foreign Minister, Eduard Schevardnaze, that the conference had shaken the Iron Curtain and

---

[3] Süß W. 1999: 71.

that the Berlin Wall was an obstacle to the unification process in Europe.[4] Hence Honecker's speech.

The new thinking in the Soviet Union since Gorbachev's accession to power in 1985 was undoubtedly a major factor behind the collapse of the communist system in the GDR, as was the reform process in Poland and Hungary, all of them manifestations of the general crisis affecting the communist world. These factors are but one part of the equation, however. The disintegration of the SED – and with it the MfS – must also be seen as part of a wider series of developments: the Soviet retreat from its East European empire; the emigration movement; the gathering strength and determination of the East German opposition groups; the loss of faith in the state social-ist project; the obduracy and the loss of confidence of the ruling elites; and the stalled modernisation and technological flaws of the command economy. The German factor, too, played a crucial part: the powerful attraction of the superior living standards of West Germany; the SED regime's ambivalence to nationhood in a divided Germany; and the adroit manoeuvres of Chancellor Kohl after the fall of the Berlin Wall. All these factors were interlinked, their significance varying at different stages of the East German revolution. Their nature and role will be examined in the next section, mainly on the basis of materials in the Stasi files, before looking at the disintegration of the Stasi in the late autumn of 1990.

POPULAR DISSATISFACTION

Throughout the four decades of communist rule in East Germany, the MfS had tracked popular opinion for signs of rebellion on the lines of June 1953 as well as monitoring attitudes to SED domestic policies, the standard of living and the GDR's foreign relations, especially with West Germany. The MfS was not the only agency involved in this task. The SED and the other political parties also gathered data and a Central Committee Institute for Public Opinion Research, which existed between 1964 and 1979, provided the Politbüro and other leading organs with information about citizens' views.[5] One other significant body, the Central Institute for Youth Research in Leipzig, monitored the attitudes and opinions of young people. The Insti-tute's longitudinal studies are particularly crucial for assessing the precipitous fall in support for the SED and the socialist cause during the 1980s. While the Institute's research is not without methodological flaws, the declassified findings indicate a rapid decline between 1985 and 1989 in young people's approval of aspects of the system after the broad consensus of the 1970s. The mass defection can be measured by the collapse in adherence to basic tenets of

---

[4] Süß W. 1999: 92–3.
[5] See Niemann H. 1993.

official socialist culture, such as a belief in the eventual victory of socialism over capitalism. Identification with the GDR also fell sharply. Between the mid- and late 1980s, the percentage of apprentices and young workers who felt a strong attachment to the GDR declined from 51 per cent and 57 per cent to 18 per cent and 19 per cent respectively, whereas the proportion of those who had virtually no affinity with their country rose by 28 points and 13 points respectively.[6]

PETITIONING THE STASI

Among other declassified materials now available for tracing popular attitudes are the *Eingaben* or petitions which, according to GDR law, entitled East Germans to address their complaints and concerns, mainly in writing but also orally, to the appropriate body or individuals. Among the main addressees were Honecker and Mielke, the Council of State, the MfS and the mass media. East Germans made full use of their right, with almost every GDR household, at least in statistical terms, submitting a petition between 1949 and 1989.[7] The contents of *Eingaben* varied according to the addressee. Thus the Council of State was primarily involved in matters arising from legislative questions and the MfS dealt with security issues. The most frequent themes running through the petitions are complaints about the poor quality of housing, restrictions on travel or emigration to the West, and the inadequate supply of consumer goods.[8]

The petitions, according to the SED, demonstrated the trust of the population in their state and provided citizens with a flexible and effective instrument to resolve their problems. In the absence of administrative courts and a pluralistic political system, the petitions did at least offer East Germans an opportunity to exert pressure on the representatives of state and party, and many grievances were settled. However, the records of the MfS indicate that the official line on petitions contained much wishful thinking: the materials reaching the ministry were often redeployed for security purposes, whether for checking contacts with the West or for pursuing 'hostile-negative' forces. One illustration of MfS manipulation is the case of a check in 1983 by a local MfS unit in Kamenz on an *Eingabe* from parents whose son had failed to secure an apprenticeship as a sailor. An internal investigation confirmed the parents' suspicion that the Stasi lurked behind the rejection on account of the family's contacts in the West. The officers in Kamenz insisted that the decision should not be reversed and that the parents be advised to break off their Western links.[9]

---

[6] Dennis M. 2000: 270.
[7] Mühlberg F. 1999: 7.
[8] Merkel I. 1998: 14, 22, 25.
[9] MfS ZA, AS, no. 209/86, pp. 34, 46, 53.

Of the petitions reaching the Stasi some were addressed directly to the ministry, the remainder were passed on by other bodies on account of their security implications. In 1988, 698 *Eingaben* and letters were sent to the MfS, 315 more than in 1986, and over 31,000 arrived via Honecker's Central Committee office and the Council of State's Department for petitions. The latter figure represented a sharp increase over the approximately 7,000 in 1980.[10] The focus of the petitions was on everyday matters such as poor housing, problems at work, neighbourhood concerns and the reintegration of prisoners into society. They also dealt with the more sensitive political issues of visits to the West, the alternative political culture and complaints against officialdom, such as telephone tapping, passport control and interrogations by the MfS. Given that they record in a vivid and highly personal manner some of the innermost concerns of East Germans, the petitions have been likened to an 'ethnographic diary'.[11] Even though they tended to record disturbances in daily life rather than its normal flow, no objective reader could have continued to attach much credibility by the end of the 1980s to the notion that Honecker's much-vaunted 'unity of social and economic policy' was sustaining a social consensus between regime and population.

While some of the complaints in the petitions appear to have little direct political import, they nevertheless reflect the irritations with life under state socialism. The grievance of a Berliner about a broken telephone at the time when his partner went into labour and the police refusal to help draw attention to the inadequacies of the telephone network and the pettiness of state bureaucracy.[12] An anonymous letter to the MfS from Neustadt in Saxony in 1985 was disparaging about conditions at work: the belittling of critics as 'grumblers'; the misuse of business trips abroad for tourism; the prevalence of 'personal connections'; and the widespread corruption arising from payments in hard currency for services by craftsmen. The MfS and the central organs of state should, he demanded, deal with those who misuse their positions, not those who draw attention to the problems.[13] Bribery and corruption were the theme of another petition in 1985 which revealed a veritable mafia at an engineering trading company in the Pankow district of East Berlin. The firm had been purchasing secondhand cars and spare automobile parts from state-owned enterprises and state organs, including cars seized from their owners by MfS units, and selling them on at inflated prices to private buyers.[14] A convoluted story concerned a doctor at the University of Rostock's clinic for women and his appeal, in 1984, against the rejection of his application to spend some time working in a developing country. In consequence, he

---

[10] MfS ZA, Sekretariat des Ministers, no. 361, pp. 6, 13, 61.
[11] Mühlberg F. 1999: 8.
[12] MfS ZA, AS, no. 119/88, p. 10. The complaint was sent on 9 January 1985.
[13] MfS ZA, AS, no. 98/88, pp. 126–30.
[14] MfS ZA, HA XVIII, no. 7820, pp. 1–2, 7–9. The year was 1985.

claimed that he had been downgraded to the status of a second-class citizen. Security checks revealed that, on the instructions of the ministry, he had been removed from the university's list of cadres with the right to travel abroad on account of his Western contacts, his sexual affairs with women and bringing pornographic literature into the GDR from the Netherlands.[15] Finally, a resident of Leipzig, a married woman with four children, erupted at the police's refusal of her request to visit Marburg in West Germany: 'In this state we give every skiver, everybody who has done something wrong or been condemned the chance to prove themselves and yet many people don't learn their lesson – but for me I've never put a foot wrong in all my life – for me all doors are closed'.[16]

The elements of defiance and protest which resonate among many of the *Eingaben* are not easily reconciled with the popular image of the GDR as a harsh dictatorship presiding over a cowed and conformist society. While some writers were adroit at expressing their grievances and many others focused on non-political issues, some of the petitions reaching the MfS were nevertheless blunt and openly critical of malpractices and unsatisfactory conditions. In 1984, a department head in the research and development unit of a car-body works accused the Stasi of having blocked his promotion, or so he believed, despite his dedication to the welfare of society and the goals of party and state.[17] A regular petitioner from Birkenfelde, who had been imprisoned in 1964 for six months on a charge of embezzlement, argued that while he did not mind being a stoker or a watchman, he did object to unqualified 'yes-men' having positions of responsibility. 'The stupid govern better' was his ironic conclusion.[18] Finally, although the list could be extended, a hospital worker, who was also engaged in social work for the Protestant churches, drew attention to the paradox of being observed by the Stasi but, because of his positive attitude towards the GDR, had to face accusations from his colleagues of being an IM. 'Here', he concluded, 'the dog is somehow biting its own tail' and 'It is a vicious circle that I'm being drawn into'.[19] Little did he know that he was not under observation by the MfS.

Nor was the Stasi a petition-free zone. Stasi personnel, especially younger members, frequently complained about the poor quality of their apartments, an indicator that even an elite body like the Stasi was also caught up in the everyday problems of society. In 1988, among the *Eingaben* sent by MfS employees 20 concerned accommodation problems and 26 objections to decisions by superior officers, including disciplinary measures.[20] Another

---

[15] MfS ZA, AS, no. 282/87, pp. 204, 246–50.
[16] MfS ZA, AS, no. 113/88, p. 68. Our translation.
[17] MfS ZA, AS, no. 107/88, p. 140.
[18] MfS ZA, AS, no. 111/88, p. 139.
[19] MfS ZA, AS, no. 115/88, p. 144.
[20] MfS ZA, Sekretariat des Ministers, no. 361, p. 8.

trigger for an *Eingabe* was official rejection of a request to undertake a visit to West Berlin or the Federal Republic because the petitioner was related to a member of the MfS or had once been an employee of the ministry.[21] It was not unusual for staff to enlist their parents' help. The parents of a full-time informer (HIM) complained on her behalf that: 'We can't understand why young comrades who sacrifice their youth and all their energy for the security of the state have to live in degrading conditions. Not without reason has our party declared the housing programme is at the heart of social policy'.[22] The woman lived with her husband and two children in a tiny apartment; her husband was also a full-time informer.

ZAIG: ASSESSING THE POPULAR MOOD

While the individual petitions offer fascinating insights into personal attitudes and actions, the key Stasi agency for evaluating and delineating the contours of popular opinion was the Central Assessment and Information Group (*Zentrale Auswertungs- und Informationsgruppe* – ZAIG) and its offshoots, the Assessment and Information Groups (AKGs) in the Regional Administrations and the District Service Units. ZAIG digested and collated information from its myriad sources and despatched reports and indicators on the mood of the population and specific events to the leadership of the Stasi as well as to the party and state elites, notably Honecker, Krenz, Stoph and Mittag. The actual distribution list varied according to the nature of the topic addressed in the report. Other SED organs at regional and district level were also in receipt of pertinent information.[23] Although the ZAIG reports cannot be regarded as GDR-representative and were coloured by the ministry's Marxist-Leninist ideology and SED policy preoccupations, they provide invaluable and sometimes highly critical insights into popular thinking. The format of most reports was initially to paint a positive picture of the popular mind before turning to the problem areas.

Despite the generally positive gloss, the grievances of the populace at large as well as of specific social groups pervade the ZAIG reports. Along with the petitions, these reports capture a society which, the steamroller impact of state socialism notwithstanding, was characterised by perceptible cleavages of social status, age, gender, political position and access to Western goods. Take just two examples: older workers and pensioners carped at the unwillingness of many younger people to take on positions of responsibility despite their higher standard of living. The state's social policy, they complained, had

---

[21] MfS ZA, Sekretariat des Ministers, no. 361, p. 33.
[22] MfS ZA, AS, no. 113/88, p. 92. The latter was sent to the MfS on 25 April 1985. Our translation.
[23] Gieseke J. 1998: 40.

made life too comfortable for young people.[24] Secondly, a host of complaints concerned the divisive effect of unequal access to Deutschmarks and the Intershops. It was a standard argument among those who did not have Western currency that they worked more conscientiously and had a more positive attitude to the socialist system than those who acquired Deutschmarks through family connections or by providing services which were not easily found in the public sector, such as plumbing and car maintenance.[25] Resentment was also expressed about the many privileges enjoyed by leading SED functionaries,[26] even though their true extent did not become public knowledge until Honecker was overthrown.

While it awaited the galvanising impact of Gorbachev's reforms and the erosion of communist power elsewhere in the Soviet empire to translate grievances among East Germans into calls for radical change, the ZAIG materials provide indicators of some of the preconditions which led to the fall of communism. As already mentioned, the main complaints concerned the inadequacy of supplies to the population and poor housing. These were sensitive matters as the leitmotif of the Honecker regime was the provision of higher living standards, especially better housing, on the basis of greater economic efficiency. Yet despite the construction of new high-rise flats and fundamental improvements in heating systems and toilets and despite the high level of subsidies for rents, transport and many consumer items, East Germans continued to give vent to their anger. Their frustration was exacerbated by their awareness of the superior provision in the West. Just how out of touch Mielke was with popular feeling can be seen from the minister's condemnation in August 1989 of the ingratitude of the emigrants for scorning the benefits of socialism.[27]

The mood of the population can be traced in ZAIG's weekly surveys (*Wochenübersichten*) and information bulletins (*Hinweise*). The latter were overviews of the current situation and tended to home in on one broad theme, often reproducing the criticisms of a number of social, political, economic and cultural groups. The weekly surveys were usually divided into separate sections, which focused on specific events, such as accidents at work or illegal attempts to leave the GDR. The issue of endemic shortages is a thread running through these reports, especially at times of acute economic difficulties as in the late 1970s and early 1980s, when the GDR had to tighten its belt because of the sharp rise in oil prices and the ballooning hard currency indebtedness. Complaints about shortages and waste were, of course, not new but feelings were exacerbated by the gloomy international economic climate and contributed to the gradual undermining of the fragile social

---

[24] MfS ZA, ZAIG, no. 4175, 'Hinweise', 29 May 1984, p. 4.
[25] MfS ZA, ZAIG, no. 4119, 'Hinweise', 17 February 1977, pp. 3–4.
[26] MfS ZA, ZAIG, no. 4158, 'Weitere Hinweise', 17 April 1981, p. 14.
[27] Süß W. 1999: 182.

consensus of the 1970s.[28] One report, compiled in January 1979, encapsulates popular reactions to the disruption caused by bad weather to transport and consumer and energy supplies: 'After the initial appreciation of certain restrictions in all regions, especially in the central and southern ones, there is now widespread incomprehension that a few days of hard frost and snowfall can have such effects on all aspects of life'.[29] The reports in the mass media of the successful development of modern technology were contradicted by reality: 'Technology is useless when 20 cm of snow, as in the central and southern regions, produce a catastrophe in the economy'.[30] Towards the close of 1979, the state's manipulation of prices, whereby certain commodities were transferred into higher price categories, resulted in long queues for goods in short supply and widespread dissatisfaction with the negative impact on living standards.[31] Given that criticism was fiercer and more outspoken than hitherto, ZAIG assessors testified to an 'overall dwindling trust on the part of its people in the party and in the economic policy of the GDR (especially trade and price policy)'.[32]

The consumer supply problems assumed an even greater urgency in the early 1980s when the emergence of the independent trade union, the so-called 'counterrevolutionary' Solidarity, in neighbouring Poland set the alarm bells ringing in East Berlin. The GDR's rulers were worried not only by the threat posed by such a movement to the Communist monopoly on power but also because the dislocation of supplies and price rises in the GDR might provoke similar unrest and destabilise the SED system. MfS reports from the autumn of 1980, when Solidarity was beginning to organise strikes and undermine the administrations of Gierek and Kania, lent some substance to SED and MfS worries. Long-time SED members and experienced labour activists warned that great care was needed in order to prevent similar developments being triggered off in the GDR if union functionaries continued to be insensitive to workers' grievances and if the disruptive activities of 'hostile-negative forces' were not contained.[33] However, popular opinion, at least according to ZAIG reports, did not anticipate that the GDR would share the fate of Poland, partly because the MfS and the other security forces were likely to take preventive action and partly because, for all its problems, the GDR was regarded as having the superior social and economic system. Although the SED provided some material assistance to the beleaguered

---

[28] A Stasi assessment of the social consensus in this vein can be found in MfS ZA, ZAIG, no. 4082, May 1972, pp. 1–3.

[29] MfS ZA, ZAIG, no. 4165, 'Hinweise', 8 January 1979, p. 4. Our translation.

[30] Ibid. Our translation.

[31] MfS ZA, ZAIG, no. 4480, 'Wochenübersicht', Berlin, 5 November 1979, pp. 58–9.

[32] MfS ZA, ZAIG, no. 4480, 'Wochenübersicht', Berlin, 19 November 1979, p. 149. Our translation.

[33] See the various reports in August and September 1980 in MfS ZA, ZAIG, no. 4151, pp. 19, 31, 33, 40, 52.

Polish government, its campaign against Solidarity, which was also designed to stoke up traditional anti-Polish feeling, was not without resonance among the East German population. In late August 1980, the MfS noted considerable popular antipathy to aiding Poland for fear that it might cause consumer supply shortages in the GDR. The Poles, it was believed, had brought the desperate situation upon themselves through their own 'apathy' and 'laziness'.[34]

Although the end of the communist power monopoly in Poland lay several years in the future, endemic problems could not be erased by the declaration of martial law. Nor could those of the GDR be solved by Western credit injections. Schalck-Golodkowski utilised his Bavarian contacts to negotiate two massive credits from West German *Land* and private banks of 1 billion DM and 950 million DM in 1983 and 1984 respectively, thereby boosting the creditworthiness of the GDR in the eyes of foreign banks. East German reactions were mixed. According to ZAIG, 'progressive forces', meaning SED supporters, welcomed the credit agreements as they strengthened the GDR economy and demonstrated that the country was a 'trustworthy partner'. Yet even this group had reservations: the credits increased the GDR's dependence on the FRG and plunged the country deeper into debt.[35] Furthermore, as it was generally believed that the credits were linked to concessions by the SED on emigration to the West, they feared for the internal stability of the GDR. When Honecker's visit to West Germany finally went ahead, in September 1987, it undoubtedly boosted his international reputation and appeared to seal the GDR's position as a separate and sovereign state. ZAIG, however, drew attention to the other side of the coin: young people interpreted the visit as a sign that the Berlin Wall and the traditional negative image of West German imperialism were both redundant.[36]

MASS EMIGRATION

The widespread dissatisfaction with the regime fuelled a mass exodus which almost brought the GDR to its knees in 1953 and 1961, and would finally do so in 1989. Although the building of the Berlin Wall had bought the SED some breathing space in 1961 and helped the party to rebuild the shattered economy and establish an uneasy social contract with the population in the later 1960s and early 1970s, the emigration pressures did not vanish. Indeed, with the advent of détente and the signing of the Helsinki Accords ratified by the Conference on Security and Cooperation in Europe in 1975 (see Chapter 2), the emigration movement gathered momentum. The Accords committed the Soviet Union, the GDR and the other East European allies to promote

---

[34] See the reports on the reaction of the East German population to events in Poland in MfS ZA, ZAIG, no. 4151, pp. 14, 48.
[35] MfS ZA, ZAIG, no. 4158, 31 July 1984, pp. 54–6.
[36] Dennis M. 2000: 181.

Table 14.1 Reasons and motives for leaving the GDR; comparison between the 1984 and 1989 émigrés

	Percentage of the émigrés	
	1984	1989
Lack of freedom to express one's own opinion	71	74
Limited opportunities for travel	56	74
To be able to shape one's own life	(not included)	72
A lack of or unfavourable future prospects	45	69
Political pressures/regimentation and tight control by the state	66	65
Poor supply situation	46	56
Uniting of the family	36	28
Unfavourable career opportunities	21	26

The 1984 survey took place between the end of March and early April 1984: 500 emigrants at the Gießen emergency camp responded to a questionnaire. As in 1989, all persons were aged 18 years or over. The 1989 data were collected between 29 August and 11 September 1989 from written responses by a sample of 537 emigrants.

Source: Hilmer R. and Köhler A. 1989: 1385.

the cause of human rights in return for Western recognition of the 'inviolability' of Europe's post-war boundaries. This provided individuals and groups within the GDR with a lever to extract permission from the authorities to leave the GDR. Collective applications were made on various occasions during the 1980s and some applicants resorted to staging silent marches of protests in town centres.

The SED was soon confronted by a mass movement which it was increasingly unable to control. Official records show a six-fold increase in the number of applicants under pensionable age between 1980 and the second half of 1989.[37] In numerical terms, 21,500 applied to leave in 1980, 53,000 in 1985 and 113,500 in 1988. In a vain attempt to defuse the situation, the regime allowed over 21,000 of its citizens to leave in the first three months of 1984. By the end of the year, about 35,000 had been given official permission to leave and a further 6,000 had fled the country. *In toto*, between the building of the Berlin Wall and the end of 1988, 616,000 left for the West, of whom as many as 235,000 (38 per cent) managed to leave without the permission of the authorities. Although West German researchers found that political considerations such as 'lack of freedom to express one's own opinion' narrowly outweighed material factors in propelling the 1984 and 1989 emigration waves (see Table 14.1), the great exodus undoubtedly reflected the failure of the GDR to tackle its systemic defects and to reverse the pull exerted by West German living standards and political pluralism.

[37] On the statistics of the emigration movement, see Eisenfeld B. 1995a: 192–3, 203, 21 and Eisenfeld B. 1995b: 50.

The MfS sought to stem the tide by means of the Central Coordinating Group (*Zentrale Koordinierungsgruppe* – ZKG) and its regional branches.[38] When it was first set up, in 1976, the emphasis was on combating 'illegal' flight from the GDR and the so-called criminal traffickers in human beings. The focus shifted, especially after 1983, towards reducing the numbers applying to leave the country. The latter were supposedly inspired by external forces opposed to socialism and détente, notably Amnesty International and the International Society for Human Rights in Frankfurt am Main. In carrying out its tasks, ZKG cooperated closely with, among others, ZAIG, HV A, Main Department VI (passport control and tourism), and Main Department VII (counterintelligence in the Ministry of the Interior and the People's Police). As the exodus pressures mounted, so did the size of ZKG. Between 1976 and the end of 1986, it grew from the original three to six departments. Department 1 dealt with stemming the emigration pressures within the GDR, whereas Department 4 concentrated on West Germany, including the refugee centre at Marienfelde in West Berlin. ZKG's highly qualified staff rose from 20 in 1976 to 185 in October 1989 and in the Regional Coordinating Groups from 84 to 261 over the same period. As part of its general strategy, the SED allowed periodic increases in legal emigration and from 1986 onwards extended the categories of citizens who were allowed to go to the FRG on urgent family business, with the latter being interpreted in a much more generous manner than before. The boomerang effect of the new policy did not escape ZAIG: 'According to current information, the supply level in the GDR and in the FRG is being compared more and more frequently especially by people returning from journeys on urgent family business and the supply situation in the FRG is being praised. In some cases these comparisons lead to doubts about the productive capacity of the GDR's economy as a whole and the ostensible superiority of the capitalist production system is being underlined'.[39] The point about the reinforcement of perceptions was apposite as most East Germans were able to tune into West German TV programmes to form favourable impressions of life in the West. Despite the rapid expansion of ZKG and the heavy price paid by many of those applying to leave the GDR – interrogation, charges of treasonable activity, imprisonment, job discrimination, the withdrawal of driving licences – the MfS failed to halt the emigration movement and, in the summer of 1989, exit via Hungary and Czechoslovakia coalesced with the voice of the street to topple the SED monolith. The trickle of East Germans fleeing to the West after the barbed wire separating Hungary and Austria was cut on 2 May 1989 turned into a torrent when, on 10 September, the liberalising Hungarian government, to the fury of the SED, suspended its bilateral agreement with the GDR and opened the Iron Curtain in the East.

---

[38] Eisenfeld B. 1995a: 3–13, 21–6, 34–5, 49.
[39] MfS ZA, ZAIG, no. 3605, 'Weitere Hinweise', 8 September 1987, p. 73. Our translation.

GORBACHEV, REFORM AND OPPOSITION

Mikhail Gorbachev's accession to the post of General Secretary of the Communist Party of the Soviet Union in March 1985 acted as a catalyst for reform and change in the GDR. Honecker and the SED leaders were not unduly worried by Gorbachev's initial ideas on the modernisation of the Soviet Union, both economically and politically, by means of economic reconstruction (*perestroika*) and openness (*glasnost*). However, they became alarmed by, and then bitterly opposed to, his plans when it became apparent in the autumn of 1986, and particularly after the CPSU's Central Committee plena in January and June 1987, that Gorbachev was engaged in a massive overhaul of the Soviet Union's obsolescent structures. This was a momentous development for although the Prague Spring had shown how the administrative-command system might be reformed, the Soviet Union had then been the enemy of reform rather than, as in the later 1980s, a motor of radical change. The SED leadership sought to restrict the circulation of reformist ideas from the Soviet Union by ordering the censor to cut key passages from Gorbachev's speeches and to ban, in October 1988, the German issue of *Sputnik*, the Soviet monthly digest, which contained sharp criticism of the Hitler–Stalin non-aggression pact of 1939 and of the KPD's failure to co-operate with the SPD against Hitler. The banning of *Sputnik* precipitated widespread and bitter protests among the GDR population. ZAIG reported that East Germans, both SED and non-party members, felt that they had been 'rendered politically immature'.[40]

The most disturbing development in the eyes of Honecker and his associates was Gorbachev's reformulation of the Soviet Union's relations with its Warsaw Pact allies and the West, which entailed the erosion and then the *de facto* abandonment of the Brezhnev Doctrine in the summer of 1989. The latter became apparent when Gorbachev asserted before the Council of Europe in July 1989 the 'right of all countries to unimpeded independence and equal rights'. Although the Soviet leader had informed both Honecker and Kohl one month earlier that the Soviet Union would not abandon the GDR, it was apparent that thinking in Moscow on the German question was in a state of flux as the Soviet reformers strove for closer economic and political ties with West Germany and the USA. Whereas Gorbachev's preferred option seems to have been a form of *perestroika* for the GDR, some Soviet reformers were thinking the unthinkable. Vyacheslav Daschichev, a member of the Institute of the Economy of World Socialism, contrasted the inferior economic performance of the GDR's administrative-command system with that attained by the FRG's market economy and liberal political system, and he advocated the gradual drawing together and eventual reunification of the two German states.

---

[40] Süß W. 1999: 101.

As early as August 1985, ZAIG was reporting to Mielke, Mittig and Neiber that the new Soviet leader was, in the opinion of politically engaged GDR workers and management cadres, undertaking the kind of critical assessment of the Soviet Union's economy which was necessary in the GDR.[41] With Gorbachev becoming ever more radical and the SED gerontocracy more dogmatic and more obstructive, the Soviet leader's confrontation with the deficiencies of the administrative command system found 'widespread support' in the GDR. The SED leaders' counterargument that the GDR had to tread cautiously as it stood on the dividing line between NATO and the Warsaw Pact was rejected and greater openness was advocated in order to restore workers' loss of trust in the SED.[42] The unpopularity and counterproductive nature of Honecker's opposition to Gorbachev's course, no matter how the SED leader sought to cloak it in superficial approval of change in the Soviet Union, can be seen in popular reactions to the SED Party Congress in 1986. Whereas 'the remarks of comrade Gorbachev enjoyed great resonance among broad sections of the population' as regards the reform programme agreed by the XXVIIth Soviet Communist Party Congress,[43] many East German management cadres and members of the scientific-technical intelligentsia castigated the SED Party Congress for its failure to address the GDR's serious economic problems – the administrative methods of economic management, breaches of work discipline, manipulation of economic plans and so forth.[44] Gorbachev's new thinking was contrasted with that of the SED, whose approach produced 'apathy and indifference' and 'high-handedness and arrogance'.[45]

Gorbachev's policy of *glasnost* and *perestroika*, as well as the flowering of even more radical reform in Poland and Hungary, was an enormous boost to the small autonomous political groups in the GDR. Reform in the Soviet Union and Eastern Europe legitimised calls for political change and the promotion of human rights in the GDR and and it encouraged civil rights groups to emerge from their niches. However, despite these developments, not only did the opposition remain divided between the would-be emigrants and the 'voice' dissidents but the autonomous groups and critical church circles were numerically weak. Furthermore, the ministry continued to target the groups as it regarded them as one of the main channels for political underground activities and political-ideological diversion. The imperialist powers, notably the USA, the FRG and Great Britain were, it was believed, using the groups to subvert and ultimately destroy socialism by the propagation of notions of democratisation, liberalisation and political

---

[41] MfS ZA, ZAIG, no. 4518, 'Hinweise', 8 August 1985, pp. 59–60.
[42] MfS ZA, ZAIG, no. 4518, 'Hinweise', August 1988, pp. 102–3.
[43] MfS ZA, ZAIG, no. 4518, 'Weitere Hinweise', 20 April 1986, p. 50.
[44] Ibid., pp. 50–51.
[45] Ibid., p. 14.

pluralism.[46] While ZAIG appreciated that no consensus existed among the groups on an alternative model of society, its assessors were antipathetic to what they saw as the groups' 'attacks' against the foundations of socialism through the 'demagogic' use of concepts such as *glasnost* and their demands for a fundamental reform of socialism.[47] In condemning the groups' notions of a renewal of socialism, the MfS and the SED leaders were acting in accordance with their Marxist-Leninist viewpoint but, ironically, were undermining those very forces which, in late 1989 and early 1990, were seeking to reinvent the GDR as an independent and reformed state. For it was from among those autonomous groups and church circles that the citizens' movements and the new political parties emerged in September as part of the first foundation wave – notably New Forum, Democracy Now, Democratic Awakening and the Social Democratic Party – which sought to devise a Third Way between SED-style state socialism and the capitalist system of West Germany.

THE STASI IN TURMOIL

Important studies by Walter Süß and Jens Gieseke of the Gauck Authority's research unit have demonstrated that the MfS remained largely intact both organisationally and ideologically until early October 1989, and that members were determined to preserve their elite status and privileges. Wanja Abramowski, a captain in HV A until his departure in April 1988, recalls that in the 1980s the MfS staff were 'loyal to most of the top SED leaders and to the entire hierarchy. They identified with Marxism-Leninism as well as with socialist reality and accepted unconditionally the existing mechanisms of power'.[48] Despite murmurings, especially among younger staff, about the SED's negative attitude to Gorbachev's reforms and despite the existence of a limited reform potential in the ministry, Mielke, an unreconstructed hard-liner set the tone. The minister was opposed to *perestroika* and Gorbachev's opening to the West, fearing that such a course could only benefit the imperialist enemy.[49] In an important speech in December 1988, Mielke warned that in the difficult year ahead the GDR would be under pressure from three sides. Two of these sources were traditional – the imperialist enemy and internal oppositional forces – but the third, reform in the Soviet Union and several other socialist states, denoted the sea change in GDR–Soviet relations. Mielke's deputy, Mittig, underlined this point in the same month: 'By the misuse of the words *glasnost* and *perestroika* people hope in general for greater ideological effectiveness of demagogic demands for freedom and human rights . . .'.[50]

---

[46] Mitter A. and Wolle S. 1990: 46, 50.
[47] Ibid., 51–2.
[48] Abramowski W. 1992: 213.
[49] Süß W. 1999: 98–9, 105–8.
[50] Cited in ibid., 106. Our translation.

By the middle of the year, Mielke was becoming extremely nervous about the growing pace of democratisation in Hungary and Poland. Solidarity had scored an overwhelming victory in the elections to the *Sejm* at the beginning of June when it won 99 out of the 100 seats contested, a vivid demonstration that power was slipping away from the Communists. In Hungary, under pressure from the liberal wing of the Communist Party under Pozsgay and the centrists under Grosz, Kadar had stepped down as General Secretary in May 1988. At the beginning of the following year, a Law on Associations legitimised numerous new political groupings, some of whom, like the Free Democrats, were pushing for a Western parliamentary democracy and a free market economy. Mielke conceded that 'the many attempts by anti-socialist forces in Poland and Hungary as the legal opposition to undermine and destabilise the power of the working class have also encouraged hostile opposition forces and groupings to come forward more and more openly and provocatively with the same objective in our country too'.[51] However, he insisted that no concessions be made as regards the crucial question of power and the leading role of the SED.[52] And he concluded on a totally unfounded and anachronistic note that under the banner of the October Revolution 'all the conditions were created to continue the victorious struggle in today's class conflict . . .'.[53]

Yet neither the SED nor the Stasi could afford to ignore the growing crisis in East Germany, which manifested itself in the concession, albeit secretly, for the withdrawal in April 1989 of the order to the GDR border guards to shoot persons attempting illegally to cross the border.[54] In the following month, the Hungarians started to relax controls on their border with Austria, before, in September, dismantling the Iron Curtain. The latter action gave a powerful boost to flight from the GDR and led to a merging between 'exit' and 'voice' as it encouraged civil rights groups to emerge from the confines of the alternative political culture. The most significant of the new groups – New Forum – issued a manifesto on 9 September calling for a widespread discussion in society on reform. Ten days later, it applied, in vain, for official recognition as an association. The ministry was caught up in the contradictions of SED policy and the problems of society were piercing its protective shield. It was becoming increasingly difficult to sustain the traditional image of the class enemy in the West at a time when Honecker, Mittag and Schalck-Golodkowski were courting politicians such as the arch-conservative Minister President of Bavaria, Franz-Josef Strauß, as well as West Germany businessmen, in order to keep the GDR economy afloat. The visit of Honecker to the FRG in September 1987 and the joint SED/SPD document 'The

---

[51] From Mielke's speech on 29 June 1989 in Otto W. 2000: 680. Our translation.
[52] Ibid., 670.
[53] Cited in ibid., 685. Our translation.
[54] Süß W. 1999: 148–54.

Conflict of Ideologies and Common Security', an ideological *hors d'oeuvre* to the visit, also unnerved the Stasi. The SED/SPD document agreed on the need for open debate on the competition between the two world systems, accepted that each system was capable of reform, and advocated that the presentation of each side be done in a realistic manner rather than through the propagation of enemy images.[55] As one Stasi officer stated in his 1989 dissertation: 'Can you hate the opponent with whom you are cooperating? Doesn't maintaining peace also serve the purpose of maintaining the imperialist system? ... Will there ever be an imperialism that can exist without lying about and slandering socialism? Is not our struggle for peaceful coexistence and cooperation hopeless?'[56]

Nor could the MfS fall back on the mantra that 'to learn from the Soviet Union is to learn to be victorious' for Gorbachev's radical critique of the Soviet system, which confirmed many of the criticisms hitherto dismissed as Western propaganda, was destroying the ideological and political pillars of the MfS as well as of the entire *ancien régime*. Wolfgang Schwanitz confirms this when recalling, in 1990, that from about the middle of the 1980s, a 'starkly increasing contradiction' developed between everyday life and Central Committee reports, a contradiction which was sharpened by *perestroika* in the Soviet Union.[57] In consequence, Mielke was tilting at windmills when he called for greater political-ideological work in the MfS and the reinvigoration of traditional communist attitudes.[58]

Furthermore, as the MfS was directly involved in stemming the demographic exodus, the intractable problems of GDR society and politics found their way into the very heart of the ministry and helped undermine its sense of exclusivity. Former MfS members, mainly conscripts in the Guard Regiment, and their relatives joined the exodus and as the ministry was entrusted with the task of dissuading would-be émigrés from abandoning the GDR, it could no longer ignore the growing discrepancy between everyday reality and the 'virtual socialism' of the state media. This was but one of the factors which would undermine the ministry's unity and erode traditional ideological tenets. In September, the record of a meeting of MfS members of the SED basic organisation in Main Department III noted that a considerable number 'are convinced that not only political-ideological diversion has had its effect but that social problems and contradictions in our development have also played a part and should not be underestimated'.[59]

On the eve of communism's collapse, the Stasi's options for dealing with opposition groups, dissenters and would-be émigrés were narrowing.

---

[55] The full English text is printed in *Foreign Affairs* **27** (26), 10 September 1987, pp. 205–7.
[56] Cited in Gieseke J. 2000: 464–5. Our translation.
[57] Cited in ibid., 457.
[58] Ibid., 436.
[59] Cited in Süß W. 1999: 191. Our translation.

Decomposition remained the favoured course, and the ministry continued to deploy top IMs such as Schnur and Böhme among the alternative political groups. But in good Chekist fashion, the MfS sometimes resorted to open repression. Soon after Honecker had returned from his visit to West Germany, the security forces raided the Zionskirche in East Berlin, where the illegal periodical *Grenzfall* and the ecological church newsletter *Umweltblätter* were printed, and arrested members of the Initiative for Peace and Human Rights. Although these and other activists were soon released after public demonstrations at the church, a second and more ruthless phase was inaugurated with the arrest of some 200 activists both before and after protests at the official rally in January 1988 commemorating the death of Rosa Luxemburg and Karl Liebknecht. Among those arrested were the songwriter and singer Stefan Krawczyk, his wife Freya Klier and Vera Wollenberger. This unleashed waves of protest and support; unexpectedly, all were released from jail. Several were deported to the West, among them Krawczyk, Freya Klier, Wolfgang Templin and Bärbel Bohley. The crackdown may have pleased the conservative elements in the SED, but it did nothing to resolve the underlying contradictions facing party and state.

A similar dilemma resurfaced in the summer and autumn of 1989 when the SED and the security forces began to run out of ideas on how to preserve communism. As Honecker and Mielke were unable, either psychologically or politically, to implement even a limited reform which might have brought them some relief, rumours spread that force might be used in a GDR version of Beijing's Tiananmen Square massacre. Honecker's wife, Margot, the Minister of People's Education, had stated in public that socialism might have to be defended 'with weapon in hand'.[60] However, as the Soviet Union made it clear to Honecker that the 400,000 Soviet troops in the GDR would remain in barracks and as the SED leadership was reluctant to run the risk of civil war and international ostracism, regime violence tended to be sporadic and hesitant. Mielke's deputy, Mittig, acknowledged that the use of penal legislation, a favoured option with which the MfS had sought to combat the opposition groups in the summer of 1989, had not succeeded. And rather than create martyrs, he stressed the need to continue the well-tried decomposition measures against the leading opposition figures and the groups.[61]

The uncovering in March 1990 of Wolfgang Schnur (IMB 'Dr Ralf Schirmer') of Democratic Awakening and Ibrahim Böhme (IMB 'Maximilian') of the Eastern Social Democratic Party as informers and later revelations of the involvement with the Stasi of prominent individuals such as Manfred Stolpe (IM 'Sekretär), Lothar de Maizière (allegedly IM 'Czerni'), the chairman of the National Democratic Party Günter Hartmann (IMS 'Harry') and the General Secretary of the Eastern CDU Martin Kirchner (IME 'Hesselbarth')

---

[60] Süß W. 1999: 128.
[61] Ibid., 222–3.

have given rise to a conspiracy theory of the revolution. According to this version, the activities of the citizens' movements in the early stage of the revolution were largely steered by the Stasi and its numerous agents as part of a broader scheme to remove Honecker, whose intransigence was regarded as endangering the SED power monopoly. The informers, so it would seem, were not only subverting the new groups but Honecker too! There is also irrefutable evidence that after the failure of the security forces in the summer to quell the protests and movements by the selective use of arrests and imprisonment, the Stasi deployed its informers as *agents pacifiteurs* rather than as *agents provocateurs*. A report issued by the head of the Dresden Regional Administration at the end of November reveals that between 80 and 100 IMs had been planted in the citizens' movements.[62] Although the Stasi was undoubtedly successful in infiltrating the citizens' movements, the conspiracy theory is unsatisfactory. It exaggerates the ministry's ability to influence the powerful forces generated by the mass exodus, the citizens' movements and the demonstrators. Rather than steering developments, the Stasi tended to be reactive and its leaders' plans were often confused and uncertain. In these circumstances, informers like Schnur and Böhme were caught between the cross-currents of reaction and reform: while personally not unsympathetic to elements of reform, their main function was to apply the brakes on the process of change.

The SED and MfS leaders were anxious that the GDR's 40th anniversary should pass smoothly in East Berlin before the eyes of the assembled guests, the most notable being Gorbachev, especially on the main day of celebration, 7 October. However, the police and MfS forces were unable to suppress the cries of protest and spontaneous demonstrations against the SED despite the mass arrests and the use of gratuitous violence. Other demonstrations and arrests took place in Leipzig, Dresden, Karl-Marz-Stadt, Potsdam, Halle and elsewhere. It is estimated that about 3,500 persons were arrested between 4 and 9 October.[63] The key moment was the night of 9 October in the Saxon city of Leipzig when some 70,000 protestors gathered for what had become the customary Monday night demonstration after the early evening service in the Nikolai church. Two days prior to the demonstration, the Defence Minister, Heinz Keßler, had issued an order for the NVA to be made fully combat ready. Mielke, too, had hatched plans for crushing the demonstration, including the use of special Stasi forces and the workers' militia. On the day before the demonstration, Mielke reminded heads of service units that those 'who regularly carry arms are to have their weapons on them at all times according to the given requirements'.[64] By the evening, security forces with live ammunition were waiting in readiness in the narrow side streets;

---

[62] Süß W. 1999: 566, 576–9, 585–6, 701–3.
[63] Gieseke J. 2000: 479.
[64] See the telegram containing this instruction in Otto W. 2000: 687.

hospitals had been warned to prepare beds for the wounded. A letter had already been planted in the 6 October edition of the local Leipzig daily SED organ, the *Leipziger Volkszeitung*, from the commander of a workers' militia group condemning the misuse of the church service by enemies of the state and asserting that members of the militia were prepared to put a stop to counterrevolutionary actions. He concluded ominously: 'If needs be with weapons in their hands'.[65] While there was no doubt that the demonstration could have been put down by force and that Mielke was not averse to such a solution, the SED and the security forces were not in fact intent on this kind of course. They hoped that threats and rumours of force would intimidate the protestors. It was a high-risk strategy and it could have misfired if clashes had occurred inadvertently. That a bloody outcome was avoided was due to a number of reasons: the political infighting among the SED elites in East Berlin aimed at bringing about the removal of the old guard; the self-discipline of the crowd and the appeal for non-violence made in the churches and by six local luminaries; the confinement of Soviet troops to their barracks; and the risks attendant on the outbreak of civil war. Furthermore, the view was widespread among the Stasi and security forces that to use force against workers would demonstrate the hollowness of the SED claim to be the party of the working class.[66]

THE END OF THE STASI

With force no longer a realistic option, the hardliners were soon removed from power. On 18 October, Egon Krenz, with Mielke's unenthusiastic and opportunistic support, succeeded Honecker as head of the SED and the Council of State in a vain and desperate attempt by the SED to arrest the slide into powerlessness. Krenz's calls for dialogue in society fell on deaf ears and on 6 November an estimated 500,000 braved pouring rain in Leipzig to demand a new travel law and an end to the SED's leading role in society. Two days earlier, an even larger crowd had gathered on Alexanderplatz in East Berlin for a demonstration coordinated by the Artists' Federation. The SED and MfS were only able to organise a damage limitation exercise, a clear sign of the growing weakness of the *ancien régime*. Even though Stoph, Hager and other members of the old guard were ejected from the Politbüro, and Hans Modrow, who was known to have some reform leanings, was appointed Chairman of the Council of Ministers, the colourless Krenz appeared to be reacting to events and too inclined to half measures to convince people that he was an East German Gorbachev. With the mass exodus and popular protests gathering momentum and the SED grassroots becoming increasingly

[65] Neues Forum Leipzig 1990: 63.
[66] Süß W. 1999: 745.

restless, Krenz, in a confused manoeuvre, allowed the Berlin Wall to be opened on the night of 9–10 November. The opening of the Wall, which had become only a matter of time, compounded rather than relieved Krenz's problems. Even before Krenz resigned as General Secretary on 3 December, the legitimacy crisis of the SED regime was so deep that unification was rising rapidly towards the top of the political agenda. This is caught in the shift in calls on the streets from 'We are the people' in the early stages of the revolution to 'We are one people'. The latter was a reference to the concept of one German nation. Although Modrow laboured hard to prevent the absorption of the GDR by its powerful West German neighbour, the parliamentary election in March 1990 ended in a resounding victory for the conservative coalition of the East German CDU leader Lothar de Maizière. The GDR moved rapidly along the path to economic and monetary union in July and then political unification on 3 October 1990, when the five new *Länder* of East Germany were incorporated into the FRG.

The MfS had no option but to follow the course of 'defensive liberalisation'[67] set in motion by Krenz and continued with greater vigour by Modrow, and it also had to face the anger of the crowds and calls for its dissolution. During the burgeoning demonstrations, the cries of 'Power to the people forever, SED never!', 'Stasi out, Stasi out!' and 'Your days are numbered!' encapsulated the double rejection of the party and its sword and shield, a mood which turned into fury when the scale of Stasi surveillance and the corruption among the old elites began to make the headlines. There could, however, be no recourse to arms. As the deputy head of the Rostock's Regional Administration, Colonel Amthor, stated: 'We must not shoot, we'll destroy the current development . . . even if in the face of abuse and insults our hearts bleed and our trigger finger itches'.[68]

Mielke was an early victim of popular ire and of the SED's ejection of its old leaders. He resigned from the Politbüro and as minister on 3 November. Ten days later in a rambling valedictory speech at a televised session of the *Volkskammer*, a confused and irritated Mielke was revealed as a latter-day Wizard of Oz. He aroused derision and anger by his failure to express regret and by his pathetic protestation 'But I love you all'. The disoriented MfS staff were appalled at Mielke's abject performance, believing that he had undermined the ministry's sense of mission and the 'good cause'. In a letter to the President of the *Volkskammer* on the following day, the SED party organisation in the MfS distanced itself on behalf of all members of the Stasi from Mielke's statement and criticised him for his failure to accept personal responsibility for what had happened and for presenting a false picture of the ministry's work.[69] Bewilderment was combined with arrogance in the

---

[67] The term is used by Süß in Süß W. 1999: 465.
[68] Cited in Gieseke J. 2000: 503. Our translation.
[69] Cited from the document in Otto W. 2000: 702.

statement by one officer from Halle: 'We had hope right up to the last day. It had to be a mistake, perhaps it was even a huge joke. Now we can only look on in complete incomprehension as the so-called people refuse to stop yelling.'[70] Three days before the opening of the Berlin Wall, Mielke's number two, Mittig, had been equally arrogant in an interview with *Neues Deutschland*: 'The total surveillance state, the ubiquitous spy system exist only in the imagination of the Western media. The Ministry of State Security does not keep the people under surveillance. It cooperates with the citizens . . .'.[71]

As for Mielke, he was thrown out of the SED on 3 December 1989, imprisoned four days later and released on health grounds in March 1990 from the Berlin-Hohenschönhausen jail, where he had spent several weeks in solitary confinement in the hospital wing. Although he escaped prosecution for various charges during the next few years, including one relating to the shootings at the Berlin Wall, on grounds of ill-health, he was sentenced to six years' imprisonment in 1993 for the murder of two policemen in 1931. However, he was released two years later when he was diagnosed as senile. He died in June 2000, after having spent most of the intervening period in a spacious flat in the vicinity of the Hohenschönhausen jail.

Following a suggestion by the Collegium of the ministry, a successor to the Stasi – the Office for National Security (*Amt für Nationale Sicherheit* – AfNS) – was set up by the Modrow government on 17 November. One of Mielke's four deputies, Wolfgang Schwanitz, was elected by the *Volkskammer* to be its new head. As a member of the old officer corps, he could not, however, wipe the slate clean, thereby prompting accusations that the AfNS, dubbed the 'Nasi', was the MfS under a different name. He attempted to strike an unsatisfactory balance between the old and the new system of domestic counterintelligence: to retain the core of the officer class and as many informers as was possible while creating a new constitutional and legal basis for the AfNS and reducing the full-time staff by a half, above all in the District Service Units. In addition, the new organisation was to be divested of some of the Stasi's peripheral functions, such as passport control. At an early stage in the downsizing process, one officer lamented in November that: 'After leaving the organisation our comrades, as skilled MfS workers, are forced to go from door to door begging for integration in our society. The social situation of a high proportion of us has deteriorated and we have the feeling that we are the whipping boy of the nation'.[72] The demoralisation and disillusionment in the ranks was fuelled by revelations in the press from 1 December onwards of the privileged life-style of the SED leaders, feelings which also turned many MfS staff against their own leaders.[73] On

---

[70] Cited in Fricke K. W. 1991: 71. Our translation.
[71] Cited in Süß W. 1999: 459. Our translation.
[72] Cited in ibid., 551. Our translation. By the beginning of December, the AfNS had lost about 6,000 staff: ibid., 554.
[73] Ibid., 597–9.

6 December, most of the top generals and colonels – among them Mittig, Neiber, Kienberg and Kleine at central level and Schwarz (Erfurt), Hummitzsch (Leipzig) and Dangrieß (Gera) at regional level – were dismissed.

With citizens' committees occupying the offices of the AfNS in a number of towns such as Gera to prevent the destruction of Stasi files and with the Central Round Table in East Berlin demanding its dissolution, the Council of Ministers finally succumbed to the pressure on 14 December and decided to disband the AfNS. The Modrow government's subsequent efforts to transform HV A into a separate foreign intelligence service of 4,000 members under Werner Großmann as well as creating an Office for the Protection of the Constitution with a staff of 10,000 under the former head of the Frankfurt/Oder Regional Administration, Major General Heinz Engelhardt, also had to be abandoned – on 12 January 1990.[74] Three days later, a citizens' committee, in conjunction with the police and the Procurator General, assumed responsibility for security matters at the Stasi headquarters in East Berlin. That evening, several thousand protesters, in circumstances which are not entirely clear, stormed the building and destroyed some of the materials, despite demonstrators' demands for people to see their individual files. On the day of the occupation, the Central Round Table had received a detailed report from government sources of the finances, operations and the number of staff employed by the Stasi.[75] The dismantling of the AfNS continued until Modrow lost power in March 1990; some officers were dismissed, a few others found shelter in jobs in public administration. At the last session of the Central Round Table in mid-March, it was reported that 96 per cent of MfS regional staff and 87 per cent at headquarters had been removed.[76] The disorientation among the ranks and the rapidity of the ministry's fall led to three major generals in Regional Administrations – Gerhard Lange, Horst Böhm and Peter Koch – committing suicide in January, February and May respectively.[77] HV A remained active for a while longer than the AfNS, being granted a period of grace until 30 June 1990; it used this time to destroy virtually all of its files. The slow and erratic process of putting the AfNS to rest was coordinated by Peter-Michael Diestel, the Minister of the Interior in the de Maizière government, with the assistance of the State Committee for the Dissolution of the Former MfS/AfNS. The process was completed with German unification in October.[78]

---

[74] Gieseke J. 2001: 241–2.
[75] Fricke K. W. 1991: 73.
[76] Wolfe N. T. 1991: 128.
[77] Fricke K. W. 1991: 74.
[78] Gieseke J. 2001: 241–3.

Chapter 15

THE STASI LEGACY

OPENING THE STASI FILES

One of the most controversial issues during the East German revolution was whether or not to open the Pandora's box of microfilm, discs, tapes and documents which had survived destruction by the MfS. The question of access sometimes cut across the lines of political parties and citizens' movements, although the latter were generally in favour of opening the files. Needless to say, former MfS employees, some of whom were used by the government in the dismantling of the ministry, hoped for their closure. A cogent case could be made for both opening and restricting access. If access were strictly limited or the files destroyed, privacy would be protected, wounds in East German society perhaps healed without sensationalist disclosures and a witch hunt for agents, and a line therefore drawn under the past. It was also argued that the dubious records of a secret police were inappropriate for assessing and making judgements on the disparate reasons for an individual's collaboration with the Stasi and on complex social and political processes.[1] Pastor Rainer Eppelmann, who became Minister of Defence and Disarmament after the March 1990 elections to the *Volkskammer*, also had serious reservations, fearing that the new political freedoms would be jeopardised by 'denunciations, revelations, and acts of revenge'. The Minister of the Interior, Diestel, warned that the Stasi records – 'these products of evil' could not be used to determine innocence and guilt as 'there were only two [types of individuals] who were truly innocent in this system, the newborn child and the alcoholic'.[2] Diestel's chief, Minister President Lothar de Maizière,

---

[1] Werner Fischer, a member of Alliance '90 and a key figure in the dismantling of the AfNS, was an advocate of confronting the past through access to the files. He recognised, however, that this was a highly complex process as not all Stasi employees were criminals and that many in the SED, the bureaucracy and the neighbourhood apartments had, 'directly or indirectly, willingly or unwillingly, helped to make it possible for this repressive apparatus to function'. Cited in Sa'adah A. 1998: 93.

[2] The statements by Eppelmann and Diestel are both from McAdams A. J. 2001: 61.

even went so far as to predict murder and manslaughter if the files were opened.[3] On balance, representatives of the West German government favoured closure, partly because they wished to avoid revelations about secret service practices. Some, like the Interior Minister Wolfgang Schäuble, wondered whether it would not be better to concentrate on the reconstruction of the GDR rather than becoming embroiled in heated controversies over the millions of East Germans who had been connected with the Stasi in so many different ways.[4]

The case against destruction, closure or tight restrictions on access was, on balance, the more persuasive: individuals had the right to discover how they had been pursued and persecuted by the Stasi; the files were needed to determine criminal charges, to assess people's suitability for political and administrative posts and to provide evidence in connection with claims for rehabilitation and compensation; and ex-Stasi operatives should be deprived of their 'intellectual ownership' of the contents of the files. The files, it was also argued, were an essential tool in the reconstruction of the past and in avoiding the kind of delays which were symptomatic of the historical re-working of the Nazi era. Joachim Gauck, the head of the agency responsible for the Stasi records, reflected on another important aspect:

> The goal is that people who were long oppressed should be able to carry forward the liberation that they dreamed about and struggled for in the streets – through a process of memory and coming to terms [with the past]. People who were previously oppressed and deprived of autonomy should take possession of their former rulers' knowledge. They should become [active participants in shaping their own understanding] and – in this way – come more to find themselves. They should become more free, for the tasks of tomorrow.[5]

Despite widespread opposition by numerous politicians, as well as by Western intelligence agencies concerned about the lifting of the lid on the clandestine practices of security services, the Unification Treaty between the GDR and the FRG granted rights of access for specified purposes and provided for central control of the files by an independent commissioner and for the

---

[3] De Maizière would later come under suspicion of having served as an IM. While he denied this accusation, he admitted that he had entered into contact with the Stasi but insisted that it was only in connection with his work as a solicitor. Although the files concerning IM 'Czerni' have not survived, information in the Gauck Authority indicates that de Maizière, like IM 'Czerni', lived at the same address in East Berlin, owned property in Tornow, was a member of the Federal Synod of the Evangelical Church and had access to information from the solicitors' association in East Berlin. This does not, of course, prove that IM 'Czerni' was necessarily aware that the Stasi regarded him as an IM and it fails to reveal what might have been the motivation behind his contacts with the MfS. See Süß W. 1999: 581.

[4] McAdams A. J. 2001: 62.

[5] Cited in Quint P. E. 1997: 230.

records to be kept in the East.[6] Although the principle of access was in line with the view of the East German parliament, the initial negotiations between the two governments ran into widespread criticism from parliamentary deputies and civil rights groups. The original *Volkskammer* law on the Stasi records of 24 August had envisaged far more generous access to the files and had assigned greater rights of control to the individual eastern *Länder*. Furthermore, fears in the GDR that the Unification Treaty negotiators intended to transfer the materials to the Federal Archive provoked a hunger strike and an occupation of the former Stasi headquarters in the Normannenstraße by prominent members of the citizens' groups. Ratification of the treaty was in jeopardy. A compromise was eventually reached in the form of a supplement to the Unification Treaty, which incorporated the basic principles of the *Volkskammer* law and provided for the storage of the files in central and regional depositories in East Germany in recognition of the fact that they were an integral part of the East German past. Bowing to pressure from the citizens' groups, the supplement also allowed broader access for those affected by the files on condition that the interests of third persons were respected.

THE LAW ON THE RECORDS OF THE STASI

The comprehensive regulation of the Stasi records was left to the all-German Bundestag. This took the form of the Law on the Records of the Secret Service of the Former German Democratic Republic. The law, which was passed by an overwhelming majority in the Bundestag, came into force on 29 December 1991. At the same time, the former Rostock pastor and *Volkskammer* member for Alliance '90, Joachim Gauck, was confirmed as head of the Federal Authority for the Records of the State Security Service of the Former GDR (BStU) by the Bundestag. He had been in charge of the *Volkskammer* committee responsible for the dissolution of the Stasi and, since 3 October, had occupied the interim post of the Federal Government's Special Commissioner for the Stasi Records. In accordance with the Stasi Records Law, the Federal Commissioner holds office for five years, although tenure can be renewed for another period. The Commissioner serves several masters in that he or she is elected by the Bundestag, is appointed by the Federal President and is subject to the supervisory authority of the Minister of the Interior. The files are administered by the central agency, whose main offices are located in the eastern part of Berlin, near Alexanderplatz. Branch offices have been set up in the *Länder* of Berlin, Brandenburg, Mecklenburg-West Pomerania, Saxony, Saxony-Anhalt and Thuringia.

The aims of the act basically follow those of the original *Volkskammer* law, that is, to enable individuals to access information stored by the Stasi on their

---

[6] On the negotiations and discussions in the summer of 1990, see Quint P. E. 1997: 233–4.

person while at the same time providing protection against the violation of individual rights and privacy; to promote the historical, judicial and political appraisal of the MfS and the GDR; to provide public and private bodies with access to information in criminal prosecutions, in particular those connected with Stasi operations; to assist in the screening of individuals for jobs; and to help in the rehabilitation of victims of Stasi persecution.[7] However, the Bundestag went one stage further than the *Volkskammer* by allowing for individuals to acquire copies of their files. The Bundestag thus sought to strike the difficult balance between the risks to privacy and the pursuit of social justice on the basis of the records of a secret service, many of which had been gathered in an illegal manner. Several provisions were introduced to realise this goal. First, while all individuals, whether from the former GDR or elsewhere, are entitled to find out whether the files contain information about them, 'data subjects', that is, victims of Stasi operations, are provided with greater access to the information in their files than the full-time staff, agents and former 'beneficiaries' of the ministry. The term 'beneficiary' refers to those persons who benefited in various ways from the Stasi, for example, cash payments or protection from criminal prosecution. Secondly, although the data subjects have full access to information about their persons, the law provides for the protection of identities by rendering anonymous other victims and third parties identified in their files. On the other hand, if the identities of Stasi officials and informers can be proved, then their names can be communicated to the victim. The act also allows access to information for determining whether a criminal prosecution is appropriate, particularly for crimes committed in connection with an individual's employment with the MfS or other security and penal authorities.

Finally, the most contentious issue of all concerned the decision to allow for the use and publication of Stasi documentation by the media as well as for purposes of political education and historical reappraisal. Full access was granted to those records which contain no personal data, to duplicates in which the personal data have been 'depersonalised' by BStU staff, and to data regarding Stasi employees, unless they were younger than 18 years of age. The provision also applies to contemporary historical personages, political office holders or public law officials while in office but not to data subjects or third parties. A 'third party' is defined as someone who was neither a victim nor a perpetrator but about whom the Stasi collected information. However, if data subjects give their written consent, then access is also allowed to materials relating to them. Although researchers and the media were therefore given exceptional access to the records concerning so-called contemporary historical personages as well as public officials, a bar was placed on access to all records if, to quote section 32, 'publication of the records would impair the

---

[7] On the legislative details in this and the following paragraph, see the *Act Regarding the Records of the State Security Service* 1991: 4–5, 12–17, 20–21, 25.

overriding legitimate interests of the persons involved'.[8] The latter notwithstanding, historians, including the BStU's own research staff, and the media have been active in publishing important contributions about officers and IMs, the structure of the ministry and the surveillance of society.

THE WORK OF THE BStU

A brake was temporarily applied on research and publication as a result of the appeal by former Chancellor Helmut Kohl against the BStU's plans to publish Stasi transcripts of his intercepted telephone conversations. Kohl's defence, that this would infringe his privacy and dignity and that he merited protection as the victim of illegal eavesdropping, was accepted by the Berlin Administrative Court in July 2001. Kohl's action was highly regrettable in that his own administration had pushed the original Stasi Records Act through the Bundestag in the face of many objections to the very clauses which had come to trouble Kohl so deeply. For most observers, the ex-Chancellor was misusing a not unfounded care for the dignity of the individual behind a less exalted concern that the Stasi tapes might contain further revelations of the corrupt and illegal use of party donations by himself and several CDU associates. While the BStU's appeal against the Berlin Administrative Court's decision was turned down by the Federal Administrative Court in March 2002, an amendment to the Stasi Records Act passed by the Bundestag in July 2002 restored access to the files of public figures for journalists and historians using the materials for historical purposes. This removed a fundamental threat to the use of the BStU archive. However, the whole case serves as an illustration of the tension between two basic rights in the original 1991 Act – that of the individual to privacy and that of the public to pertinent information regarding the operations and structure of the MfS.

Given the volume of work entailed, it is hardly surprising that the BStU has grown into one of the largest administrative organs in east Germany. It grew rapidly from about 600 employees to 2,777 in May 1992, of whom 95 per cent came from east Germany.[9] Applications to consult the files and requests for information by individuals, the media, public and private bodies and researchers have flooded in: a peak of 587,325 in 1993 and a low of 253,529 in 2000.[10] On average, 10,000 requests, about half of which are new, are received each month to consult the files. Although many applications concern personal files, the BStU is also involved in collating and disseminating data relating to criminal prosecutions and the vetting of officials. In

---

[8] *Act Regarding the Records of the State Security Service* 1991: 31.

[9] *Vierter Tätigkeitsbericht* 1999: 89.

[10] For the details, see the BStU webpages http://www.bstu.de/taetigkeit/seiten/2-1-2-2-1-2-1.htm and http://www.bstu.de/taetigkeit/seiten1-4.htm

addition to these tasks, the BStU has to classify and repair documents and to conduct political education work with schools. The demand for permission to use the archive for purposes of historical research is high, 541 applications in 1993 and 651 in 2000.

Earlier chapters in this book have examined the relevance of the BStU holdings for the history of the GDR and have shown the extent of the Stasi's surveillance of individuals and institutions. Just to refer back briefly to two aspects – Stasi operations against the internal 'enemies' and the motivation and actions of both IMs and officers – serves to pinpoint some of the main difficulties in using the archival materials both for reappraising the ministry's history and for assessing the suitability of individuals for office and their liability for criminal actions. With regard to collaboration with the Stasi, it is vital to differentiate between the various levels of complicity, say between those who made their apartment available for clandestine meetings and those who reported on the intimate details of colleagues' and friends' private lives and opinions. There is also the difficult matter of persons who were, at various times, both victims and perpetrators, and it is also necessary to bear in mind the kind of motives and pressures which lay behind compliance and collaboration. Not only do the records sometimes fail to clarify motives but they may be so incomplete that an individual's actions cannot be recon- structed from them. In some cases, they are inaccurate and misleading, as in the case of those wrongly accused of being IMs. Finally, some IMs have claimed, not without justification, that they did not consciously and willingly cooperate with the Stasi; and even the registration of an IM by a controller may have been done, albeit rarely, without the consent and knowledge of an individual.

Such considerations are crucial for the historical record and for an indi- vidual's moral and personal reckoning with his or her past but they are also integral to the screening for jobs and criminal investigations. In the latter cases, the BStU, as an administrative organ, has a responsibility to provide private corporations and public bodies with the pertinent data. It is not, however, an investigative and prosecuting body and nor does it make recom- mendations on dismissals. By February 1997, according to estimates by the BStU, 42,066 people had been dismissed from the civil service and around 12,800 non-civil servants removed from their jobs on account of their Stasi connections.[11] Few former full-time officers have become civil servants. In the absence of clear criteria for past culpability and present suitability, the screening process has been flawed and inconsistent. Much has depended on local circumstances. The conservative government of the *Land* Saxony tended to take a harder line towards ex-Stasi employees and IMs than that of the *Land* Brandenburg, where Manfred Stolpe's SPD held sway. And as regards other public authorities and private firms, much depended on the availability

---

[11] McAdams A. J. 2001: 73.

of suitable alternative employees.[12] On the other hand, as McAdams has shown, the courts have adopted a differentiated approach to Stasi activities and taken into account mitigating circumstances in cases of appeals against dismissals. Indeed, a frequent criticism of the official reckoning with the past is that personnel changes have been insufficient in many areas of society. Siegfried Suckut of the BStU has estimated that 75 per cent of those teachers who worked for the Stasi remain in the profession.[13] And as for the Stasi's own officers, of the preliminary judicial inquiries, 2,255 (97.9 per cent) had been abandoned by January 1998, and only 12 officers sentenced.[14]

While SED Politbüro members such as Krenz and Schabowski have been jailed for indirect participation in manslaughter relating to the border regime, the difficulties in a judicial reckoning with the past are well exemplified by the failure to convict Mielke on a charge other than the offence which he committed in 1931. The BStU is a crucial source of information for agencies investigating criminal offences committed by public bodies and individuals during GDR times. Among the main offences are manslaughter at the German–German border, perversion of justice, wrongful detention and trespass. Although sentences have been imposed on some GDR leaders, many critics contend that the punishment does not fit the crime and that too few cases are pursued. Thus while most border guards who have been brought to trial have been sentenced, only a small number have been jailed. In addition to securing appropriate evidence from Stasi and other official sources, the problems of a judicial reckoning with state crime are compounded by the question of whether legislation can be applied retrospectively to crimes and abuses committed by the leaders and functionaries of the SED regime. Even the modification of the prohibition against retroactivity by the Basic Law of the FRG and the Unification Treaty by means of convictions based primarily within the framework of a reinterpretation of GDR law still leaves many loopholes and underscores the dilemma of judging offences committed under a dictatorship by means of the instruments of a *Rechtsstaat*.

COERCIVE POWER, COGNITIVE WEAKNESS: A FINAL ANALYSIS

In her assessment of the failure of the Stasi to prevent the collapse of the SED and GDR, Christiane Lemke has highlighted the Stasi's lack of any cognitive power in contrast to its well-equipped coercive power.[15] Although she exaggerates the latter and underestimates the former, her observations provide a helpful starting point to an evaluation of the overall role and influence of

---

[12] McAdams A. J. 2001: 73–85.
[13] Raue P-J. 1998: 137.
[14] Müller-Enbergs H. 1998: 281.
[15] Lemke C. 1992: 44.

the Stasi. In terms of coercive power and intelligence gathering capability, the MfS was undoubtedly well endowed. As was seen in earlier chapters, it had at its disposal a Guard Regiment several thousand strong, a well-stocked arsenal, a network of prisons and internment camps as well as close links with the GDR military, police and the workers' militia. In the background stood some 400,000 Soviet troops stationed in the GDR as well as regular contacts with its Soviet equivalent, the KGB. There could thus be no doubt that the MfS – along with the other coercive forces – was fully capable of a Chinese solution to the problem represented by GDR's small opposition groups and civil rights activists. Its highly disciplined, well-paid and ideologically sound officers constituted an efficient steering mechanism and a bulwark of SED rule. The 176,000 IMs, the ministry's most effective weapon in the struggle against 'hostile, negative and decadent forces', provided Mielke and his officers with the eyes to penetrate the nooks and crannies of GDR society and to answer the crucial intelligence question of 'Who is who?'. Although blackmail and other forms of coercion were deployed to recruit IMs and other contact persons, many East Germans were by no means unwilling collaborators. In the Federal Republic, HV A's dense network of spies, which included several thousand West German citizens, enabled Markus Wolf to penetrate the highest echelons of West German politics and society. Even the Chancellor's office was not immune to IMs and telephone tapping. In other words, both at home and abroad, the MfS enjoyed the semblance of an omnipresent and semi-omniscient agent of post-totalitarian rule in the Honecker era. In a relatively small and closed society like the GDR, it was able to turn these attributes into a series of highly successful operations against the burgeoning alternative political culture and it infiltrated and weakened the literary, artistic and education spheres. It protected the state's doping programme in sport, safeguarded the economy, provided enterprises with scientific and technical know-how from the West, and stamped down hard on skinheads, football hooligans and punks.

Yet, despite its intellectual property amounting to tens of thousands of kilometres of documentation and tapes and despite its elaborate checks on the accuracy of its data, the ministry was plagued by the cognitive problems typical of all intelligence agencies as well as being caught up in the contradictions of SED policy and in the frail legitimacy of the GDR as the weaker of the two German states. The latter was particularly pertinent at a time when the MfS was extending its scope from classical secret police and security activities during the 1950s to the all-embracing societal mission of the later decades. But, first, a few comments on the commonality of intelligence service problems.[16] While a powerful case can certainly be made for the need for secret internal and external intelligence operations both in war and peace, care must be taken not to overestimate the intelligence services' efficiency

---

[16] See Rusbridger J. 1989: 2–15; Knightley P. 1987; Herman M. 1996.

and prowess. Although precise figures are usually lacking, secret services are often well supported. The Czarist secret services, including the *Okhrana*, were by far the richest among their contemporaries, and one spy, Colonel Alfred Redl, head of Austrian counterespionage, is reputed to have earned about $500,000 over ten years.[17] It is, after all, in the interest of the secret services to justify escalating but often hidden budgets and the mystique surrounding the services in order to ensure their success against the threats posed by enemies at home and abroad. As James Rusbridger has pointed out, 'just as turkeys do not vote for Christmas the intelligence fraternity are not going to admit that there is less for them to do in peacetime'.[18] Thus opponents of government policy may be branded as subversives and vast resources are devoted to tracking them down and to the collection of a mountain of trivia. In the field of scientific-technical espionage, much effort is expended on collecting data which soon becomes obsolescent and freely available. The intelligence services' lack of transparency makes it difficult to assess whether governments and other budget-holders are getting value for money. Honecker claimed, after his fall from power, that he had perfectly good alternative sources in the Western media to the information supplied by the MfS.[19] He may, however, have had a better idea of the scope of the MfS budget than he was prepared to admit. If he had more straightforward ways of acquiring information – and there is no real reason to dispute this assertion as untypical of the situation in other countries – then, it should be asked, why did he condone the expansion of the Stasi?

The MfS, like the KGB, was an intelligence squirrel. Intelligence was based primarily on human sources like the IMs, although other forms of intelligence such as signals intelligence and photographic intelligence were not ignored. While all three sources have advantages and drawbacks, human intelligence was the bread and butter of the service and was fully utilised by the supreme controller, Mielke, in the tireless pursuit of omniscience. But while ZAIG was adept at producing succinct reports on security issues and the mood of the population, Mielke lamented in his rambling speech before the *Volkskammer* on 13 November 1990 that this kind of information was not always taken seriously by his comrades in party and state.[20] The sheer mass of material not only threatened to overwhelm the ministry's operatives – inundation being the price to pay for very long ears – but also compounded the problems inherent in cognitive analysis and operationalisation. This is not primarily an issue concerning the accuracy of data – the MfS, it is generally recognised, was diligent in checking for accuracy – but the obstacles to

---

[17] Laqueur W. 1985: 224.
[18] Rusbridger J. 1989: 2.
[19] The MfS, it should be noted, drew heavily on West Germany's printed media such as the daily press and weekly magazines like *Stern* and *Der Spiegel*.
[20] Herles H. and Rose E. 1990: 194.

analysis and the attendant flaws and errors. During the Cold War, the failure of Western analysts, the present writer not excepted, to predict the sudden collapse of communism in the GDR and Eastern Europe in 1989 was mirrored by the same forecasting failure of GDR intelligence and the East's long-term misperception that the future belonged to communism.

A typology of the shortcomings and failures of intelligence should take into account defects in the collection and analysis of data as well as in the 'consumer's' perception and utilisation of reports submitted by the 'producers'. In the case of the GDR, the chief producer of data assessments was ZAIG and while the ultimate consumer was Honecker and members of the Politbüro, the MfS was both producer and consumer. The flaws inherent in the intelligence process whether in an open or closed society are manifold: consumers' avoidance of information which conflict with preconceptions and from a desire for 'good news'; the difficulties in identifying and prioritising data at the collection stage; perceiving the 'enemy' in one's own image; striving for cognitive consistency; perseverance with initial conceptions and existing policies; and the bureaucratic tendencies of a security service towards routine and conservatism. In addition, the overproduction of data makes it difficult for hard-pressed policymakers to digest and use intelligence unless it is supplied in a succinct and intelligible manner.[21] The list could be extended. Although the East German policymaking process was less dependent on the kind of professionalisation of intelligence analysis than was practised in the USA, many of the kind of problems mentioned above are applicable. One thread running through this book is relevant in this context: Marxist-Leninist ideology, even if much of its pioneering élan had been eroded, created a world in which peace activists, ecologists, punks, skinheads, rock enthusiasts and critical Marxist intellectuals were perceived as subversives of various hues who had to be identified by an army of spies in their midst and then suppressed by means appropriate to the level of the perceived threat and to the latitude allowed by the political situation. Thus in the era of détente, decomposition rather than physical force was the preferred method. While the Stasi could congratulate itself on keeping the lid on the opposition groups, it was suppressing a critical potential which might have rejuvenated the GDR, and left it better prepared to face the challenges of unification and transformation. A plethora of instructions, regulations and training courses ensured that the ministry's staff operated according to the rigid friend–foe image of the world of the Cold War. This dichotomy was certainly not peculiar to the MfS, one has only to think of J. Edgar Hoover of the FBI, but was propelled by the older guard on the SED Politbüro, as represented by Honecker, Mielke himself and Hager, and constituted an insuperable impediment to reform.

However, intelligence gathering, collation and analysis have to be linked to the political system in which they are set. And here the fundamental weaknesses

---

[21] Herman M. 1996: 228, 231; Laqueur W. 1985: 91–103, 269–92, 342.

and dilemmas of the Stasi become palpable. The Stasi was embedded in a regime which demanded conformity over creativity and was inherently insecure
because of its position on the front line in the Cold War and the systemic
rivalry with the more powerful FRG. As far as the MfS is concerned, the
frailty of the GDR's polity turned it into a pessimistic Cassandra in its perception of a threat from an omnipresent internal and external enemy, but, on
the other hand, the strength of its mission and a belief in the ultimate demise
of imperialism encouraged the spread of an optimistic Pollyanna syndrome.[22]
In the end, the reputedly ultra-efficient Stasi, which was called upon to prop
up an ultra-inefficient system of socialism, was overwhelmed by its plethora
of tasks and was caught up in the general crisis of communism in the 1980s.
Its economic functions illustrate this well, as does its abject failure to stem the
emigration movement. Thus even though the communist world possessed in
the MfS and the KGB more ruthless and efficient services than did the West,
these bodies both exemplified and perpetuated communism's inherent defects.

---

[22] On the relevance of the Cassandra and Pollyanna syndromes to the world of intelligence, see Laqueur W. 1985: 280–81.

BIBLIOGRAPHY

Abramowski W. (1992) 'Im Labyrinth der Macht. Innenansichten aus dem Stasi-Apparat' in Florath B., Mitter A. and Wolle S. (eds), *Die Ohnmacht der Allmächtigen. Geheimdienste und politische Polizei in der modernen Gesellschaft.* Ch. Links Verlag, Berlin, pp. 212–33.

Act Regarding the Records of the State Security Service of the Former German Democratic Republic (Stasi Records Act) (1991) Der Bundesbeauftragte für die Unterlagen des Staatssicherheitsdienstes der ehemaligen Deutschen Demokratischen Republik, Berlin.

Ahrberg E. (1998) 'Wiedergutmachung, Überzeugung, Anpassung' in Behnke K. and Wolf J. (eds), *Stasi auf dem Schulhof. Der Mißbrauch von Kindern und Jugendlichen durch das Ministerium für Staatssicherheit.* Ullstein, Berlin, pp. 199–218.

Amnesty International (ed.) (1989) *German Democratic Republic. Sweeping Laws – Secret Justice.* Amnesty International, New York.

Andert R. and Herzberg W. (1991) *Der Sturz. Honecker im Kreuzverhör.* Aufbau-Verlag, Berlin and Weimar.

Andrew C. (1997) 'Nachrichtendienst im Kalten Krieg: Probleme und Perspektiven' in Krieger W. and Weber J. (eds), *Spionage für den Frieden? Nachrichtendienste in Deutschland während des Kalten Krieges.* Günter Olzog Verlag, Munich, pp. 23–48.

Andrew C. and Gordievsky O. (1991) *KGB. The Inside Story of its Foreign Operations from Lenin to Gorbachev.* Sceptre, London.

Andrew C. and Gordievsky O. (1992) *More 'Instructions from the Centre': Top Secret Files on KGB Global Operations, 1975–1985.* Frank Cass, London.

Andrew C. and Mitrokhin V. (1999) *The Mitrokhin Archive: The KGB in Europe and the West.* Penguin, London and New York.

Ash T. G. (1997) *The File. A Personal History.* HarperCollins, London.

Auerbach T. (1999) *Einsatzkommandos an der unsichtbaren Front. Terror- und Sabotagevorbereitungen des MfS gegen die Bundesrepublik Deutschland.* Ch. Links Verlag, Berlin.

Badstübner R. and Loth W. (eds) (1994) *Wilhelm Pieck – Aufzeichnungen zur Deutschlandpolitik 1945–1953.* Akademie Verlag, Berlin.

Bauer M. and Priebe S. (1996) 'Psychische Störungen infolge politischer Repressalien in der DDR – die Berlin-Studien' in Priebe S., Denis D. and Bauer M. (eds), *Eingesperrt und nie mehr frei. Psychisches Leben nach politischer Haft in der DDR.* Steinkopff, Darmstadt, pp. 35–42.

Behlert W. (1994) 'Die Generalstaatsanwaltschaft' in Rottleuthner H. et al., *Justiz in der DDR. Einflußnahme der Politik auf Richter, Staatsanwälte und Rechtsanwälte.* Bundesanzeiger Verlagsgesellschaft, Cologne, pp. 287–349.

Behnke K. (1995) 'Lernziel: Zersetzung. Die "Operative Psychologie" in Ausbildung, Forschung und Anwendung' in Behnke K. and Fuchs J. (eds), *Zersetzung der Seele. Psychologie und Psychiatrie im Dienste der Stasi.* Rotbuch Verlag, Hamburg, pp. 12–43.

Beleites J. (1999) 'Der Untersuchungshaftvollzug des Ministeriums für Staatssicherheit der DDR' in Engelmann R. and Vollnhals C. (eds), *Justiz im Dienste der Parteiherrschaft. Rechtspraxis und Staatssicherheit in der DDR.* Ch. Links Verlag, Berlin, pp. 433–65.

Berendonk B. (1992) *Doping. Von der Forschung zum Betrug.* Rowohlt Taschenbuch Verlag, Reinbek.

van Bergh H. (1965) *ABC der Spione.* Ilmgau Verlag, Pfaffenhofen.

Bergmann C. (1997) 'Zum Feindbild des Ministeriums für Staatssicherheit der DDR', *Aus Politik und Zeitgeschichte,* 5 December, (50), pp. 27–34.

Bergmann G. (1993) 'Wahrheit und Gerechtigkeit scheinen Stiefkinder der Menschheit zu sein', *Zwie-Gespräch,* (14), pp. 1–11.

Besier G. and Wolf S. (1992) *Pfarrer, Christen und Katholiken. Das Ministerium für Staatssicherheit der ehemaligen DDR und die Kirchen.* Neukirchener Verlag, Neukirchen-Vluyn, 2nd edn.

Blum W. (1986) *The CIA: A Forgotten History.* Zed Books, London and New Jersey.

Bohnsack G. (1997) *Hauptverwaltung Aufklärung: Die Legende stirbt. Das Ende von Wolfs Geheimdienst.* Edition ost, Berlin.

Brehmer, H. (1991) 'Antisemitismus im Geheimdienst', *Zwie-Gespräch,* (3), pp. 25–8.

BStU (1994) *Das Arbeitsgebiet 1 der Kriminalpolizei. Aufgaben, Struktur und Verhältnis zum Ministerium für Staatssicherheit.* BStU, Berlin.

Bundesministerium der Justiz (ed.) (1994) *Im Namen des Volkes? Über Justiz im Staat der SED. Katalog zur Ausstellung des Bundesministeriums der Justiz.* Forum Verlag, Leipzig.

Büscher W. and Wensierski P. (1984) *Null Bock auf DDR. Aussteigerjugend im anderen Deutschland.* Rowohlt Taschenbuch Verlag, Reinbek.

Buthmann R. (2000) *Hochtechnologien und Staatssicherheit. Die strukturelle Verankerung des MfS in Wissenschaft und Forschung der DDR.* BStU, Analysen und Berichte, no. 1, BStU, Berlin.

Chapman B. (1970) *Police State.* Pall Mall, London.

Childs D. and Popplewell R. (1999) *The Stasi. The East German Intelligence and Security Service.* Macmillan, Basingstoke and London.

Colitt L. (1995) *Spymaster.* Robson Books, London.

Corino K. (ed.) (1995) *Die Akte Kant. IM 'Martin', die Stasi und die Literatur in Ost und West.* Rowohlt Taschenbuch Verlag, Reinbek.

Dallin D. J. (1956) *Die Sowjetspionage.* Verlag für Politik und Wirtschaft, Cologne.

Deckname 'Lyrik'. Eine Dokumentation von Reiner Kunze (1990) Fischer Taschenbuch Verlag, Frankfurt am Main.

Dennis M. (1993) *Social and Economic Modernization in Eastern Germany from Honecker to Kohl.* Pinter, London.

Dennis M. (2000) *The Rise and Fall of the German Democratic Republic 1945–1990.* Longman, Harlow.

Deutscher Bundestag (ed.) (1995) *Enquete-Kommission 'Aufarbeitung von Geschichte und Folgen der SED-Diktatur in Deutschland',* 9 vols in 18 parts. Nomos Verlag, Baden-Baden, and Suhrkamp Verlag, Frankfurt am Main.

Diewald-Kerkmann G. (1995) *Politische Denunziation im NS-Regime oder Die kleine Macht der 'Volksgenossen'.* Verlag J H W Dietz Nachfolger, Bonn.

Dirksen H-H. (2000) '"Zeugen Jehovas müssen verschwinden!" Der vergebliche Kampf der Staatssicherheit' in Yoman G. (ed.), *Im Visier der Stasi. Jehovas Zeugen in der DDR.* edition corona, Niedersteinbach, pp. 15–23.

Documentation (1980) 'Code of Criminal Procedure of January 12, 1968, in the version of the third amendment of June 28, 1979', *Law and Legislation in the German Democratic Republic,* (1–2), pp. 19–130.

Eisenfeld B. (1995a) 'Die Ausreisebewegung – eine Erscheinung widerständigen Verhaltens' in Poppe U., Eckert R. and Kowalczuk I-S. (eds), *Zwischen Selbstbehauptung und*

Anpassung. Formen des Widerstands und der Opposition in der DDR. Ch. Links Verlag, Berlin, pp. 192–223.

Eisenfeld B. (1995b) *Die Zentrale Koordinierungsgruppe Bekämpfung von Flucht und Übersiedlung* (Anatomie der Staatssicherheit. MfS-Handbuch III/7), BStU, Berlin.

Eisenfeld B. (1999) 'Rolle und Stellung der Rechtsanwälte in der Ära Honecker im Spiegel kaderpolitischer Entwicklungen und Einflüsse des MfS' in Engelmann R. and Vollnhals C. (eds), *Justiz im Dienste der Parteiherrschaft. Rechtspraxis und Staatssicherheit in der DDR.* Ch. Links Verlag, Berlin, pp. 347–73.

Eltgen H. (1995) *Ohne Chance: Erinnerungen eines HVA-Offiziers.* Edition ost, Berlin.

Elsner E-M. and Elsner L. (1992) *Ausländer und Ausländerpolitik in der DDR.* hefte zur ddr-geschichte, no. 2, 'Helle Panke', Berlin.

Engelmann R. (1995) 'Zum Quellenwert der Unterlagen des Ministeriums für Staatssicherheit' in Henke K-D. and Engelmann R. (eds), *Aktenlage. Die Bedeutung der Unterlagen des Staatssicherheitsdienstes für die Zeitgeschichtsforschung.* Ch. Links Verlag, Berlin, pp. 23–39.

Engelmann R. (1997) 'Diener zweier Herren. Das Verhältnis der Staatssicherheit zur SED und den sowjetischen Beratern 1950–59' in Suckut S. and Süß W. (eds), *Staatspartei und Staatssicherheit. Zum Verhältnis von SED und MfS.* Ch. Links Verlag, Berlin, pp. 51–72.

Evans R. J. (1997) *Rituals of Retribution. Capital Punishment in Germany, 1600–1987.* Penguin, London.

Fingerle S. and Gieseke J. (1996) *Partisanen des Kalten Krieges. Die Untergrundtruppe der NVA 1957–62 und ihre Übernahme durch die Staatssicherheit.* BStU, Berlin.

Fischer R. (1948) *Stalin and German Communism. A Study in the Origins of the State Party.* Oxford University Press, Oxford.

von Flocken J. and Scholz M. F. (1994) *Ernst Wollweber. Saboteur – Minister – Unperson.* Aufbau-Verlag, Berlin.

Foitzik J. (1998) 'Organisation und Kompetenzstruktur des Sicherheitsapparates der Sowjetischen Militäradministration in Deutschland (SMAD)' in von Plato A. (ed.), *Sowjetische Speziallager in Deutschland 1945 bis 1950. Band 1: Studien und Berichte.* Akademie Verlag, Berlin, pp. 117–31.

Förtsch E. (1999) 'Science, Higher Education, and Technology Policy' in Macrakis K. and Hoffmann D. (eds), *Science under Socialism. East Germany in Comparative Perspective.* Harvard University Press, Cambridge, Massachusetts, and London, pp. 25–43.

Frank R. (2002) 'Stasi im Westen. Eine Tagung der BStU', *Deutschland Archiv,* **35** (1), pp. 122–5.

Franke W. W. (1995) 'Funktion und Instrumentalisierung des Sports in der DDR: Pharmakologische Manipulationen (Doping) und die Rolle der Wissenschaft' in Deutscher Bundestag (ed.), *Enquete-Kommission 'Aufarbeitung von Geschichte und Folgen der SED-Diktatur in Deutschland',* Vol. III/2, Nomos Verlag, Baden-Baden, and Suhrkamp Verlag, Frankfurt am Main, pp. 904–1143.

Fricke K. W. (1984) *Die DDR Staatssicherheit.* Verlag Wissenschaft und Politik, Cologne, 2nd edn.

Fricke K. W. (1991) *MfS intern. Macht, Strukturen, Auflösung der DDR-Staatssicherheit. Analyse und Dokumentation.* Verlag Wissenschaft und Politik, Cologne.

Fricke K. W. (1992) 'The State Security Apparatus of the Former GDR and its Legacy', *Aussenpolitik. German Foreign Affairs Review,* **41** (4), pp. 153–63.

Fricke K. W. (1997) 'Ordinäre Abwehr – elitäre Aufklärung? Zur Rolle der Hauptverwaltung A im Ministerium für Staatssicherheit', *Aus Politik und Zeitgeschichte*, 5 December, (50), pp. 1–16.

Fricke K. W. (2001) 'Stasi-Veteranen melden sich zu Wort', *Deutschland Archiv*, **34** (4), pp. 560–63.

Fuchs J. (1997) *Unter Nutzung der Angst. Die 'leise Form' des Terrors – Zersetzungsmaßnahmen des MfS*, BF informiert, no. 2, BStU, Berlin.

Fuchs J. (1998) 'Die Ohnmacht der Kinder' in Behnke K. and Wolf J. (eds), *Stasi auf dem Schulhof*, Ullstein, Berlin, pp. 177–98.

Furian G. and Becker N. (2000) *'Auch im Osten trägt man Westen'. Punks in der DDR – und was aus ihnen geworden ist.* Verlag Thomas Tilsner, Berlin.

Gast G. (1999) *Kundschaftlerin des Friedens. 17 Jahre Top-Spionin der DDR beim BND.* Eichhorn, Frankfurt am Main.

Gauck J. (1998) 'Vorwort' in Behnke K. and Wolf J. (eds), *Stasi auf dem Schulhof. Der Mißbrauch von Kindern und Jugendlichen durch das Ministerium für Staatssicherheit.* Ullstein, Berlin, pp. 7–11.

Geiger H. (1993) 'Die Inoffiziellen Mitarbeiter. Stand der gegenwärtigen Erkenntnisse' in BStU (ed.), Analysen und Berichte, Reihe B, no. 3, pp. 41–71.

Geipel G. L. (1999) 'Politics and Computers in the Honecker Era' in Macrakis K. and Hoffmann D. (eds), *Science under Socialism. East Germany in Comparative Perspective.* Cambridge, Massachusetts, and London, pp. 230–46.

Gellately R. (1996) 'Denunciations in Twentieth-Century Germany: Aspects of Self-Policing in the Third Reich and the German Democratic Republic', *Journal of Modern History*, **68** (4), pp. 931–67.

Gieseke J. (1995) *Die hauptamtlichen Mitarbeiter des Ministeriums für Staatssicherheit.* (Anatomie der Staatssicherheit. MfS-Handbuch IV/I), BStU, Berlin.

Gieseke J. (1998) *Das Ministerium für Staatssicherheit 1950 bis 1989/90. Ein kurzer historischer Abriß.* BF informiert, no. 21, BStU, Berlin.

Gieseke J. (2000) *Die hauptamtlichen Mitarbeiter der Staatssicherheit. Personalstruktur und Lebenswelt 1950–1989/90.* Ch. Links Verlag, Berlin.

Gieseke J. (2001) *Mielke-Konzern. Die Geschichte der Stasi 1945–1990.* Deutsche-Verlags-Anstalt, Stuttgart and Munich.

Gill D. and Schröter U. (1991) *Das Ministerium für Staatssicherheit. Anatomie des Mielke-Imperiums.* Rowohlt, Berlin.

Grande D. and Schäfer B. (1996) 'Interne Richtlinien und Bewertungsmaßstäbe zu kirchlichen Kontakten mit dem MfS' in Vollnhals C. (ed.), *Die Kirchenpolitik von SED und Staatssicherheit. Eine Zwischenbilanz.* Ch. Links Verlag, Berlin, pp. 388–404.

Grasemann H-J. (1996) 'Die politische Justiz in der Ära Honecker' in Bundesministerium der Justiz (ed.), *Im Namen des Volkes? Über die Justiz im Staat der SED. Wissenschaftlicher Begleitband zur Ausstellung des Bundesministeriums der Justiz.* Forum Verlag, Leipzig, pp. 197–208.

Grieder P. (1999) *The East German leadership 1946–1973. Conflict and Crisis.* Manchester University Press, Manchester and New York.

Gries S. and Voigt D. (1998) 'Jugendliche IM als Forschungsfeld der "Wissenschafter" des Ministeriums für Staatssicherheit der DDR' in Behnke K. and Wolf S. (eds), *Stasi auf dem Schulhof. Der Mißbrauch von Kindern und Jugendlichen durch das Ministerium für Staatssicherheit.* Ullstein, Berlin, pp. 103–23.

Großmann W. (2001) *Bonn im Blick. Die DDR-Aufklärung aus der Sicht ihres letzten Chefs.* Das Neue Berlin Verlagsgesellschaft, Berlin.

Hacke G. (2000) *Zeugen Jehovas in der DDR. Verfolgung und Verhalten einer religiösen Minderheit.* Sächsisches Druck- und Verlagshaus, Dresden.

Haendke-Hoppe-Arndt M. (1995) 'Wer wußte was? Der ökonomische Niedergang der DDR' in Helwig G. (ed.), *Rückblicke auf die DDR*. Verlag Wissenschaft und Politik, Cologne, pp. 120–31.

Haendke-Hoppe-Arndt M. (1997) *Die Hauptabteilung XVIII: Volkswirtschaft.* (Anatomie der Staatssicherheit, MfS-Handbuch, III/10), BStU, Berlin.

Hasselbach I. (1996) *Führer-Ex. Memoirs of a Former Neo-Nazi.* Chatto and Windus, London.

Henke K-D. (1993) 'Zu Nutzung und Auswertung der Stasi-Akten', *Vierteljahreshefte für Zeitgeschichte*, **41** (4), pp. 575–87.

Herles H. and Rose E. (eds) (1990) *Vom Runden Tisch zum Parlament.* Bouvier Verlag, Bonn.

Herman M. (1996) *Intelligence Power in Peace and War.* Cambridge, Cambridge University Press.

Hertle H-H. and Gilles F-O. (1995) 'Stasi in der Produktion – Die "Sicherung der Volkswirtschaft" am Beispiel der Struktur und Arbeitsweise der Objektdienststellen des MfS in den Chemiekombinaten' in Henke K-D. and Engelmann R. (eds), *Aktenlage. Die Bedeutung der Unterlagen des Staatssicherheitsdienstes für die Zeitgeschichtsforschung.* Ch. Links Verlag, Berlin, pp. 118–37.

Hilmer R. and Köhler A. (1989) 'Der DDR läuft die Zukunft davon. Die Übersiedler-/ Flüchtlingswelle im Sommer 1989', *Deutschland Archiv*, **22** (12), pp. 1383–93.

Hockenos P. (1993) *Free to Hate. The Rise of the Far Right in Post-Communist Eastern Europe.* Routledge, New York and London.

Horschig M. (1999) 'In der DDR hat es nie Punks gegeben' in Galenza R. and Havemeister H. (eds), *Wir wollen immer artig sein . . . Punk, New Wave, HipHop, Independent-Szene in der DDR 1980–1990.* Schwarzkopf & Schwarzkopf Verlag, Berlin, pp. 17–40, 2nd edn.

Joestel F. (1999) 'Verdächtigt und beschuldigt. Statistische Erhebungen zur MfS-Untersuchungstätigkeit 1971–1988' in Engelmann R. and Vollnhals C. (eds), *Justiz im Dienste der Parteiherrschaft. Rechtspraxis und Staatssicherheit in der DDR.* Ch. Links Verlag, Berlin, pp. 303–27.

Johnson L. K. (1996) *Secret Agencies. US Intelligence in a Hostile World.* Yale University Press, New Haven and London.

Kabus A. (1993) *Auftrag Windrose. Der militärische Geheimdienst der DDR.* Neues Leben, Berlin.

Kaiser P. and Petzold C. (eds) (1997) *Boheme und Diktatur in der DDR. Gruppen, Konflikte, Quartiere 1970–1989.* Verlag Fannel and Walz, Berlin.

Kallinich J. and de Pasquale S. (eds) (2002) *Ein offenes Geheimnis. Post- und Telephonkontrolle in der DDR.* Edition Braus, Heidelberg.

Karau G. (1995) *Stasiprotokolle. Gespräche mit ehemaligen Mitarbeitern des 'Ministeriums für Staatssicherheit' der DDR.* dipa-Verlag, Frankfurt am Main.

Kaufmann B., Reisener E., Schwips D. and Walter H. (1993) *Nachrichtendienst der KPD 1919–37.* Dietz Verlag, Berlin.

Kinner K. and Richter R. (eds) (2000) *Rechtsextremismus und Antifaschismus. Historische und aktuelle Dimensionen.* Karl Dietz Verlag, Berlin.

Klessmann C. (1998) *Zeitgeschichte in Deutschland nach dem Ende des Ost-West Konflikts*. Klartext Verlag, Essen.

Knabe H. (1990) 'Politische Opposition in der DDR. Ursprünge, Programmatik, Perspektiven', *Aus Politik und Zeitgeschichte*, 22 January, (1–2), pp. 21–32.

Knabe H. (1997) 'Die Stasi als Problem des Westens. Zur Tätigkeit des MfS im "Operationsgebiet"', *Aus Politik und Zeitgeschichte*, 5 December, (50), pp. 3–16.

Knabe H. (1999) *Die unterwanderte Republik. Stasi im Westen*. Propyläen, Berlin.

Knabe H. (2000) 'Strafen ohne Strafrecht. Zum Wandel repressiver Strategien in der Ära Honecker' in Timmermann H. (ed.), *Die DDR – Recht und Justiz als politisches Instrument*. Duncker and Humblot, Berlin, pp. 91–109.

Knightley P. (1987) *The Second Oldest Profession*. Pan Books, London and Sydney.

Koehler J. O. (1999) *Stasi. The Untold Story of the East German Secret Police*. Westview Press, Boulder, Colorado.

Kolinsky E. (2000) 'Unexpected Newcomers: Asylum Seekers and other non-Germans in the New Länder' in Flockton C., Kolinsky E. and Pritchard R. (eds), *The New Germany in the East*. London, Frank Cass, pp. 148–64.

Korfes G. (1990) '"Seitdem habe ich einen dermaßenen Haß". Rechtsextremistische Jugendliche vor und nach der "Wende" – exemplarische Biographien' in Heinemann K-H. and Schubarth W. (eds), *Der antifaschistische Staat entläßt seine Kinder. Jugend und Rechtsextremismus in Ostdeutschland*. Cologne, PapyRossa Verlag, pp. 64–76.

Krenz E. (1990) *Wenn Mauern fallen. Die Friedliche Revolution: Vorgeschichte – Ablauf – Auswirkungen*. Paul Neff Verlag, Vienna.

Krivitsky W. G. (1992) *I Was Stalin's Agent*. Ian Faulkner Publishing, Cambridge.

Krone T., Kukutz I. and Leide H. (1997) *Wenn wir unsere Akten lesen. Handbuch zum Umgang mit den Stasi-Unterlagen*. BasisDruck Verlag, Berlin, 2nd edn.

Krüger-Potratz M. (1991) *Anderssein gab es nicht: Ausländer und Minderheiten in der DDR*. Waxmann, Münster.

Labrenz-Weiß H. (1998) *Die Hauptabteilung II: Spionageabwehr*. (Anatomie der Staatssicherheit. MfS-Handbuch, Teil/7), BStU, Berlin.

von Lang J. (1991) *Erich Mielke. Eine deutsche Karriere*. Rowohlt, Berlin.

Laqueur W. (1985) *World of Secrets. The Uses and Limits of Intelligence*. Weidenfeld and Nicholson, London.

Lemke C. (1992) 'Trials and Tribulations: The Stasi Legacy in Contemporary German Politics', *German Politics and Society*, no. 26, pp. 43–53.

Los M. and Zybertowicz A. (2000) *Privatizing the Police State. The Case of Poland*. Macmillan, Basingstoke and London.

Macrakis K. (1999) 'Espionage and Technology Transfer in the Quest for Scientific-Technical Prowess' in Macrakis K. and Hoffmann D. (eds), *Science under Socialism. East Germany in Comparative Perspective*. Harvard University Press, Cambridge, Massachusetts, and London, pp. 82–121.

Madloch N. (2000) 'Rechstextremistische Tendenzen und Entwicklungen in der DDR, speziell in Sachsen, bis Oktober 1990' in Kinner K. and Richter R. (eds), *Rechtsextremismus und Antifaschismus. Historische und aktuelle Dimensionen*. Karl Dietz Verlag, Berlin, pp. 63–145.

Mählert U. (1998) '"Die Partei hat immer recht!" Parteisäuberungen als Kaderpolitik in der SED (1948–1953)' in Weber H. and Mählert U. (eds), *Terror. Stalinistische Parteisäuberungen 1936–1953*. Schöningh, Paderborn, pp. 351–457.

Marquardt B. (1995) 'Die Zusammenarbeit zwischen MfS und KGB' in Deutscher Bundestag (ed.), *Materialien der Enquete-Kommission 'Aufarbeitung von Geschichte und Folgen der SED-Diktatur in Deutschland'*, vol. 8, Nomos Verlag, Baden-Baden, and Suhrkamp Verlag, Frankfurt am Main, pp. 297–33.

Marxen K. (1999) '"Recht" im Verständnis des Ministeriums für Staatssicherheit der DDR' in Engelmann R. and Vollnhals C. (eds), *Justiz im Dienste der Parteiherrschaft. Rechtspraxis und Staatssicherheit in der DDR.* Ch. Links Verlag, Berlin, pp. 15–24.

McAdams A. J. (2001) *Judging the Past in Unified Germany.* Cambridge University Press, Cambridge and New York.

McElvoy A. (1993) *The Saddled Cow. East Germany's Life and Legacy.* Faber and Faber, London.

Meckel M. and Gutzeit M. (1994) *Opposition in der DDR. Zehn Jahre kirchliche Friedensarbeit – kommentierte Quellentexte.* Bund-Verlag, Cologne.

Merkel I. (ed.) (1998) *'Wir sind doch nicht die Meckerecke der Nation!' Briefe an das Fernsehen der DDR.* Schwarzkopf & Schwarzkopf Verlag, Berlin.

MfS und Leistungssport (1994) BStU: Reihe A. Dokumente, no. 1, BStU, Berlin.

Michael K. (1999) 'Macht aus diesem Staat Gurkensalat: Punk und die Exerzietien der Macht' in Galanza R. and Havemeister H. (eds), *Wir wollen immer artig sein . . . Punk, New Wave, HipHop, Independent-Szene in der DDR 1980–1990.* Schwarzkopf & Schwarzkopf Verlag, Berlin, pp. 72–93, 2nd edn.

Miller B. (1999) *Narratives of Guilt and Compliance in Unified Germany.* Routledge, London and New York.

Mitter A. and Wolle S. (eds) (1990) *Ich liebe euch doch alle! Befehle und Lageberichte des MfS Januar–November 1989.* BasisDruck, Berlin.

Müggenberg A. (1996) *Die ausländischen Vertragsarbeitnehmer in der ehemaligen DDR.* Die Bundesbeauftragte der Bundesregierung für die Belange der Ausländer, Bonn.

Mühlberg F. (1999) *Informelle Konfliktbewältigung. Zur Geschichte der Eingabe in der DDR.* Dissertation, Technische Universität Chemnitz.

Müller K-D. (1997) '"Jeder kriminelle Mörder ist mir lieber . . ." Haftbedingungen für politische Häftlinge in der Sowjetischen Besatzungszone und der Deutschen Demokratischen Republik und ihre Veränderungen von 1945–1989' in Gedenkstätte für die Opfer politischer Gewalt Moritzplatz Magdeburg (ed.), *'Die Vergangenheit läßt uns nicht los . . .' Haftbedingungen politischer Gefangener in der SBZ/DDR und deren gesundheitliche Folgen.* Oktoberdruck, Berlin, pp. 7–127.

Müller-Enbergs H. (1993) 'IM-Statistik 1985–1989', BF informiert, no. 3, pp. 1–64.

Müller-Enbergs H. (1995a) 'Inoffizielle Mitarbeiter – eine Skizze', *Horch und Guck*, (1), pp. 1–16.

Müller-Enbergs H. (1995b) 'Warum wird einer IM? Zur Motivation bei der inoffiziellen Zusammenarbeit mit dem Staatssicherheitsdienst' in Behnke K. and Fuchs J. (eds), *Zersetzung der Seele. Psychologie und Psychiatrie im Dienst der Stasi.* Rotbuch Verlag, Hamburg, pp. 102–29.

Müller-Enbergs H. (1996) *Inoffizielle Mitarbeiter des Ministeriums für Staatssicherheit. Richtlinien und Durchführungsbestimmungen.* Ch. Links Verlag, Berlin.

Müller-Enbergs H. (ed.) (1998) *Inoffizielle Mitarbeiter des Ministeriums für Staatssicherheit. Teil 2: Anleitungen für die Arbeit mit Agenten, Kundschaftern und Spionen in der Bundesrepublik Deutschland.* Ch. Links Verlag, Berlin.

Müller-Enbergs H. (1999) 'Zum Umgang mit inoffiziellen Mitarbeitern – Gerechtigkeit im Rechtsstaat' in Deutscher Bundestag (ed.) *Materialen der Enquete-Kommission 'Überwindung der SED-Diktatur im Prozess der deutschen Einheit'*, vol. IV/2, Nomos Verlag, Baden-Baden, and Suhrkamp Verlag, Frankfurt am Main, pp. 1335–98.

Müller-Enbergs H. (2000) 'Zur Kunst der Verweigerung. Warum Bürger nicht mit dem Ministerium für Staatssicherheit kooperieren wollten' in Kerz-Rühling I. and Plänkers T. (eds), *Sozialistische Diktatur und psychische Folgen. Psychoanalytisch-psychologische Untersuchungen in Ostdeutschland und Tschechien*. edition diskord, Tübingen, pp. 165–95.

Naimark N. M. (1995) *The Russians in Germany. A History of the Soviet Zone of Occupation*. Harvard University Press, Cambridge, Massachusetts, and London.

Neubert E. (1993) *Vergebung oder Weißwäscherei. Zur Aufarbeitung des Stasiproblems in den Kirchen*. Herderbücherei, Freiburg im Breisgau.

Neues Forum Leipzig (1990) *Jetzt oder nie – Demokratie! Leipziger Herbst '89*. C. Bertelsmann, Leipzig and Munich.

Niemann H. (1993) *Meinungsforschung in der DDR. Die geheimen Berichte des Instituts für Meinungsforschung an das Politbüro der SED*. Bund-Verlag, Cologne.

Niethammer Lutz (1997) 'Die SED und "ihre" Menschen. Versuch über das Verhältnis zwischen Partei und Bevölkerung als bestimmendem Moment innerer Staatssicherheit' in Suckut S. and Süß W. (eds), *Staatspartei und Staatssicherheit. Zum Verhältnis von SED und MfS*. Ch. Links Verlag, Berlin, pp. 307–40.

Offenberg U. (1998) *'Seid vorsichtig gegen die Machthaber'. Die jüdischen Gemeinden in der SBZ und der DDR 1945 bis 1990*. Aufbau-Verlag, Berlin.

Otto W. (2000) *Erich Mielke – Biographie. Aufstieg und Fall eines Tschekisten*. Karl Dietz Verlag, Berlin.

Peter R. (1992) 'Wir haben das eigene Volk zum Feind gemacht', *Zwie-Gespräch*, (7), pp. 24–8.

Pirker T., Lepsius M. R., Weinert R. and Hertle H-H. (eds) (1995) *Der Plan als Befehl und Fiktion. Wirtschaftsführung in der DDR. Gespräche und Analysen*. Westdeutscher Verlag, Opladen.

Podewin N. (1995) *Walter Ulbricht. Eine neue Biographie*. Dietz Verlag, Berlin.

Pollack D. (1999) 'Modernisation and Modernisation Blockages in GDR Society' in Jarausch K. (ed.), *Dictatorship as Experience. Towards a Socio-Cultural History of the GDR*. Berghahn, New York and Oxford, pp. 27–45.

Poppe U., Eckert R. and Kowalczuk I-S. (eds) (1995) *Zwischen Selbstbehauptung und Anpassung. Formen des Widerstands und der Opposition in der DDR*. Ch. Links Verlag, Berlin.

Przybylski P. (1991) *Tatort Politbüro. Die Akte Honecker*. Rowohlt, Berlin.

Quint P. E. (1997) *The Imperfect Union. Constitutional Structures of German Unification*. Princeton University Press, Princeton, NJ.

Quoirin M. (1999) *Agentinnen aus Liebe. Warum Frauen für den Osten spionierten*. Eichborn, Frankfurt am Main.

Raschka J. (1999) 'Die Entwicklung des politischen Strafrechts im ersten Jahrzehnt der Amtszeit Honeckers' in Engelmann R. and Vollnhals C. (eds), *Justiz im Dienste der Parteiherrschaft. Rechtspraxis und Staatssicherheit in der DDR*. Ch. Links Verlag, Berlin, pp. 273–302.

Raschka J. (2000) *Justizpolitik im SED-Staat. Anpassung und Wandel des Strafrechts während der Amtszeit Honeckers*. Böhlau Verlag, Cologne, Weimar and Vienna.

Raschka J. (2001) *Zwischen Überwachung und Repression – Politische Verfolgung in der DDR 1971 bis 1989*. Leske & Budrich, Opladen.

Raue P-J. (1998) 'Demokratie und Diktatur in Deutschland. Rückblick auf ein Jahrhundert und einen viertägigen Kongreß in Bogensee', *Zeitschrift des Forschungsverbundes SED-Staat*, (6), pp. 144–8.

Reichenbach A. (1992) *Chef der Spione. Die Markus-Wolf-Story*. Deutsche Verlags-Anstalt, Stuttgart.

Reinartz K. (1999) 'Die Sportpresse und ihre Lenkung' in Teichler H. J. and Reinartz K., *Das Leistungssportsytem der DDR in den 80er Jahren und im Prozeß der Wende*. Verlag Karl Hofmann, Schorndorf, pp. 357–404.

Reiner R. (1992) *The Politics of the Police*. Harvester, New York, 2nd edn.

Reinke H. (1996) 'Staatssicherheit und Justiz' in Bundesministerium der Justiz (ed.), *Im Namen des Volkes? Über die Justiz im Staat der SED. Wissenschaftlicher Begleitband zur Ausstellung des Bundesministeriums der Justiz*, Forum Verlag, Leipzig, pp. 239–47.

Reinke H. (1997) 'Policing Politics in Germany from Weimar to the Stasi' in Mazower M. (ed.), *The Policing of Politics in the Twentieth Century*. Berghahn, Providence and Oxford, pp. 91–106.

Reuth R. G. (1992) *IM Sekretär. Die 'Gauck-Recherche' und die Dokumente zum Fall Stolpe*. Ullstein, Berlin.

Richie A. (1998) *Faust's Metropolis. A History of Berlin*. HarperCollins, London.

Richter H. (2001) *Die Operative Psychologie des Ministeriums für Staatssicherheit der DDR*. Mabuse-Verlag, Frankfurt am Main.

Richter P. and Rösler K. (1992) *Wolfs West-Spione. Ein Insider-Report*. Elefanten Press, Berlin.

Rieckert A., Schwarz A. and Schneider D. (1990) *Stasi intim. Gespräche mit ehemaligen MfS-Angehörigen*. Forum Verlag, Leipzig.

Rieker P. (1998) '(Un-)Heimliche Jugend' in Behnke K. and Wolf J. (eds), *Stasi auf dem Schulhof. Der Mißbrauch von Kindern und Jugendlichen durch das Ministerium für Staatssicherheit*. Ullstein, Berlin, pp. 305–24.

Rosenberg T. (1995) *The Haunted Land. Facing Europe's Ghosts After Communism*. Vintage, London.

Ross G. C. (2000) *The Swastika in Socialism. Right-Wing Extremism in the GDR*. Verlag Dr Kovac, Hamburg.

Roßberg K. (1996) *Das Kreuz mit dem Kreuz. Ein Leben zwischen Staatssicherheit und Kirche*. Edition ost, Berlin.

Rottleuthner H. (1994) 'Zur Steuerung der Justiz in der DDR' in Rottleuthner H. et al., *Steuerung der Justiz in der DDR. Einflußnahme der Politik auf Richter, Staatsanwälte und Rechtsanwälte*. Bundesanzeiger Verlagsgesellschaft, Cologne, pp. 9–66.

Rüddenklau W. (1992) *Störenfried. ddr-opposition 1986–1989. Mit Texten aus den 'Umweltblättern'*. BasisDruck, Berlin.

Runge I. and Stellbrink U. (1990) *Markus Wolf: 'Ich bin kein Spion'. Gespräche mit Markus Wolf*. Dietz Verlag, Berlin.

Rusbridger J. (1989) *The Intelligence Game*. The Bodley Head, London.

Sa'adah A. (1998) *Germany's Second Choice. Trust, Justice and Democratization*. Harvard University Press, Cambridge, Massachusetts, and London.

Sandford J. (1983) *The Sword and the Ploughshare: Autonomous Peace Initiatives in East Germany*. Merlin Press/European Nuclear Disarmament, London.

Schabowski G. (1990) *Das Politbüro. Ende eines Mythos. Eine Befragung.* Rowohlt Taschenbuch Verlag, Reinbek.

Schalck-Golodkowski A. (2000) *Deutsch-deutsche Erinnerungen.* Rowohlt Verlag, Reinbek.

Schell M. and Kalinka W. (1991) *Stasi und kein Ende. Die Personen und die Fakten.* Ullstein, Frankfurt am Main and Berlin.

Schleicher H-G. and Engel U. (1996) 'DDR-Geheimdienst und Afrikapolitik', *Aussenpolitik. Zeitschrift für internationale Fragen*, **47** (4), pp. 399–409.

Schlomann F-W. (1984) *Operationsgebiet Bundesrepublik. Spionage, Sabotage und Subversion.* Universitas Verlag, Munich.

Schlomann F-W. (1993) *Die Maulwürfe: Noch sind die unter uns, die Helfer der Stasi im Westen.* Universitas Verlag, Munich.

Schmeidel J. (1995) *'Shield and Sword of the Party'. Internal Repression, Exterior Espionage and Support for International Terrorism by the East German Ministry for State Security 1970–1989*, Cambridge University PhD.

Schmidt A. (1995) 'Gegenstrategien. Über die Möglichkeit sich zu verweigern' in Behnke K. and Fuchs J. (eds), *Zersetzung der Seele. Psychologie und Psychiatrie im Dienst der Stasi.* Rotbuch Verlag, Hamburg, pp. 158–77.

Schmidt I. (1992) 'Ausländer in der DDR – Ihre Erfahrungen vor und nach der Wende' in Heinemann K-H. and Schubarth W. (eds), *Der antifaschistische Staat entläßt seine Kinder. Jugend und Rechtsextremismus in Ostdeutschland.* Cologne, PapyRossa Verlag, pp. 64–76.

Schmidt M. (1993) *The New Reich. Violent Extremism in Unified Germany and Beyond* (trans. D. Horch). Hutchinson, London.

Schmidt-Eenboom E. (1993) *Schnüffler ohne Nase. Der BND – die unheimliche Macht im Staate.* Econ, Düsseldorf, Vienna and New York.

Schmole A. (1996) 'Frauen und MfS', *Deutschland Archiv*, **29** (4), pp. 512–25.

Schmole A. (2001) 'Frauen im Ministerium für Staatssicherheit (MfS)', *Horch und Guck*, **10** (2), pp. 15–19.

Schröter U. (1994) 'Die Spannbreite der IM-Tätigkeit', *Zwie-Gespräch*, (23), pp. 1–13.

Schröter U. (1995) 'Das leitende Interesse des Schreibenden als Bedingungsmerkmal der Verschriftung – Schwierigkeiten bei der Auswertung von MfS Akten' in Henke K-D. and Engelmann R. (eds), *Aktenlage. Die Bedeutung der Unterlagen des Staatssicherheitsdienstes für die Zeitgeschichtsforschung.* Ch. Links Verlag, Berlin, pp. 40–46.

Schüle A. (2002) 'Vertragsarbeiterinnen und -arbeiter: "Gewährleistung des Prinzips der Gleichstellung und Nichtdiskriminierung"', *1999. Zeitschrift für Sozialgeschichte des 20. und 21. Jahrhunderts*, **17** (1), pp. 80–100.

Schumann S. (1998) *Die Parteiorganisation der SED im MfS.* (MfS-Handbuch, III/20), BStU, Berlin.

Schürer G. (1996) *Gewagt und verloren. Eine deutsche Biographie.* Frankfurter Oder Editionen, Frankfurt an der Oder.

Schwan H. (1997) *Erich Mielke. Der Mann, der die Stasi war.* Droemer Knaur, Munich.

Schwarz J. (1994) *Bis zum bitteren Ende. 35 Jahre im Dienste des Ministeriums für Staatssicherheit. Eine DDR-Biographie.* GNN-Verlag, Schkeuditz.

Sélitrenny R. and Weichert T. (1991) *Das unheimliche Erbe.* Forum Verlag, Leipzig.

Siebenmorgen P. (1993) *'Staatssicherheit' der DDR. Der Westen im Fadenkreuz der Stasi.* Bouvier, Bonn.

Siegler B. (1991) *Auferstanden aus den Ruinen. Rechtsextremismus in der DDR.* edition TIAMANT, Berlin.

Spennemann N. (1997) 'Aufbauhelfer für eine bessere Zukunft. Die vietnamesischen Vertragsabreiter in der ehemaligen DDR' in Hentschel T., Hischberger M., Liepe L. and Spennemann N., *Zweimal angekommen und doch nicht zu Hause. Vietnamesische Vertragsarbeiter in den neuen Bundesländern.* Reistrommel, Berlin, pp. 8–20.

Spitzer G. (1998a) *Doping in der DDR. Ein historischer Überblick zu einer konspirativen Praxis.* Sport und Buch Strauß, Cologne.

Spitzer G. (1998b) 'Im Schattenbereich. Inoffizielle Mitabeiter im Sport: Fallstudie Leipzig' in Hartmann G. (ed.), *Goldkinder. Die DDR im Spiegel ihres Sportes.* Forum Verlag, Leipzig, pp. 188–204.

Stasi Akte 'Verräter'. Bürgerrechtler Templin: Dokumente einer Verfolgung 1993, Spiegel Spezial, no. 1, Spiegel-Verlag, Hamburg.

Stern C. (1963) *Ulbricht, A Political Biography.* Pall Mall Press, London.

Stiller W. with Adams J. (1992) *Beyond the Wall: Memoirs of an East and West German Spy.* Brassey's, Washington.

Stokes R. G. (2000) *Constructing Socialism. Technology and Change in East Germany 1945–1990.* The Johns Hopkins Press, Baltimore and London.

Suckut S. (ed.) (1996) *Das Wörterbuch der Staatssicherheit. Definitionen zur 'politisch-operativen Arbeit'.* Ch. Links Verlag, Berlin.

Suckut S. (1997) 'Generalkontrollbeauftragter der SED oder gewöhnliches Staatsorgan? Probleme der Funktionsbestimmung des MfS in den sechziger Jahren' in Suckut S. and Süß W. (eds), *Staatspartei und Staatssicherheit. Zum Verhältnis von SED und MfS.* Ch. Links Verlag, Berlin, pp. 151–67.

Süß S. (1999) *Politisch mißbraucht? Psychiatrie und Staatssicherheit in der DDR.* Ch. Links Verlag, Berlin.

Süß W. (1995) ' "Schild und Schwert" – Das Ministerium für Staatssicherheit und die SED' in Henke K-D. and Engelmann R. (eds), *Aktenlage. Die Bedeutung der Unterlagen des Staatssicherheitsdienstes für die Zeitgeschichtsforschung.* Ch. Links Verlag, Berlin, pp. 83–97.

Süß W. (1996) *Zu Wahrnehmung und Interpretation des Rechtsextremismus in der DDR durch das MfS.* BStU, Reihe B: Analysen und Berichte, no. 2, BStU, Berlin.

Süß W. (1997) 'Zum Verhältnis von SED und Staatssicherheit' in Herbst A, Stephan G-R. and Winkler J. (eds), *Die SED. Geschichte – Organisation – Politik. Ein Handbuch.* Dietz Verlag, Berlin, pp. 215–40.

Süß W. (1999) *Staatssicherheit am Ende. Warum es den Mächtigen nicht gelang, 1989 eine Revolution zu verhindern.* Ch. Links Verlag, Berlin.

Tantzscher M. (1995) ' "Was in Polen geschieht, ist für die DDR eine Lebensfrage" – Das MfS und die polnische Krise 1980/1' in Deutscher Bundestag (ed.), *Materialien der Enquete-Kommission 'Aufarbeitung von Geschichte und Folgen der SED-Diktatur in Deutschland',* vol. V/3, Nomos Verlag, Baden-Baden, and Suhrkamp Verlag, Frankfurt am Main, pp. 2601–760.

Tantzscher M. (1998) ' "In der Ostzone wird ein neuer Apparat aufgebaut". Die Gründung des DDR-Staatssicherheitsdienstes', *Deutschland Archiv,* **31** (1), pp. 48–56.

Templin W. and Weißhuhn R. (1991) 'Initiative Frieden und Menschenrechte' in Müller-Enbergs H., Schulz M. and Wielgohs J. (eds), *Von der Illegalität ins Parlament. Werdegang und Konzepte der neuen Bürgerbewegungen.* Ch. Links Verlag, Berlin, pp. 148–65.

Timm A. (1993) 'DDR-Israel: Anatomie eines gestörten Verhältnisses', *Aus Politik und Zeitgeschichte,* 22 January, (4), pp. 46–54.

Vierter Tätigkeitsbericht des Bundesbeauftragten für die Unterlagen des Staatssicherheitsdienstes der ehemaligen Deutschen Demokratischen Republik 1999 (1999). BStU, Berlin.

Villain J. (1990) *Die Revolution verstößt ihre Kinder. Aussagen und Gespräche zum Untergang der DDR*. Zytlogge, Berne.

Vinke H. (ed.) (1993) *Akteneinsicht Christa Wolf. Zerrspiegel und Dialog. Eine Dokumentation*. Luchterhand Literaturverlag, Hamburg.

Vollnhals C. (1994) 'Das Ministerium für Staatssicherheit. Ein Instrument totalitärer Herrschaftsübung' in Kaeble H., Kocka J. and Zwahr H. (eds), *Sozialgeschichte der DDR*. Klett-Cotta, Stuttgart, pp. 498–518.

Vollnhals C. (1996a) 'Die kirchenpolitische Abteilung des Ministeriums für Staatssicherheit' in Vollnhals C. (ed.), *Die Kirchenpolitik von SED und Staatssicherheit. Eine Zwischenbilanz*. Ch. Links Verlag, Berlin, pp. 79–119.

Vollnhals C. (1996b) 'Zugleich Helfer der Opfer und Helfer der Täter? Gegenwärtige und historische Sperren für die evangelische Kirche bei der Aufarbeitung ihrer DDR-Vergangenheit' in Vollnhals C. (ed.), *Die Kirchenpolitik von SED und Staatssicherheit. Eine Zwischenbilanz*. Ch. Links Verlag, Berlin, pp. 434–46.

Vollnhals C. (1999) '"Die Macht ist das Allererste". Staatssicherheit und Justiz' in Engelmann R. and Vollnhals C. (eds), *Justiz im Dienste der Parteiherrschaft. Rechtspraxis und Staatssicherheit in der DDR*. Ch. Links Verlag, Berlin, pp. 227–71.

Wagner B. (1995) *Jugend – Gewalt – Szenen. Zu kriminologischen und historischen Aspekten in Ostdeutschland. Die achtziger und neunziger Jahre*. dip, Berlin.

Wagner H. (1993) 'Kirchen, Staat und politisch alternative Gruppen' in Dähn H. (ed.), *Die Rolle der Kirchen in der DDR. Eine erste Bilanz*. Olzog Verlag, Munich, pp. 104–26.

Waibel H. (1996) *Rechtsextremismus in der DDR bis 1989*. PapyRossa Verlag, Cologne.

Walther J. (1996) *Sicherungsbereich Literatur. Schriftsteller und Staatssicherheit in der Deutschen Demokratischen Republik*. Ch. Links Verlag, Berlin.

Weber H. (1969) *Die Wandlung des deutschen Kommunismus: die Stalinisierung der KPD in der Weimarer Republik*. Europäische Verlags Anstalt, Frankfurt am Main.

Weber H. (1990) *'Weiße Flecke in der Geschichte'. Die KPD-Opfer der Stalinschen Säuberungen und ihre Rehabilitierung*. Isp-Verlag, Frankfurt am Main, 2nd edn.

Weber H. (1998) 'Schauprozeßvorbereitungen in der DDR' in Weber H. and Mählert U. (eds), *Terror. Stalinistische Parteisäuberungen 1936–1953*. Schöningh, Paderborn, pp. 459–85.

Wegmann B. (1997) *Entstehung und Vorläufer des Staatssicherheitsdienstes der DDR*. hefte zur ddr-geschichte, no. 46, 'Helle-Panke', Berlin.

Weinke A. (2000) 'Stasi und Strafrecht: Ein dunkles Kapitel' in Timmermann H. (ed.), *Die DDR – Recht und Justiz als politisches Instrument*. Duncker & Humblot, Berlin, pp. 141–61.

Weitz E. D. (1997) *Creating German Communism, 1890–1990: From Popular Protest to Socialist State*. Princeton University Press, Princeton, New Jersey.

Werkentin F. (1995) *Politische Strafjustiz in der Ära Ulbricht*. Ch. Links Verlag, Berlin.

Werkentin F. (1997) 'Zur Dimension politischer Inhaftierungen in der DDR 1949–1989' in Gedenkstätte für die Opfer politischer Gewalt Moritzplatz Magdeburg (ed.), *'Die Vergangenheit läßt uns nicht los . . .' Haftbedingungen politischer Gefangener in der SBZ/DDR und deren gesundheitliche Folgen*. Oktoberdruck, Berlin, pp. 129–43.

Wernicke T. (1992) *Staats-Sicherheit – ein Haus in Potsdam*. Potsdam-Museum, Potsdam.

Wiedmann R. (1996) *Die Organisationsstruktur des Ministeriums für Staatssicherheit 1989.* BStU, Berlin.

Wilkening C. (1990) *Staat im Staate. Auskünfte ehemaliger Stasi-Mitarbeiter.* Aufbau-Verlag, Berlin and Weimar.

Wolf M. (1991) *Im eigenen Auftrag. Bekenntnisse und Einsichten.* Schneekluth Verlag, Munich.

Wolf M. with McElvoy A. (1997) *Man without a Face. The Memoirs of a Spymaster.* Jonathan Cape, London.

Wolf M. (1998) *Spionagechef im geheimen Krieg. Erinnerungen.* Econ Taschenbuch Verlag, Munich.

Wolfe N. T. (1991) *Policing a Socialist Society. The German Democratic Republic.* Greenwood Press, New York, Westport, Connecticut, and London.

Wolffsohn M. (1997) *Meine Juden – eure Juden.* Piper, Munich and Zürich.

Wolle S. (1998) *Die heile Welt der Diktatur. Alltag und Herrschaft in der DDR 1971–1989.* Ch. Links Verlag, Berlin.

Wollenberg E. (1951) *Der Apparat – Stalins Fünfte Kolonne.* Ruhrländische Druckerei J. März, Essen.

Wollenberger V. (1992) *Virus der Heuchler. Innenansicht aus Stasi-Akten.* Elefanten Press, Berlin.

Wunschik T. (1997) *Die maoistische KPD/ML und die Zerschlagung ihrer 'Sektion DDR' durch das MfS.* BStU, Berlin.

Wunschik T. (1999) 'Der DDR-Strafvollzug unter dem Einfluß der Staatssicherheit in den siebziger und achtziger Jahren' in Engelmann R. and Vollnhals C. (eds), *Justiz im Dienste der Parteiherrschaft. Rechtspraxis und Staatssicherheit in der DDR.* Ch. Links Verlag, Berlin, pp. 467–93.

Wüst J. (1996) 'Die IGfM im Visier von Antifa und Staatssicherheit' in *Jahrbuch Extremismus und Demokratie*, vol. 8, Nomos Verlag, Baden-Baden, pp. 37–53.

INDEX